The Making of Modern Africa

Volume 2   The Twentieth Century

A.E. Afigbo B.A., Ph.D.
Professor of History, University of Nigeria at Nsukka

E.A. Ayandele B.A., Ph.D.
Formerly Professor of History, University of Ibadan

R.J. Gavin M.A., Ph.D.
Professor of History, University of Ulster

J.D. Omer-Cooper M.A.
Professor of History, University of Otago, Dunedin

This edition revised in collaboration with
Robin Palmer B.A., Ph.D.
Professor of History, University of Malawi

Longman

Longman Group UK Limited,
Longman House, Burnt Mill, Harlow,
Essex CM20 2JE, England
and Associated Companies throughout the world.

First published 1971
New edition 1986
Seventh impression 1992

Set in 10/12 pt Plantin (monophoto)

Printed in Hong Kong
WP/07

ISBN 0-582-58509-0

Contents

Part two
Northern Africa E.A. Ayandele

6 The Maghreb 138

Part three
Southern and Central Africa J.D. Omer-Cooper

7 South Africa from the South African War to the apartheid election of 1948   165

8 South Africa from the introduction of apartheid to the introduction of the multiracial constitution 199

9 Central Africa, *c.* 1900–53 233

10 Central Africa since 1953 264

Part four
Middle Africa R.J. Gavin

13 Middle Africa since independence R. Palmer

Index

List of Maps

Acknowledgements

The publishers are grateful to the following for permission to reproduce photographs in the text:

Associated Press Limited for pages 78, 216 and 267; Barnabys Picture Library for page 316; BBC Hulton Picture Library for pages 90, 174, 202, 241 and 311; Black Star Publishing Co. Limited for page 123; Camerapix Hutchison Library Limited for pages 64, 68, 134 and 135; Camera Press Limited for pages 33, 46, 51, 71, 104, 144, 162, 207, 221, 222, 225, 280, 281, 332, 334, 352, 354, 355, 359, 360 (left and right), and 361; J. Allan Cash Photo Library for pages 110 and 265; Collins Publishers for page 11; Department of Antiquities for page 255; Mary Evans Picture Library for page 81; Ghana Information Service for page 29; John Hillelson Agency for pages 199 and 209; Imperial War Museum for page 324; Institute of Ethiopian Studies for page 132; Mansell Collection for pages 182 and 298; Marie-Louise Martin, University of Birmingham for page 304; National Archives of Zimbabwe for page 239; Peter Obe/West Africa Magazine for page 63; Oxford University Press for page 30; Photo Source for pages 48, 97, 154, 268, 278, 337 and 342; Popperfoto Limited for pages 129, 248, 252, 327, 345 and 347; Public Record Office for page 94; Jean Ribiere for page 43; United Press International for page 359 (right); University of Ibadan Library for page 22; H. Roger Viollet for pages 4, 18 and 25; Zimbabwe Information Service for page 274; Zimbabwe Herald/Elizabeth York for page 273.

The publishers regret that they have been unable to trace the copyright holders of photographs appearing on pages 16, 62, 146, 150, 151, 168, 200, 205 and 295 and would welcome any information enabling them to do so.

The cover photograph shows Kenneth Kaunda addressing a mass rally and was reproduced by kind permission of the Zambia Information Services.

1 European administration and the growth of nationalism in West Africa (c. 1900–39)

The German colonies

German rule in West Africa only lasted a few years for in the course of the First World War Britain and France seized Togoland in 1914 and Kamerun (the Cameroons – now Cameroon) in 1916. Germany had spent part of the peaceful years between 1884 and 1914 defining the boundaries of these two colonies and imposing her rule on their peoples. Though German civil administration had little time to leave permanent impressions in West Africa, its distinctive features deserve to be highlighted. In the area of political administration pure and simple, the Germans were no better and no worse than their British and French counterparts or rivals in West Africa. At least so much can be said with reference to their rule in Togoland. They recognized that, for the usual good reasons which are spelt out in the sections dealing with French and British administrations, they could not rule their colonial subjects directly. The result was that where they found some chiefs of standing in existence, for example in the region of Misahohe, they made use of them in local administration. But where such chiefs did not exist, for instance in the Lomé region, they created them by appointing former soldiers, court clerks and interpreters as chiefs. These chiefs had their own courts for the settlement of minor civil disputes. They also had the power to arrest criminals, to collect taxes and to recruit labour for building and maintaining roads and railways. To enable German officers to understand the working of local indigenous law and custom in order to guide the chiefs aright, two German experts were appointed to carry out research into Togolese traditional law and customs as a first step to getting them codified. But before the work could be concluded the First World War broke out, leading to the liquidation of German rule by the French and the British.

In its other aspects German colonial administration was marked by energetic and imaginative action. The aim was to make the German colonial presence pay rich dividends. To this end every effort was made to promote agricultural production by encouraging the establishment of large-scale plantations of cocoa, coffee, tobacco, cotton and rubber on modern lines by German businessmen. In Kamerun there were forty-eight such farms, owned by 200 Europeans and worked by 18 000 Africans by 1913. In Togoland there were only three such farms. Here, by contrast, an effort was made to encourage peasant production by Togolese farmers. German agricultural experts were brought in to teach the people modern methods, especially through running schools of agriculture at Nuatja in Togoland and at Victoria, Yaoundé and Dschang in Kamerun.

At the same time effort was put into the building of modern roads and railway systems to ensure cheaper and more efficient evacuation of the resources of the colonies to the coast. For Togoland three railway lines were planned and executed. The first was the Lomé–Anécho line (44 kilometres) begun in 1902 and completed in 1905. Then followed the Lomé–Palimé line (119 kilometres) begun in 1904 and completed in 1907. Finally came the Lomé-Blitta line (270 kilometres) which was begun in 1908. By 1914 this line had been completed as far as Atakpamé (170 kilometres). It was later to be completed by France which 'inherited' that part of partitioned German Togoland. In Kamerun two main lines were planned, but only the line from Bonaberi (near Douala) to N'kongsamba (160 kilometres) was completed. The one from Douala to Widimenge (360 kilometres) was less than halfway through by 1913.

Side by side with this energetic economic policy went the introduction of western education. Here the colonial government worked in collaboration with the missions who dominated primary education. The government was more active in technical education. In Togoland, for example, it ran three of the four technical schools in existence by 1914. German colonial education has been described as more enlightened than that of the British or the French because of its emphasis on practical training as distinct from literary education. Also primary education was free. So was technical education but graduates of the technical colleges were bonded to serve the government for at least three years.

On the whole German colonial administration would appear to have held out much hope for rapid economic and social development, especially for the Togolese. But its methods were brutal, as it depended largely on forced and poorly paid labour. The French and the British were later to exploit this weakness to the full in their bid to discredit the German colonial record and justify their seizure of German colonies. However, it would appear that in retrospect the former German colonial subjects do not exactly share this bleak view of the German record. Much as they regret and resent the harshness of the regime they seem to think that the takeover by the French and the British slowed down their development.

In 1919 the League of Nations divided each of the two former German West African colonies into two. The eastern portion of each went to France while the western portions went to Britain. Britain's share of Togoland was administered as part of the Gold Coast (modern Ghana), while her share of Kamerun was renamed the Cameroons and administered as part of Nigeria but effectively in two separate units which reflected the administrative division of Nigeria itself. The Southern Cameroons were administered as part of Southern Nigeria, and the Northern Cameroons as part of Northern Nigeria. France administered Togo and Cameroun separately from her other colonies in West and Equatorial Africa. By and large, however, Britain and France extended to these mandated territories the same basic policies as they applied in their West African colonies. The main differences were that their administration of these mandates was under the general supervision of the League of Nations and that France could not extend to them some of the more obnoxious aspects of her policy such as forced labour. Just as in the case of the scramble, therefore, the history of European administration in West Africa is largely the history of French and British administrations.

The French colonies and the policy of assimilation

Senegal was France's first colony in West Africa. In 1893 the Ivory Coast and Guinea, in 1900 Dahomey (now Benin) and in 1904 Soudan were created as separate colonies. The interior regions of French West Africa continued under military administration until after the First World War when the colonies of Niger, Upper Volta (now Burkina Faso) and Mauritania were created. (In 1932 Upper Volta was 'partitioned' between Soudan, the Ivory Coast and Niger, but was restored as a separate colony in 1948). France thus carved up her vast West African empire into eight colonies. In spite of this, however, she applied to all of them virtually the same administrative and economic policies. To understand properly the pattern of French administration in West Africa it is necessary to analyze the theories which lay behind it.

Up to the beginning of the general European scramble for colonies in Africa French administration in West Africa was based entirely on the theory of assimilation. As a result of the French Revolution which started in 1789 Frenchmen had come to believe that all men were equal. They had also made a declaration which conferred the right of French citizenship on every inhabitant of a French colony. This latter measure derived from the fact that France believed that her culture and civilization were the best in

3

the world and that it was her mission to admit her colonial peoples into this rich heritage. This end, France believed, was to be attained by teaching the colonial peoples the French language, by subjecting them to French laws and by giving them French civil and political rights. Throughout French West Africa, the French applied assimilation in full only in Senegal, the only West African colony she possessed at the time when this theory enjoyed unchallenged ascendancy. Thus in 1848 France conferred French citizenship on the Senegalese and also gave them the right to elect a representative, called a Deputy, to the French National Assembly (the lower house of the French Parliament) in Paris. From 1848 to 1913 (except between 1852 and 1871 when Senegalese representation in the National Assembly was suspended altogether) it was usually a resident Frenchman who was elected Deputy. But in 1914 the first full-blooded African Deputy, Blaise Diagne, was elected and he held the position until his death in 1934. Also in accordance with the policy of assimilation Senegal was given the French system of local government based on *communes*. In 1872 there were only two communes in Senegal – St Louis and Gorée. In 1880, the commune of Rufisque, and in 1887 the commune of Dakar, were created. Each commune was endowed with a council which was elected by all its adult males, and a mayor who was the

Blaise Diagne, Senegal's Deputy, 1914–34

4

president of the council. In 1879 another council was created, the *Conseil du Sénégal*, which was made up of representatives from all the communes of Senegal and had the duty of levying taxation and regulating the use of public property.

The four communes of Senegal remained peculiar in French West Africa. All their indigenous inhabitants were French citizens and enjoyed the same civil and political rights as Frenchmen. Whereas people born in other parts of French West Africa could become French citizens only if they could read, write and speak the French language well, were known to be very loyal to France and had worked for a number of years in the civil service, those who were born in these four communes automatically became French citizens. They were called the *originaires*, that is, those who became French citizens by virtue of their birth. Also while French citizens from elsewhere in West Africa came under French law, the citizens of the four communes remained under Muslim law, a very special concession.

From the 1880s, however, the theory of assimilation came under vehement attack. As French rule and influence expanded in West Africa and elsewhere, France came into contact with very strongly organized African states whose cultures were still intact since they had not been influenced by centuries of contact with Europe. The French found it difficult to sidetrack completely the traditional authorities in these areas as they had done in Senegal where the people had been very greatly influenced by centuries of intercourse with France. Also in this period French expansion in West Africa was primarily for economic purposes, to find markets for her goods and raw materials for her industries. French businessmen therefore came to attack the policy of assimilation because it disorganized indigenous society and thus hampered the rapid economic exploitation of tribal areas. They also feared that assimilated colonists could become serious economic rivals. They doubted whether it would be possible to assimilate all the inhabitants of French West Africa. In any case, they argued, Africans were a different branch of the human family and therefore could not be properly absorbed into French culture. As a result of all this vigorous opposition, by 1905 France ceased to be completely committed to the policy of assimilation, though its influence remained strong. In its place the French people developed the doctrine of *association*. According to the advocates of this doctrine French colonial policy would respect the culture of her dependent peoples and allow each group to develop in its own way, rather than force them to adopt French civilization and culture. To achieve this aim France would as much as possible govern each group through its traditional political institutions. Though *association* influenced later French colonial policy it never completely dominated it.

Chiefs and administration in French West Africa

It was however largely as a result of this theory that the rest of French West Africa came to have local government institutions which were markedly different from those of Senegal. There was no longer any question of proclaiming all French West Africans French citizens and giving them French local government institutions. Outside Senegal therefore the French made an attempt to govern their subjects through local chiefs. They recognized three grades of chiefs. Firstly there were those they called *chefs de province* (the equivalent of paramount chiefs in British colonies) who were usually the successors of the more prominent and influential chiefs of the pre-colonial days. Secondly there were the *chefs de canton* (district heads) who were in most places ordinary people of ability whom the French appointed to that position. To start with, the canton was an artificial administrative unit created by the French; it did not correspond to any ethnic boundary. Lastly there was the *chef de village* or the village head who was often the traditional head of his community. The village chief was responsible for collecting the taxes imposed by the government and was expected to maintain law and order, arrest criminals and organize relief in times of disaster, for instance during floods or locust invasions. It also was his duty to ensure that surplus food was stored up for use in times of scarcity, and to maintain the roads in his area of authority. The district head or *chef de canton* kept the register of taxpayers in his canton, reported on how much each village had paid, helped the government in conscripting people for the army and in recruiting forced labour for the road or for any other public work. This was the system of local government in French West Africa outside Senegal which some people have described as 'direct rule' in order to distinguish it from indirect rule which is said to have been the British system. This description is not very accurate but we cannot go into the complicated controversy about it here. Later in the chapter we shall bring out the main differences between the French and British systems.

French administration in West Africa had one other distinguishing characteristic. It was highly centralized. The French believed in a strong and centralized government. As a result of their own bitter experiences they had come to the conclusion that strong local government bodies constituted a danger to a state. The French also believed in efficiency and uniformity and it was felt that if these two ideals were to be achieved, then government must be run from a common centre. In West Africa the French were lucky that their territories formed one continuous block for this meant that they could easily be administered from one capital. The passion for centralization visibly affected French administration of their territories in West Africa.

Every French colony in West Africa was divided into units called *cercles* (provinces) each of which was under a political officer called the *commandant*. A big *cercle* was usually further split into units called *sub-divisions* each of which was under an officer called a *chef de sub-division* (this officer corresponded to the district officer in British territories). The latter officer was responsible to the *commandant* who in turn was responsible to the Lieutenant-Governor who was the head of the administration in a colony. Each Lieutenant-Governor was assisted in his work by a council which he was expected to consult on certain issues touching the colony, especially revenue and expenditure. A decree of 1920 created another council, called the *privy council*, which advised the Lieutenant-Governor. All Lieutenant-Governors were responsible to the Governor-General in Dakar who was the administrative head of all French West Africa. It was the duty of this officer to see that decrees issued by the French Ministry of Colonies and laws passed by the French parliament which concerned West Africa were carried out. He alone had the right to correspond with the Ministry of Colonies, and for this reason all other officers in West Africa had to work according to his direction. Sometimes, however, owing to difficulties of communication the Lieutenant-Governors and the officers under them enjoyed more initiative and powers in practice than they were allowed in theory. At one time the Governor-General was the same person as the Lieutenant-Governor of Senegal, but in 1904 the two offices were separated, and the headquarters of the Governor-General was moved from St Louis to Dakar. The Governor-General had a body called the *Conseil de Gouvernement* which advised him. This council met once a year to hear government policy from the Governor-General and to discuss the federal budget as well as the budget of each colony. French West Africa was thus a federation of territories linked together through the Governor-General to the government of metropolitan France.

These were the main features of French government in West Africa until the end of the Second World War. Post-war changes will be discussed in Chapter 2. Senegal was given another local government body in 1920. The *Conseil-Général du Sénégal* (General Council of Senegal) dealt only with the affairs of the four communes. A body which would deal with matters affecting both the communes and the hinterland later became necessary. It was to meet this need that in 1920 the French Ministry of Colonies authorized the creation of a *Conseil Colonial* (Colonial Council) comprising *citoyens* (citizens) from the four communes and *sujets* (subjects) from the hinterland. This council had the duty of approving the budget of the Lieutenant-Governor of Senegal, of legislating on the control of public property and of making recommendations in matters of taxation. In 1929 Gorée ceased to be an independent commune and became part of Dakar.

In the last paragraph we talked of French citizens and subjects. French subjects could be called second-class 'citizens'. They were not culturally assimilated to France; French civil and criminal law did not apply to them; they could be polygamists, which citizens could not be; they came under the summary judicial system known as the *indigénat* which did not apply to French citizens. Under this system, for instance, a subject could suffer arbitrary arrest and summary trial at the hands of an administrative officer. Again, whereas a citizen was exempt from compulsory labour, a subject was not, and a subject could be forced to serve for a longer period in the army than a citizen. This division of French West Africans into first- and second-class human beings continued until after the Second World War.

Patterns of British colonial administration

The British, like the French, believed that their culture and social institutions were the best in the world. But unlike the French they also believed that their African subjects were so backward that they could not benefit from the introduction of these 'highly' developed institutions amongst them. In fact they held that any attempt to force Africans to adopt the British political system and practices would only lead to disintegration and disaster. But at the same time the British believed that Africans should be introduced to what they called modern ideas of government, by which they meant British ideas of government. The question was how to do this without causing African culture and society to break up completely. Somehow the British convinced themselves that the best method was to 'purify' African institutions and govern Africans through them. Practices like human sacrifice, slave dealing and slavery, twin murder and secret societies were to be suppressed. After this reform had been carried out new ideas of government and development were to be gradually introduced into African society through what remained of the traditional system.

This was not the only reason why the British chose to govern their African subjects through local African political institutions. On most occasions the British found that they had not enough men to control effectively the areas they brought under their rule. This situation arose partly because the British government was not prepared to spend much money on the colonies, and partly because the climate in some areas of West Africa made service there unpopular among the British people. Also

8

the latter did not forget that they came to West Africa mainly to satisfy their economic needs. They wanted to create markets for their goods and to encourage West Africans to produce those raw materials which they needed. In order to do this it was not necessary to abolish everything African. The British therefore decided not to involve themselves more than was necessary in the business of governing their West African colonies.

For these reasons they governed these colonies by means of a system popularly known as indirect rule. The British claimed that under this system they did not rule their West African subjects directly, but through those local chiefs and elders by whom the people were being governed in the days before the colonial era. There was no single British officer who introduced this system throughout British West Africa. We have seen in Volume I how George Maclean cooperated with Fante chiefs in maintaining law and order on the Gold Coast. His example was continued by those who succeeded him. In 1878 the authorities of the Gold Coast Colony passed an ordinance which authorized the chiefs of the colony and their councillors to make bye-laws on local matters, and to form courts in which they would try those who broke any of these bye-laws. The chiefs and their councils were also given the right to try civil and criminal cases which were not of a very serious nature. Though the British exiled Prempeh of Asante and his leading chiefs in 1896 they recognized the minor chiefs and tried to use them in local government.

In the region of what was to become Nigeria the same policy was being carried out. Here it was traders who started it all. We have already seen how along the Niger Delta they co-operated with the local chiefs through the Court of Equity. When the Royal Niger Company was empowered to rule Northern Nigeria, it attempted to do so in a fashion that did not undermine the authority of the emirs of the region. Under the Niger Coast Protectorate the example of the Court of Equity was continued. Institutions called Native Councils and Minor Courts were formed and given the power to make bye-laws, to regulate local matters and to try certain classes of cases. The members were all supposed to be traditional chiefs, but in the region later known as Eastern Nigeria they were not. In this area certain individuals were compelled by the British to become chiefs. These people were given 'certificates of recognition' which were called warrants. For this reason these men were popularly known as warrant chiefs. Apart from trying cases and passing bye-laws the warrant chiefs also recruited and supervised the men who built the main roads and government stations. In the same way the Lagos government in the 1890s created Native Councils in Yorubaland which comprised local chiefs and carried out duties very much like those which chiefs in other parts of British West

Africa carried out. In the protectorates of Sierra Leone and The Gambia British political officers also did their best to make use of indigenous chiefs in local government.

Thus by 1900 the policy of using African chiefs in local government was already well established in British West Africa. In that year Sir Frederick Lugard became the High Commissioner of the Protectorate of Northern Nigeria. Like other British Governors and High Commissioners in West Africa he found that he had not enough European officers to administer the region effectively. The Protectorate was not only very extensive, but also there were no good roads. Lugard was therefore happy to find that the emirs had centralized governments which he could use easily and cheaply. And since the Fulani emirs did not resist British conquest very vigorously Lugard had no fears in using them. The emirs for their part were happy to find that the British did not intend to displace them completely and so cooperated with Lugard who told them plainly that he would respect their rules of succession as well as their religion. He also allowed them to impose and collect taxes as before and to try cases in their Muslim courts. He issued the Native Courts Proclamation to legalize and define their judicial powers; and allowed them to have their own prisons where those convicted in the Native Courts served their terms. In each province he created what he called a Protectorate Court to serve as a court of appeal from the Native Courts. The Protectorate Court was presided over by the Resident and was the highest court to which the case of an indigenous Northerner could go. In this way Lugard sought to prevent the application of English law to Northern Nigerians. In 1904 he got the chiefs to pay a quarter of the revenue they collected from taxation to the central government while using the remainder for their private purposes.

Lugard left Northern Nigeria in 1906. Between 1906 and 1911 those who succeeded him went further in developing his particular method of using chiefs in local government. They got the chiefs to agree to the formation of what were called Native Treasuries into which they paid a part of the remaining three-quarters of the sum they collected from direct taxation. The revenue which came through the Native Courts in the form of fees and fines also went into the Native Treasuries. All this money was to be used in providing local amenities and in paying those employed by the local government. Under each emir there were a number of district heads and under the latter village heads. If the British wanted something done they told the emir who passed the order on through the district heads and village heads who in turn got their people to carry it out.

By means of this system Britain succeeded in bringing the large area of Northern Nigeria under control very quickly and cheaply. It was largely because of this success that the British concluded that of all methods of

Sir Frederick (later Lord) Lugard

ruling Africans through their chiefs, Lugard's was the best. In this however they forgot that this so-called success owed a great deal to the nature of the political system then existing in Northern Nigeria. In 1912 Lugard returned to Nigeria as Governor of both Northern and Southern Nigeria and in 1914 brought the northern and southern portions of the country under one administration. At once he condemned the other attempts which had been made in Southern Nigeria to rule through local chiefs. Because the approach in Southern Nigeria differed from that in Northern Nigeria he concluded that it was not indirect rule and that therefore it was pernicious. He then tried to impose his northern system on Southern Nigeria. Among the Yoruba people this meant that he gave the obas more powers than they had had in traditional law and custom. His attempt to levy taxation after the Northern Nigerian fashion caused much resentment and led to a riot among the Egba in 1918 in which lives were lost. In the area east of the Niger he singled out some warrant chiefs and made them paramount chiefs overnight. This led to great confusion. He also wanted to introduce direct taxation there but failed. The confused situation which Lugard left behind east of the Niger later led to a serious anti-government movement in Aba in 1929 known in Igbo as *Ogu Umunwanyi* (the 'Women's War') in which many women were shot down by government forces.

Lugard retired from Nigeria in 1919 and in 1922 published his famous book, *The Dual Mandate in Tropical Africa*, in which he discussed in great detail the theory of his particular method of ruling Africans through their chiefs. By this time Lugard had become very famous as a great colonial administrator. Even the League of Nations invited him to give advice on how dependent peoples should best be governed. The British concluded that many of their administrative problems in West Africa would be solved if all their West African colonies adopted Lugard's own principles of indirect rule. From 1931 local government legislation in the Gold Coast Colony sought to apply these principles to the Fante. From 1935 they were applied to the Asante, from 1939 to the Sierra Leone Protectorate, from 1933 to The Gambia Protectorate. In this way Lugard's own particular method of using chiefs in local government became more famous than those of the other administrators who long before him had also in their own different ways used chiefs in local government. As we shall see later all the hopes which the British placed on Lugard's type of indirect rule were to be sadly disappointed.

French and British administrations compared

There were two major differences between the British and French methods of using African chiefs in local government. The first was that the British tried as much as possible to see that all the chiefs they used were traditional rulers, whereas the French were not particular on this point. As we have already seen the canton chief was usually not a traditional chief.

However, this does not mean that the British did not sometimes make the mistake of using people who were not traditional chiefs. We have already seen that in what later became Eastern Nigeria they created artificial warrant and paramount chiefs to whom they gave excessive powers and the same was true of parts of the Northern Territories of the Gold Coast. In the non-Muslim parts of Northern Nigeria they created artificial district heads and in this way caused much resentment among the people. In Western Nigeria they gave the obas more powers than they usually had and since this made the obas independent of their traditional councils it tended also to make their position somewhat artificial.

The second main difference between the British and French methods was that the British were more inclined to respect the chiefs under them and to give them more powers than the French did. This did not mean that where the British found a chief difficult to control they did not discipline him. The result of this second difference between the French and British systems was that the French system led to more efficient government. The French officer looked into everything a chief under him did, while the British officer left too much in the hands of the local chief, believing that a certain amount of inefficiency, corruption and even oppression must be tolerated if African chiefs must be used at all. It is, however, noteworthy that ultimately the French and British methods virtually led to the same result. They caused African chiefs to lose their traditional character. African chiefs became independent of their people and instead came to depend on their colonial masters. They also ceased to perform many traditional functions which the French and the British regarded as uncivilized. Since it was through them that changes were introduced into African society, the chiefs too became greatly changed in the process.

The British pattern of central government in their West African colonies also differed from that of the French. The British administered each of their four colonies separately. This was partly because the British colonies were so widely scattered that they could not be efficiently administered from one centre. Earlier attempts to do so had failed. In the 1820s the British had attempted to administer the Gold Coast and The Gambia from Freetown, but this was soon abandoned as unsatisfactory. After 1865 they had also tried to administer Lagos, the Gold Coast, Sierra Leone and The Gambia from a common capital. This too had failed. But the fact that Britain administered each of her West African colonies independently did not prevent her from applying to them the same kind of governmental system. We have already seen how in each colony an attempt was made to rule the Africans through their chiefs. Later still Lugard's particular method of indirect rule was applied to all of them. In the same way Britain divided each of her West African territories into two main sections. The first was the coastal region in which European influence had been present for a long time. To this region she first applied the so-called Crown Colony system of government. The main feature of this system was that the Governor passed laws for the colony with the advice of a legislative council dominated by government officials. Behind the colony, that is in the interior, was the section usually known as the protectorate which was inhabited by people who had not been under European influence for long. For these people the Governor legislated by proclamation, that is without the advice of any group of people supposed to represent the inhabitants of the protectorate. It was only after many years that the colony and the protectorate areas in each British West African territory were brought under the same legislature. One or two examples could be given.

In 1874 a legislative council was established for the Gold Coast Colony. It had the power to pass laws for the colony, to set up local government bodies, to levy taxation and to encourage the provision of amenities. But it was not until 1946 that the Ashanti (Asante) Protectorate and the Gold Coast Colony came under the same legislative council. The Northern Territories of the Gold Coast continued to be outside the area of authority of this body until 1951. In Nigeria the Colony of Lagos got a legislative council in 1862. In 1914 Lugard modified this body, renamed it the Nigerian Council and gave it the power to discuss matters affecting the whole country. Eight years later, however, Governor Clifford removed Northern Nigeria from the area of authority of this body which he reconstituted and renamed a legislative council. It was not until 1946 that the whole country was again brought under the authority of a central legislative body.

The British, unlike the French, did not attempt to pass laws in London for all their West African colonies. On the contrary the Governor of each territory drew up laws according to the needs of his particular area. But before these laws were applied they were sent to the Secretary of State for the Colonies in London for his approval. It is therefore not surprising that many of the laws of British West African colonies tended to be based on the same principles. In a later section in this chapter we shall examine the reactions of West Africans to these two patterns of European rule.

Economic policies and developments

British and French attitudes towards the economic development of their West African colonies were very similar. Each of the two powers was concerned with encouraging West Africans to produce raw materials for her home industries. Both knew very well that the export of these raw products would bring more money into the hands of West Africans, and that with this money the latter would become increasingly able to buy more and more European manufactured goods. French and British economic policies in West Africa were thus very selfish; they were designed to benefit mainly the colonial powers. Throughout their years of rule in West Africa these powers spent their time promoting the production of export crops, but never attempted to encourage the increased production of locally consumed staple foods. There were research centres which sought to improve the yield of rubber, palm trees, cocoa, cotton and other cash crops, but none which tried to discover cheaper and better ways of growing and storing yams, cassava, millet and other local foodstuffs. For the same reason neither of these powers was interested in establishing industries in their West African colonies. Attempts which were made by local French officials to create industries in territories under their charge were vehemently opposed by French businessmen who feared that colonial industries would rival the home industries of France. Consequently cocoa, timber, palm oil, groundnuts, leather, cotton and rubber were grown in West Africa and sold to European businessmen at very cheap rates. They took these crops home, processed them and brought the finished products back to West Africa to sell at a great profit.

From the beginning of their rule, therefore, these powers took such steps as they believed would help them realize their economic aims. They abolished trade by barter as well as indigenous currencies because they said these did not make for quick business. Trade by barter was slow while indigenous currencies were too cumbersome to be carried about easily and conveniently. In place of these the colonial powers introduced their own currencies which helped to increase the speed of economic transactions. If trade was to flourish it was also necessary to have efficient means of communication. West African rivers were not all navigable for long distances nor all the year round. The Niger and the Senegal, for instance, could be navigated by fairly big steamers up to certain points for only three months in the year. The main rivers of the Gold Coast – the Volta and the Pra – were even more limited for purposes of communication. France and Britain therefore decided early on to build railways and modern motor roads in their West African possessions as a means of improving communications. Between 1882 and 1906 the French built a railway line, 510 kilometres long, from Kayes on the Senegal to Bamako on the Niger to link the upper Niger and the Senegal. As the port of St Louis did not prove very suitable for modern ocean-going vessels, the French built a railway to link it with Dakar which had a better harbour. By 1923 the French had built another line connecting this Dakar–St Louis line to the Kayes–Bamako line. From their other stations along the coast they built other lines to promote easy access to the Sudan. These lines, which started from Conakry in Guinea, Abidjan in the Ivory Coast and Cotonou in Dahomey sought to reach the Niger, but only the one from Guinea succeeded in getting to one of the tributaries of this great river.

The British were equally vigorous in building railways in their West African colonies. The Gambia, a small country, needed no railway line since it was satisfactorily served by the river from which it derives its name. The British therefore merely built roads to feed the river. The Gambia was also lucky in having a good natural harbour in Bathurst (now Banjul). Railway construction began in Sierra Leone in March 1896, in the Gold Cost in 1898, and in Nigeria in 1896. By 1932 there were about 500 kilometres of railway in Sierra Leone, 800 kilometres in the Gold Coast and 3000 kilometres in Nigeria. Like the railways of French territories those of British West Africa were built to serve specific purposes. The Y-shaped railway system of Sierra Leone tapped the palm oil producing regions of the country. In the Gold Coast the line from Sekondi-Takoradi to Kumasi passed through the gold mining areas and was useful for transporting the heavy equipment needed for mining gold at great depths. The eastern line from Accra to Kumasi passed through the pioneer cocoa-producing regions. In Nigeria the lines from Lagos and Port Harcourt not only passed through the palm belts of the south but also traversed North-ern Nigeria from which the British obtained groundnuts as well as hides and skins. Roads were also built to supplement these railways, while ports

Railway construction in the Gold Coast

and harbours were improved. This revolution in communications did not only serve economic purposes. It enabled the French and the British to move soldiers and policemen easily to any region where their rule was challenged by force of arms. It also made it possible for a political officer to supervise the administration of a large district.

The recruitment and control of labour was an important aspect of the economic policy of the colonial powers, especially the labour needed for building roads and railways. The key to an understanding of the attitude of the imperial authorities in this matter was their strongly held belief that Africans are naturally lazy and would not work unless compelled to do so by circumstances. As one European put it, what the African likes best is 'to do nothing for six days in the week and to rest on the seventh.' French and British solutions to this so-called problem of the African's unwillingness to work were similar in many respects. Basically it was to force the African to work whenever and wherever free labour was not available.

The pressure on the African was to be exerted directly and indirectly. The direct method relied on laws and regulations which required chiefs to recruit their subjects to work even against their will on government projects—roadmaking, railway building, carrying the European officer and his property or the luggage of the military and the police from one place to another. Most times this labour was unpaid, or when paid the rate was fixed without reference to fair market rates. This method of making labour available for the needs of the colonial government was adopted in those areas where it was considered unwise or impossible to impose direct taxation for the time being.

The indirect method of compelling labour to come forward was the imposition of direct taxation. Direct taxation was considered a good social and economic tonic. Not only was it capable of compelling farmers to increase their productivity in order to produce surpluses for the market and thus raise the money they needed for paying the tax. It also compelled people to take up paid work with the government, commercial firms and even with the missions in order to earn the cash with which to pay their taxes. For the most part the indirect method was used in those areas such as the former Muslim states, where taxation was already long established by the time of the imposition of European rule. But as time went on, especially as the resistance to forced labour grew, it was introduced to even such small-scale societies as were found in south-eastern Nigeria where the institution was totally unknown and heartily detested.

The colonial powers had yet a third method of meeting their labour needs. One of the advertised aims of the colonialists in West Africa was the abolition of slave trade and slavery. Now as they imposed their rule on West Africa both the French and the British freed many former slaves, or in any case gathered together runaway slaves. The French created what they called 'villages of liberty' in which they settled such former slaves, while the British had their freed slave homes in Northern Nigeria. The French 'villages of liberty' were misnamed. In plain language they were reservoirs of labour often strategically placed along main roads. The inmates did not even have freedom of movement. They were also ready sources of conscripts for the army especially during the First World War. The British freed slave homes in Northern Nigeria were run on more humane lines. The inmates were given some rudimentary education and taught handicrafts and domestic science according to their sex. But all the same they were a ready source of domestic servants for European colonial officers.

By and large the British record on this issue of forced labour was far better than that of the French. But the German record, already discussed, was by far the harshest in West Africa. But there is no doubt that such labour policies achieved the objectives for which they were adopted. Africans were compelled to move out of the more quiet retreat of their villages into the towns in search of work. Apart from this rural-urban migration which did not always involve long-range travel, there were also region to region or even colony to colony migrations. Igbo labourers, for instance, not only moved into such budding urban centres as Aba, Umuahia, Port Harcourt, Enugu and Onitsha all within Igboland but also travelled to Benin and Yorubaland, to work in the rubber and cocoa plantations. As time went on they also travelled to the Cameroons and to Fernando Po under the French and the Spanish respectively. Similarly

Forced labour on the road between Cotonou and Porto Novo (Dahomey) in 1933

peasants from the French Sudan and Upper Volta which grew few cash crops had to travel to Senegal, Ivory Coast and the Gold Coast to work in groundnut, coffee and cocoa plantations.

Apart from helping to build railways, roads and harbours Britain and France did little else of permanent significance to promote economic development in West Africa. For a long time France had no money to spend on her colonies, while her businessmen were reluctant to invest their capital in West Africa. British businessmen were more liberal than their French counterparts in this respect but their half-hearted efforts did not produce any remarkable change. From 1929 the British government started to set aside a sum of one million pounds annually for the purpose of supplementing the scanty resources of all her colonies. But this sum turned out to be too small to serve any great purpose. The result was that the colonies continued to depend on money raised locally. However, 1940 brought a great change in British policy for in that year Britain passed the Colonial Development and Welfare Act which enabled her to set aside £5 million annually for the developmennt of her dependent territories. Another sum of £500 000 was set aside to promote research. In 1945 another Act was passed which authorized the British government to spend the sum of £120 million on her colonies in the period 1945–55. To enable this sum to be distributed according to need, the colonies were asked to submit their development plans for that ten-year period. Nigeria proposed to spend £53 million in the period and of this sum £23 million was to come from the Colonial Development and Welfare Fund. Sierra Leone planned to spend £5.24 million of which £2.9 million was to come from Britain; The Gambia £2 million of which £1.3 million was to come from Britain; and the Gold Coast £75 million of which £3 million was to come from Britain. The Gold Coast was at the time the richest British West African territory and so received proportionally least of all. In 1946 the French followed the British example by passing a law which enabled their government to set up its own colonial development fund from which grants were made to French West Africa. It has been estimated that under this arrangement French West Africa received from France four times the sum of money which Britain spent on her West African territories in the years after the war.

Results of colonial economic policies

On the whole British and French economic policy in West Africa produced similar results. In the first place the chief source of revenue for both the French and British colonies remained the export of raw materials. In the second place the greater part of the foreign trade of these colonies was in the hands of their metropolitan countries. The French were the worst offenders in this matter. To discourage other European nations from entering into direct trade with their dependencies they imposed very high tariffs on non-French goods. Britain did not adopt exactly the same method, but somehow her businessmen dominated the trade of her West African colonies. Also the inhabitants of British West Africa came to believe that only British goods could be of good quality. Goods from other places were indiscriminately despised as cheap and inferior. In the third place developments in both French and British West Africa were concentrated in the forest or coastal areas of the south or centre, rather than the northern savannas. The rich regions of French West Africa were the Ivory Coast, Senegal, Guinea and Dahomey in that order. The other four colonies remained very poor. In British West Africa the Gold Coast was the richest owing to her cocoa and gold which came from the south and centre. The greater part of Nigeria's revenue came from cocoa, palm produce, timber and rubber which are all southern products. The chief export of Northern Nigeria was groundnuts which in 1950 amounted to about one-sixth of Nigeria's total exports.

This difference in the economic development of the Sudanic and forest regions is not surprising. The Sudan is not thickly populated, and thus lacks manpower. Its soil is also drier and poorer than that of the forest zone and it is distant from the coast. Since the colonial powers were not prepared or able to undertake extensive development schemes and transport improvements, the region with the natural advantages of thicker population density, richer soil and proximity to harbours remained economically in advance. This explains why British West Africa was relatively richer than French West Africa. As we have already seen, French West Africa lay mainly in the drier and poorer Sudan, while British West Africa lay mainly in the wetter and more fertile forest zone. Another important result of French and British economic policy in West Africa is the fact that the economic development of the region has depended entirely on peasant enterprise. Though Europeans were the first to grow coffee and bananas in a place like the Ivory Coast, the growth and export of cash crops in West Africa now lies entirely in the hands of West Africans. They own the plantations and they supply the labour. It was once thought that Africans were very lazy but the continued increase of export crops from West Africa produced by Africans themselves without forced labour has proved this assumption to be false. Europeans found the West African climate very trying. They also discovered that almost all the land was occupied. For these reasons they made very few attempts to seize the land from the people as they did in North, East and Southern Africa. In this situation they had no alternative but to allow the people to occupy and cultivate their land and export their products. The last important result of the French and British attitude to the economic development of West Africa is the fact that the industrialization of the region had to wait till after independence (see chapter 3).

Since for a long time neither Britain nor France was ready to spend much money on the development of their West African territories, the colonial governments remained too poor to provide adequate social services. Hospitals and schools remained few in number and ill-equipped, most of them having been built and maintained by missionary societies. Many areas lacked roads, while many of the roads which were built were not properly maintained. The British in West Africa were noted for narrow and winding roads. Proposed railway schemes were not carried out in full owing to shortage of funds. It is true that the colonial powers brought a number of improvements to West Africa yet one can say that if they had been less selfish and grudging in their economic and social policies they would have brought about even more rapid development.

The rise of nationalism in West Africa

In the period of colonial rule nationalism in West Africa meant almost entirely a refusal to submit to foreign rule, and it took different forms at different times. We have already seen how West African peoples and their rulers tried at first to prevent by force of arms the imposition of European rule. In this they failed for reasons we have already discussed. But the story did not end there. The colonial powers soon adopted the trick of dividing the ranks of their African opponents by persuading or forcing West African chiefs to co-operate with them in the work of ruling the region. In areas where chiefs were readily found the strategy succeeded to a great extent. But in those places where it was not easy to say who was a chief, the traditional rulers, who were usually suspicious of the newcomers, successfully avoided co-operating with them. The ordinary people, who were thus in many places left leaderless, continued the resistance to foreign rule in different ways. Many of them refused to have anything to do with the new ways of the colonial powers and instead tried to live their lives as their fathers had done. From time to time this group of people rose in open rebellion, for example against taxation, the Native Courts, oppressive road work, or even the newly created chiefs imposed on some of them, but they were usually easily suppressed by the colonial army and police. What was more it was impossible to boycott the new ways completely. Some might refuse to go to church, or to take cases to the new and alien

Chiefs in Northern Nigeria 'agreeing' to submit to British rule

courts or to send their children to school or even to dress in the new fashions, but they could not refuse to use the new currencies or the new roads, or even to hear or see new things which they would normally not want to hear or see. Others reacted in a different way. They felt that the colonial powers had been able to defeat them because of the many new and wonderful feats which they could perform. These Africans therefore concluded that the best thing to do was to send their children to school and workshops to learn these new ways and techniques in order to be able to meet the white man on equal grounds. Unfortunately, however, many of those who were sent to learn the white man's ways came back to want things which their fathers did not quite like. This, however, is a different story and cannot be told here. The relevant aspect from our standpoint here is that they came back well-equipped to fight colonial rule. It is how this group fought and defeated their colonial masters that we are concerned with here and in much of Chapter 2.

We have already seen in Volume 1 how European activity along the coast of West Africa, especially missionary enterprise, led to the rise of a group of West Africans who were educated along European lines. As European rule expanded and as the missions spread their influence into the interior this class grew in number. British West Africa produced more people educated according to European tradition than French West Africa. At first this may seem surprising since the French tried to assimilate their subjects to French culture while the British did not. The explanation lies in the fact that the French did not give enough encouragement to missionaries working in their colonies. Ever since the Revolution of 1789 the French people had come to distrust the Church. From 1903 the French government refused to give financial assistance to mission schools in its colonies and in its West African territories allowed education to be taken over by the colonial government. Since the French had not enough money to spend on their colonies this meant that many French West Africans had a limited chance of receiving western education. In British West Africa the situation was different. The British gave the missionaries a free hand, except in certain of the Muslim areas where the colonial government did not want to offend the prevailing religion. Since various missionary bodies competed with one another in the establishment of schools, many British West Africans had a chance of receiving western education of one kind or another. This was one of the reasons why the struggle for political power between the new West African élite and the colonial powers started earlier in British than in French West Africa.

Also the élite in French West Africa was better treated by its colonial masters than its counterpart in British West Africa. Its members got well-paid jobs in the administration, and as civil servants were in no position to criticize the government. Those who were not employed in West Africa even found employment in France itself. Thus they did not experience racial discrimination and in fact those who attained a certain level of education and showed loyalty to France were, as we have already seen, given French citizenship and enjoyed the same civil and political rights as Frenchmen. In Senegal the élite enjoyed the honour of being represented in the French National Assembly. This sometimes meant that protests against the colonial régime were heard more in Paris than in West Africa. Furthermore, for the few who were not happy under the French régime there was very limited scope for political agitation, which was banned until 1946. French political officers had at their disposal the *indigénat* which gave them wide powers over those labelled as troublesome subjects. As a result of all this, opposition to French rule was very limited. A few African journalists in Paris or Senegal or Cotonou asked for the abolition of the *indigénat* and for the removal of the difference between citizens and subjects. Some of those who were qualified to become citizens refused to do so in order to retain their African status. Some of these also developed an interest in African history and culture to show that Africa had a civilization of her own.

The élite in British West Africa had every reason to protest against

British rule. British officers treated its members with contempt and often referred to them insultingly as 'black Englishmen' or 'apes in trousers'. The British argued that because of its western education the new African élite was not qualified to lead its people or to speak for them. Britain, it was argued, would prepare her African subjects for self-government through the system of indirect rule, because it was the chiefs rather than the new élite who were the natural leaders of the masses. This policy offended the educated elements for various reasons. In the first place it meant that they would not find employment in local government since it was believed that indirect rule had no need for men educated beyond the most basic level. The lawyers were not allowed to practise in the Native Courts, and in the protectorates senior administrators acted as prosecution, judge and jury in courts which barred African lawyers from representing defendants as they were able to do in magistrates' courts and superior courts in 'Colony' areas such as Lagos and the Gold Coast Colony. In the second place the new élite felt that indirect rule was a very slow method of preparing Africans for self-government. The chiefs were generally illiterate, conservative and ignorant of the modern methods of government which the new élite wanted to introduce. The latter soon come to the conclusion that the British ruled indirectly because they wanted to rule their West African subjects for ever.

The legislative councils were another source of conflict between the new élite and the British colonial administrations. These bodies were expected to advise the Governors on how to govern Africans yet the majority of the members were European political officers. The few Africans who were members were all nominated by the Governors until the 1920s, and generally the Governors chose those whom they felt would not violently criticize their administration. The new élite accused the British of hypocrisy. If the government was honest, they argued, it would allow Africans to choose those who should represent them and, furthermore, Africans should form a majority in the body that helped to decide their future. Since the British refused to employ the élite in large numbers in the central government or at all in local government, many British West Africans who went to the universities took to professions like the law, medicine and engineering which they could practise on their own. As these men did not depend on the government for their livelihood they could criticize and abuse the government as much as they liked. And as many of them were lawyers who liked argument they found fault with everything the government said or did and sometimes with what the goverment did not say or did not do.

There were also other factors which in this period contributed significantly to the rise of nationalism in West Africa. One of these was the First

World War which exposed many of the weaknesses in the colonial system. For one thing the war caused much economic and social dislocation in West Africa. The prices of locally produced goods such as cocoa, palm oil, palm kernels, cotton and coffee, fell because these could not easily be shipped to Europe and because European consumption declined as available income was invested in the war effort. For similar reasons the volume of European goods imported into West Africa fell as a result of which they were sold at exorbitant prices. In other words as the earning capacity of West Africans fell, they were called upon to pay more for those European goods which they were beginning to regard as necessities.

Thus socially and economically West Africans were dragged into a war which did not actually concern them. But beyond that they were made to fight in it too thereby shedding their blood and even losing their lives. West African soldiers fought the Germans not only in Togoland and the Cameroons, but also in East Africa and Europe. Many able-bodied men who were not soldiers participated in the war as carriers. When those of these men who survived came home at the end of the war they were no longer prepared to accept the old conditions without protest. Even members of the educated élite who supported the French and the British

French West African troops (*tirailleurs sénégalais*) on their way to the front in France during the First World War

against Germany pressed for concessions as the price of their support. Blaise Diagne, for instance, campaigned in favour of the French war effort in West Africa. But he also used his position and standing in the French National Assembly to secure the passage of the *Loi Diagne* which sought to protect the political rights of the four communes against threats from the colonial authorities.

Another important factor which helps to explain the growth of nationalism in West Africa in this period was the rise of pan-Africanism through the efforts of prominent American and West Indian blacks such as Dr W.E.B. Du Bois, George Padmore, Marcus Garvey and Henry Sylvester Williams. These black intellectuals were concerned to fight the ideology of white supremacy on which European rule in Africa as well as European suppression of blacks in the New World was based. In particular Garvey's flamboyant Universal Negro Improvement Association, with its slogans of 'Africa for Africans' and 'Back to Africa' attracted many educated West Africans who took steps to form branches along the west coast. These activities on the world platform, especially the Pan-African Congresses of the period (1900, 1919 etc) kept the question of the rights of the black man *vis-à-vis* the white races constantly in view and under discussion. Their full implications for West African nationalism were not worked out until much later.

There was thus one significant similarity between nationalism in French and British West Africa during this period. It was first and foremost an élite movement which did very little to exploit the seething discontent of the masses, who were denied education, and for the most part access to such other social services as hospitals. And since the élite were concentrated in the more modernized urban centres, the movement was also limited to the coast. In British West Africa the storm centres of agitation were Bathurst, Freetown, Accra, Lagos and, to some extent, Calabar and Port Harcourt. As far as French West Africa was concerned it was the four communes of Senegal, to a limited extent Porto Novo in Dahomey and then, strangely, Paris.

After this general introduction to the subject of nationalism in West Africa, we shall now examine specific nationalist activities in the region, taking the case of French West Africa first.

Nationalist activities in French West Africa

As we have seen, the French régime in West Africa was less liberal than that of the British and gave less scope for the rise of organized agitation for more political rights and participation in government for Africans.

Nonetheless there was a measure of political activity and agitation. For this purpose French West Africa could be seen as falling into two political regions. In the first region were the four communes of Senegal whose politics was closely integrated with that of metropolitan France under the old policy of assimilation. The political life of this region revolved around the election of the single Deputy who represented these four communes in the French National Assembly. Between 1848 and 1913 this Deputy was either a Frenchman or a *métis* (a man of mixed African and European descent). In 1914 the first full-blooded African Deputy was elected in the person of Blaise Diagne, a Wolof and a former customs official who had served in many parts of French West Africa and even in Gabon. Married to a French woman, he began by using the grievances of the four communes as the platform on which he and his party, the Republican-Socialist Party, came to power and dominated the politics of these communities for the next twenty years. There were two phases of his career.

First was the radical phase covering the years 1914 to 1922. During this phase he took the opportunity of his co-operation with France to secure the political rights of the citizens in the communes. He secured the lifting of press censorship, the grant to Africans of the right to form and organize political parties as well as the building of schools and hospitals. In this period he also associated himself with the pan-African movements, participating in the Pan-African Congress of 1919. He spoke of the rights of African peoples to self-government and against the monopoly which French merchants had established over the Senegalese economy. But also in this phase he showed himself prepared to support the French. He supported conscription during the war and campaigned extensively in French West Africa in favour of recruitments into the army in his capacity as Commissioner-General of the Republic for the Recruitment of Troops in Black Africa.

The second phase of his career covered the years 1923 to 1934 and was characterized by increasing collaboration with the French at the expense of the Africans. He declared himself a Frenchman first and a black man second. He reached an agreement with French merchants by which he stopped attacking them. In 1930 he defended forced labour before an International Labour Organization investigation. The next year he accepted appointment in the French government as under-secretary of state for the colonies. He began to detach himself more and more from his country and people. The result was that his younger and more radical followers deserted him out of disgust and began opposing him back home in Senegal. In 1925, 1928 and 1932 he encountered stiffer opposition at the elections than he had hitherto faced. And it has been suggested that even though he won, this was the result of official intervention on his side. By the time he died in 1934, he had ceased to speak for his people. How far his career should be discussed as part of the history of West African nationalism is really in doubt.

Outside the four communes, the rest of French West Africa formed the second region in terms of the history of nationalism in this period. This vast region came under the brutal *indigénat* régime where the Africans were given no political rights, where the overwhelming majority of the people were subjects, a kind of second-rate Frenchman and where the status of citizen was very difficult to attain. Even the right to protest or to go on strike was denied.

But in spite of these harsh rules, or even because of them, there was seething discontent which occasionally came into the open as visible protests against French rule. For instance there were strikes in Senegal in 1925 and 1927, and in Soudan in 1925 and 1938. But the most noteworthy stand against the French during this period was made by Louis Hunkanrin of Dahomey. In Dahomey education had made rapid progress and the colony produced many educated people which it exported as civil servants to other parts of French West Africa. Hunkanrin began as a follower of Blaise Diagne but deserted him when Diagne entered that phase of his career marked by close collaboration with France. A former civil servant, he lost his job in 1910 but then fought for the French in Europe during the war. After the war he spent some time in Paris in French radical circles before returning home and founding in Dahomey a branch of the Ligue des Droits de l'Homme (League of the Rights of Man), which was a metropolitan organization. Being suspect to the administration, he was blamed for the Porto Novo riots of 1923 and exiled to Mauritania.

But with respect to the future development of nationalism in French West Africa, the important events were taking place during this period not in West Africa, but in Paris. Here educated French West Africans who found no scope for political expression back home congregated after the war. Some of them were former soldiers. They moved in French radical circles, even toying with communism. Highly educated, these people were the cream of French assimilated West Africans. They played an important part in the cultural and literary movement that led to the creation of the philosophy of *Négritude* and establishment of the journal *Présence Africaine*. The fact is that though highly Frenchified, they continued to feel the need to identify with their African background and culture. They had, so to speak, seen the limits of assimilation. They could not attain full self-realization through that policy. They had therefore to begin making the return journey to the culture of mother Africa. The most distinguished of these men, whether as poet, scholar, linguist or statesman, was Senghor, of whom more will be heard in the next chapter.

Nationalist activities in British West Africa

We have already seen how early in this struggle with the colonial powers the Sierra Leone élite adopted the tactics of grouping themselves together as a means of achieving their ends. The practice grew in strength as the

J.E. Casely Hayford

Members of the 1920 National Congress of British West Africa delegation to London. *From left to right, seated*: H.C. Bankole-Bright (Sierra Leone), T. Hutton-Mills (Gold Coast), Chief Oluwa (Nigeria), J.E. Casely Hayford (Gold Coast), H. Van Hein (Gold Coast). *Standing*: J. Egerton Shyngle (Nigeria), H.M. Jones (The Gambia), Herbert Macaulay (Nigeria), T.M. Oluwa (Nigeria), F.W. Dove (Sierra Leone), E.F. Small (The Gambia).

struggle spread from Sierra Leone to the rest of British West Africa. In 1897 the educated elements in the Gold Coast Colony and their chiefs formed the Aborigines' Rights Protection Society led by J.W. Sey, its President. The purpose of this society was to protest against a law which the government wanted to pass to control the rate at which people sold their lands to foreign companies. Some people thought that the British wanted to seize their land, while some of the lawyers knew very well that if the law were passed they would not have enough land cases. Yet land cases were, and are, very lucrative. This was a time when the new élite and the chiefs could agree, as indirect rule had not yet succeeded in creating a division between the two groups. The Aborigines' Rights Protection Society succeeded in preventing the passage of the obnoxious law. In 1917 many educated elements from the different parts of British West Africa came together and formed the National Congress of British West Africa under the leadership of J.E. Casely Hayford, a Gold Coast lawyer and journalist. The Congress insisted that Britain should give each of her West African colonies a legislative council in which half the members would be elected Africans. It also demanded that the African members of the council should alone have the power to impose taxation, that chiefs should be left under the control of their peoples as in days gone by, that Britain should give Europeans and Africans equal chances in the civil service and that a university should be established in British West Africa. In 1920 the Congress sent a delegation to London to try to persuade the Secretary of State for the Colonies to grant these points, but the requests were refused. The Governors of the Gold Coast and Nigeria refused to listen to the Congress because, they claimed, the members had no right to speak for their fellow Africans. By this time the new élite and the chiefs no longer agreed. The chiefs of the Gold Coast even sent a delegation to London to tell the Secretary of State that the Congress did not speak for them. Sir Hugh Clifford, the Governor of Nigeria, left nothing unsaid to make the Congress look ridiculous. He made fun of the idea that either West Africa or Nigeria could be a nation.

After attacking the Congress very bitterly Sir Hugh Clifford in Nigeria and Sir Gordon Guggisberg in the Gold Coast came round to grant the educated elements of the coastal cities the right to elect some of the African members of the legislative councils. In 1922 Clifford abolished Lugard's Nigerian Council which had proved useless and in its place created a legislative council for Lagos and Southern Nigeria. Of the ten African members four were to be elected, three from Lagos and one from Calabar. The Gold Coast constitution was likewise revised in 1925, and Accra, Cape Coast and Sekondi were given the right to elect their representatives to the council. However the legislative councils continued to be dominated by European officials. In Nigeria twenty-seven out of forty-six members of the council were government officials and only ten were Africans while the other nine were Europeans representing various commercial interests. The Gold Coast council contained sixteen officials, five other Europeans representing commercial interests and nine Africans. In the Gold Coast there was another feature of the council which offended the new élite. Six out of the nine Africans were chiefs who by this time had come to be regarded as stooges.

With the coming of these revised constitutions the National Congress of British West Africa started to decline. The educated elements in Nigeria and the Gold Coast concentrated their attention on fighting the elections to their respective legislative councils. For this purpose Herbert Macaulay formed in 1923 the Nigerian National Democratic Party which from then on dominated Lagos politics until 1938 when it was eclipsed by the Nigerian Youth Movement whose origins go back to 1934.

Thus by the time the Second World War came in 1939 the educated élite in British West Africa had not achieved much in their fight against colonial rule. They were handicapped by many things. The British were still convinced that the new élite had neither the ability to govern nor the right to speak for its fellow Africans and so held it in contempt. To some extent members of the élite were responsible for the way in which they were treated. They confined their activities to the highly westernized urban cities of the coast – Calabar, Lagos, Accra, Cape Coast, Freetown and Bathurst and thus failed to make any attempt to rouse their country-men in the interior. Also their demands made them appear self-seeking. Rights to be employed in the civil service, representation in the legislative council, employment of Africans in the judiciary, the establishment of a university – these were all demands which benefited members of their class and which the majority of the people in the interior could not understand. None of them called for the end of alien rule. It was not until 1938 that the Nigerian Youth Movement asked that Nigeria be granted 'complete autonomy within the British Empire'. Then the nationalist leaders of these years – apart from individual radicals like the Sierra Leonian, I.T.A. Wallace-Johnson – were mostly moderates. Since they did not ask or press for much they received only limited concessions. Furthermore the political groups which fought the nationalist battles of these years were not really modern political parties. The Aborigines' Rights Protection Society of the Gold Coast, the National Congress of British West Africa, the Nigerian National Democratic Party; each was a loose collection of gentlemen dominated by a single personality. They all lacked proper organization and discipline. However, they prepared the way for the rise later of modern political parties.

But even before the Second World War came there were signs of change in the tactics of the new elite, as seen in the activities of an American-educated Igbo, Nnamdi Azikiwe. This remarkable man came back from the United States in 1934, and after failing to get a job under the Nigerian government went to the Gold Coast where from 1935 to 1937 he edited a newspaper, the *African Morning Post*. In 1937 he came back to Lagos and established his most influential newspaper, the *West African Pilot*. Azikiwe differed from the politicians who preceded him in two ways. He was radical and inclined to use violent language against the Europeans and thus won the admiration of his fellow Africans who were happy to see one of themselves who could speak plainly to the white masters. In the second place he was the first to attempt to get the people in the interior to take part in the modern political struggle. To this end he made his newspapers cheap and established dailies at Ibadan, Onitsha, Port Harcourt and Kano and in this way got many more people to know what the fight between the new élite and the British was all about. After the Second World War another American-educated West African, Kwame Nkrumah, did precise-

Nnamdi Azikiwe

ly the same thing in the Gold Coast. However the fact remains that when the Second World War came the colonial powers in West Africa still felt as secure as ever. In the then British West Africa there were still educated men who enjoyed humming the song 'British Empire Shall Never Perish'. But the war brought about a complete change in the situation. How this change came about and its consequences will be dealt with in Chapter 2.

2 The triumph of nationalism in West Africa

New forces making for increased nationalist agitation

The Second World War affected the nationalist movement in West Africa in two main ways. First, by the end of it many more people had started to take part in the nationalist struggle than had done so in the years before 1939. Secondly, the agitation became more vigorous and continuous than before. Even in the French territories the outlook of the élite became greatly changed, largely as a result of political developments in neighbouring British colonies which soon made the French-speaking West African élite ask first for internal self-government and then for independence.

In the course of their conflict with Hitler the Allied Powers had framed their propaganda in such a way as to rouse peoples in different parts of the world against Germany. For instance in Article 3 of the Atlantic Charter the Allies promised to respect 'the right of all peoples to choose the form of government under which they will live'. This declaration was welcome to all colonial nationalists as they believed it to mean that at the end of the war they would have the right to ask for, and be granted, self-government and independence. At the same time the Americans gave much encouragement to colonial nationalists by openly attacking imperialism and supporting the demands of oppressed peoples for justice and self-government. To the influence of the United States must be added that of the Soviet Union which started campaigning openly for colonial independence on the floor of the United Nations Organization. Whereas the British Prime Minister, Winston Churchill, wanted Article 3 of the Atlantic Charter to be applied only to European peoples, the Americans said it applied to all peoples throughout the world. Even within Britain there were men and women who raised their voices against imperialism. The Labour Party, for instance, came out in favour of granting all dependent peoples the right of self-determination. Also the activities of the West African Students' Union (WASU) in London strengthened the demands of the nationalists at home.

Through the WASU, which was formed in 1925, West African students pressed their demands for political reform through public lectures and lobbying for the support of sympathetic statesmen and members of parliament. Apart from helping to intensify the nationalist agitation WASU provided training in political organization and leadership for many of its members. Some of these came back later to become leading statesmen in their different countries.

The war also caused a certain amount of economic expansion in West Africa for after the Allied Powers had lost control of the Far East in 1941 they came to depend on Africa to a greater extent than before for many of the raw materials which they needed either in industry or for feeding their peoples. This changed economic situation caused a rapid increase in the export and import trade of West Africa and brought much money to her peoples. The population expanded, new urban centres sprang up and more people were sent to school. Part of the end result was that a large section of West African peoples came under unsettling influences which made them more difficult to control than before, and more ready to listen to the propaganda of the new élite against alien rule. As the war drew to a close thousands of West African ex-servicemen came back with new ideas and attitudes as well as with stories which showed that Europeans were ordinary flesh and blood, and that some indeed worked as stewards, cooks, cleaners or even lived by begging. Much of the respect and fear which European administrators had excited before 1939 had disappeared by the end of the war.

The nationalists used this new and favourable situation to great advantage. They did not forget that because they had so far paid attention only to the coastal towns their right to speak for the people in the interior had been challenged. They therefore campaigned for, and secured, increasing support from the masses both along the coast and in the interior. The élite were further favoured by the fact that many trade unions had come into existence during the war years. As the cost of living rose in those years the workers formed unions to enable them to help each other and agitate for increased wages without being victimized individually. These unions became ready and formidable instruments in the hands of the nationalists for bringing pressure on colonial governments. To strengthen their hands further, the élite formed properly organized political parties which had branches all over the country and newspapers in the urban centres for making their points of view known to the people. The roads and railways which the colonial governments had built to serve economic and administrative needs were now put to nationalist advantage. Improved communication made it easy for a political party to maintain contact with its many branches and to plan and carry out extensive campaigns.

Changing attitudes of France and Britain

We can therefore say that by 1945 the ground had been well prepared for the final stages of the political struggle between the nationalists and the colonial administrations. Even before the war ended there were signs that the latter, especially the British, had become aware of the need to grant more political rights to their dependent subjects. This change of attitude on the part of the colonial powers helps to explain why the nationalists were able to secure one concession after another without having to use physical coercion. Britain led the way in the business of admitting her colonial élite to the heritage of political power in her West African territories. In 1942, for instance, some unofficial members of the legislative councils of the Gold Coast and Nigeria were given seats on the Governors' executive councils which formerly contained officials only. The same development took place in Sierra Leone in 1943 but not until 1947 in The Gambia. As a result of this concession Africans were able to take some part in the discussion of government measures and proposals before they came to the legislative council. But this concession did not satisfy the nationalists for the unofficial elements in the executive council were too few to influence official policy appreciably. Furthermore, since they were made to take an oath not to reveal what was discussed in the executive council, these men could not give their fellow African unofficial members the benefit of their inside knowledge of government policy.

Constitutional revisions in British West Africa

Immediately after the war the constitutions of the Gold Coast and of Nigeria were further revised. The most important concession in these new constitutions introduced in 1946 was the fact that Africans were given an elected majority in the legislative council. Sierra Leone and The Gambia reached the same stage in 1951 and 1954 respectively. However, this constitution aroused much criticism from the nationalists in the Gold Coast and Nigeria. In the first place the new élite bitterly attacked the fact that only a small fraction of the African unofficials was directly elected while the larger fraction was elected indirectly by the Native Authorities which the élite neither liked nor trusted. In the second place the executive council was not reformed: African membership was not increased and the unofficials in it were not given any specific functions to perform. The constitutional revisions of 1946 in the Gold Coast and Nigeria therefore merely gave Africans an increased opportunity of taking part in the discussion of government business, rather than the right to help in framing and carrying out policy which was the very thing the nationalists wanted. In Nigeria there were two other reasons why the constitution was vehemently attacked. One of these was that the Governor, Sir Arthur Richards, introduced the new constitution without consulting the political leaders of the nation, let alone the common people. The nationalists regarded this as a slight. In the second place the fact that under the constitution Nigeria was divided into three regions each of which had its own house of assembly and an executive council offended those nationalists who felt that Britain was deliberately trying to weaken the country by dividing it into three semi-autonomous units.

In 1951 the constitution was further revised in the Gold Coast and Nigeria, in 1953 in Sierra Leone and in 1954 in The Gambia. The aim of this revision was to give the nationalists some responsibility for taking official decisions and for carrying them out; in short it was the first real step towards transforming the Governor's executive council into a modern cabinet. The African members of the executive council were increased in number and given ministerial positions though not all of them were attached to specific departments. In the Gold Coast, for instance, the executive was made to consist of the Governor who was president, Kwame Nkrumah who was Leader of Government Business, eight other African ministers, six of whom had portfolios, and three European officials who also held ministerial positions. The legislative assembly was reconstituted to comprise thirty-eight members elected directly by the people and thirty-seven elected indirectly by the Native Authorities. There were four aspects of this revised constitution which failed to satisfy the nationalists. The first was the presence in the executive council of European officials who did not in any way represent the people. The second was the fact that the executive was not responsible to the legislature, that is that the members of the legislature could not force all the members of the executive to resign at once, though they could force an individual minister to resign. The executive remained responsible to the Governor who could dismiss it. The third shortcoming of the constitution was that the ministers who had portfolios did not enjoy the right to make policies for their departments; policy-making remained the responsibility of the European heads of those departments. The duty of the African ministers was to answer questions about their departments in the legislature, to introduce matters touching their departments in the council of ministers and to co-operate with the European heads of their departments in carrying out policies approved by the government. The fourth complaint against this constitution was that the members of the legislature were not all directly elected.

However, slowly but steadily these shortcomings were removed. In the Gold Coast the constitution was revised again in 1954. In the first place the executive became an all-African cabinet presided over by a Prime Minister who chose from his supporters in the legislature those who were to work with him. The Prime Minister had the right to dismiss or replace any of his ministers and the whole cabinet remained in office for as long as it had the support of the majority in the legislature. The ministers became directly responsible for their departments, though owing to lack of experience they tended to depend a great deal on the European permanent secretaries. Nigeria attained the same position in 1957, Sierra Leone and The Gambia in 1958 and 1962 respectively.

The remaining complaint which the nationalists had against the legislature was removed in 1954 in the Gold Coast and Nigeria when it was conceded that all members of the legislature in each of these two countries had to come in by direct election. This concession was a major victory for the élite. We have already seen that there was a time when Britain thought that it was to the traditional rulers and not to the new élite that she would eventually hand over political power in West Africa. Even after the war Britain had entertained the idea of enabling the chiefs to share in political power at the centre as shown in the constitutions she granted the Gold Coast and Nigeria in 1946 and 1951. This 1954 concession, therefore, was a confession by Britain that she had hoped for too much from indirect rule and that her previous policy towards the new élite was unwise. Even in Sierra Leone and The Gambia where the chiefs continued to be directly represented in the legislature, political power passed into the hands of the new élite with the granting of internal self-goverment.

British colonies gain independence

From internal self-government the next, and the last, stage in the victory of the new élite over the British was full independence with which each of these four territories got absolute control over its own internal and external affairs. On 6 March 1975 the Gold Coast attained this stage under the name of Ghana. Nigeria followed on 1 October 1960, Sierra Leone on 27 April 1961 and The Gambia on 18 February 1964.

Since British policy after the Second World War favoured the granting of political power to the nationals of her West African colonies, on the surface it seems strange that the conflict between the nationalists and Britain not only continued but in fact became more bitter than in the years before 1939. There were two reasons for this. The first was that both groups could not agree on how soon self-government and independence should come. Britain believed that it would take some time since she felt she still had to train the nationalists in the business of running a modern state. The nationalists on their side were impatient with the official approach and accused the British of hypocrisy. They refused to accept the view that they were not already well-equipped to exercise political power. In the second place, as we have just seen, Britain still believed that the Native Authorities which she had nurtured with so much care must be made to take an important part in central government. This again was unacceptable to the new élite which felt that the chiefs were too ignorant and too conservative to play any useful role in the political and economic development of a modern state. They accused the British of adopting this policy in order to prolong their rule in West Africa. These were the issues at the root of the bitter clashes between the British and the nationalists which took place in the period 1945 to 1954 in the Gold Coast and Nigeria. Constitutional progress in Sierra Leone and The Gambia took place not necessarily as a result of the efforts of the nationalists there, but at times in response to developments in the other two British West African territories.

France grants political rights to her colonies

In less than two decades after the Second World War French rule in West Africa was likewise at an end. The French, like the British, showed themselves prepared to grant their colonies in West Africa more and more political rights after 1945. But whereas self-government and independence in English-speaking West Africa came as a result of pressure from the nationalists, in French-speaking West Africa the initiative came from the French themselves. In 1944, for instance, General Charles de Gaulle called a meeting of France's colonial governors at Brazzaville to recommend what French colonial policy should be after the war. Though the conference denied that France could ever grant self-government to her colonies in Africa, it made important recommendations on how to reform French colonial administration. It advised the abolition of forced labour and of the *indigénat*. It also recommended that the powers of the Governor-General be reduced in order to give more powers to the administration in each territory. It suggested the setting up of an elected assembly in each colony to help the Lieutenant-Governor, and of a central council (*Grand Conseil*) to which all territories in French West Africa would send representatives. The conference also recommended that French West Africa should be represented in the constituent assembly which would draw up a new constitution for France after the war. The goal of post-war French colonial policy was the implementation of these suggested reforms.

French West Africa participated in the constituent assembly which met

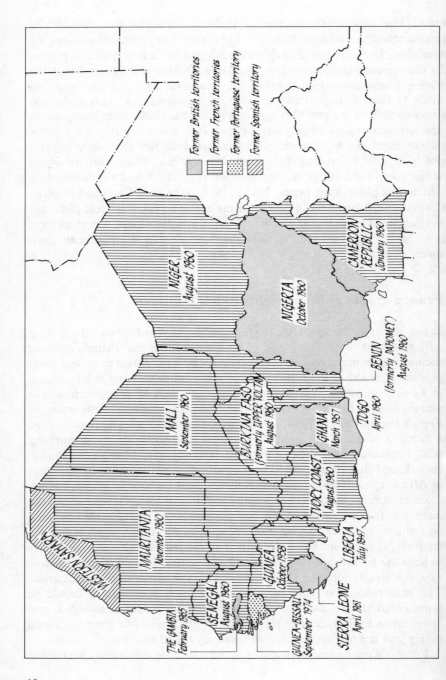

Former British territories
Former French territories
Former Portuguese territory
Former Spanish territory

WESTERN SAHARA

MAURITANIA
November 1960

MALI
September 1960

NIGER
August 1960

NIGERIA
October 1960

CAMEROON
REPUBLIC
January 1960

THE GAMBIA
February 1965

SENEGAL
August 1960

GUINEA
October 1958

GUINEA-BISSAU
September 1974

SIERRA LEONE
April 1961

LIBERIA
July 1847

IVORY COAST
August 1960

BURKINA FASO
(formerly UPPER VOLTA)
August 1960

GHANA
March 1957

TOGO
April 1960

BENIN
(formerly DAHOMEY)
August 1960

after the war. In the constitution which the assembly drew up the French empire was reorganized and renamed the French Union, consisting of metropolitan France, the overseas departments (for example, Martinique and Guadeloupe) and the overseas territories in which category French West Africa was included. All French West Africans were declared citizens and in this way the distinction between citizens and subjects disappeared. Forced labour was abolished, while a later decree abolished the *indigénat*. Also an elected assembly, known from 1952 as the Territorial Assembly, was set up for each colony. This assembly had more extensive powers in French Togo and Cameroun than in the rest of French West Africa. In 1947 a federal council known as the *Grand Conseil* was set up under the High Commissioner (the former Governor-General) at Dakar. In addition to all these concessions at the local level French West African colonies were given the right to elect deputies to represent them in the French National Assembly and the Senate as well as in the Assembly of the French Union.

These reforms soon turned out to be inadequate. The French Ministry of Colonies continued to legislate for French West Africa and in doing so was not bound to take the advice of its deputies. The social reforms which were decreed were not carried out quickly: for instance the *indigénat* took time to disappear. Though all West Africans were declared French citizens, a new distinction was made between French citizens of French status and French citizens of local status. The former were subject to French law and so were considered superior to the latter who remained subject to their indigenous law. What was more, the territorial assemblies had only limited powers especially outside Togo and Cameroun. The élite in French West Africa in this period thus asked for increased powers for the assemblies, the introduction of democratic practices into the administration and for equality of social and political rights with Frenchmen. They did not, however, ask for self-government, nor were they ready to attack the administration as vigorously as their counterparts in British West Africa did. Therefore after 1946 France paid little attention to the question of political development in her West African territories for nearly a decade.

Independence in French West Africa

It was largely due to happenings in British West Africa that France came to grant a further instalment of political rights to her colonies in 1956. In that year Félix Houphouët-Boigny, an Ivory Coast Deputy to the National Assembly, who was given a cabinet post, helped France in framing the *loi cadre* 'outline law' which gave the French government extensive powers to legislate detailed political reforms in West Africa. A series of decrees issued under the *loi cadre* by the French Ministry of Colonies granted a form of internal self-government to each territory. Each Territorial Assembly was granted the power to elect, from among its members, a council of ministers which under the presidency of the Governor (the former Lieutenant-Governor) constituted the executive for the territory. The minister who had the largest vote in the assembly was made the vice-president. The council of ministers resigned if it was defeated in the assembly. Each Territorial Assembly was given the right to pass laws for its area of authority on such subjects as agriculture, health, primary and secondary education, internal trade and civil service, each of which came under a minister. Subjects like defence, foreign affairs, currency and economic development remained in the hands of the metropolitan government, and laws passed on them were carried out under the direction of the High Commissioner. In Togo and Cameroun because of their status as territories under United Nations trusteeship the reforms went a little further. Togo became an autonomous republic within the French Union in 1956. But though it was given a prime minister its assembly had the same powers as those of other French West African territories. Cameroun attained the same status as Togo in 1957.

De Gaulle's referendum

These changes satisfied a large section of the new élite in French West Africa, but a few radicals insisted on full independence. Then in 1958 de Gaulle became French President, and in the new constitution which he published in July that year he decided to transform the French Union into the French Community. He saw the community as a sort of French Commonwealth of Nations, but unlike the British Commonwealth it was to be under the effective control of France. It was to have an executive council which would be made up of de Gaulle (president), a number of French cabinet ministers and the prime minister of each of the member states. This council would deal with issues of common interest to the community like defence, foreign affairs and economic policy. This constitution was to be approved by a referendum in September and the French West African territories had to choose between voting 'Yes' and becoming autonomous republics within the community, or voting 'No' and attaining immediate independence outside it. De Gaulle made it clear that any territory which chose the latter course would at once lose French economic and technical aid. Since the economies of the French West

A poster for the French West African referendum of 1958

African territories were closely tied to that of France this threat succeeded in forcing nearly all of them to vote in favour of the constitution. Only Guinea voted 'No' and became independent overnight. Because of this France withdrew all assistance to Guinea and even refused to accord her diplomatic recognition. In November 1958 the other territories became autonomous states within the community. But by this time complete independence had became the ultimate end which the new élite in these states had in view. Thus in 1959 Senegal and Soudan, which had meanwhile formed the Mali Republic, asked for an amendment of the constitution of the community in such a way as to allow them to achieve full independence without losing their membership of the Community. This amendment was made and by November 1960 all the former French West African colonies had become fully independent states. With the exception of Guinea, all the erstwhile French West African colonies remained closely linked with France through agreements on such subjects as technical assistance, defence, currency and economic aid. Togo and Cameroun also attained independent status about the same time as the other French territories. In 1960 when the United Nations decided to end its trusteeship of these two territories, Togo immediately became independent. Cameroun followed suit in 1961 after uniting to form the Cameroon Republic with the Southern Cameroons which had voted to remain outside the Federation of Nigeria.

Political parties in British West Africa

An interesting feature of the politics of the post-war years in West Africa was the tendency for members of the élite to fight among themselves almost as bitterly as they fought their colonial masters. The reasons for this development varied from place to place and can be best understood by a study of the relationship which existed among the various political parties which came into existence within each territory at this time. We can start with the Gold Coast which was the first West African colony to attain independence.

From the days of the Mankessim constitution (see Volume 1) to those of the Aborigines' Rights Protection Society and of the National Congress of British West Africa, the new élite in the Gold Coast had seemed to present a united front against the British. But with the coming of the post-war political concessions disagreements set in. In 1947 the new élite had formed the United Gold Coast Convention (UGCC) in response to the challenge of the Burns Constitution of the previous year. This party aimed at using all constitutional and legal means to press for self-government for the Gold Coast 'within the shortest time possible'. In 1948 Dr Kwame Nkrumah was invited to become its Secretary-General. But it soon became clear that his attitude to political agitation was quite different from that of the foundation members of the UGCC. The latter wanted to carry on in the leisurely manner which had characterized nationalist politics before

1939. They wanted to concern themselves with the colony and perhaps with Asante, but certainly not with the Northern Territories or the region beyond the Volta or with British Togoland. In short they had no plans for making politics an affair of the whole country and of the masses. Nkrumah on the other hand had contrary ideas. He wanted to call up the masses and to make the nationalist movement nationwide. For this purpose he sought the support of the trade unions and established newspapers at Sekondi, Cape Coast and Accra to inform the people. He also undertook tours of different parts of the country during which he gave public lectures to educate the masses. Because he believed in militant politics he set up the 'Committee on Youth Organization' which mobilized the youth of the country and affiliated them to the party. What was more, Nkrumah believed in achieving 'self-government now' rather than 'within the shortest time possible'. This radicalism proved too much for the leisurely gentlemen who had founded the UGCC and they started planning to expel its author. But on 12 June 1949, a day before before his planned expulsion, Nkrumah took the radical elements out of the UGCC and formed the Convention People's Party (CPP).

In 1954 the Gold Coast attained full internal self-government under the CPP which derived most of its support from the Colony area. As soon as it appeared that the British were about to hand over political power to the CPP government, parties sprang up in various parts of the country to protect local ethnic interests. Already by 1954, there were about four such sectional parties in existence in the Gold Coast. The Northern Peoples' Party rose to defend the Northern Territories against southern domination. The Togoland Congress Party wanted British Togoland separated from the Gold Coast and united with French Togo. The National Liberation Movement which was based in Asante fought for Asante 'national' interests. In particular it was opposed to the CPP's policy of using the national income derived mainly from Asante cocoa for the development of the whole country. A Muslim Association Party which derived its support from Kumasi and the Colony area was formed to protect the interests of the Muslims. The most important result of this rise of mutually opposed parties in the Gold Coast was that the new élite became divided on whether the country should have a federal or a unitary government. Those from Asante and the Northern Territories wanted a federation because they thought it would give them protection against the Colony area. It was the CPP alone that stood for a unitary constitution. The conflict between these two aims was in fact responsible for the fact that the Gold Coast did not become independent before 1957. And even when independence came in 1957 the constitution stipulated that regional assemblies had to be set up for regions which wanted them as a means of allaying ethnic group fears.

Kwame Nkrumah with his first post-independence Cabinet

Similar things happened in the rest of British West Africa. In Nigeria the Nigerian Youth Movement (NYM) broke into two factions in 1941 as a result of conflicts between its Igbo and Yoruba members. In 1944 one of the factions formed the National Council of Nigeria and the Cameroons (NCNC) under the leadership of Herbert Macaulay. When the latter died in 1946 the party came to be led by Nnamdi Azikiwe. By the time of the Macpherson Constitution in 1951 the NCNC derived its greatest following from among the Igbo. The Yoruba therefore felt that if they were to be saved from Igbo domination they must have a party that could speak for them. It was largely this fear that brought the Action Group with Obafemi Awolowo as its major leader into being in 1951. In the same way the Fulani and Hausa élite of Northern Nigeria feared that if they did not organize their own party, independence would merely transform British rule into 'southern rule'. Their answer to this supposed threat was the formation of the Northern Peoples' Congress (NPC). At one stage, in 1953, the enmity between the southern parties and the NPC nearly split Nigeria into two nations. The three parties came to agree on a federal constitution for the country as the best means of preserving unity and ensuring that no single ethnic group dominated the others. This arrangement did not solve these problems as subsequent Nigerian politics clearly showed. Not all Northern Nigerians, however, belonged to the NPC. There were a few radical elements who regarded the NPC as the party of backward-looking conservatives and autocrats. It was such men who formed the Northern Elements Progressive Union under Mallam Aminu Kano to press for democracy and rapid economic development in Northern Nigeria.

In Sierra Leone, and to a lesser extent in The Gambia, the conflict was mainly between the more westernized coastal colony areas and the more conservative inland protectorates. The Sierra Leone People's Party (SLPP) which became the dominant party in Sierra Leone derived its main support from the Protectorate.

Political parties in French West Africa

In French West Africa there were two main sources of disagreement amongst the élite and these are clearly brought out in the history of the Rassemblement Démocratique Africain (RDA) which was the most powerful political party in French West and Equatorial Africa. The RDA was formed in October 1946 at Bamako under the leadership of Félix Houphoüet-Boigny of the Ivory Coast. The African delegates to the French National Constituent Assembly had felt that they would be in a better position to exert a strong influence on French politics if they acted as a group. What was more, they wanted to fight the conservatives in the assembly who were not enthusiastic about colonial reform. Therefore they summoned a congress of political, trade union and youth leaders at Bamako in 1946. The French government, fearing that the Communist Party would gain undue control over the Bamako congress, used its influence to keep some of the deputies away from it. For instance the Senegalese deputies – Lamine Guèye and Léopold Senghor – were prevailed upon not to attend. When the RDA allied with the Communist Party, Senghor and the other African deputies who refused to join it came together and formed the parliamentary party known as the Indépendants d'Outre-Mer (Overseas Independents – IOM). This was the party of moderates and was allied to the French Socialist Party. Thus after the Second World War the élite of French West Africa came to be openly split into radical and moderate groups.

Up to 1950 the RDA enjoyed a measure of internal harmony and stability, but after that date it started to experience severe strains first because of ideological differences and then because of conflicting attitudes too the issue of federation in French West Africa. After 1950 Houphoüet-Boigny came to favour compromise with the French government in place

Félix Houphouët-Boigny, President of Ivory Coast, with President Charles de Gaulle of France

of the alliance with the French Communist Party. This policy of compromise was not acceptable to the Secretary-General of the RDA, Gabriel d'Arboussier, who led the radical wing of the party which favoured open defiance of France. The ensuing conflict soon led to the expulsion of the radicals. A further split among the élite followed as a result of the *loi cadre* of 1956. Houphouë-Boigny was in favour of breaking up the federation of French West Africa. The Ivory Coast, as the richest French territory in West Africa, understandably did not like the way revenue derived from her crops was used for the development of the whole federation. Senegal was the second richest but she benefited from the fact that Dakar was the federal capital and so favoured maintaining the federation intact. Houphoüet-Biogny supported the *loi cadre* because it weakened federal authority by giving each territory self-government. His ideal was independence for each territory and then federation with France. But other RDA leaders, especially Sekou Touré of Guinea, wanted the federation maintained and strengthened and then granted complete independence of France. Senghor also favoured federal unity because he hoped that a united French-speaking West Africa would be in a stronger position to negotiate with France than any individual territory. France on her side wanted to break up the federation as she preferred dealing with each territory separately to dealing with the federation as a unit. An attempt in 1958 to bring all political parties in French West Africa together failed owning to this disagreement on the federal issue. When the RDA refused to accept any compromise the small territorial parties came together and formed the Parti du Regroupement Africain (PRA).

Before the internal conflicts in the RDA could be resolved de Gaulle introduced his famous constitution for the French Community in 1958. This turned out to be the parting of the ways. The RDA leaders in Guinea opted for immediate independence. The other territories in voting for the status of autonomous republic within the community helped in breaking up the federation. After 1958, however, federation still remained a burning question in the politics of the former French territories. In December 1958 the PRA, which strongly continued to support the idea of federation, succeeded in getting Senegal, Soudan, Dahomey and Upper Volta to agree to the formation of a Mali federation. But before this verbal agreement could become practical politics Houphouët-Boigny and France brought pressure to bear on Dahomey and Upper Volta to stay out of the proposed union. In spite of this setback Senegal and Soudan went ahead to form the Mali federation in April 1959. In May the Ivory Coast sought to counterbalance the influence of this new bloc by forming the Conseil de l'Entente (Entente Council), a loose economic union, with Upper Volta, Niger and Dahomey. In August 1960 the Mali federation broke up,

Senegal withdrew leaving the name 'Mali' for the former Soudan. The idea of a French-speaking West African federation thus eluded its enthusiasts. Like its English-speaking counterpart the French-speaking élite found itself uncompromisingly divided as the prospect for enjoying political power became brighter.

The independence movement in Portuguese West Africa

As already mentioned in Volume 1, Portugal did not seize the opportunity of the general European partition of Africa to increase her holdings in West Africa. Portuguese West Africa thus meant no more than the small enclave of Guinea-Bissau and the Cape Verde Islands. To give an idea of the area concerned it may be mentioned that Guinea-Bissau, the main territory, had a population of only about 650 000 people. This population was split into many ethnic groups with each ethnic group being further split into small mutually autonomous communities.

On these little enclaves Portugal imposed what was certainly the most brutal regime in colonial West Africa. To the end it rested on naked military might. Not surprisingly it had to be overthrown by means of an open war of attrition. Portugal allowed no scope whatever for political expression to her colonials. The right to form trade unions or to strike was denied. Nor did she invest in the development of the territories. Even the bauxite which was found there could not be mined because Portugal had no money to invest in its exploitation. The economy rested mainly on agriculture, especially the cultivation of groundnuts. This was done in large European plantations worked mainly by means of forced labour. Both the government and private European farmers could recruit forced labour without let or hindrance until 1928 when a so-called Native Labour Code was passed. This restricted the use of forced labour to government projects. But in practice private farmers continued to flout the law with the support of local officials.

To make matters worse Portugal adopted a policy of systematic cultural suppression. She banned the use of local languages in schools as part of her policy of asimilation. But the policy of assimilation was a mere pretence since little scope existed for real education. Yet only those who attained a certain prescribed level of education and had imbibed a certain amount of Portuguese culture could be assimilated. In the event by 1960 only about eleven colonials had qualified to be conferred with Portuguese citizenship. Also only few colonials participated in the administration.

The export economy was in the hands of the Portuguese, indeed under the monopoly control of one Portuguese company which was thus able to

Amílcar Cabral

squeeze the people as much as it liked. So harsh was the regime that Guinea-Bissau which had little population to spare lost about 50 000 people to other West African territories between 1930 and 1970 by emigration. Cape Verde lost about 4000 in the same way in the 1950s.

This unbearable regime could not continue unchallenged for ever, especially in the light of what was happening in the rest of colonial West Africa at the time. And the challenge came in 1958, centred around the person of Amílcar Cabral.

Cabral, who came from Cape Verde, was one of the few people from

Portuguese Guinea to have been well educated. While in Portugal he had come into contact with a number of other Portuguese colonial subjects, especially from Angola, whose education had awakened in them a deep resentment of Portuguese colonial policy and oppression. One of these was Agostinho Neto, the future leader of the Movimento Popular de Libertação de Angola (Popular Movement for the Liberation of Angola – MPLA) in Angola. Cabral and his colleagues became interested in the activities of the radical groups in Europe, especially the Marxist wing of them. Through this contact and through the reading of Marxist classics he became a revolutionary committed to improving the social and economic circumstances of the people. He was, however, convinced that European Marxism would not fit the conditions existing in Africa. The need existed, he felt, to work out a version of that ideology which could better serve the needs of the toiling masses of Africa.

In 1950 Cabral returned to Guinea-Bissau from Portugal. As an agricultural expert he gained an appointment in the Ministry of Agriculture and was deployed as a field officer to carry out an agricultural census of the colony for his department. This posting was of great use to him. It gave him the opportunity to gain a first-hand knowledge of the land and its people and to build up intimate contact with the peasants and rural labourers. In 1953, by which date a few more educated Africans had returned to Guinea-Bissau, he championed the formation of a nationalist movement called the Movimento de Independência Nacional da Guiné Portuguesa (Movement for National Independence of Guinea — MING). The aim was to co-ordinate the efforts of all educated Africans who were revolted by the Portuguese regime and to create some political consciousness amongst the people.

The going was difficult and the movement achieved very little at first. In 1956, however, it was decided to convert the group into a formal political party which was named the Partido Africano da Independência da Guiné e Cabo Verde (African Party for the Independence of Guinea and Cape Verde – PAIGC). The party's programme was independence by all means. But not until 1959 did its activities come into the open in consequence of a dock-workers' strike which the Portuguese suppressed with great brutality.

Predictably the Portuguese responded to the emergence of PAIGC with violent repression in the hope of overwhelming Cabral and his party militarily. But this was not to be. Cabral and his men had done their groundwork well. Also the international atmosphere of the 1950s was quite different from that in which the Portuguese had imposed their rule in the first place. The reasons for the failure of the Portuguese to withstand the challenge of PAIGC were many.

Of these factors, probably the most important was the organization and working of the PAIGC itself. The party organized for guerrilla warfare which depends on hit-and-run tactics rather than for conventional warfare depending on large armies, positional manoeuvres and heavy armament. And the terrain of Guinea-Bissau was well-suited for guerrilla warfare. It is marshy and forested for the most part and thus unsuited for the manoeuvres of large armies such as those that the Portuguese used. After 1958 when Sekou Touré's Guinea became independent, Cabral and his men made Guinea their adminstrative headquarters. They they trained revolutionary activists and fighters who were sent back to Guinea-Bissau to mobilize the people effectively against the government. To retain the loyalty of the people his men gave exemplary leadership and identified themselves with the people and their suffering. And as the war progressed and some territories were captured from the colonial forces PAIGC took every opportunity to give the people concrete rewards for their sacrifices and some idea of what an independent Guinea-Bissau had in store for them. To this end schools and hospitals were built while young men and women were sent to such friendly countries as the Soviet Union for training in relevant professions.

Another important factor was foreign support. The PAIGC recognized from the beginning that it could not face Portugal alone, and so set out to win as much foreign sympathy and support as possible. And it was lucky in the fact that the emerging African states were committed to the liquidation of all forms of colonialism in the continent. Mention has already been made of Sekou Touré's vital support which among other things enabled the party to set up a government in exile. Arms and other material supports were received from China, the Soviet Union and other communist countries. These landed in Sekou Touré's Guinea before being shipped to Guinea-Bissau. From the temporary headquarters a fierce and withering propaganda warfare was waged on Portugal. Other African countries also gave Cabral and his colleagues moral and some material support and helped with propaganda. The Organization of African Unity (OAU) also gave support, helping to take the matter to the United Nations.

A third important factor was the fact that Portugal was hampered by similar armed conflicts in her other African colonies. The result was that her resources were rather overstretched. At one time she had about 75 per cent of all her armed forces in the colonies fighting to sustain a situation which even her friends recognized as untenable. The strain of the war soon began causing stress and division at home, especially as the government was an unpopular dictatorship. Conflicts and disillusionment arising from this running sore of colonial wars were to lead, in 1974, to a military coup which overthrew the hated dictatorship.

By the 1960s the case of PAIGC was no longer new to world opinion. Cabral and his colleagues spoke and wrote extensively exposing the evils of Portuguese colonialism and advertising the military and other successes of their party – the union it had forged with the masses, its ability to bog down the Portuguese army which was superior in numbers and equipment, its control of the provinces and so on. It soon became clear that Portugal could not win the war. In addition the international propaganda against her reached such a pitch that the term 'Portuguese colonialism' stank in the nostrils of even Portugal's sympathizers.

By 1973 the PAIGC had won such successes that it felt itself strong enough to proclaim the independence of Guinea-Bissau. And such was the international sympathy it had that many nations immediately recognized the sovereign status of the new state. In April 1974 there was the coup in Portugal. The new government decided to cut Portugal's losses and so began pulling her forces out of Guinea-Bissau. When this was completed in September the same year, Portugal faced the accomplished fact by recognizing her former colony as a sovereign state. Unfortunately Cabral did not live to see this event. He had been assassinated in January 1974. But his work had not been in vain.

3 West Africa since independence

Two phrases summarize the history of West Africa since independence. These are 'the search for political stability' and 'the search for economic development'. It is a matter for argument whether the triumphant nationalists fully appreciated at first the immensity of these problems, and that the struggle to find solutions to them was going to prove more difficult and more long-lasting than the campaign against the colonial masters. In this battle against disintegration and poverty bitter experiences were to show that the ability to make fiery speeches would not be enough as it had been in the campaign against the imperialists. In this chapter we shall examine the nature of each of these two major problems and the efforts which have been made to find solutions to them. We shall also deal with various developments which led in the direction of regional co-operation.

The search for stability

The problem of internal stability and internal political unity in the new independent West African states was closely bound up with the problem of the form of government. It had been assumed by most people that these countries would adopt and run the same kind of political system and government as their former colonial masters did in their own countries. This assumption was the explanation for the kinds of constitutions which these states were given or made to adopt during the final stages of decolonization.

The Anglophone West African states were thus expected to operate what has come to be known as the Westminster parliamentary system of democracy characterized by the existence of two main parties which would alternate between being in government and being in opposition, as well as by a politically neutral civil service, armed forces and judiciary. The Francophone states were for their part expected to operate the French kind of presidential democracy with its principle of proportional representation. Under this system each party was represented in parliament in proportion to the total number of votes it scored at an election. That is to say assuming that a weak party scored only a quarter of all the votes cast at the elections, it would be entitled to have a quarter of the seats in the national assembly. But in the British system such a party could have no representation at all in parliament even if it scored one-third of the votes in all the constituencies.

The two systems both had weaknesses. That of the British has been described as based on the principle of 'winner-take-all', that is to say the winning party takes all the positions and privileges which go with being the government of the day. The others have to content themselves with being patient in the hope of winning the next time, as in a football match. Where patience and maturity were lacking this system was bound to break down fast and as we shall see this was the case in Anglophone West Africa. The French system, by contrast, encouraged the growth of a multiplicity of parties. Consequently French governments have tended to be based on coalitions of rival parties sharing different ideologies. The result has usually been frequent breakdowns of such coalitions and governments and equally frequent elections. In a new nation whose unity is shaky and where the people want a government that can bring rapid development this kind of political system would be considered an expensive luxury. Again as we shall see this was the case in Francophone West Africa. France can afford it because over the centuries she has evolved a united nation with a stable and efficient public service able to carry on with the work of maintaining law and order, and administering development programmes while phrase-mongering politicians indulged in the game of forming unstable coalitions and fighting frequent elections.

But it was not only the weaknesses inherent in these two systems that made them break down so rapidly in the West African region. Equally important in explaining their rapid demise were the internal conditions of the West African states. In the first place each of these states was an artificial creation of a colonial power. None was a nation properly so-called. On the contrary each was a hotchpotch of ethnic nationalities all of which were still fully aware of the differences between them. It has been argued that this ethnic awareness or ethnic nationalism (often called tribalism) was a creation of the period of colonial rule which brought these various peoples forcibly together and made them struggle amongst themselves for the few jobs in government, the limited opportunities in private enterprise and for the limited places existing in schools and hospitals. Whatever the case, the factor of ethnic rivalry leading to ethnic antagonism was present in each of these states and must take part of the blame for the failure of the political constitutions with which West African states attained independence.

There was yet another internal factor which is best described as the political style of West African politicians. Without exception they made being in government another business that must be made to pay. It brought rich material rewards through the taking of bribes, and the outright stealing of public funds. It brought prestige and respect. A nonentity of yesterday who managed to find himself in political office quickly became the centre of attraction and of excessive official pomp. He would now enjoy free government quarters, government-paid servants and, for the heads of government, police and military outriders in addition to a fat salary which was unrelated to his actual contribution to the well-being of the state. This fact led to a situation in which once a party came to power, whether by fair or foul means, it sought to keep it for ever, like the True Whig Party of Liberia had kept exclusive monopoly of political power from 1877 to 1980.

This had two major consequences. One was that those parties which found themselves out of government, and therefore in opposition, feared exclusion from power for all time. They consequently became impatient and so sought to take every available action to gain power at the expense of the party in government. The methods adopted by such parties included the whipping up of ethnic or tribal consciousness and the use of unorthodox election methods usually leading to violence and rigging. Where these methods and the systematic vilification of their opponents failed to achieve the end in view, they at times resorted to conspiracy, assassination and the instigation of the armed forces to take over control of the state. To preserve themselves in office the parties in power used all the machineries of government at their command to suppress the opposition. The result was a perversion of the purposes for which the police, the judiciary and even the army were established. Government contracts and appointments were reserved only for the supporters of the party in power as if all others were not full-blooded tax-paying citizens of the state.

The other consequence of this political style was the alienation of the generality of the people from the politicians. The wealth, pomp and arrogance of the politicians was contrasted unfavourably with the humble appearance of the former colonial rulers many of whom had done their work in shorts and on bicycles, in the end retiring from service as relatively poor men. To make matters worse the dawn of independence was accompanied by worsening economic and social conditions. Even the production of staple foods fell as young men fled to the towns in search of white-collar jobs. Prices rose while the few infrastructures provided by the colonialists deteriorated. Meanwhile the same flamboyant, dishonest and incompetent politicians imposed what they called austerity budgets – austerity for the people but luxury for themselves. Above all the violence which now characterized politics began making life unbearable. Political-party thugs became a common sight in the towns and it was only a short step from political thuggery to armed robbery as Nigeria has found out to her dismay.

The one-party system

The reaction of West African states to this alarming deterioration of political life was almost uniform. It took the form of the creation of one-party systems as distinct from the multi-party system with which, as we showed in Chapter 2, these states attained independence. It was hoped that a one-party system, to which all politicians would belong could adequately settle the problems discussed above – the problems of tribalism and party political warfare. All would thus share in the rewards which governing brought and be happy ever after. Also all ethnic groups would be represented both in the party and in government, and thus each would get a fair share of what Chief S.L. Akintola of Nigeria called 'the national cake'.

Apart from these rather specious arguments for the one-party system, there were others. It was maintained that the one-party system was more in accord with African sensibilities and traditions. Governments in traditional Africa were based on consensus rather than on organized rivalry and competition between different groups in the society. In the one-party system consensus would be achieved through internal debate, discussion and compromise. Without public controversies and confrontations amongst politicians, nobody would lose face, thus making it possible for harmony and brotherly love to reign. It was also argued that a one-party system was better suited to the needs and circumstances of poor countries like the West African states, which were anxious to develop rapidly and had not the necessary manpower for attaining this development. Because they were in a hurry, they could not find the time for long public debates and because they lacked manpower they wanted everybody positively involved in governing rather than leaving some to waste in the political wilderness of opposition. Finally it was argued by the Marxist-oriented groups that a multi-party system can only exist in a society divided between property owners and workers. In Africa, it was said, the only division was between colonialists and the colonized. Therefore now the colonialists had gone no real cause existed for division. All the people who had jointly suffered the humiliation of being the colonized, were now called upon to come together to develop their society.

The drive for the one-party system was simple and swift though leading to results other than harmony and brotherly love. The various trade unions and youth groups which had worked hand-in-hand with the political parties during the struggle for independence were compelled to sink their differences and form central organizations. This trend was most marked in Francophone West African states. From 1956 these different organizations were being amalgamated into central monolithic bodies and being subordinated to the leading political parties. The same trend was not entirely absent from Anglophone West Africa. Nigeria made strenuous but unsuccessful efforts to persuade her different trade unions to amalgamate into one central union. Kwame Nkrumah's Ghana was more successful in this respect. Even though the different Ghana unions were closely associated with the leading party, the Convention People's Party (CPP) from the critical days of the nationalist struggle, they were compelled in 1963 to form one central body which would ostensibly speak with one voice for all Ghananian workers. This central body was then brought directly under the party machinery.

But the critical step was the absorption of all small parties, or in any case all those in opposition, by the party in government. Where possible this was done through the application of gentle and indirect pressure – that is by the creation of situations which made the existence of such parties rather untenable and unrewarding for the members. In Sekou Touré's Guinea, in Mali and Ivory Coast such persuasion worked. In any case many politicians were reluctant to stay in opposition to be discriminated against in the distribution of jobs and government contracts. Elsewhere persuasion and mild pressure failed, thus making it necessary to use harsher methods. In Upper Volta, Niger, Cameroon, Togo, Dahomey (now Benin) and Mauritania rival political parties were banned outright. In Ghana the existence of opposition parties was not abolished by law, but government authority was used openly to destroy them. Immediately after independence the CPP government took strong action against all those who were suspected of constituting a threat to the peace and unity of Ghana. Foreigners who were suspected of meddling in Ghanaian politics were deported while parties which were accused of promoting sectional interests were declared illegal and unco-operative chiefs were destooled. When these measures failed to eliminate all forces considered a threat to the government, the infamous Preventive Detention Act of 1958 was passed. Under this law the government could keep anybody it suspected of subverting the state in detention for up to five years without a trial. The CPP government used this power to such effect that by the early 1960s Ghana became in effect, though not in law, a one-party state in which Nkrumah and his CPP ruled supreme, but still not unchallenged. In 1964 a rigged referendum sanctioned the formal creation of a one-party state.

In The Gambia, the received constitution had more life in its than in most other West African states, but that was because the so-called opposition was and remains so weak as not really to pose a serious challenge to the dominant party. In Sierra Leone, Sir Albert Margai's Sierra Leone People's Party would neither abolish the opposition nor tolerate it. In Nigeria the situation was more complex. The received constitution survived as long as it did (six years) because neither of the three major ethnic groups – the Hausa-Fulani of the north, the Yoruba of the west and the Igbo of the east – each of which had its own political party, as already shown, could swallow up the others. Preoccupied with their three-cornered conflict, they could not come together to destroy the smaller parties representing the minority ethnic groups. In fact the Action Group of the Yoruba and the National Council of Nigeria and the Cameroons (NCNC) of the Igbo competed between themselves for the support and 'love' of these minority parties. The Northern People's Congress (NPC), sure of its might, ostentatiously stayed away from the contest for 'minority' support. Also ruling out any likelihood of a single-party system in Nigeria was the fact that each of the three leading parties had at least a regional government which it controlled. The NPC had firm control of the North while the Action Group controlled the Western Region. The NCNC started with control of the Eastern Region, but with the creation of the Mid-West Region in 1963 controlled that government also.

But neither the one-party model, nor the Nigerian model based on the unstable equilibrium of many parties could guarantee peace and stablity. The one-party system merely drove the opposition underground or overseas, there to hatch plot after plot to overthrow the government by force. The result was that treason trials became a common occurrence in many states. Professor K.A. Busia, who fled Ghana and took teaching positions in European universities and who was so much beloved by the west as an intellectual and a liberal, became the symbol of Asante ethnic nationalism in opposition to Nkrumah and the CPP whose base lay mainly in southern Ghana. Bullet-proof vests and swarms of policemen became a feature of Nkrumah's public appearances.

In Nigeria while the regions had stable governments at least for a time the story was different at the centre. There the government was formed by a coalition of the NPC (the senior partner) and the NCNC with the Action Group and its allies in frustrated opposition. The cracks in the system became manifest in 1962 over an attempt to take a census of the nation. The fact that the NCNC joined the Action Group in attacking the conduct of the census and the figures returned which 'showed' that a majority of Nigerians lived in the North seriously weakened the basis of the coalition.

Meanwhile Obafemi Awolowo, the leader of the Action Group and of the oppostion at the Federal House, was accused of attempting to overthrow the federal government. He was tried and imprisoned. To make matters worse the Action Group cracked up at its home base, the Western Region, where Awolowo quarrelled with his deputy Akintola who was then the Premier of the region. In all this confusion the NPC–NCNC coalition collapsed. The NPC now allied with Chief Samuel Akintola who in 1964 had formed his own party, the Nigerian National Democratic Party (NNDP). The NCNC turned round and allied with the Action Group which it had earlier sought in alliance with the NPC to liquidate. The battle lines were clearly drawn. There was no longer any confidence amongst political colleagues. Communal riots began to erupt in different parts of the country especially in the Western Region and among the Tiv of the Middle Belt.

Military coups

Once again the reaction of West African states to this breakdown of the received independence constitutions was fairly uniform. It took the form of intervention by the armed forces in politics contrary to the tradition which the colonial rulers had sought to hand down which required them to maintain neutrality in politics. An exhaustive mention of all the coups and counter-coups, assassinations and attempted assassinations which followed would make a tedious catalogue. The endless search for alternative governments which would reconcile all groups and ensure progress, as well as the agony of these societies can be fully illustrated by reference to a few cases. Togo set the ball rolling in 1963 with the assassination of President Sylvanus Olympio, the first of its kind in independent West Africa. The army hesitated to take over and so installed another civilian president in the person of Nicholas Grunitzky. But within two years the hesitation evaporated and so it took over in 1965. In January 1966 President Maurice Yaméogo of Upper Volta was said to have resigned thus 'enabling' the army to assume the government. By 1966 it was the turn of Anglophone states. There was the January coup in Nigeria followed by the one that toppled Nkrumah's government in Ghana in February. Then in July the same year there was a counter-coup in Nigeria. Sierra Leone then joined in with two coups in quick succession, the first in March 1967 overthrowing the civilian government and the second in April 1968 reinstalling a civilian government under Siaka Stevens. The same year Nigeria drifted into the civil war which lasted for three years until 1970. After that she had another coup in 1975 and an attempted one in 1976 which, though it failed, led to

Coup day in Ghana, 24 February 1966

the death of General Murtala Mohammed and the accession to power of General Olusegun Obasanjo. A period of civilian rule beginning in 1979 was brought to a close late in 1983 by a coup which installed a government led by General Muhammed Buhari. In Mali there was a coup in 1968 which brought Lieutenant Moussa Traoré to power.

In Upper Volta the army returned power to the civilians in 1970 only to turn round the next year to share power with the politicians in a diarchy. Nor did this peculiar remedy ensure peace for there was a further coup in 1974 which overthrew the diarchy and installed Colonel Sangoulé Lamizana as head of state. In 1983 Lamizana was himself overthrown in a coup led by Captain Thomas Sankara, whose regime changed the name of the country to Burkina Faso in 1984. In 1974 Lieutenant-Colonel Seyni Kountché took over power in Niger in the wake of the disastrous Sahelian drought which wrecked that nation's economy and exposed the political brankruptcy of the politicians. Meanwhile the military in Ghana had returned power to the civilians in 1969 under Busia, who was Nkrumah's arch-rival, only to take over again in 1972. Ghana was to see other, even more startling coups. The first, led by Flight-Lieutenant Jerry Rawlings in 1979 recalled some former army heads of the Ghana governments from

The military hand over, Nigeria, October 1979: General Olusegun Obasanjo with President Shehu Shagari

retirement and executed them along with General Frederick Akuffo, the incumbent head of state whom Rawlings had overthrown. After handing over to a civilian government led by President Hilla Limann in 1979, Rawlings returned to power in a new coup at the end of 1981. Nor was Liberia to be left out. In 1980 Master Sergeant Samuel K. Doe overthrew the political dominance of the True Whig Party which had lasted 113 years.

At first the military takeover of government in West Africa, as in other parts of Africa, was regarded as a short sharp remedy for the kind of abnormal situation sketched above. But after nearly twenty years, it is no longer regarded as 'short' or as a 'remedy', even though it has grown sharper and bloodier. Indeed it is now considered an intrinsic part of West African political culture. Soldiers are now considered the logical alternative to politicians. A Canadian professor of politics has indeed described African politics as 'a continuing dialogue between soldiers and politicians'. Nigerians have come to refer to the army humorously, but correctly, as 'the khaki politicians' as distinct from civilians who are referred to as 'the *agbada* politicians'. Dr Nnamdi Azikiwe, the doyen of Nigerian politics, has even seriously advocated that Nigeria should adopt that system of government in which civilian politicians and the armed forces share power.

Why is the military becoming a permanent feature of the West African political scene? The reasons are not far to seek. The factors of ethnicity, political corruption, refusal on the part of politicians to tolerate opposition or to accept the verdict of the electorate with good grace are still very much in evidence. Indeed they have tended to grow worse as these divisive tendencies have penetrated the armed forces and the judiciary which at independence were to some extent immune from them. Furthermore many army officers who held political power enjoyed every minute of it and became very rich as a result. Coups, even though they are risky, have therefore became attractive to their younger colleagues. If one succeeded in the attempt he would exercise immense political power, grow rich, and even wreak vengeance on his superiors who had denied him rapid promotion. To make matters worse political scientists drilled it into the heads of the soldiers that they are at least as good as the politicians at governing. They have been told they are as educated as the politicians, if not indeed better trained, and that at least they have discipline. And discipline is one of the qualities needed for mobilizing the people for economic and social reconstruction.

As a result everywhere in West Africa that a civilian government is in power, the politicians and their supporters continue to look over their shoulders almost all the time to see if the soldiers are coming. At the same time disgruntled politicians, journalists and university men continue to document and advertize widely the failures of those in power which in their view would justify military takeover of government.

Flight-Lieutenant J.J. Rawlings

The search for economic development

The search for economic development is closely linked with the search for political stability. The nationalists regarded economic development as the next logical step to take after achieving political independence for two reasons. In the first place political independence would be a hollow prize unless every citizen could be sure of a full stomach, good health, good education and decent shelter. And in any case much of the bitterness of national politics derived from the fact that resources are scanty and cannot go round all the persons and groups that hunger for them. If there is enough to share, there will be fewer things to wrangle over. In the second place a sound economic base is necessary to consolidate political independence. Unless a people can take their economic destiny in their own hands, and run it successfully they will not have the means to defend their independence in a brutal and competitive world. Should the economy fall into foreign hands, political independence could easily be subverted. The same would be the case should the people remain poor and therefore disenchanted and disgruntled.

It was for these reasons that right from the morrow of independence the leaders of the new states of West Africa began to emphasize the need for economic and social development. While they thought of what measures to take in order to realize this objective they sought to convey the urgency of this search to the people and to mobilize them for hard work. The slogan 'Seek ye first the political kingdom and all else will be added unto you' was likely to be misunderstood in certain quarters to mean that with political independence West Africa would enter the millennium of material plenty for little work. Thus in places like Upper Volta and Ivory Coast laws were passed authorizing the government to draft men and women of more than eighteen years of age into specified jobs for two years. Those who were found obstructing the drive were to be placed under house arrest. In some other places like Senegal units of the army were used to push through urgent development projects. In other states politicians contented themselves with speeches on the need for hard work and thrift. Nigerian leaders have continued to call on Nigerians to 'rededicate themselves anew' to patriotic hard work and service. Thus the political will was there from the beginning. But economic laws, at least in West Africa, have so far resisted the spell of political determination.

Before we go on to examine the methods which the statesmen have used in the search for social and economic development, the results achieved and the obstacles on the road to the desired economic revolution, it will be necessary to attempt first a brief analysis of the character of the West African economy at the time independence was attained.

West African economies at independence

At independence the economy of West African states was largely dependent on the production and export of raw materials. These included agricultural products like cocoa from Ghana, Nigeria and Ivory Coast; groundnuts from Nigeria, The Gambia and Sierra Leone; palm produce from Nigeria, Ghana, Benin (Dahomey), Sierra Leone; coffee from the Ivory Coast and so on. Mineral products included tin and petroleum from Nigeria, diamonds from Ghana and Sierra Leone, gold from Ghana and so on. The industrial sector was grossly underdeveloped since the colonial powers had deliberately neglected this in order to ensure that these territories remained as markets for their manufactured goods and a source of supply for the raw materials needed by their industries. However, the point must be made that at that time the agricultural sector was fairly strong, even though the prices paid for agricultural produce were beginning to decline steeply. But at least many of the countries were self-sufficient or nearly so in the staple foods of the people.

Another feature of the West African economy at that time was the poor infrastructural base. Roads were few, poorly aligned, narrow and poorly maintained, especially in Anglophone West Africa. The rail lines were few, single track and the gauge narrow. Telecommunications barely existed. And what was more what existed of these infrastructures had been constructed with limited objectives in mind. One of these was the military and political one of being able to move police and troops quickly or being able to maintain easy contact within the administration. The other objective was to be able to move raw materials from the interior to the coast for shipment overseas. The need to link areas of staple food production to markets or urban areas to rural communities was hardly considered.

One other feature which should be mentioned is the wide variation in potential wealth which existed amongst the states. Economists have divided West African countries into three groups. First are the potentially rich nations like Nigeria, Ghana, Ivory Coast, Sierra Leone and Senegal. Then there are the desperately poor nations many of which are located on the edge of the desert (the Sahel), where the soil is poor and the climate severe, with periodic droughts to make things worse. Among these countries are Mauritania, Chad and Mali for which France has remained the paymaster. 'Aid' has also come from international organizations. Then in between the two polar extremes are countries like The Gambia, Guinea, Benin, Liberia and Togo. One or two examples here will illustrate the point. Ivory Coast and Ghana in the potentially rich group have a *per capita* income of $345 and $286 a year respectively. Mali and Burkina Faso (formerly Upper Volta) in the desperately poor group have a *per capita* income of $54 and $57 a year respectively. These figures are mere statistical averages. That means that in a place like Mali there are many people whose annual income is less than $54!

Development plans

The strategy which the states adopted for attaining the much desired 'economic takeoff', as it is called in the jargon of economists, is that of drawing up and implementing development plans. The concept and practice of development planning arises from the belief of modern social scientists that the laws which guide social and economic change can be identified, controlled and guided by man. This is different from the belief of their nineteenth-century predecessors who argued that economic and social conditions were regulated by an unseen hand. Thus instead of interfering, government was to maintain law and order and allow private individuals to sort out their economic and social fortunes through free competition. Development plans arrogate to government the main initiative in economic and social development. This means that if the government is unstable, incompetent, corrupt or all three, the economy and the social services suffer severely.

Development plans of varying durations have been launched – some for fifteen years, some for ten, others for five. The first major plan launched by Nkrumah's Ghana in 1963 was for seven years. Nigeria's first plan was for seven years (1962–8). After that five-year plans came to be preferred. The second Nigerian plan lasted from 1970 to 1974 and the third from 1975 to 1980. Just as the durations of the plans have tended to vary from country to country and from plan to plan, the objectives aimed at have also tended to vary. Thus Ghana's 1963 plan was said to aim at starting the process which would transform Ghana into a socialist society within twenty years. Nigeria's second plan claimed, in grandiloquent language, that its aim was to create 'a united, a strong and self reliant nation, a land of bright and full opportunities for all citizens and a free and democratic society.' This was in the first flush of the oil boom when it was boasted that money was no problem to Nigeria. So it can be understood if Nigeria's leaders thought they could scale the skies.

Judged by the gap which today still exists between these grandiose, vague and idealistic objectives and actual levels of development attained, the plans must be written off as having completely failed, not only in Nigeria and Ghana, but throughout West Africa. But before we examine the reasons for this uniform failure it will be necessary to discuss what these plans sought to do in each sector of the economy.

Agriculture

We take first the agricultural sector. As already stated this is the main sector of the economy, at least in the sense that it is said to engage more than 70 per cent of the population. In these plans provisions were made for the establishment of schools and institutes for teaching and research in agriculture to add to the work already being done in the faculties of agriculture in the few existing universities. There were also provisions for the expansion of field and extension services, for distribution of fertilizers and insecticides to farmers, for increased food production campaigns and for the diversification of cash crops to fight dangerous dependence on a single crop. To some extent Sierra Leone has been most successful in this last regard. To her traditional crops of palm oil and ginger, Sierra Leone has added cocoa and coffee. The Gambia, which was expected to collapse economically unless she federated with Senegal, has managed to survive by expanding groundnut production and creating a tourist industry.

By and large it cannot be said that the dangers which faced agriculture at independence were fully appreciated by statesmen, who believed their economic salvation lay in industrialization. The result has been not only that earnings from agriculture have declined partly because of unstable world prices and partly because of a fall in production in certain areas. But

An oil refinery in Nigeria

also the point has now been reached at which few West African countries can feed themselves, not even so-called rich Nigeria which now spends huge proportions of her external reserves importing rice, frozen fish and meat and – what is more humiliating – palm oil. The food crisis in West Africa has reached a point where such countries as can have launched emergency measures to meet the situation. In 1972 Ghana was forced to launch Operation Feed Yourself (OFY). Nigeria followed in 1976 with an Operation Feed the Nation (OFN). In 1980 Nigeria renamed her own programme the Green Revolution and relaunched it. But to find a programme and a catchy name for it is different from solving the problem of hunger!

Industry

Then we come to the other major sector, industry. As already mentioned this was believed to hold the key to 'economic take off'. Here much has been hoped for but very little has been done, let alone achieved for reasons which will be examined below. The general approach has been the creation of industries which would achieve 'import substitution', that is the establishment of industries which would manufacture and market locally goods that would otherwise be imported. These, it is hoped, would create jobs, conserve foreign reserves and process agricultural produce locally. The weakness of this strategy is now becoming clear. Much agricultural produce continues to be exported and thus to suffer from erratic international markets. The local products are generally more costly than imported products and in any case are insufficient and not of good quality. So smuggling of banned items has become a major industry undermining these substitute industries.

The pattern taken by this form of industrialization can be illustrated by reference to Nigeria which of all West African countries has had the kind of money needed for financing these projects. Between 1962 and 1965 Nigeria set up about forty-six of these small industries under the first plan, that is more industries that the country had throughout the hundred-odd years of colonial rule. But statistics can be deceptive. When set against the area and population of the country this was like a small drop in a mighty ocean. More have been set up subsequently, especially since the end of the civil war. To illustrate the nature of these industries a few can be mentioned. They include cement factories (at Nkalagu, Ewekoro, Calabar, Benue), a salt refinery (Ichoko), petroleum refineries (Port Harcourt, Warri, Kaduna), beer breweries in nearly every state of the federation with some states like Imo and Lagos having several. There are also textile factories (for example at Aba, Kaduna and Asaba), flour mills, plastics factories and so on. None of these factories produces enough for Nigeria's needs, let alone exports that would earn foreign exchange. The textile factories do not even have enough local cotton to feed them, and yarn has to be imported from abroad. And when it cames to beer, all the ingredients, except water, are imported from abroad. What it is hoped will mark the breakthrough in Nigerian industrialization is the steel industry being built at Ajaokuta which was scheduled to be opened in 1980 but had still not begun production in 1983.

Infrastructure

The third major sector which we shall discuss here is that of infrastructure – especially communication and power on which so much depends, whether one is thinking of agriculture or of industry. We have already examined the limitations of the infrastructural base of the West African economy at independence. These were promptly recognized and tackled to improve the movement of goods and services and to meet the energy needs of the entire society. The Gambia, for instance, devoted 51 per cent of its first plan and 61 per cent of its second and third plans to the improvement of communications by road, water, air, telephone, telegraph and so on. Consequently it now has a moderately successful tourist industry. The same kind of attention has been paid to communications in other parts of West Africa. Even the colonial railways are being extended and plans made for their modernization at least in the Ivory Coast, Ghana and Nigeria. In Nigeria in particular air services have expanded tremendously with even medium-range businessmen conducting their affairs by air. All the state capitals in the federation are being linked by air. In all these cases the aim has been the same – to link region to region, urban area to urban area, urban area to rural area and food-producing areas to centres of food consumption. It can be said that progress has been much more noticeable here than in other sectors, but much still remains to be done.

Energy

Then there is the question of energy for industry, for agriculture and for domestic use. In Nigeria there are plans and talk of major industries for thermal generation of electricity and for research into solar and nuclear energy. But these remain hopes for the future. It is water resources which have been and are being harnessed throughout the West African region

The Volta Dam, Akosombo, Ghana

where such resources exist. The building of dams has flourished with Nkrumah's Ghana setting the pace when she built the Volta Dam at Akosombo. This began producing electricity in 1966, supplemented in 1982 by a second dam downstream at Kpong. The Ivory Coast has built two dams, Nigeria has built one (at Kainji) and proposes others on the Benue, Imo and Ikpoba rivers. The Niger Republic is also proposing one on the upper Niger which Nigerians fear will imperil the Kainji project if implemented. These dams have served many purposes. They provide water for irrigated agriculture, for the generation of electricity as well as artificial lakes for fishing. The lake at Akosombo (Ghana) is said to be the third largest man-made lake in the world. Apart from the dams river basin commissions have also been set up for the Senegal and Niger rivers and Lake Chad to regulate the use of these bodies of water by the nations that border them. Internally Nigeria has on her own set up various river basin

commissions have also been set up for the Senegal and Niger rivers and development. Experience has shown that as always too much hope was placed on some of the projects. It was thought Akosombo would transform Ghana industrially and that Kainji would meet all Nigeria's power needs. But neither proved to be the case. Moreover poor rainfall in the late 1970s and early 1980s seriously affected water levels and thus led to greatly reduced power production.

Social development

Closely related to economic development is the development of social services especially as the manpower needed for the economy needs to be well-trained, well-fed, adequately sheltered and healthy. This involves the expansion of educational facilities; the building of hospitals, clinics and maternity units; the training of doctors, nurses, midwives and paramedicals; the implementation of large-scale housing programmes; the provision of good drinking water and a fight against infectious diseases.

Unfortunately West African statesmen tended at first to underplay the importance of social development forgetting that the life and welfare of the citizen are the bedrock of a sound economy and a stable state. The only social service whose importance they recognized early on was education because it was needed to produce the men to plan and implement the economic takeoff. And even here the tendency at first was to concentrate on so-called high-level manpower – those needed to draw up and implement development plans. Consequently old universities were expanded and scholarships floated both for those studying at home and for those who had no placement in local universities to study abroad in western Europe, America and Eastern Europe. New universities were also built. Between 1960 and 1975 Nigeria set up eight new universities, while Ghana set up two, and Ivory Coast, Guinea, Sierra Leone and Liberia set up one each. Nigeria has since set up three new federal universities in Imo, Benue and Bauchi and projected five new ones including an Open University for distance studies. The member states of Nigeria are also beginning to compete amongst themselves over the building of state universities. The situation in Nigeria is heading for that in America, especially as private individuals, such as Dr Nnanna Ukegbu of Imo State, are claiming the right and making plans to build private universities. Below the universities, various colleges of technology for so-called middle-level manpower have also been built especially in Nigeria. Those poor states such as Mali, Burkina Faso and so on which have not the money to expand their own resources in this regard, have taken advantage of resources in neighbouring countries by sending their young people there to study.

The expansion of universities would have been meaningless without the expansion of facilities at the secondary and primary school levels. The statistics here are harder to obtain and like all statistics from Africa patently unreliable. Only projections are available. Nigeria, for instance, launched her universal primary education scheme in 1976 planning for three million schoolchildren and some 400 000 schoolteachers. When the scheme took off it was found everything had been underestimated with a place like Imo State alone recording something like 1.5 million schoolchildren. The system began from the start to burst at the seams, and quality was sacrificed to quantity. A similar thing happened with the secondary schools.

While something is being done to increase the number of West African children of school age who are actually in school very little has been done for adults most of whom are illiterate. Various West African universities have extramural and evening classes. Not only is the range of these limited, but most times they are concerned to help people reading for the General Certificate of Education examinations at the ordinary and advanced levels or examinations equivalent to that. The result is that these facilities thus serve mainly secondary-school leavers seeking to improve their qualifications for university admission. It is only now that Nigeria is making bold plans to tackle this problem by establishing an open university which will provide opportunities for lifelong education.

The importance of improved health care has also been recognized and plans laid by these states to increase the ratio of doctors, nurses, midwives and other medical workers to the population and to build many more hospitals providing beds for the sick. Here again statistics are difficult to obtain and quite unreliable. In the third development plan, the Nigerian government aimed to produce enough doctors to ensure that by 1980 there would be one doctor for every 14 000 Nigerians. Now nobody knows how far this has been realized. But the health situation in West Africa remains quite poor. In many favoured areas, sick people have still to cover upwards of 200 kilometres to reach a hospital, nurses are still made to prescribe medicines for patients while many hospitals and medical centres have no drugs and even no water! Private pharmacists and medical quacks continue to operate flourishing businesses. After turning up their noses at traditional medicine men, statesmen are now making plans to recruit them into the fight against disease.

With respect to water supply and housing one can only say plans have been drawn and continue to be drawn for improvement. Traditionally governments limited their attention in these area to the needs of the urban areas. And it has often been said that it is this neglect of the rural areas which is responsible for the increasing shift of population from the villages to the towns. The result has been that excessive pressure has been brought to bear on the few social facilities in the towns. And many of them can no longer cope. Thus it is common to see that taps are dry in the towns, drains are blocked and overflowing, there is inadequate sewerage, and that most people live in makeshift shacks. But in spite of that the towns continue to be preferred to the rural areas. That, perhaps, is the best comment on the state of social services in the new countries of West Africa where the population continues to outstrip resources and managerial skill.

Yet the point being made here must be stressed. The rulers of independent West Africa have achieved more in twenty years than the colonial powers did in about a hundred years, especially with respect to promoting economic and social development. A comparison of West Africa around 1960 and West Africa today makes this clear even to a blind person. What is being said is that more could have been achieved with more prudent management and greater honesty. It is also being said that there is an uncomfortable gap between what leaders planned to achieve and what they have actually achieved. This raises the question: why the gap?

Obstacles to economic development

There are more intractable problems on the road to economic development than were initially recognized. Experience has shown that economic development in this century, especially for the so-called nations of the Third World, is a kind of vicious circle which it requires the strength of a Titan to break. First we have the problem posed by political instability, the details of which we discussed above. Here only the economic effects will be mentioned. The rapid rise and fall of regimes has meant lack of continuity in planning and in implementation. It has also meant that foreign investors have been made doubly wary about sowing where they may not reap – or where they may reap charges of having been involved in plots and counter-plots. Two examples will further illustrate the economic effects of instability. Ghana's seven-year plan was launched in 1963 but before it took off Nkrumah's government came under siege from its opponents who bombed and sabotaged him right and left. In 1966 Nkrumah was overthrown. The new government declared Ghana insolvent and abandoned this plan. Similarly Nigeria's first plan was launched in 1962, the year that saw the beginning of the internal crisis that led to the civil war. Indeed it can be said that by 1964 the country's future was vibrating so precariously in the balance that the attention of her statesmen came to be focused on how to preserve the nation and avoid a civil war. They failed in the second and nearly failed also in the first. With the civil war the plan collapsed and even what little progress was made in a third of the country (the former Eastern Region) was reduced to rubble with bombs liberally supplied by Britain and the Soviet Union.

A second major factor is lack of manpower of the right calibre and quantity. Colonial education was not designed to prepare West Africans for such a period of feverish economic development as we have been witnessing. What educated people there were lacked the technical knowledge and skill to plan and carry through the kind of development programmes which now became the order of the day. For the most part statesmen have had to rely on administrators trained for routine leisurely administration. The first major effort made to rectify this situation emphasized the production of science teachers. But even now science and mathematics teachers remain in short supply. Even more scarce are engineers, statisticians and factory operatives.

There is also the question of the quality and orientation of the élite which runs these programmes. Doctors do not want to serve in the rural areas, engineers angle for posting at headquarters so that they can work in air-conditioned offices; statisticians are too few and too lazy to cross-check personally the figures they work with, while technical personnel in the private sector are satisfied to work as agents and frontmen of foreign companies. To make the situation worse the so-called experts are no more honest than the politicians with whom they compete in defrauding the state.

Allied to this has been a chronic lack of capital, except perhaps in Nigeria where petroleum came to the rescue. Those countries which have depended mainly on the export of agricultural produce have been particularly hard hit as seen in the case of Ghana. Some money has come in from the exploitation of minerals like bauxite (in Guinea) diamonds and iron ore (in Sierra Leone), gold (in Ghana) and so on. But because this is dependent largely on foreign companies and technical personnel, products are mainly processed abroad and the full financial benefit is not kept within West Africa. At one time much hope was placed on foreign 'aid' but it has been discovered that this is politically dangerous without being economically profitable. The cost of repaying loans and servicing them, and of paying the salaries of the experts who execute the projects to which the loans are usually tied turns out to create more burdens than the loans settle. The generation of capital from within has not been easy. This requires honesty and discipline which are in very short supply in many West African countries. In any case in spite of their ostentatious living members of the West African middle class are actually quite poor. For the most part they are public servants dependent on monthly salaries which run out before the middle of the month. Without savings they cannot invest. Indeed it is a vicious circle. For it is the same civil servants whose salaries swallow up much of the national budget. Thus, for instance, in Benin civil service salaries take up about 65 per cent of the annual budget. For Senegal it was 47 per cent in the 1960s and for Ivory Coast where civil servants constitute 0.5 per cent of the nation it is 58 per cent.

There are other contributory factors. These include the lack of adequate statistics for proper planning. In Nigeria, for instance, it is not even known how many people are being planned for. Every effort so far made to take a scientific census has led to failure and very serious political trouble. Other economic and social statistics are also poor. Then there is the sin of locating economic projects on political rather than on rational economic grounds. Economic and social projects are regarded as vote catchers. Hence politicians tend to locate them with an eye on the next elections. Even civil servants are not immune from this. Their concern is with their local areas. In this regard the eastern axis of Nigeria, inhabited by the Ijo, Efik-Ibibio, Igbo, Benue Plateau and Gongola peoples is likely to remain a relatively underdeveloped region of Nigeria. The result is uneven development.

Finally there is the question of markets. Except probably for Nigeria, none of these countries has a large enough internal market to absorb the products of a really large industry. It is not only that populations are small by modern world standards, but because of general poverty, purchasing power is low. The result is that industries have to remain on a small scale for as long as the countries do not come together in a real economic community which will make heavy industries economically feasible. Right now it is widely believed that only heavy industries can bring the desired economic takeoff. That requires co-ordination so that there is no unnecessary multiplication of industries of the same type. A beginning is being made in tackling this problem through the infant Economic Community of West African States (ECOWAS).

The search for regional co-operation

To some extent the colonial powers had laid some of the foundations for the emergence of at least two large blocs or communities in the West African region which with further negotiation could come together as one economic bloc. French West Africa was administered as a unit. Even though towards independence the French favoured the balkanization of the federation for selfish political reasons, the French language and common French political institutions remained as bases on which a common stand could be forged. Though the British had abandoned the idea of administering their holdings as a unit from the later part of the nineteenth century, the English language, the West African Currency Board and the West African Court of Appeal were common institutions that again appeared to point in the direction that could lead to the formation of an Anglophone West African community.

But the tendency on the morrow of independence was for each of these links to break down leaving only the link of common speech within each group. As part of their anxiety to consolidate the unity of their new states, politicians began with emphasizing the separate identity of their 'nations', even at the risk of alienating neighbouring states. In the colonial days, for instance, it was usual for a man from one colonial territory to work in another territory under the same colonial power. Sierra Leoneans, for example, worked and felt at home throughout the British territories. This practice was even more highly developed in French West Africa which was run as one administration. A large proportion of the Africans employed by the French came from Senegal and Benin (Dahomey) where western education was more highly developed.

But with independence the tendency was for non-nationals to be expelled or at least forced to leave because of discrimination. In 1959 many civil servants of Benin origin who were deployed in Senegal were forced to leave the country. The matter got to such a point that the President of the Republic of Benin had to visit Senegal for discussions with his counterpart. When in 1961 Southern Cameroons (now part of the Cameroon Republic) became independent, Nigerian civil servants and businessmen were forced to leave the country. Unilaterally Kwame Nkrumah pulled Ghana out of the West African Currency Board.

There were also other elements of strain. The differing colonial experiences of the former French and English colonies constituted a major obstacle between the two groups, especially the problem of language which at the time appeared insurmountable. France was also accused of deliberately working to keep her former colonies away from the embrace of the Anglophone states. Even within the latter there were elements of strain. Relations between Nigeria and Ghana were far from warm. Ghana was at the time the richest independent state in West Africa thanks to cocoa and her relatively small population. This tended to make her people arrogant – or so Nigerians and some other West Africans thought. It was also suspected that Nkrumah was uncomfortable about the size of Nigeria and would have liked Nigeria to attain independence as three different countries. There was also a temperamental and psychological gap between Nkrumah and Abubakar Tafawa Balewa, with Nkrumah being more ebullient, more radical and more decidedly cut out for the leadership of Africa. For these reasons and more the first few years of independence did not give much hope for meaningful economic unity within the West African region.

The first few moves in this direction would appear to have been made for political and sentimental reasons, and naturally did not last. There was for instance the Ghana–Guinea Union of 1958 which Mali joined in 1960 and which was supposed to lead to political unity. The main achievement of this move was that it gave Guinea some of the moral, psychological and financial support to survive the shock treatment administered to her by the French for voting 'No' in General de Gaulle's 1958 referendum (see Chapter 2).

Two attempts to build closer unity amongst the Franchophone states in 1959 have already been mentioned. Again what these achieved one cannot say. Not until 1963, by which time the different statesmen were becoming sure of their grips on their states, did significant moves begin along the lines of limited economic co-operation. Thus in 1963 there was an agreement between The Gambia and Senegal on currency matters, air services and trade, and in 1982 a confederation of the two countries was formed.

The expulsion of aliens, Nigeria, January 1983: Ghanaians at the port of Lagos await sea transport home

There was also the Niger River Commission between Nigeria, Mali, Upper Volta and Niger on the use of the waters of the Niger river and the overall development of that waterway. The following year there were two other such agreements – the Lake Chad Basin Commission between Nigeria, Niger, Chad and Cameroon; and the Senegal Basin Commission between Senegal, Guinea, Mali and Mauritania.

In retrospect all the above arrangements now look like preparatory steps towards the formation of ECOWAS which came into being in 1975. The organization originated in a small way in 1972 as a bilateral agreement between Nigeria and Togo. After some quiet diplomacy and more wide-ranging consultations there was a meeting of the fifteen nations concerned in 1974 which cleared the way for the signing of the treaty on 28 May 1975. All the West African States are members with the exception of Chad and Cameroon. The treaty provides for co-operation in many areas of economic and social endeavour. It provides for the abolition of visas and other obstacles to free movement between the member states, the setting up of technical and specialized commissions of mutual interest, joint industrial developments, co-operation in agriculture and communications and in cultural matters. A lot of hope has been placed on ECOWAS and many think that if it succeeds, it will open the door to West African economic development and integration. The ordinary Nigerian worker, however, is already beginning to fel the pinch of free movement of persons in the form of fierce competition from workers from other West African states who stream into Nigeria expecting to find streets paved with gold. Consequently the Nigerian dailies are being regularly inundated with complaints against ECOWAS. In 1983 the Nigerian government responded by expelling at short notice hundreds of thousands of foreign workers – a move scarcely likely to promote greater unity in the region.

4 Egypt

After their military occupation of Egypt in 1882, the British imprisoned or exiled the leaders of the 'Egypt for the Egyptians' movement and set about reorganizing Egyptian society. According to the constitution proclaimed in the Organic Law of 1883, under which Egypt was ruled until 1912, the Khedive was to continue to be the head of the administration and to 'choose' ministers who were to be responsible to him. A Legislative Council and an Assembly were established to enable Egyptians to participate in the running of their affairs. The British also asserted that in law and in theory Egypt was still a part of the Ottoman empire and as such recognized the suzerainty of the Sultan of Constantinople.

But events revealed a situation different from the British declaration. The actual head of Egyptian administration was the British Agent and Consul-General, to whom the Khedive was no more than a puppet who should do the bidding of the British. The Egyptian ministers, exclusively people of Turkish origins, were no more than figureheads, under the effective control of the British inspectors who controlled all departments. The Turco-Egyptian 'ministers' constituted the Council of Ministers contemptuously described by a British official as 'this collection of supine nonentities and doddering old pantaloons'. The constitution was by no means liberal; it was a step backward, compared with the vocal, assertive and mainly elected Assembly that was abolished by the British. The Sultan of Turkey was given no voice in the affairs of Egypt which, in all but name, was an integral part of the British empire.

Lord Cromer's administration

Of all the heads of the British administration in Egypt from 1883 to 1922 the best known is Evelyn Baring, 1st Earl of Cromer, whose tenure of office covered the years 1883 to 1907. In Cromer's book *Modern Egypt* and in most of the works on Egypt by British writers, Cromer is portrayed as a

Lord Cromer

first-class administrator and financier who created modern Egypt by organizing a highly efficient civil service, a judiciary that dispensed justice
without fear or favour, and who conferred unexampled prosperity on
Egyptians by his fiscal reforms and by the building of the Aswan Dam. He
is also credited with educating the Egyptians in a way that made it possible
for them to manage their affairs successfully when Egypt became an
independent territory.

This view of Cromer, and indeed of British administration in Egypt, is very one-sided. Cromer certainly deserves credit in many respects and none can doubt that he was an efficient financier. A member of the Baring family that had loaned money to Ismail Pasha, Cromer had had administrative experience in India before he assumed the control of Egypt. He combined commercial and financial ability. He saw his task in Egypt as primarily financial. In this respect, from the viewpoint of British interests, his administration was a huge success. Foreign debt was largely disposed of during his reign and the Suez Canal was well run. Cromer organized the finances of Egypt so well that the country came to depend upon its own resources from 1888 onwards. In 1882 the Khedive could not pay interest on his loans; by 1906 Egypt was able to pay interest on her foreign loans and reduce her debts by £10 million. Cromer achieved this by reorganizing the accountancy section of the Finance Ministry so that money was not wasted and by increasing the productive capacity of Egypt. Between 1883 and 1906 the annual revenue available to the Egyptian Treasury rose from £4.5 million to about £11.5 million, in spite of the lowering of taxes.

Also to his credit Cromer's policies enabled Egypt to produce more crops by improving irrigation. He did this by building the Aswan Dam, which was completed in 1902 at a total cost of £3.5 million. The dam stored sufficient water to irrigate the Nile Valley the whole year round. This meant that whereas previously farmers had only been able to grow one crop a year, at flood time, now they would be able to grow two or even three crops a year on the same piece of land. Famine, which used to bring disaster to a large section of the population in years of a low flood, was no longer a serious danger. Indeed the Aswan Dam has been so crucial to the economic life of Egypt that in the 1950s President Nasser determined on the building of a new, higher dam which would greatly extend the area of irrigated land. The results of Cromer's decision to build the dam appeared early: an area of 200 000 hectares in Upper Egypt was converted to perennial irrigation. The cultivated area rose from 2 million hectares in 1877 to 3.2 million hectares in 1906. The yield of cotton and sugar crops trebled in ten years. Henceforward Egypt depended upon the export of cotton, in the same way that Ghana and Western Nigeria came to depend on the export of cocoa.

But Cromer's achievements are, however, being differently assessed by Egyptians today. His economic policy, they argue rightly, centred on agriculture, that is the production of specific crops – particularly cotton – for European manufacturers. They contend, with some justification, that the economic policy that would have been in the best interests of Egypt would have encouraged industrialization as well, as Muhammad Ali had attempted to do and as independent Egypt has been doing since 1922. The best evidence for this criticism of Cromer's economic policy is to be found in the encouragement given to the cultivation of cotton of which Egypt was producing one of the best varieties. By 1912 cotton accounted for 80 per cent of Egyptian exports. One would have thought that a textile industry would have been in the interest of Egyptians. Indeed in the 1890s a group of Englishmen attempted to establish local textile factories in Egypt. These factories would have competed with the Lancashire factories aimed at the Egyptian consumer market. But the Cromer administration killed the venture by imposing 8 per cent excise duties on locally manufactured goods, the tax being equivalent to the tariff on imported goods. Cromer also imposed an 8 per cent customs duty on imported coal in order to prevent the industrialization of Egypt and he killed the tobacco industry in the country with a threat of heavy fines. Many Egyptians argue further that although Cromer made Egypt solvent, he did not pay off the entire debt of Egypt in his long period of rule, but when Egyptians resumed the control of their affairs they were able to pay off their country's debt at a much faster rate.

It is also argued that Cromer's successful running of the Suez Canal conferred no benefits upon Egypt. After the British occupation all revenue from the canal was drained out of Egypt; millions of pounds, one and a half millions annually to the British, went out every year as dividends to the foreign shareholders of the International Suez Company. From 1880 to 1936 the government of Egypt did not receive a penny for the use of its territory or in return for its original investment of £16 million in the canal.

Also, while Egyptians do not question the efficiency of Cromer's administration they argue that it was British, rather than Egyptian, in personnel and that Cromer wilfully neglected the education of Egyptians. The ministries of finance, justice and education, the army and the police, were all staffed in the senior posts by British subjects. The number of British officials increased from 286 in 1896 to 662 in 1906. Egyptians were employed as junior clerks only, in spite of the existence of a corps of well-educated individuals who had received university education in Europe. The civil service policy was described as British heads and Egyptian hands.

It is true that Cromer did not want a western form of education to thrive in Egypt. He spent only 1.5 per cent of the total revenue of the country on education and health. Even the modest education programme that he planned was not properly carried out. It was left to the nationalists to organize schools at their own expense. Cromer argued that a western form of education would be bad for the British administration: it would create a band of disgruntled individuals who would wish to get rid of the British rulers. He believed that all that Egypt needed was vernacular education for the masses, with secondary education to produce a sufficient number of Egyptians to do the lower-grade clerical and technical jobs and no more. He had an intense hatred for the idea of university institutions for Egyptians. There was no question of his encouraging the three higher institutions of learning that had been founded under Ismail to achieve university status by western standards. These institutions, which could easily have been turned to advantage, were the law school, the school of medicine and the engineering school.

One must stress that Cromer believed that by discouraging the development of higher education he was acting in the best interests of the Egyptian masses. It was his conviction that to foster the growth of a tiny minority, the educated élite – a group of people whose political and social aspirations were not necessarily identical with those of the masses – would be to throw the latter into the hands of demagogues incapable of ruling. Cromer believed that the administration of the country should not be left in the hands of the largely secularized élite who would misgovern the country. He held the view that for a long time British administration was best for Egyptians; that it was not only benevolent but enlightened and that it was only under the gradual tutorship of the British that Egyptians could learn the rules of administration of the modern state. He expected Egyptians to submit to British rule and tutorship with gratitude.

The revival of the nationalist movement

However the Egyptian masses never showed much gratitude towards the British. By 1891 the nationalist movement, stimulated and led by the minority élite for whom Cromer had unrelenting contempt, had reappeared. The nationalists were divided into two distinct groups from the last decade of the nineteenth century. There were the 'Constitutionalists' who were made up of the ruling class of Turkish, Armenian and Circassian Egyptians with whom the British preferred to co-operate rather than with the pure Egyptian nationalists. They desired that the Khedive should rule 'constitutionally' through themselves, and wanted the British to withdraw from the country gradually. They took offices under Cromer and they hated the extremist nationalists, most of whom were pure Egyptians. They formed the *Umma* party and aired their views through their most important newspaper, *Moayyah*. The other group of nationalists were more radical in their demands and were led by lawyers, doctors, teachers and junior government officials. They were mainly of *fellah* (plural *fellahin:* peasant) origin and they hated the British. The racial and social differences between the two groups of nationalists became more marked after the attainment of independence by Egypt in 1922. The radicals were led by people like Mustapha Kamil and Saad Zaghlul. They formed the Nationalist Party. Two of their influential papers were *al-Liwa* and *al-Alam*. Through their newspapers they disseminated their ideas in French and Arabic, educating the masses about the evils of prolonged British occupation, the autocratic tendencies of the Khedive and the necessity of Arabic being taught in schools.

There are clear reasons for the resurgence of nationalist agitation in the last decade of the nineteenth century. Taking the statements by British politicians at their face value and the manner in which their country was occupied, the nationalists believed that British occupation would be of very short duration. Between 1882 and 1907 Britain made more than a hundred declarations and pledges of her intention to evacuate Egypt but with every year her hold upon the country became tighter and tighter. These declarations and pledges were intended for the consumption of France and other European powers who did not accept the suzerainty of Britain over Egypt until the first decade of the twentieth century. After 1888 it began to appear that the British would stay on in Egypt indefinitely. By 1906 Cromer was already urging the British government to declare a protectorate over Egypt. The nationalists were stung by the fact that the Egyptians were paying the cost of the army of occupation of their country as well as the cost of the alien administration forced upon it. There was also the maintenance of Khedival authority by the British, a very bitter pill for the radical nationalists to swallow. To them Khedival authority symbolized oppression, tyranny and corruption. It meant putting in power the alien Turks and Armenians and minority Copts at national and local levels. In the provinces, districts and villages it was these Turco-Egyptians who were appointed as rulers by the Ministry of Interior. These Turco-Egyptians despised the Egyptians, kept themselves socially apart, used the Turkish language, were self-indulgent and corrupt.

Nationalism also revived on the Sudan question. The nationalists had never liked the 1885 evacuation of the Sudan which, it will be remembered, had been a Turco-Egyptian appendage since 1821. In the early 1890s when Menelik II of Ethiopia was threatening to divert some of the Nile waters away from Egypt, many nationalists advocated a reconquest of the Sudan. In 1896 Lord Kitchener led an army, the bulk of which was Egyptian, into the Sudan. Out of the total cost of £2 354 000 entailed by the expedition Egypt provided £1 554 000, and Britain only £800 000. Nevertheless the Condominium established in the Sudan in 1898, which in theory meant that both Britain and Egypt were to administer the Sudan, was in practice no more than a British administration, a disguised form of British annexation of the Sudan. The Sudan was financially and administratively separated from Egypt, and when on 27 January 1906 the railway from Khartoum to Port Sudan was opened, it also acquired economic independence. This made it clear that the Sudan had not in any way come under Egyptian control and was described by the popular press in Cairo as 'the day of Egypt's funeral'. To add to the grievances of the Egyptians, the British made Egypt contribute financially to the administration of the Sudan from the date of its reconquest until 1936.

Many external developments strengthened Egyptian nationalism. Before the Anglo-French Agreement of 1904, in which France recognized Britain's claims to Egypt, the French had welcomed nationalists, many of whom studied law in France, where their anti-British feelings had strengthened. Leaders like Mustapha Kamil disseminated anti-British feelings through the French press, denouncing the British occupation and asking the British to withdraw from Egypt as well as from other Arab countries. The success of Japan in the Russo-Japanese war in 1905 was an encouragement to the nationalists. They began to think that they too could defeat British imperialism as Japan had forestalled Russian imperialism. In the following year, to the surprise of British rulers in Egypt, the nationalists and the press indicated support for Turkey in the dispute over Taba in the Gulf of Aqaba which both Turkey and Britain claimed. The Sultan, who claimed ownership of the entire Sinai Peninsula, sent in troops and there was danger of war between Britain and Turkey. Edward Dicey, correspondent in Cairo of the *Daily Telegraph*, estimated that 90 per cent of the people of Egypt would have risen for the Sultan if war had broken out.

The Suez Canal

By the beginning of the twentieth century the Suez Canal had become a burning issue for the nationalists. In 1880 the rights to 15 per cent of the net profit, which in the original contract with de Lesseps should have gone to Egypt as a 'rent' for the territory through which the canal passed, had been senselessly and ruinously sold away by the French and British controllers for the meagre sum of £4 million. Henceforth millions of pounds flowed to Britain and France without a single penny going into Egypt's treasury. The nationalists could forget neither this diversion of money nor the trickery that had led to the original contract. In 1910 Butros Ghali, the Coptic Prime Minister, acted against the national interests of Egypt when he agreed to, and put before the Legislative Assembly, a proposal by the International Suez Company which sought to extend the contract of the company by forty years for a sum of £4 million and a profit of 5 per cent whenever the company realized in a year £100 000 000 net profit. The anger of the nationalists was unconcealed in the Assembly where the proposal was thrown out. So enraged were the Egyptians that a fanatic assassinated the prime minister, who could do nothing right in the eyes of the Egyptians. In 1899 he had signed the Condominium Agreement and had been prime minister at the time of the notorious Dinshawai incident in 1906 which was of major significance to the development of Egyptian nationalism.

The Dinshawai incident

The Dinshawai incident of 1906 is an event which is remembered even today. In the small village bearing this name a party of Englishmen went pigeon-shooting. Contrary to tradition, the officers had not sought permission to shoot the pigeons, which were a means of livelihood to the people. Incensed by this, and by the fact that a barn caught fire from the gun of one of the officers, the villagers flogged the latter and an Egyptian woman was seriously wounded. The officers managed to escape from the village to the camp but one of them, Bull, dropped dead. In spite of the fact that the medical report on Bull certified that he had died of sunstroke, the British authorities decided to treat the case as one of premeditated murder. Very harsh measures were taken. A special tribunal tried the villagers for murder. Both the composition of this tribunal and its proceedings were a travesty of justice. All fifty-two accused were examined within half an hour, that is thirty-four seconds per man, just time enough for the accused to give his name and age. The charge of premeditated murder was upheld. Four of the men were condemned to death and were hanged in the presence of the other villagers; two were sentenced to penal servitude for life and others to various terms of imprisonment.

The Egyptians were outraged by this unblushing demonstration of injustice and riots broke out in Cairo and in the provinces. Anti-British feelings rose to fever height, doing far more for the nationalist cause than the press and oratory had done for nationalist awakening since the British occupation. Secondary-school boys and the *fellahin* became infected with the nationalist spirit. Indeed the *fellahin* composed this folk-ballad:

> They fell upon Dinshawai
> And spared neither man nor his brother,
> Slowly they hanged the one and flogged the other,
> It was a gloomy day when Zahran was killed,
> His mother from the roof watched, while tears from her were spilled,
> His brother, O you people, stood by him,
> And gazed till his eyes grew dim.

The ghost of Dinshawai was haunting Cromer when he resigned as the British ruler in Egypt in 1907. The nationalists were delighted at his resignation. In the words of *Al-Ahram* of 12 April 1907, Cromer was 'a violent destroyer and a tyrant. He destroyed the Egyptian Sudan and built an English Sudan. He destroyed the Egyptian ministry and built an English advisory body'.

The nationalist movement gained in strength under Gorst, Cromer's successor. Like Cromer, Gorst treated the nationalists with contempt but allowed them free use of the spoken and written word. It was under Lord Kitchener, who successed Gorst in 1911, that the nationalists came under the sledgehammer as Kitchener enacted measures designed to paralyze the nationalist movement. In that year he enacted the Criminal Conspiracy Act, the Press Censorship Act and the School Discipline Act. In the fact of these severe measures some nationalists were imprisoned and others were exiled. Nevertheless, nationalist sentiment grew stronger. In 1913 Kitchener dismissed the General Assembly because it dared to ask for the establishment of a representative parliamentary system of government. However, he discovered that the nationalist movement could not be destroyed. After the death of Mustapha Kamil in 1908 national consciousness was being aroused through the writings of Ahmad Lutfi al-Sayyid, who edited the newspaper *al-Jaridah* from 1907 to 1915.

The First World War

The outbreak of the First World War further poisoned Anglo-Egyptian relations. In December 1914 Egypt was formally proclaimed a British Protectorate. Sir Arthur MacMahon was appointed High Commissioner, the office of Agent and Consul-General being abolished. Britain placed the Egyptian Foreign Office under the new British High Commissioner, deposed Abbas II, abolished the Khedival title and chose Hussein Kamil, a member of the royal family, as Sultan of Egypt. Because Egyptians, religiously one with the Turks and like the latter intensely anti-British, were pro-Turkey, a power fighting on the side of Germany, the British proclaimed martial law and rounded up Egyptians whose tendencies appeared dangerous to them.

To Egyptians the word Protectorate, *Himaya*, had a very unpleasant meaning. According to the Quran it is the duty of Muslims, the true believers, to 'protect' Christians, 'people of the Book'. Now, to the horror of the Egyptians, 'Christian' British claimed that they would be 'protecting' Egyptian Muslims. To the Egyptians this was turning the world upside down, infidels 'protecting' the faithful.

Although the Egyptians did not feel that they had a stake in the issues that led to the outbreak of the war, they saw their country being turned into a base for all British military operations in the Middle East. The army of occupation became in effect the government of the country. Moreover, the Egyptians suffered many hardships throughout the war. Much against their wish they were forced to contribute to British success. Egyptians were conscripted as porters, their foodstuffs were taken from them and their camels were seized at low prices. They were forced to build roads and barracks in Egypt and Syria. About 135 000 Egyptians took part in the Syrian campaign, 8500 men in Mesopotamia and 10 000 in France. Furthermore, a collection for 'Christian' Red Cross funds was somehow converted into a forced levy on a Muslim people.

The war had economic effects on the country. Cotton was cultivated at the expense of subsistence crops, thus making foodstuffs very expensive. Moreover the price being paid for cotton was the lowest in Egypt's experience; and yet this was the time when the British administration demanded higher taxes from the people.

Saad Zaghlul

The nationalist leader who spoke on behalf of the Egyptians in these years was Saad Zaghlul. Born in 1857 he had been a disciple of the late-nineteenth-century modernizing nationalists, Jamal al-Din al-Afghani and Sheikh Muhammad Abduh. They had denounced the ultra-traditional faith of the 'old turbans' and had argued that Islam, far from turning its back on modern science, should play an innovating role in an increasingly technological world. Saad Zaghlul participated in the Arabi Pasha 'rebellion' and was jailed. He studied law and then took office in the British administration. In 1906 he was made minister in charge of education and in 1910 he was given control of the Ministry of Justice. In 1913 he resigned his ministerial appointment and became bitterly anti-British. He demanded the abolition of the privileges afforded to European residents enshrined in the treaties known as Capitulations which European powers had signed with Turkey since the sixteenth century, and called for constitutional reforms, improvements in education and agriculture and, above all, the independence of Egypt.

The behaviour of the British in the Middle East outraged the nationalists. In 1916 France, Britain and Russia signed the Sykes–Picot Agreement, according to which these powers would partition the Turkish empire after the war. Egypt, Hijaz in the Arabian Peninsula and Iraq were embittered by the revelation of this secret agreement by the Russian

Saad Zaghlul

revolutionary government in 1917. Egyptians believed that Britain would not hesitate to absorb Egypt into her empire if this Agreement were to be put into effect. The nationalists also noted that Britain was encouraging Sharif Hussein of the Hijaz to revolt against the Sultan of Constantinople, with the promise that independence would be given him after the war. The nationalists in Egypt could not see how Britain could give independence to Hijaz, the most backward country in the Middle East, and deny it to their country, the most advanced. Furthermore, the principle of self-determination, which meant the right of a people to decide for themselves how they were to be ruled, which was being advocated by President Woodrow Wilson of the United States, was proclaimed by the British, through the High Commissioner in Egypt, in the Declaration to the Seven. Although Egypt was not specifically mentioned in this document it was stated that the self-determination principle would apply to the Ottoman empire.

It is not surprising then that after the war Saad Zaghlul led a delegation to the British High Commissioner, claiming the right to send delegates to the Peace Conference in Paris. To their shock the High Commissioner, Sir Reginald Wingate, did not recognize their claims and refused them permission to go to Paris. When the High Commissioner insisted that the three-man delegation of Saad Zaghlul was not really representative the Egyptian nationalist made his famous speech:

> Do we have to ask a nation whether it wants independence? Ours is the oldest of civilizations. Our ancestors have handed down to us indisputable social virtues. Our civic sense is there for everyone to see. One can see it in our respect for the rule of law, our even temper and identity of outlook. To ask a nation like this whether it is agreed on independence is an affront to it.

It is worth noting that the delegation – 'Wafd' – gave its name to the most popular political party in Egypt from 1922 to 1950.

Zaghlul and other leaders were deported to Malta for a short while, and as a result tension was heightened. The *fellahin* felt that they had every cause to hate the British. Not only had the cost of living risen very high but the lowest price within their memory was being paid for cotton, and taxation was crushingly heavy. The educated people were shocked that the British did not think they were mature enough to rule themselves. Thus the ground was prepared for Zaghlul to succeed where Arabi Pasha had failed. Zaghlul associated the *fellahin* and the townsmen with the nationalist movement and gave the country a political party in the modern sense.

The Milner Commission

The Egyptian people resorted to violence in 1919. Such severe riots broke out in the Delta towns and Upper Egypt that the British had to import special troops to restore law and order. The British government decided to send a commission to inquire into the situation in the country. The man who led this Commission was Viscount Milner, by no means a liberal. He was instructed to suggest the best form of constitution by which Egypt could be ruled within the Protectorate system.

The Milner Commission was not well received by the nationalists. They had formed the Committee of Independence after Zaghlul's deportation and they boycotted the Commission completely. Having studied the charged atmosphere on the spot Milner came to the conclusion that the nationalist movement was not just an organization of a few disgruntled educated Egyptians. He could not have been unaffected by the wave of terror which broke out again a few weeks before he arrived in Egypt. On 22 November a British officer was murdered; the following day four British soldiers were fired at and wounded; the following January, Sirry Pasha, a member of the Cabinet, was attacked with a bomb; the next month an attempt was made on the life of Shafiq Pasha, Minister of Agriculture.

Egypt becomes self-governing, 1922

In the circumstances the British decided to release Zaghlul and his associates. Zaghlul was summoned to London for negotiations with Milner. Both sides found it difficult to reach an agreement. The British would not grant full independence to Egypt. Zaghlul was asked to give a guarantee to protect British interests in Egypt, to recognize Britain's right to station an army of occupation there, to approve clauses that would give Britain rights of protecting foreigners in Egypt and to leave Egypt's foreign policy in the hands of the British. Zaghlul refused to accept the British terms and the negotiations ended inconclusively. In 1921 disturbances broke out again. In the following year the British government unilaterally granted self-government to Egypt but retained control of foreign policy, defence – both of Egypt and the Suez Canal – and of the protection of minorities, including the protection of the small but powerful minority of Europeans with business interests in Egypt.

Obviously this was not a satisfactory declaration to the Egyptian nationalists. By it the British only gave with one hand what they took away with the other. In the circumstances, however, the nationalists could do nothing but accept the measure of independence that had been forced on them. In the following year a constitution on the British pattern was established and Fuad, the Sultan, became King. He was expected to behave like a parliamentary monarch, choosing ministers from a popularly elected parliament. Nevertheless between 1923 and 1952 the constitution never worked, simply because the kings, Fuad up to 1936 and Faruk from

1936 to 1952, did not intend to be constitutional rulers. They wished to be autocrats who would both reign and rule, irrespective of the wishes of the electorate as expressed in the parliamentary elections. The kings hated the Wafd which was the most popular of the political parties, usually won the elections, and wished the kings to rule like their British counterparts. In the first year of the promulgation of the constitution King Fuad violated it and he did so again in 1928; in 1930 he suspended it altogether. Between 1937 and 1952 King Faruk ruled by martial law for eleven years.

Then there was also the fact that the kings allowed their fear of the Wafd to drive them to adopt a pro-British attitude and thereby support British interests in the country. They hoped that in this way the British would become a counterforce to the Wafd which was intensely anti-British. The Wafd wanted full independence for Egypt and complete exclusion of British influence. As a result of the pro-British attitude of the kings the British High Commissioners became a decisive voice in the affairs of the country. In 1924, after the murder in Cairo of Sir Lee Stack, the Governor-General of the Sudan, the High Commissioner influenced King Fuad to force Zaghlul, the first Prime Minister of independent Egypt, to resign. In his place was appointed Abdul Ziwar, a man who did not control a majority of votes in parliament. From 1925 to 1930 parliament was dissolved because it would not support the measures favoured by the king. In 1930 the king dissolved parliament permanently and used as his advisers the Palace Party, an organization of conservative big landlords who exacted high rents from their peasant tenants and hated the Wafd. It is not surprising, then, that hostility began to build up against the king as a result of his autocratic tendencies. The feeling became strong that it was the British who continued to rule Egypt through the king and that the centre of power was London and not Cairo. By 1952, when a military coup ousted King Faruk from authority, the Egyptian people had lost faith in the monarchy and Faruk's enforced abdication evoked little sympathy.

Egypt becomes independent, 1936

In 1936 the Wafd, which in that year was swept into power in an election, succeeded in strengthening Egypt's position through negotiations with the British. What brought both sides to decide to iron out their differences was the invasion of Ethiopia by Italy and Britain's need of Egypt's support. Britain feared that Italy might plan to revive the Roman empire in Africa and in the process employ Egypt against Britain. Naturally the nationalists made reduction of Britain's control over Egypt the condition

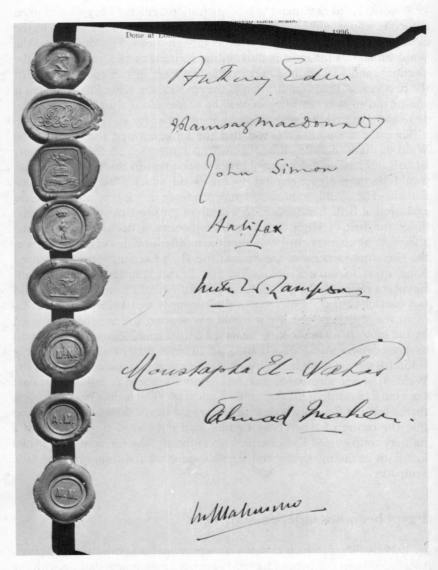

The signatures to the Anglo-Egyptian Treaty of 1936. Signatories included Lord Halifax, Anthony Eden, Sir Miles Lampson and Mustapha El-Nahas

on which they agreed not to ally with Italy against Britain. The 1936 Anglo-Egyptian Treaty confined British power to the Suez Canal zone. Also the number of British troops in the country was limited and provision for the treaty's revision was made. By the treaty of 1936 Egypt became an independent nation. She joined the League of Nations (the predecessor of the United Nations) and the system of Capitulations, under which foreigners were exempt from Egyptian law and taxation, was brought to an end. Yet Britain still had a firm hold on Egypt, for the treaty now gave her a legal right to protect the Suez Canal and to station British forces on Egyptian territory. It also provided for British defence of Egypt against aggression and for Egyptian assistance to Britain in the event of war. In 1951 this treaty was formally abrogated by a Wafdist government. Negotiations continued from 1947 to 1952 but the British did not evacuate the canal zone until after the termination of the monarchy.

The Second World War

The Second World War had an enormous impact on Egypt as it did upon the whole African continent. It brought fighting and mobilization, economic hardship and near-famine, political change and humiliation, yet it also sowed the seeds of later more radical nationalism and socialism.

The war raged across North Africa from 1940 to 1944. Britain was afraid that the Suez Canal, her gateway to India, the Far East and Australia, might fall into the hands of the Axis powers, Germany and Italy, which controlled neighbouring Ethiopia, Somalia and Libya. With the help of African and Indian soldiers, the British drove the Italians out of Ethiopia and Somalia in 1941, but the Germans reinforced the Italians in Libya and then invaded Egypt in 1942, penetrating to within 100 kilometres of Alexandria. At this point King Faruk attempted to appoint as Prime Minister Ali Maher, whom the British considered was far too friendly towards Italy and Germany. The British then surrounded Faruk's palace with tanks, forcing him to capitulate in the most humiliating manner, and to appoint the pro-British Wafd leader Mustapha El-Nahas as Prime Minister. By this time the Wafd Party had become somewhat conservative and was dominated by the wealthy landlords. The British had got their way, and soon recovered to win one of the decisive battles of the war, at El-Alamein, after which the Germans and Italians were pushed westwards across Libya. But the long-term political cost to the British was enormous. By so clearly revealing their contempt for Egyptian independence, the British finally undermined the position of the monarchy and the Wafd Party in the eyes of the younger nationalists while also seriously prejudicing their own future position in the Suez Canal. They became still more unpopular when they and the Americans supported the birth, in Palestine, of the Jewish state of Israel in 1948 – an event which was to dominate subsequent Egyptian history.

Economically, the war had brought inflation, shortages, near starvation in 1944–5, greater wealth to a few but increasing hardship and poverty to many, especially poor peasants who found themselves increasingly forced to work for the large landowners. By the end of the war in 1945 Egypt was clearly ripe for revolution. Eighty-five per cent of the population were landless, while over a third of the cultivable land was owned by a mere 0.5 per cent of the population. The mass of the people suffered disease and grinding poverty, while the ruling elite was ostentatiously wealthy and grossly corrupt. The question was, who was going to lead the revolution which seemed inevitable?

The Muslim Brotherhood

The leading contenders were the Muslim Brotherhood and the army. The Muslim Brotherhood had been founded in 1927 by Hasan al-Banna. It rejected all modernization and instead sought revival through a purified, fundamentalist Islam. The Muslim Brotherhood set up schools, co-operatives, hospitals and textile factories, and tried to secure the social, economic and political advancement of its members. (Similar, though secular, movements were springing up elsewhere in Africa at this time, for example among Afrikaners in South Africa and Kikuyu in Kenya.) The Muslim Brotherhood regarded the British as usurpers and urged all Muslims to take part in a jihad against them. A terrorist wing, started in the 1940s, was responsible for many political assassinations. By 1946 it claimed a membership of about one million. After the first Arab–Israeli war of 1948, in which the Arabs were defeated and the Egyptian monarchy still futher humiliated, Faruk and his government feared that the Muslim Brotherhood would seize power. The Brotherhood was therefore banned and al-Banna was assassinated in 1949. However the organization survived the banning and remained politically active.

The Free Officers and the 1952 coup

Meanwhile in the army a group of young lower-middle-class officers under Gamal Abdul Nasser, calling themselves the Free Officers, had been plotting in secret since about 1944. They were particularly angry and bitter at the incompetence and cowardice of the Egyptian political and military leadership during the war against Israel in 1948, in which many young officers had acted with great bravery. They aimed to abolish the monarchy and the old corrupt political clique, to attack the power of the landowners and bring about much-needed agrarian reform, and to rid the country of foreign influence. In short, they wanted a social revolution. Some were members of the Muslim Brotherhood and some were Marxists, but most of them, including Nasser and Anwar Sadat, had no party label and could best be described as radical nationalists.

After a series of crises, the Free Officers seized power on 23 July 1952 in a coup in which only two people were killed and seven injured. The old order collapsed without resistance, Faruk abdicated and went into exile, and the country became a republic in 1953. The young officers, realizing the need for a more senior officer to act as a figurehead and give their movement greater respectability at home and abroad – they were afraid that the British might invade from the Suez Canal – appointed Muhammad Neguib as their nominal leader, though he was not involved in the planning of the coup. At the time of the coup the most formidable political force was the Muslim Brotherhood. The Muslim Brotherhood had applied

The Egyptian Military Revolutionary Council after the proclamation of a republic in 1953. Included in the picture are, *seated, second from left*, Gamal Abdul Nasser, *third from left*, Muhammad Neguib, *extreme right*, Anwar Sadat

much political pressure which had greatly undermined the old regime and thus facilitated the army coup. It therefore expected to be rewarded in the new order. But its conservative, theocratic outlook was quite incompatible with the beliefs of the more modern, forward-looking army officers who favoured a secular state. A confrontation seemed inevitable. Nasser and his colleagues grew steadily more impatient with the conservatism of Neguib. Neguib allied with the Muslim Brotherhood, but when a member of the Brotherhood was convicted of trying to assassinate Nasser in October (there is a suspicion that he was 'framed'), the Muslim Brotherhood was dissolved, Neguib was disgraced, and Nasser's Revolutionary Command Council (RCC) assumed total control of the political destiny of Egypt.

The RCC wanted to bring about fundamental changes in Egyptian society. Because Nasser adopted a non-aligned position in the East–West conflict (which was then an unusual thing to do), because he advocated state intervention in the economy, and because he received Russian aid to build the Aswan high dam, many western observers labelled him a 'communist'. This was an entirely false description. When Nasser and his fellow officers came to power they started to deal with Egypt's many serious problems on an entirely unplanned, day-to-day basis. Later, and partly as a consequence of his dealings with the west and with local wealthy capitalists, Nasser moved in a consciously socialist direction. But after his death in 1970 his colleague and successor Anwar Sadat, confronted by serious economic problems and the effect of the world recession, began to undo many of the earlier socialist measures. Nasser was the first to experiment with socialism in Africa. Later, countries such as Tanzania, Ethiopia, Mozambique and Angola would follow. It is therefore interesting to look at Nasser's attempts to change Egyptian society and the obstacles he encountered. We shall also look at his relations with African nationalists, with the imperial and superpowers, and with Israel.

Economic reforms

The RCC was deeply conscious of the decades of oppression which the Egyptian people had suffered and it believed that they were entitled to some compensation for this past suffering. The military regime was thus extremely popular in its early days, but it aroused high expectations which in the event proved difficult to fulfil. This 'crisis of expectations' was to confront all African governments as they achieved independence in the 1950s and 1960s. Nasser's government sought to expand industrialization, to produce an increasing number of goods which had hitherto been imported, to broaden the base of the economy and thus not have to rely too heavily on the export of cotton, and to ensure that control over the economy was in Egyptian rather than foreign hands. A series of apparently sweeping socialist measures were taken between 1961 and 1963. The government nationalized all banks and insurance companies, all cotton exporting and ginning firms and pharmaceutical factories, and took over, wholly or in part, several hundred smaller industrial and trading companies. Six hundred of the country's wealthiest families, mostly Copts and Jews, had their property sequestered (taken away). An attempt was made to prevent people earning more than £5000 per annum. Henceforth, private enterprise was to be relegated to a minor role and a chain of government retail shops replaced private traders. The working day was reduced to a maximum of seven hours so that more people could be employed, on a shift basis. The cost of food and other basic commodities as well as bus and train fares and house rents were kept down by government subsidies. It was hoped to achieve a substantial redistribution of wealth.

But laudable though these measures and the objectives which lay behind them may have been, they soon encountered problems. The new regime had no alternative but to employ the old, largely corrupt, bureaucracy to implement the new measures. Like many of the white civil servants in Zimbabwe in the 1980s, the Egyptian bureaucracy disliked the changes and did its best to obstruct them. Overstaffing, inefficiency and corruption proved extremely difficult to eradicate from the civil service. New, efficient and incorruptible administrators were bitterly disliked by those who had served the old regime. Because of overstaffing, there was often an extreme unwillingness to make decisions in the lower levels of the bureaucracy, while corruption remained rife among the customs officials, the police and elsewhere. The country also lacked skilled, top-level management to implement the reforms. It proved impossible to enforce the £5000 maximum wage, as civil servants and others found ways of doubling their salaries through 'allowances' of various kinds. Those running the government retail shops were frequently both inefficient and rude. Some held back items to sell privately on the black market. Long queues were not uncommon. Moreover, it soon became apparent that the reforms benefited the urban working class far more than the *fellahin* who comprised some 70 per cent of the population. There was a danger of a 'labour aristocracy' being created, fed by cheap food, lacking in discipline, hard to sack and even harder to motivate. In the event, the plans for industrialization proved to be over-ambitious. The Helwan steel works, built with Russian backing, seldom operated to full capacity and its products proved unable to compete in price with imported steel. People preferred to buy prestige imported goods even when local products were superior in quality. Egyptian industry proved unable to increase exports sufficiently to outweigh the people's propensity to buy imported consumer goods. Egypt's defeat by Israel in the 1967 war was a major disaster for the economy; the Suez Canal was blocked for eight years. By the 1970s there were clear signs that a new privileged class, based on office rather than property or land, was beginning to emerge. It was a class largely indifferent to the plight of the masses and hence likely to resist any more far-reaching reform.

Attempts at land reform encountered similar problems and were far less radical than they at first appeared. Within weeks of the military coup of 1952 the new government determined on land reform, initially to break the political power of the large landowners, who had dominated the old regime. Under the Agrarian Reform Decree no-one was allowed to own

Egypt today

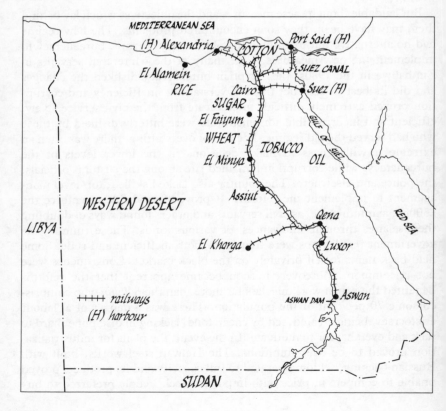

more than 200 *feddan* (84 hectares) of land; this was subsequently reduced to 100 *feddan*. No foreigners were to be allowed to own land. 'Surplus' land from the large estates was to be taken over by the government, the former owners paid some compensation, and people resettled on government co-operatives. Rents were to be reduced and a minimum agricultural wage introduced. The new Aswan high dam (completed in 1970) would increase the amount of irrigable land.

All this was again laudatory especially when set against the background of what had gone before. Because Egypt has virtually no rainfall, all the cultivable land along the Nile Valley needs to be irrigated. This small cultivable area, around 3 per cent of the total area of the country, has therefore always attracted a dense population. Land had become scarce, expensive and profitable. From 200 *feddan* a landowner could expect to derive an annual profit of £4000. For basic subsistence two *feddan* were needed. Yet in 1952 some two million people owned less than one *feddan* and one and a half million families owned no land at all! There had been a substantial increase in renting, in the cost of rents, and in absentee landlordism over the previous twelve years. Again, there was a crisis of expectations among the landless.

In practice the land reforms produced a significant but not a radical redistribution of income. The very large estates disappeared, but the estates of the middle- and upper-middle class landowners remained intact, as did much of their local political influence. Landowners found ways of evading the new laws by secretly distributing parcels of land out amongst different branches of their families. Less than 200 000 families were resettled on expropriated land. The minimum agricultural wage proved impossible to enforce in a country with widespread rural unemployment. The initial rent reductions benefited some four million people, but as population pressure mounted steadily landowners found ways of reimposing higher rents. Some of the government co-operatives floundered amidst corruption and inefficiency. The Aswan high dam extended the irrigated area by half a million hectares and increased cultivation in other areas previously farmed only seasonally. But such advances tended to be swamped by the dramatic population increase from 19 million in 1947 to 30 million in 1966, to an estimated 42 million in 1980. It was ten years before Nasser felt sufficiently secure to come out publicly in favour of birth control: he knew that Muslim leaders were strongly opposed to it.

Relations with African nationalists

The major significance of Nasser's relations with African nationalist leaders was that he offered many of them a safe haven in the 1950s and early 1960s, when such havens were hard to find. He provided office space, a modest salary, air tickets, scholarships for students, and broadcasting time on Radio Cairo. This was particularly important for Kenyan nationalists during the 'Mau Mau' Emergency, when the western media consistently supported the British colonial administration and its version of events. During these years Cairo became an important centre for African nationalists and for the dissemination of pan-Africanist ideas. Crucially, Nasser was able to arrange for the secret passage of arms from the Eastern block countries to the Front de Libération Nationale (National Liberation Front – FLN) which was fighting the French in Algeria. Many subsequent leaders owed him a great deal and they were often influenced by the example of Egypt.

The Suez crisis, 1956

One of Egypt's most striking successes – and something which other countries found difficult to emulate – was its successful struggle between 1952 and 1956 to throw off the last remains of European imperialism. This struggle should certainly be seen as an integral part of the worldwide anti-colonial movement, which was then gathering momentum.

In June 1954 agreement was finally reached whereby Britain agreed to withdraw its troops from the Suez Canal Zone, leaving the canal to be operated by the foreign-owned Suez Canal Company. Nasser was already planning the building of the Aswan high dam, and the United States had agreed to finance its construction. But in July 1956, alarmed by Nasser's increasing emphasis on Egypt's neutrality in East–West conflicts, the United States withdrew the offer. Nasser responded immediately by nationalizing the Suez Canal Company, asserting that Egypt would finance the dam from the profits. This was an extremely popular decision with the Egyptian people, long sick of foreigners dominating their affairs. But the British and the French, the main foreign powers involved, plotted with the Israelis to overthrow Nasser's nationalization. In October 1956 Israel invaded Egypt. The British and the French then moved troops into the Canal Zone, on the pretext of keeping the Israelis and Egyptians apart. This deceived no-one and amidst worldwide condemnation and much public controversy at home, the invaders were forced to withdraw. Subsequently British and French property was seized.

It was a resounding public success for Nasser, all the more sweet to those who remembered the humiliations of the past, and it did much to cement the popularity of the new regime. On a wider scale, it almost certainly persuaded the British not to get involved in such late imperial adventures again. The main losers were probably the white settlers of East, Central and Southern Africa. There was never any question after Suez that Britain would come to their rescue militarily against mounting African nationalism. The French however did not learn the lesson. They were sucked into a bloody war on behalf of the white settlers in Algeria, a war which they eventually lost. There is no doubt that the Egyptian triumph at Suez was a great landmark in the anti-colonial struggle. It encouraged nationalists everywhere, especially the FLN in Algeria. The fortunes of the old colonial powers were henceforth clearly on the wane.

Relations with the United States and the Soviet Union

In their dealings with the superpowers too, Nasser and Sadat proved extremely adept. We have already mentioned that the United States offered and then withdrew her offer to build the Aswan high dam. After the Suez crisis, the Soviet Union moved in quickly to take the place of the United States. It was the Soviet Union which financed the dam and the steel works at Helwan. But when Sadat found that the Soviet Union was reluctant to continue supplying arms to Egypt following her decisive defeat in the 1967 war, relations gradually cooled and Sadat had no compunction in expelling all Soviet military personnel in 1972. Following the much more successful war of 1973, the United States predictably stepped into the Soviet shoes and began supplying Egypt (and Israel!) with arms. The United States was also heavily involved in attempts to arrange a peace treaty between Egypt and Israel. Egypt was certainly helped, in its dealings with the superpowers, by its undoubted strategic importance in the Middle East. Nevertheless, its leaders handled the problem skilfully and provided an outstanding example of a small nation being able to manipulate the superpowers for its own ends, without abandoning either its sovereignty or its integrity.

Relations with Israel

Finally, although strictly outside the scope of this book, it is important to remember that it was relations with Israel which dominated the attention of Egyptian leaders, and some mention of this is therefore necessary. The state of Israel had been created in Palestine in 1948, following worldwide concern at the massacre of millions of Jews by the German Nazis during the Second World War. Israel was to be the long promised 'National Home' for the Jews. But the Palestinian Arabs bitterly resented the

The Aswan High Dam, built by Egypt with assistance from the Soviet Union. The Egyptian and Soviet flags fly side by side over a section of the dam

creation of the new state. War broke out immediately the state of Israel was proclaimed in 1948 and, as we have already seen, Egypt was humiliatingly defeated and thousands of Palestinian Arabs fled into exile. In 1956 the Israelis invaded Egypt, but were forced to leave in the international uproar which followed the British and French invasion. In June 1967 Nasser gambled on attacking Israel, but the Egyptians were heavily defeated and Israel occupied Egyptian territory as far west as the Suez Canal. It was a crushing blow for Nasser from which he never really recovered. His stature as a leading Third World figure declined and he died three years later. His successor Anwar Sadat was more fortunate. In the 1973 Yom Kippur war the Egyptian soldiers and air force put up their best display yet, the war was evenly contested, and the myth of Israeli invincibility was shattered. Like the Suez crisis of 1956 this success was a great boost to the President's prestige. It also enabled Sadat to move towards policies which no Arab leader had hitherto contemplated – recognition of and peace with Israel.

This shift in policy was almost certainly the result of economic difficulties. Egypt is not an oil producer of any magnitude. Consequently she did not enjoy the benefits when the major Arab oil producers dramatically raised the price of oil following the 1973 war. Egypt then began to suffer the inflationary effects of the world recession, as well as the problems arising from Nasser's earlier socialist measures. She also found the continuing need to equip herself with expensive modern weaponry against possible Israeli threats an almost crippling burden to bear. From 1975 the private sector began to be allowed back into areas of the economy previously dominated by the state. When the government reduced subsidies on basic foodstuffs early in 1977, this led to serious urban rioting. Sadat argued that peace with Israel was essential in order that money spent on armaments could be used more productively.

In November 1977 Sadat made his historic visit to Jerusalem (the Israeli leader Menachem Begin later visited Cairo). In September 1978 came the Camp David summit agreement, and an official peace treaty was signed between Egypt and Israel in March 1979. Israeli ships were allowed to use the Suez Canal for the first time in May, and Israeli troops withdrew from Sinai in two stages, in 1980 and 1982. The cost for Egypt was complete diplomatic isolation in the Arab world, though it is still too early to say whether Sadat's example might be followed by other Arab states. The cost for Sadat himself was an assassin's bullet, fired in October 1981 by a member of an Islamic fundamentalist sect. This was a reminder of the old struggle with the Muslim Brotherhood and of the fact that many Egyptians were unhappy with Sadat's pro-western and pro-Israeli policies. Sadat was succeeded by Hosni Mubarak.

5 The Sudan and Ethiopia

British domination of the Sudan

The status of the Sudan after its reconquest by Egyptian and British forces was put in precise legal terms in the Anglo-Egyptian Conventions of 1899 signed on behalf of Britain by Lord Cromer, and on behalf of Egypt by the Coptic Foreign Minister, Butros Ghali. Certain stipulations of this Condominium Agreement, as it is better known, should be noted. The Sudan, it was stated, was to be jointly administered by Britain and Egypt. The Governor-General, who was to head the armed forces and administration, was to be appointed and could be dismissed by the Khedive on the recommendation of the British government; the British and Egyptian flags were to be jointly hoisted throughout the territory; slave trading was abolished.

But from the start the British never intended to rule the Sudan jointly with Egypt. Throughout the Condominium from 1899 to 1956, no Egyptian was ever appointed as Governor-General. Only in the early years were Egyptians appointed to junior positions in the civil service of the Sudan, the British monopolizing the higher posts. As time went on, particularly after 1924, the Governor-General took decisions without prior consultation with the Khedive and even without the Khedive being formally informed. The British accepted the Condominium principle in 1899 for purely diplomatic purposes – to sweeten France's pill, to ward off possible Ottoman interference in the Sudan and to obtain international approval for the disguised annexation of the Sudan by the British empire. As time went on many British officers began to argue that Egyptians were unqualified to rule over the Sudan, partly because in the period of Turco-Egyptian administration, 1821–85, the Sudanese were exploited and badly governed and partly because, as the British officers believed, contemporary Egyptian administration in Egypt itself was corrupt and would corrupt the Sudan administration if a free hand were given to Egyptians in the Sudan. Moreover the British began to declare that their mission in the Sudan was a disinterested one: to rule in the interests of the Sudanese, establish law and order, dispense justice, develop the economy of the territory and put the Sudanese peoples on to the path of progress.

Egypt's financial contribution to the Sudan

Ironically, however, from the year of the reconquest to 1912, whenever the resources of the Sudan were inadequate to meet the requirements of the administration, the British persuaded the Egyptian government to make financial grants to the Sudan. The series of advances made by Egypt enabled the railway to be built from Atbara on the Nile to the Red Sea, and the new port of Port Sudan, with deep-water quays, to be developed north of Suakin. Later they enabled the Blue Nile to be bridged at Khartoum and the railway extended down the Gezira to Sennar and across the White Nile at Kosti. It was not until 1949 that the Sudan could pay back the loans Egypt had made to her in these earlier years. Until 1924 Egypt was also constrained by the British to maintain an army for the internal and external defence of the Sudan.

Throughout the Condominium, during which any Egyptian participation in the administration of the Sudan progressively diminished, the Sudanese witnessed the spectacle of two masters discussing and disputing with themselves the destiny of the Sudan without any consultation with the Sudanese peoples. The point must be stressed here that in these years of Condominium neither the British nor the Egyptians considered primarily the interests of the Sudanese. They both looked upon the Sudan with imperial eyes with the sole aim of treating the territory as a mere projection of their respective economic, political and strategic interests. However, it should be noted that the clash of interests of these two alien masters, which was prominently displayed on the international scene, contributed in no small measure to the nationalist awakening and to the termination of colonial rule in the Sudan.

Egyptians regarded the Sudanese as belonging to the same geographical area – the Nile valley; they liked to think of the traditional historical and economic links that had held them together in the past. But, as historians of the Sudan have shown clearly, Egypt had economic reasons for desiring to exercise influence and control over the Sudan. It was a major market for Egypt's exports, a potential field for Egypt's capital investment and for colonization by emigrants from overpopulated Egypt. Above all Egypt wanted to control the Sudan to prevent being strangled economically by Sudanese overuse of the Nile waters.

The British, too, had commercial and strategic interests in the Sudan. Several British companies invested millions of pounds in various enter-

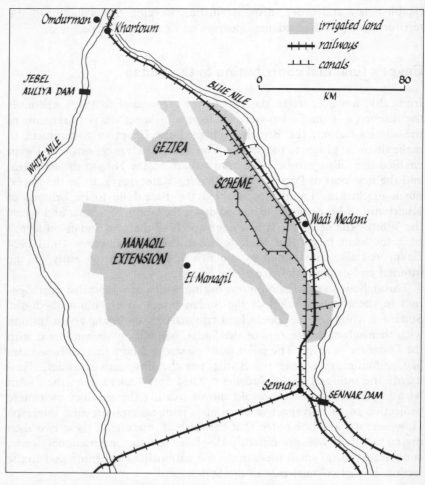

The Gezira Scheme and the Manaqil Extension, which was completed in 1961

prises. Britain valued highly the long-staple cotton of the Sudan and bought most of the Sudan's other products, including gum arabic, hides and skins, oil seeds, dates and vegetable oils. The strategic importance of the Sudan in the Scramble for Africa has been mentioned in Volume 1. Through her control of the Sudan, Britain could, and many times did, curb the excesses of Egyptian nationalism by threatening to starve Egypt of the Nile waters. Also by her occupation of the Sudan Britain was in a position to watch militarily over her interests in Middle East countries such as Iraq, Syria, Palestine and the Transjordan, and in East Africa.

Irrigation schemes

There can be no doubt that the Condominium conferred economic advantages on the Sudan. Roads and railways were constructed to facilitate transportation of products. By 1930 the Sudan had a railway system linking Wadi Halfa in the north to Sennar in the south, with a main branch to the east from Atbara to Port Sudan on the Red Sea coast. There was also a subsidiary branch southwards from Port Sudan to Sennar and another line from Sennar to El Obeid in the west, the centre of the gum arabic and cattle trades of the western provinces. Port Sudan was modernized. But the greatest economic achievement of the Condominium was the irrigation programme launched and encouraged by the administration. As early as 1904 Leigh Hunt, an American financier, was given a concession of 10 000 *feddan* (4200 hectares) at Zeidab for the cultivation of cotton and wheat. In that year he founded the Sudan Experimental Plantations Syndicate. In 1911 the administration opened the first test pumping station on 250 hectares of land rented from local native owners at Tayiba. In the Northern Region the government established seven pumping schemes between 1917 and 1928, for the irrigation of areas varying in size from 800 to 1600 hectares. These were demonstration farms which willing individuals were expected to copy. By 1947 private irrigation schemes numbered 347. In the north, dates, citrus and mango were extensively cultivated. On the White and Blue Niles, there were in 1947 over twenty-four private pump-watered fields growing fruit, vegetables, grain, forage crops and cotton.

However, the greatest feat of the Condominium was the construction of the Sennar Dam which was completed in 1925. With its canal system the dam irrigates 400 000 hectares of the Gezira plain, the triangular area between the White and Blue Niles. The crop which is grown here is cotton, the mainstay of Sudan's economy, amounting in value to between 70 and 80 per cent of the country's total exports. In 1937 the Jebel Auliya Dam, 50 kilometres south of Khartoum, work on which was begun in 1924, was completed.

It is usual for writers to praise the Gezira Scheme as the best illustration of partnership between foreign investors and Africans, illustrating in the words of Margery Perham 'how the wealthy and economically experienced nations can help the poorer peoples of the world to develop their own resources without either economic or political subordination'. There is no doubt that the Sudanese have had much to be grateful for in the Gezira Scheme compared with Africans in East Africa, Southern Africa and the Maghreb, where white settlers dispossessed Africans of their lands and forced them to become labourers, and with Africans in the former Belgian

Water stored by the Sennar Dam is fed into canals to irrigate the Gezira plain

Congo whom the Belgians exploited as labourers on European plantations. By independence in 1955 the scheme supported a quarter of a million people and produced over half the country's exports in value. But it should be stressed that by the scheme the Sudanese, original owners of the land, became tenants of the Syndicate. Each tenant was given 40 *feddan*, ten of which were used for cotton, five each for millet (the staple food grain) and fodder, the remaining twenty being left to fallow. Whatever profits were realized were shared as follows – the tenants received 40 per cent, the government (which invested £13 million in the Sennar Dam and the major canals) 40 per cent and the syndicate 20 per cent.

The point should also be made that the real gainers from the scheme were the British textile manufacturers of Lancashire who enjoyed virtual monopoly of the fine quality long-staple cotton grown in the Gezira. Moreover, the British financiers and directors controlled the Gezira plains operations through two British companies – the Sudan Plantations Syndicate Ltd, and the Kassala Cotton Company. These companies supervised the cultivation, ginning and marketing of cotton until 1950 when the extravagant concessions they enjoyed were terminated.

Distribution of the Nile waters

One point of dispute between the Condominium powers was over the distribution of the Nile waters between the Sudan and Egypt. Britain also sought to persuade Ethiopia to allow the building of a barrage to control the flow of water from Lake Tana. It was clear that unless an agreement could be reached between the British and Egyptian governments the Sudan could starve Egypt economically. For, as Colonel Helmy, one-time Secretary-General of the High Dam authority, Egypt, was quoted as saying: 'From the dawn of history Egypt has depended on the flow of the waters of the Nile as the individual depends on the circulation of the blood'. It is not surprising, then, that Egyptian nationalists were alarmed at the efforts of the British to erect barrages in the Sudan.

In 1920 an international commission considered how water should be allocated after the construction of a number of proposed dams. The majority report of the 1920 Commission recommended that Egypt's existing needs should be fully catered for. This implied that Egypt had a right to practically all low-season water, leaving Sudan to meet its needs from flood waters. It was specifically recommended that Sudan should receive water to irrigate 300 000 feddans from these flood waters. In 1925 another Commission, with British and Egyptian representatives and an independent chairman endorsed these proposals and in 1929 an agreement was reached. It was agreed that no waterworks of any kind should be built in the Sudan without the consent of the Egyptian government and that the Egyptian government was not to set up any water scheme in the Upper Nile without consultation with the Sudan. Waterwork was defined as any scheme that would reduce the volume of water flowing into Egypt. An Organization of Irrigation Department was set up in Egypt. Instead of water to irrigate a fixed area Sudan was to be allocated a specified quota of the Blue Nile flood (929 million cubic metres). This amounted to only about 4.3 per cent of Egypt's share.

There is no doubt that the 1929 Agreement favoured the Egyptians in the sense that it limited the development of irrigation in the Sudan while leaving Egypt free to develop her irrigation as fast as she pleased. Such an agreement could hardly have satisfied the Sudanese nationalists. In 1955, when the Sudan was on the eve of independence, the Sudanese government denounced the 1929 Agreement, declaring that they needed more water for expansion of the Gezira cultivation. This was the time when Egypt also required more water for the Aswan high dam project. It was not until 8 November 1959, after the Sudan was an independent country, that a satisfactory agreement was concluded, whereby Egypt was allocated two-thirds and the Sudan one-third of the annual flow of water once the high dam began to store water, in May 1964. The Sudan was also given £15 million compensation for the land in the neighbourhood of Wadi Halfa which would be flooded when the high dam was completed.

The Condominium should also be praised for improving the health of the Sudanese. Smallpox was virtually wiped out through a vaccination campaign and sleeping sickness, bilharzia, cerebro-spinal meningitis and yaws were attacked with much success.

The beginnings of a nationalist movement

A nationalist movement of the type led by a westernized élite began relatively late in the Sudan. There were several reasons for this. Perhaps the most important was the fact that internal divisions along racial, economic, geographical and religious lines were very acute and made it extremely difficult for the many peoples to think in terms of one Sudanese nation. The major division lay between the Arab, Muslim North and the black African, and partly Christian, South. There was also the division between those townsmen and countrymen closest to the Nile and those in more remote parts; the former tended to be more economically advanced, the latter more politically conservative. Finally, there was the division between the Ansar and Khatmiyya sufi brotherhoods, each with millions of followers. The Ansar were the followers and supporters of the Mahdi and his successor, the Khalifa Abdullahi; the Khatmiyya adherents were the bitterest opponents of the Mahdist regime. In the early years the Condominium tried to play one faction against the other. Aware that the Ansar were still looking for a return to the Mahdiyya the British began to support the Khatmiyya. In 1916 the head of the Khatmiyya, Sayyid Ali al-

Mirghani, was knighted. In later years when the Khatmiyya began to show pro-Egyptian leanings the British swung to supporting the Ansar under the son of the Mahdi, Abdel Rahman al-Mahdi.

Other factors that delayed the emergence of the nationalist movement in the Sudan included the existence until 1946 of different administrations for the north and south which perpetuated the cultural and racial differences between the two areas. Then there was the fact that the Condominium administration did very little to educate the people, thereby delaying the rise of an élite which in colonial Africa was often the champion and spearhead of the nationalist struggle. Government schools were few and far between. Apart from the Gordon Memorial College, which became a secondary school in 1905, the government had no other secondary school until 1946, when a second was built at Hantub in the Blue Nile Province.

It was only after the First World War that modern nationalist sentiments were openly expressed. It was only to be expected that the anti-British agitation in Egypt should have effects on the small band of westernized educated Sudanese. In the towns, in the army and in the lower ranks of the civil service, Sudanese nationals came in contact with their Egyptian counterparts and around 1921 various local nationalist leagues and societies were founded. In 1921 Ali Abdel Latif, a man of Dinka origin, who envisaged an independent Sudanese nation, formed the Sudanese United Tribes Society. He was arrested and imprisoned in the following year. Soon after his release he began to co-operate with the Egyptians and formed the White Flag League, an organization made up of young army officers, ex-students of Gordon College and government employees. This organization inspired demonstrations between June and November 1924 and riots occurred in several towns. The White Flag League was dedicated to the establishment of a Nile Valley state under the King of Egypt. There was also a mutiny of Sudanese and Egyptian soldiers. It was in this tense atmosphere that on 19 November 1924 the Governor-General, Sir Lee Stack, was assassinated in Cairo. The British seized the occasion to compel Egypt to withdraw all Egyptian officers and troops from the Sudan within twenty-four hours. Troops of the 11th Sudanese Battalion – part of the Egyptian army – sympathized with the Egyptians by mutinying and establishing themselves in the military hospital in Khartoum.

In 1936 the Graduates' General Congress was founded, comprising ex-Gordon College students and other educated Sudanese. This body informed the Condominium government that henceforth it should be regarded as the spokesman for Sudanese interests. In 1942 the Congress submitted a memorandum in which it demanded among other things from the Condominium administration recognition of the rights of self-determination for the Sudanese after the war, a special agreement with

Egypt, abolition of restrictions placed upon northern Sudanese influence in the south, Sudanization and the creation of a Legislative Council. The negative response of the administration to these demands led to a split in the Congress in 1945. Thanks to the conflict of the interests of the British and the Egyptians, the alien masters began to patronize two opposing factions, each claiming that they alone identified with and would defend the true interests and aspirations of the Sudanese.

One faction in the 1945 split became the Ashiqqa (Full Brothers) Party. This organization was led by Ismail el Azhari. In 1939 Secretary of the Graduates' Congress and the following year its President, Azhari was one of the seven founders of Ashiqqa and a strong opponent of the British colonial presence. He became committed to the 'Unity of the Nile Valley' slogan of those Egyptians who desired the political and economic integration of Egypt and the Sudan. Until 1955, when Azhari began to perceive that the interests and aspirations of Egypt and the Sudan were not necessarily identical, he leaned heavily on two main props for his support – Egypt herself and the Khatmiyya. Since 1942 Egypt had recognized in the Graduates' Congress, and later in the Ashiqqa Party, a nationalist movement that would promote unity between Egypt and the Sudan. Within the Sudan support came from the Khatmiyya, led by Ali al-Mirghani, an unbending protagonist of union with Egypt. Educated in Egypt he did not speak a word of English and regarded the British as foreign usurpers. But the pro-Egypt attitude of the Khatmiyya should be understood in another sense: with the memory of the sufferings which members of the sect had suffered under the original Mahdi, its members feared the political ambitions of the Ansar, who they believed wanted to turn the Sudan into another Mahdist state with the son of the original Mahdi as its ruler.

The other faction in the 1945 split, which developed into the Umma Party, consisted of those who still had faith in the British administration. They preferred co-operation with the British, who they hoped would grant their country independence within the Commonwealth. They did not wish to see the Sudan become an appendage of Egypt. The Umma Party came to have as its patron Sayyid Abdel Rahman al-Mahdi. Regarded at first by the British as a potential danger, in view of the large number of the Ansar in the three provinces of Darfur, Kordofan and the Blue Nile, the Condominium administration restricted his movement to the Gezira Province until after the First World War. By this time the Condominium administration had begun to see in him a possible ally and in 1926 he was knighted. In the meantime he had become wealthy through his cotton enterprise in the Gezira. His son, Siddik el Mahdi, was President of the Umma Party from its foundation in 1945 until 1958.

Moves towards independence, 1948–55

From 1948 the Sudan moved fairly rapidly towards independence. In that year a Legislative Assembly was established, to which the South sent thirteen members and the North fifty-two members. In 1951 the Egyptian government formally abrogated the Condominium Treaty of 1899 and the Anglo-Egyptian Treaty of 1936, whereby Egypt and Britain exercised joint sovereignty over the Sudan. In the same year Faruk was declared the King of the Sudan. As a result of these actions the British began to think of granting independence to the Sudan much earlier than had been contemplated. In the Anglo-Egyptian Agreement signed on 12 February 1953, Britain accepted the principle of self-determination for the Sudan and Egypt conceded sovereignty to the Sudanese, leaving them the choice between a link with Egypt or an independent Sudan. It was decided that the transitional period of self-government should not exceed three years after 'the Appointed Day' that would be announced after elections had been duly held. In the meantime the National Unionist Party, embracing the Ashiqqa and other pro-Egyptian groups, had been formed under Azhari. With the massive support of the Khatmiyya this party won the elections held in the course of the year. There is no doubt that events in Egypt influenced the results. The cause of a Sudan–Egypt union had an appeal for those Sudanese at a time when General Neguib, whose mother was a Sudanese, was at the head of the Egyptian Revolutionary Command Council. 9 January 1954, when Azhari was appointed Prime Minister, was declared 'the Appointed Day', and he appointed an all-Sudanese cabinet.

In the short period of its rule the Azhari administration made efforts to advance the Sudan in her path towards full independence. Barely a month after the cabinet had assumed office a Sudanization Committee was set up and before the end of the year the civil service was already being Sudanized. The Azhari government also desired a measure of economic independence for its country. It instructed the Gezira Board, the hitherto all-white directors of the Gezira cotton enterprise, to Sudanize its administration. It was not long, however, before the prospects of some form of union with Egypt began to fade. Many Sudanese did not approve of the deposition of Neguib by Nasser in 1954 and they also resented the brutal suppression of the Muslim Brotherhood with which they felt they shared similar beliefs. Moreover many members of the Khatmiyya in the cabinet began to clamour for unfettered independence for the Sudan. By the end of 1955 Nasser and Azhari had become antagonistic towards each other. The forces of independence became so strong in the Sudan that even Sir Sayyid Abdel Rahman had begun to ask for a Sudan completely independent of the British. In December 1955 the Republic of the Sudan thus became a sovereign state with no formal links either with Egypt or with the British Commonwealth.

Post-independence changes of government

The period after independence has not been one of political calm in the Sudan. Political parties multiplied and by 1958 there were four principal parties – the Umma, the Southern Liberals, the People's Democratic Party and the National Unionist Party. The People's Democratic Party was formed in 1956 by the Khatmiyya sympathizers who broke away from the National Unionist Party of Azhari, on the grounds that his policy tended more and more to be secular. The Southern Liberals, as the name implies, was mainly based in the largely non-Arab South and had been formed on the eve of the 1953 elections. In the 1958 elections the Umma Party had a majority of seats, but not a majority over the other parties. The result was that the Umma Party had to continue the uneasy coalition that had been made in 1956 with the People's Democratic Party, in order to form the government. Neither of the two sufi sects – the Ansar and the Khatmiyya – upon which the coalition was based, trusted each other. While they were plotting against each other – the Umma members of the cabinet making a bid to ally with Azhari and the Khatmiyya with Nasser – the army believed that the time was ripe to seize control of affairs. In November 1958 General Abboud seized power and dissolved the political parties. The army remained at the helm of affairs for the following six years. In October 1964 the army regime was overthrown by a popular demonstration which wished a return to a civil and parliamentary system of government. However, the civilians were not to govern the country for long. In May 1969, after nearly five years of factiousness among the politicians, the army struck again and General Nimeiri's National Revolutionary Council seized power.

The roots of the civil war

The major problem which the Council inherited was the civil war between the South and the North, which had started in 1955. Its roots go back to the nineteenth century. It was only then that the largely Arab Muslim North came into intensive contact with the heterogeneous African societies of the South, which included the Dinka, the Azande, the Bari and the Shilluk. This contact was unfortunately an unpleasant experience for the Southerners and not one likely to help to build a united country, for the Turco-Egyptians and Arab Northerners raided the South for slaves. This past enslavement of their ancestors by the Northerners was used by many Southern politicians to illustrate their contention that the domination of the South by the North in the civil service and in the distribution of rewards after 1954 was just history repeating itself.

In a sense the Condominium administration added fuel to the flames. For the South was until 1948 administered as a separate territory and in the 1940s some British officers even toyed with the idea of merging the South with British East Africa. In 1930 what has been described as the 'Southern Policy' came to be defined and was rigidly applied. All Northerners in administrative, technical and clerical services in the South were transferred to the North; Northerners who wished to trade in the South were refused permits; the Islamic religion was suppressed and Arabic as a school language was abolished in favour of English. European, rather than Islamic, codes of law were introduced. Christian missions, which had been allowed to operate in the South, supported this policy. In the years that followed the missionaries emphasized to their followers the danger of the North to the South.

This 'Southern Policy', which was applied for eighteen years and was comparable to certain of the more restrictive indirect rule policies elsewhere in British Africa such as in Northern Nigeria, naturally increased the fears of the Southerners about their Northern countrymen. But after 1948, when the administrative union of the South and North began, the barriers that had existed began to be removed. Northerners resumed trading activities in the South, Islam began once again to gain adherents and in government schools Arabic began to be taught. Had the North and South developed at the same rate during the period of separate administration the unification of the two areas might well have been easier than it actually was. Unfortunately the South was much less developed than the North in local government, irrigation schemes, health, education and industrial development. In the circumstances, when unification came, most of the government positions in the South came to be held by Northerners. Feelings in the South ran high against the North when the results of the Sudanization programme of the Azhari administration began to show themselves. The bulk of promotions went to Northerners.

Consequently by 1955 the Southerners, upon whose sectional feelings aggrieved Southern politicians (dismissed by the Azhari government from the posts they held in the government) played, were very much on edge. It was unfortunate that many Northern officers in the South were not discreet in their behaviour. Efforts of the Southern politicians to organize meetings and conferences were frustrated; a Southern politician was tried in a manner that gave the widespread impression that justice was not done; a demonstration by some dismissed Southern workers was met with force involving the killing of six of the demonstrators. The government did not assess the situation carefully and tactfully before issuing threats and making provocative broadcasts to people who felt that their grievances were real. The situation degenerated to the point that the Southerners in the army in the South began to sympathize with the grievances of their fellow Southerners. Revolt occurred in August 1955; three hundred Northerners were murdered and government retribution followed swiftly.

The situation simmered for years, as the North tried to impose its people and its religion upon the South. Then in 1963 the Anyanya Liberation Movement began a guerrilla campaign. Northern troops killed wan-

The Sudan today

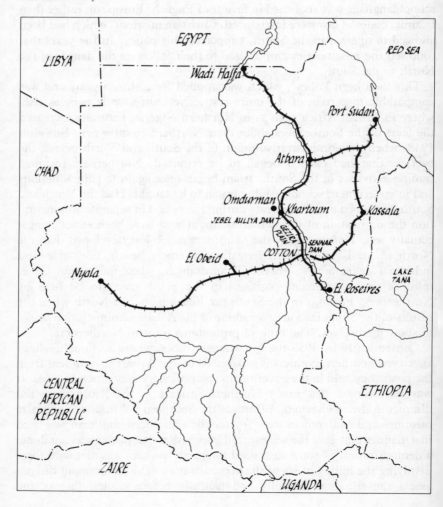

118

tonly, people fled to the bush and thousands crossed into Uganda, Ethiopia and Zaire as refugees. The government was left in control of only the main centres. The civil war dragged on until 1972 when the two sides were brought together and, with Ethiopian mediation, signed the Addis Ababa Agreement. The Anyanya were to be absorbed into the Sudanese army and stationed in the South, and Nimeiri agreed to a federal political structure, which allowed some autonomy to the South.

From 1972 until 1983 the South remained quiet, though there were border conflicts with the revolutionary Ethiopian government which overthrew Haile Selassie. During the 1970s there were at least four attempted *coups* in the Sudan, mounted by local communists or the Libyan leader Gadafy. Meantime Nimeiri moved, like Sadat in Egypt, away from his earlier revolutionary socialism towards a pro-western stance and support for moderate Arab governments in the Middle East. In 1985 he was dramatically toppled from power for reasons which included his attempt to reverse the 1972 agreement with the South.

Ethiopia under Menelik II

So much attention was demanded by the necessity of warding off European aggression and extending the frontiers of his country (see Volume 1) that Emperor Menelik II had little time for internal reforms. More than any of his predecessors he unified and expanded Ethiopia and commanded the obedience of the local rulers throughout the empire. Important, too, was the fact that he was master in his own house, dominating the European residents whom he taxed heavily. He planned to abolish slavery, reform the laws of the country and introduce compulsory education. It was Menelik II who founded Addis Ababa and made it the imperial capital; he introduced the electric light, the telephone and the postal system with stamps; he established the first government school (1905) and ordered his subjects to be vaccinated in 1898 (he built a hospital staffed by Russian and French doctors); and the Bank of Abyssinia was founded.

Haile Selassie comes to power

Unfortunately for his country Menelik's health began to fail in 1906 and for the rest of his reign – he died in 1913 – he suffered from paralysis. The two strong men who might have succeeded him, Ras Mangasha, son of Emperor John IV and Ras Makonnen, the progressive and able ruler of Harar province and a man particularly trusted by Menelik, had died in 1906. Menelik's successor was Lij Iyasu, a young man of seventeen who had little respect for some of the traditions of the 'Solomonic' throne. He outraged certain of his Christian subjects by marrying Muslim women and it has been claimed by certain of his detractors that he ultimately declared himself a Muslim. At the outbreak of the First World War he favoured the Turks and the Germans and thereby alienated the British, French, Russian and Italian diplomatic representatives in Addis Ababa. The nobility, encouraged by the Church and certain foreign legations, seized the opportunity to reassert the independence they had lost under Menelik. In 1916 Lij Iyasu was formally deposed and Menelik's daughter, Zauditu, was crowned as Empress. Dejazmatch Tafari, the son of Ras Makonnen and later Emperor Haile Selassie, became Regent.

Although Tafari was Regent and did not have a free hand to direct the affairs of the country until he ascended the throne in 1930, to a very great extent it might be said that the history of Ethiopia from 1916 to 1974 has been that of this remarkable man. Tafari was a great-grandson of King Sahela Selassie of Shoa, albeit through a woman, which technically disqualified him from the succession. Born in Harar on 23 July 1892 Tafari received his early education from French missionaries and was for several years trained in the court of Menelik, who discerned his talents. By 1911, that is when he was still under twenty, he had already been given the governorships of the provinces of Sidamo and then Harar. In 1916 Tafari was prominent among the conspirators who sought to overthrow Lij Iyasu. Ras Mikhael, the deposed Emperor's father, led the Oromo of Wello and other northerners against the Shewans and heavy fighting took place outside Addis Ababa. The rases reasserted their independence, the treasury was empty and there was no army to enforce the laws of the central government. Even after resistance had been crushed, Tafari had to contend with the opposition of the Empress and the Church who deplored his comparatively progressive outlook and modernizing tendencies. In 1928 an attempt was made to depose him as Regent. But his position became so much stronger after the crisis that he assumed the title of Negus (king). Two years later he survived the last major domestic crisis in his bid for ultimate control of affairs when he defeated Ras Gugsa, Governor of Begemder, the estranged husband of the Empress Zauditu. Soon afterwards the Ras was killed and the Empress died three days later. Tafari was crowned Emperor in St George's Cathedral, Addis Ababa, and took the name of Haile Selassie – 'Might of the Trinity'.

The monarchy in Ethiopia

Haile Selassie realized that Ethiopia could no longer be isolated from the rest of the world; that European powers which had economic interests in the country were so militarily powerful that they could not be ejected; that all over Africa European intrusion in the guise of commercial activities, missionary propaganda and technological innovation had come to stay irrespective of the predilections of the traditional rulers. Shrewdly he decided to harness these intruding forces to the progress of the state.

His enlightenment in this respect began in his Regency years. He inspired the founding of the Ras Tafari school, and sent graduates of this school abroad for higher education. He attached so much importance to education that its control remained in his hands for several decades. After the defeat of the Italians and his restoration to the throne in 1941, he built other secondary schools, including the Haile Selassie I and Orde Wingate secondary schools. In 1957 there were over 600 primary schools and twenty-four secondary schools in Ethiopia, apart from commercial, technical, agricultural and teacher-training establishments. At the apex of his educational programme was the University College of Addis Ababa inaugurated in 1951 with the Emperor as the Chancellor. It was to become the nucleus of the Haile Selassie I University (now Addis Ababa University) established in 1961.

Knowing that it would be a long time before the country would be able to produce the much-needed trained men to direct the various departments of administration and development of the country, and anxious to control the rate of change, Haile Selassie chose for a long time skilled foreigners as his advisers, but not in the way Ismail Pasha had done in nineteenth-century Egypt (see Volume 1). These foreigners, mainly Europeans, were expected to advise and train and not to be political agents or a law unto themselves. In 1931 his foreign advisers belonged to various nationalities. His Legal Adviser was a Swiss, the Foreign Affairs Adviser was a Swede, the Adviser in the Ministry of Interior was an Englishman, the Adviser on finance an American. Nor did he look to the western powers alone for financial and technical aid. In 1959 he went to Moscow, obtained an honorary LL.D. degree of the University of Moscow and secured a promise of financial and technical aid. But as late at 1960 an American was the Emperor's chief adviser on foreign affairs and the Americans were supplying him with a massive quantity of arms.

Constitutional reforms

While embarking on the development of modern education at all levels Haile Selassie was probably aware of the fact that the traditional, unmitigated absolutism of the Ethiopian monarchy would become out of date as people became educated and informed of the growth of democratic institutions in most parts of the world. The Emperor himself took the initiative in 1931 by proclaiming a constitution which, for the first time in the country's history, took the people into some degree of partnership in the government of the country. The constitution was by no means democratic to the extent of giving the people the franchise. The Emperor believed in the necessity of moving gradually in the alteration of the system of government of the country. The constitution established two chambers – the Senate and the Chamber of Deputies. Members of the former were to be appointed by the Emperor from the rases and notables while members of the nobility and local landed gentry – the *shums* – were in turn to choose members of the lower chamber. But the Emperor remained all-powerful; he was to appoint, promote, transfer, suspend and dismiss his own ministers. Under the constitution all the officers of the ministries and departments, as well as the mayors of municipalities, were responsible to him. Christianity was declared the state religion, the Emperor assuming the title of the 'Defender of the Holy Orthodox Faith based on the doctrines of St Mark of Alexandria'. The Constitution also attempted to stabilize the monarchy by regularizing the succession. Henceforward the throne was vested in the Haile Selassie family's male line.

Later, in 1955, Haile Selassie granted another constitution which gave greater powers to the Ethiopian people, through their representatives. Members of the Chamber of Deputies were to be elected by direct franchise by all Ethiopians of twenty-one years and above – although there had never been a census. The Emperor retained the power to choose all senators for a period of six years. The Lower Chamber in this constitution had the power to approve yearly budgets submitted by the various ministries, to initiate legislative proposals and constitutional amendments, to adopt various international agreements concluded by the government and to impeach government officials. However the Emperor still had veto powers over legislation passed by parliament. He initiated legislative proposals and reserved the right to determine the size, organization and responsibilities of the armed forces. The Emperor also exercised certain administrative controls over Ethiopia's Christian Orthodox Church.

Such reforms, and others which followed in the 1960s, only served to whet the appetite of the educated youth for more, whilst doing little to alter the fundamental nature of Ethiopian society. Ethiopia remained a feudal empire in which corrupt, largely Christian landlords dominated and exploited the peasantry of all religions – particularly in the southern provinces conquered by Emperor Menelik during the scramble for Africa. Despite the reforms, the Emperor remained a dictator. Economically the country was desperately backward, with few roads and virtually no de-

Haile Selassie, Emperor of Ethiopia 1930–74

velopment outside Addis Ababa and Asmara. Meanwhile demands for
self-determination grew in the former Italian colony of Eritrea (federated
with Ethiopia in 1952, but annexed as an integral part of the empire in
1962), in the Somali-inhabited Ogaden and, increasingly, in other out-
lying provinces.

External affairs

Since the last years of Menelik's reign the Ethiopian government had realized that the European powers were not prepared to respect her sovereignty if this went against their own interests, particularly economic ones. In 1894 a French company had obtained a concession for the building of a railway between Djibouti in French Somaliland and Addis Ababa. The British were concerned about their possible utilization of the Blue Nile water and Lake Tana and the River Sobat – important sources of the Nile flood so vital to the Sudan and Egypt. The Italians, who never forgot the humiliation of Adowa, still nursed political and territorial ambitions and wanted in particular to control a strip of land in Ethiopian territory linking Eritrea and Italian Somaliland and running through the fertile highlands 'to the west of Addis Ababa'. In 1906, without consultation with Menelik II, these three powers signed a Tripartite Treaty in which they paid lip-service to the independence of Ethiopia but also pledged themselves to recognize one another's 'sphere of influence' and to interfere in Ethiopia's affairs by 'protecting' their nationals 'in the event of rivalries or internal changes in Ethiopia'. Menelik replied: 'We have received the arrangement made by the three powers. We thank them for their communication and their desire to keep and maintain the independence of our government. But let it be understood that this arrangement in no way limits what we consider our sovereign rights.' In the same decade these three powers defined their boundaries in a number of treaties in a way that denied Ethiopia access to the Eritrean Red Sea coast, an area that Ethiopian rulers regarded as traditionally belonging to the empire.

Haile Selassie perceived during his Regency the imperialist intentions of the powers. In order to safeguard his country's sovereignty he pressed for the admission of his country to the international body of the League of Nations and this was finally granted in 1923. He hoped that by becoming a member of this organization, which had been formed after the First World War to maintain peace and prevent aggression by one member-state against another, Ethiopia would become immune to the dangerous ambitions of Britain, France and Italy, themselves members of the League. Hostility to the African state's application had centred on the argument that slavery and the slave trade still existed in the country.

The Italian threat to Ethiopia

Two years later it became clear that Ras Tafari had judged rightly about the threat posed by European imperialists to the Ethiopian empire when

Britain and Italy discussed how best the two powers could promote their interests in Ethiopia, at the expense of Ethiopia's sovereignty. Britain demanded Italian support for a water-control project she wanted to undertake on the shores of Lake Tana inside Ethiopia. In return the Italians wished to obtain British support, or recognition, for the construction of a railway through Ethiopia, west of Addis Ababa, to link up Eritrea and Somaliland; for exclusive Italian economic control in the west of Ethiopia and in the whole territory crossed by the proposed railway, and for economic concessions throughout the territory. In other words the Italians would constitute themselves into a state within the state of Ethiopia. Following Ras Tafari's vigorous protest to the League of Nations the British and Italians denied that they had any designs against the sovereignty of Ethiopia.

After 1925 Ethiopia's major concern in foreign affairs was the persistent Italian threat. However Ras Tafari left no stone unturned to give Italy no pretext to attack his country. In order to reduce the tension of 1925 he began to stretch hands of fellowship and friendship to Italy. The result was the Treaty of Perpetual Friendship which Ethiopia and Italy signed in 1928. It was expected to last twenty years. This treaty also provided that any disputes that might arise between the two countries should be settled by arbitration.

It was not long, however, before one clause of the treaty began to strain their relations. It was agreed that Ethiopia should use the Italian port of Assab, to be connected by a road to Dessye inside Ethiopia; the Italians were to construct the road up to the Eritrean frontier and Ethiopia the rest of the road inside the country. The Italians constructed their own part of the road but began to complain about how Ethiopia was constructing her part. Fearing the intentions of the Italians Haile Selassie decided that the road should continue to the capital, Addis Ababa. The Italians objected to any extension – a situation that would have denied them a military advantage over Ethiopia – and demanded that Italy should have control over the entire road from Assab to Dessye, that is including the stretch inside Ethiopia. The Ethiopians would not have a razor applied to their throats in this way, fearing that Italian control over the road would make their country vulnerable. The Ethiopians decided to employ Dutch engineers in the construction of their own part of the road. The Italians, however, took offence at this, claiming that there were enough qualified Italian engineers to build the road.

It is now known that as early as 1932 the Fascist ruler of Italy, Benito Mussolini, had decided to attack Ethiopia. For in that year he sent one of his principal military officers, General De Bono, to Eritrea with the object of surveying the military situation there. De Bono also spied on the state of affairs in Ethiopia and in the following year submitted a memorandum to Mussolini. In this document he described the political condition of Ethiopia as 'deplorable' and declared that it would not be difficult for Italy 'to effect the disintegration of the [Ethiopian] Empire'; it was hoped that some rases would rebel against the Emperor and thereby 'give us an opportunity to intervene'. Although Mussolini continued to deceive the world that Italy had no intention of 'territorial conquests' he had made up his mind that Ethiopia would be invaded by Italy in 1936 at the latest.

It is clear that all Italy wanted was a pretext to attack and annex Ethiopia. One came in November 1934 in the Wal Wal incident. Although the frontier between Italian Somalia and Ethiopia was ill-defined and had never been demarcated, there was no doubt that the important wells at Wal Wal were clearly within the Ethiopian Ogaden. Up till 1931 these and other wells in the deserts of Ethiopia had been used by the British, Italian and Ethiopian Somalis for their camels. Since 1929 a small military force from Italian Somaliland had occupied Wal Wal, although they had never interfered with the people from any direction using the wells. In 1931 Haile Selassie, who ever since his governorship of Harar had retained a commitment to this part of the Ethiopian empire, had sent a force of Ethiopian troops to clear the area and expel intruders. For some reason, however, the troops omitted Wal Wal. The Italians perhaps began to think that Wal Wal belonged to them for the garrison there was increased. When in November 1934 the Anglo-Ethiopian Grazing and Boundary Commission, which had set out to demarcate the frontier between Ethiopia and British Somaliland, came to Wal Wal, they were surprised to find an Italian encampment there. The British withdrew, leaving about 600 Ethiopian troops to face the much larger Italian forces. As was to be expected in such an explosive situation, shooting began, both parties accusing each other of firing first. The Ethiopians suffered the greater loss and withdrew, pursued by Italian aeroplanes which, the Ethiopians claimed, bombed the villages of Ado and Gheriogubi.

The Wal Wal incident provided Mussolini with the opportunity he had been hoping for since his seizure of power in 1922. By 1934 he had whipped up the nationalist feelings of Italians to fever heights. It was believed by many Italians that Italy was a great power which should imitate the other great powers by acquiring colonies – a 'place in the sun'. It was believed that at least parts of the Ethiopian empire held out bright economic prospects for Italy. It was argued that the country might even be richer than the highlands of Kenya which white settlers had long since occupied. Ethiopia had offended Italy by refusing to allow Italian economic activities to develop freely, and by not appointing sufficient Italian experts in the various technical and public services. It was pointed out that after 1928 only one Italian, an electrical engineer, had been appointed, whereas an Englishman had been selected as adviser for internal administration, a Frenchman for public works, another for archaeological research, and a third for foreign affairs.

Mussolini exploited the Wal Wal incident to the full. He decided to humiliate Ethiopia in a way that would enable Italy to remove what the right-wing post-soldier Gabriele d'Annunzio described as 'the scar, yes, the shameful scar of Adowa'. The demand in Italy that the humiliation of Adowa be avenged had been made for years and many Italians had been dismayed that Ethiopia had begun to be modernized along European lines in matters of communications, education, administration and military reforms, and that she had begun to organize and arm her troops 'in an up-to-date European manner', as an Italian military spokesman said. Indeed it was believed by many that the aim of Ethiopia was to expel Italy from Eritrea and Italian Somaliland along the coast, which were the only gains Italy had made in the Horn of Africa during the Scramble.

Mussolini made it clear that he would not allow himself to be bound by the provision of the 1928 treaty which, as Ethiopia pointed out, bound the two countries to refer the Wal Wal dispute to independent arbitration. He hated to think that Ethiopia should be regarded as a state with equal rights with Italy in international affairs; he would not have Italy put in the same class as Ethiopia. Mussolini dictated terms which he knew Ethiopia would never accept. Ethiopia was asked to apologize; to pay to Italy a compensation of £20,000 and to send an Ethiopian delegation to Wal Wal to salute the Italian flag there. Of course no sovereign nation would have submitted to a humiliation of that sort.

Failure of the League of Nations

It was in these circumstances that Haile Selassie turned to the League of Nations to help prevent the outbreak of hostilities. But Ethiopia was eventually to be rudely disappointed both by Britain and France, the two powers in whom Haile Selassie had reposed much confidence. In fact the British had tried to dissuade the Emperor from resorting to the League. This was a time when both Britain and France were bent on conciliating Mussolini in order to prevent him from becoming a supporter of Nazi Germany. In January 1935, that is about two months after the Wal Wal incident, the French signed a treaty with Italy, giving the latter some areas in Africa and also 25 000 out of the 34 000 shares in the Djibouti-Addis Ababa Railway. Three months later Macdonald and Flandin, prime ministers of Britain and France respectively, met Mussolini in Stresa and agreed to collaborate for peace. Britain and France were ineffective in resolving the Ethiopian crisis and Italy gained the correct impression that when the actual time of invasion came she would not face any opposition worth speaking of from the two powers.

In the meantime the League of Nations continued to prevaricate. A conciliation committee was set up but made little progress before it was overtaken by events. Later in 1935 Britain and France drew up the Zeila Agreement, according to which the signatories of the Tripartite Treaty were to supervise economic, financial and political 'reforms' in Ethiopia, 'particular account being taken of the special interests of Italy'. Although this Agreement was humiliating for Ethiopia she accepted it. Mussolini, however, refused to have any dealing with Ethiopia on terms of equality, the same reason for his rejection of the peace efforts of the League. In his view Ethiopia was a backward territory in which slavery still persisted and where a proper form of government had not been organized.

Arms embargo on Ethiopia and Italy

In 1935 Haile Selassie placed orders for arms with Belgium, Czechoslovakia, Britain and France. However at this point Britain and France announced an embargo on arms for both Italy and Ethiopia. However it was only Ethiopia that was really hit by this decision. Italy could supply her own arms, which she was already pouring into Eritrea and Italian Somaliland through the Suez Canal, still at that time under the control of the British. Haile Selassie kept on hoping that the British would not allow Italy to attack her and that in the last resort Britain would fight for her against Italy, an impression given to him by Sir Samuel Hoare, Britain's Foreign Secretary. The Ethiopian Emperor also believed that the League would intervene effectively, according to its Charter, and prevent a member state from committing an act of aggression against another member state. In both respects his hopes were destined to cruel disappointment. The British government, headed by Stanley Baldwin, decided to appease Mussolini and would not even allow British nationals to represent the League in keeping watch over the border between Ethiopia and Italian Somaliland. Britain and France signed the Hoare-Laval Agreement which would eventually have turned Ethiopia into an Italian dependency. The League then decided only on economic sanctions, denying Italy products and materials she did not really consider of crucial importance. Oil was specifically excepted.

Italy invades Ethiopia

In the meantime the Italian war machine was fully geared for a complete invasion of Ethiopia. In the view of Pietro Badoglio, the Italian general who eventually commanded the Italian forces, the objectives of the invasion were 'the utter destruction of the Abyssinian armed forces and the complete conquest of Ethiopia'. In October 1935, after inciting a number of local governors in Ethiopia to rise up against the rule of Haile Selassie, an Italian force of 120 000 began the invasion.

In a matter of seven months Ethiopia was overrun and many brutalities were committed. Many of the educated élite who were being raised by the Emperor were put to the sword; planes, artillery and poison gas were used to crush Ethiopian resistance. On 9 May 1936 Italy formally announced the annexation of Ethiopia and King Victor Emmanuel of Italy was named Emperor of Ethiopia. Haile Selasie fled his country in 1936 and lived in exile until 1941.

One important thing to note is that the League of Nations failed signally to fulfil its obligations to Ethiopia and thereby became discredited. Not long after the Italian occupation of Ethiopia member-states began to recognize the new regime and the ineffectual economic sanctions that had been announced against Italy were removed. This was in spite of the prophetic speech made before the League in Geneva by Haile Selassie on

Ethiopian chieftains preparing to fight the invading Italians

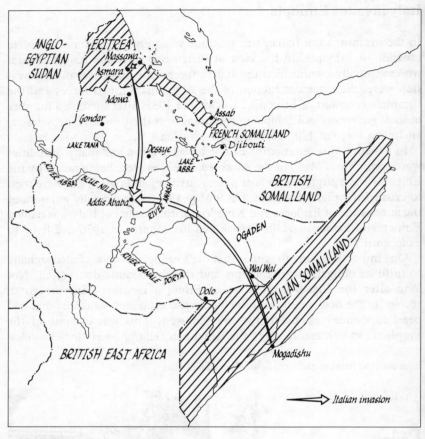

Ethiopia, showing the lines of Italian invasion

30 June 1936, in which he warned that if the League did not stand by its Charter, then 'the very existence' of the League would be in danger. He declared that what the League should uphold was 'the confidence that each state is to place in international treaties ... the value of promises made to small states, that their integrity and their independence be respected and ensured...' Italy's unpunished aggression served to encourage Hitler and brought the world closer to the brink of world war.

The Italians did not find their occupation of Ethiopia easy. Revolts against them were common and Italy's control was limited to the cities and villages where they had garrisons; there were many provinces over which the invaders had little or no control. In 1937 an attempt was made on the life of the Italian viceroy. The Italians seized the occasion to put to death about 3000 Ethiopians, mostly the educated élite and over 100 priests. Another problem was that there were no resources in Italy to sustain the Italians' heavy expenditure on roads and public works. By 1940 the Italians were fast losing their grip on their north-east African empire.

Italian forces expelled

In 1939 the Second World War had broken out and in 1940 Italy decided to fight with Germany against France and Britain. It was this situation, rather than any genuine concern for Ethiopia's independence, that made the British government decide to give military help to restore Haile Selassie to his country. Even then many British administrative officers in the Sudan, who believed that Italy would be victorious in such a war, were opposed to the idea of Haile Selassie being helped back into the country, believing that Italy might well annex the Sudan. In June 1940 Haile Selassie was taken to the Sudan. Ethiopian refugees were organized in support of the internal resistance and a patriot army armed by the British and sometimes even officered by British, French, Kenyan, South African and Australian volunteers. The empire was invaded from north and south and in January 1941, Haile Selassie also crossed the frontier into Ethiopia. By the end of the year Italy's rule in Ethiopia had come to an end. The Italian conquest of Ethiopia had aroused strong emotions among nationalists throughout Africa, Asia and in the black diaspora. Haile Selassie's return was seen as a major defeat for European imperialism.

Not all the peoples of the Ethiopian empire, however, welcomed back their former Shewan rulers. In particular the Somalis of the Ogaden had experienced under Italian rule a period of unity with their fellow Somalis in Italian Somaliland. This unity was extended in a period of British military administration which brought them together with British Somaliland under what was essentially one administration. The reluctance of Somalis living in Ethiopian territory to return to Ethiopian administration – a process which began in 1948 but was not completed in the Haud and the 'reserved area' around Jigjiga until 1955 – lay at the root of future conflict involving open warfare between Ethiopia and independent Somalia. The 'disposal' of the Italian colony of Eritrea – more economically and politically advanced than Ethiopia – was also to produce problems which federation with Ethiopia in 1952 did not solve.

The Ethiopian revolution, 1974

Despite Haile Selassie's various constitutional reforms and his attempts at modernization, it was clear that the old feudal system of imperial Ethiopia

A painting dating from the Italian-Ethiopian war, depicting Saint Michael, representing Ethiopia, trampling on the faces of Hitler and Mussolini was an anachronism. General Mengistu Neway, on being sentenced to death for his part in an attempted coup in 1960, had commented: 'Ethiopia has been standing still, while our African brothers are moving ahead in the struggle to overcome poverty.' Hosting pan-African conferences and making Addis Ababa the headquarters of the Organization for African Unity did little to stem the increasingly loud demands being made for the radical reform of Ethiopian society.

The revolution finally began in 1974. It was to be a bloody and bitter one. It started quietly enough in February with army mutinies and demonstrations by taxi drivers and others in Addis Ababa. There followed a wave of strikes, demonstrations and boycotts which gradually eroded the ability of the old regime to resist. As the central government began to collapse, peasants in the south took the opportunity to drive out the northern landlords and officials who had oppressed them for so long. Government was brought to a standstill. Then came the stunning revelation that Haile Selassie had done nothing to alleviate a famine which had begun the previous year and had cost over 200 000 lives. All mention of the famine had been suppressed, all warnings of its imminence ignored, and offers of foreign assistance refused. When these facts became widely known, much of the mystique surrounding the monarchy vanished almost overnight.

Peasant soldiers within the army, tired of fighting endless internal wars and irritated by the rewards lavished by the Emperor upon senior army officers, started to molest and arrest them. These mutinies were warmly supported by many younger, junior officers who saw prospects of quick promotion. It was they who took the lead in the formation of the Co-ordinating Committee of the Armed Forces, or *Dergue* (Committee), which assumed control over the armed forces in June. They proceeded to arrest senior officers and leading officials of the old regime. By September they felt strong enough to depose the Emperor. Haile Selassie was later to die in uncertain circumstances in prison in August 1975. The *Dergue* was increasingly influenced by radical Marxist-Leninist elements, including students who called for the formation of a peoples' government. In 1975 it began to take over large manufacturing, financial, banking and insurance institutions and promulgated radical land reform measures. All agricultural land was to be nationalized, the sale or renting of land was forbidden, and maximum holdings were fixed at 10 hectares. These measures were far more radical in the south, where the landlords had already fled, than in the north, where the land was already minutely divided and tenancy was not a major problem. Peasant associations were set up to implement land reform and to take over the running of local government. It seemed that power was really being transferred to the people. At the same time, urban land

133

Members of the Ethiopian *Dergue*: Major Mengistu Haile Mariam is in the front row on the left

was also nationalized, families were restricted to only one house each, and the rents for cheaper houses were lowered. Urban committees were set up to administer housing and other local affairs. No compensation was to be paid to rural or urban landowners who were dispossessed.

But, precisely at the point when the revolution had achieved a widespread impact throughout the country, different political factions began a period of vicious and bloody fighting. The students, just back from the countryside where they had helped to implement land reform, called upon the *Dergue* (now renamed the Provisional Military Advisory Council) to resign and make way for a revolutionary peoples' government. Since the army retained its rigidly centralized and highly authoritarian structure, the *Dergue* refused this demand and therefore the students began to launch an urban guerrilla campaign in 1977. This provoked savage retaliation from the *Dergue*, and officially sanctioned 'Red Terror' killings continued throughout the year. The emerging strong man, Mengistu Haile Mariam, became chairman of the *Dergue* in February 1978, and, with the help of timely Russian support, began the brutal extermination of all opposition within and outside the army. Over half of the *Dergue's* original membership of around 120 was killed.

The problem of the outlying provinces

The military government inherited serious problems of disaffection in the Ogaden, in Eritrea and elsewhere. In the Ogaden, in the south-east, the Somali inhabitants had resisted Shewan rule ever since their incorporation into the empire at the end of the nineteenth century, and when Somalia became independent in 1960 this greatly encouraged the Ogaden Somali. Ethiopia and Somalia were thus on the brink of war for many years. Eritrea in the north had been an Italian colony. Many of its people, especially the Muslim sections of the population, hoped for complete independence. But in 1951 the United Nations ruled that Eritrea should be federated with Ethiopia in 1952 with internal self-government. How-

Guerrillas of the Eritrean Liberation Front in action in Eritrea

ever in 1962 Ethiopia incorporated Eritrea as just another province. The Eritrean liberation movements began a struggle for independence which was still being waged in the 1980s.

Initially the new military rulers in Ethiopia raised the hopes of the various ethnic and provincial groups. They denounced the policies of the old regime, proclaimed the equality of all cultures, gave official recognition for the first time to Islam, and allowed newspapers and broadcasts to use languages other than the previously dominant Amharic. They acknowledged the right of minorities to some, as yet unspecified, degree of local autonomy. But soon the *Dergue*, which continued to be dominated by Shewan-Amharas, began to argue that since the old ruling class had now been overthrown, there was no longer any justification for 'secessionist' demands. In 1974 the Eritreans rejected an offer to restore regional self-government (which had earlier proved a sham), and the war there intensified. By 1977 the Eritreans had driven the Ethiopians out of all but three towns but massive refugee flows occurred into the Sudan.

In the Ogaden, a full-scale war had broken out – also involving Somalia. To make matters worse, other liberation movements emerged or re-emerged: in Tigrai in the north and in the Oromo and Sidama lands in the south. Since the Americans had stopped supplying arms to a self-proclaimed Marxist regime, the Ethiopian government was in a truly desperate position, and was saved from probable disintegration by a massive Russian airlift of supplies starting in 1977. With the aid of some 12–15 000 Cuban soldiers, Ethiopia launched a counter-offensive in February 1978 which drove the Somali Army out and reoccupied the Ogaden. But guerrilla war continued and by 1980 over one million refugees had fled to Somalia.

The summer of 1978 saw a massive Ethiopian offensive in Eritrea, resulting in the capture of all towns but one. Here too guerrilla war continued.

The problems of food, education and health

By 1980 the *Dergue* leaders had butchered most of their internal rivals and had regained a measure of initiative against the various secessionist and regional movements. It was thus in a position to try to concentrate more on how to provide sufficient food for the people. The decision was taken to reverse certain earlier land reforms. State collectivization was to be the order of the day. Groups were set up 'to agitate the peasantry to abandon individual cultivation and get organized into co-operatives.' Under the expansion of state collectives which followed, peasant associations were

136

forced to surrender some of their land. Those who resisted were killed. Collectivization was 'encouraged' by drastically increasing taxes on those living outside the collectives. Some former landlords were even encouraged to return and were given land, as were thousands of supposedly drought-stricken northerners who were resettled mainly in the southern provinces. In such circumstances, it is not surprising that the Oromo and other liberation fronts continued to gather support.

Ethiopia's dream of social equality in the context of equality of opportunity for all may seem impossible. The country's shift from feudal capitalism to socialism has not been easy. However the regime has made steps forward in social reform, especially in education, health and land distribution, in what is one of the world's poorest countries. The literacy rate has gone from 7 per cent to more than 40 per cent. A little more than 50 per cent of children of primary-school age are now in classes as opposed to 18 per cent in 1974 and overall school enrolment has increased by 250 per cent to more than 2.7 million. The literacy campaign which made 4 million people literate in three years is being conducted in ten languages and has been found to be so impressive that in 1981 UNESCO gave Ethiopia a special award.

The percentage of Ethiopians with access to health services has increased from 15 to 46 per cent of the estimated 32 million population, meaning that an additional 10 million people have a chance to get medical care. Land has been nationalized, and peasants no longer have to give half or more of their crop to the landlord as rent. In the urban areas access to better housing has been enhanced by provision of free land and improved financing.

Conclusion

The Ethiopian revolution illustrates the impossibility of transforming a feudal empire into a homogeneous socialist society overnight. The collapse of the old authoritarian and monolithic regime allowed new factions, which had hitherto not been allowed to exercise any authority, to compete bloodily for power. At first the largely Amharic *Dergue* had gone along with the programme of the radical Marxist intellectuals, but later, when its own supremacy was challenged, it turned brutally on all who opposed it. As in Southern Africa, the superpowers intervened in the Horn of Africa pursuing their own interests, and the warring African states and secessionist movements competed for their military support.

6 The Maghreb

Conquest, Islamic law and the settlers

The Maghreb is to a large degree a region of ethnic and religious unity. Most of its people are Arabs, though there are important Berber minorities, notably in Morocco, and the vast majority are followers of Islam. The region was colonized by three European Catholic powers. France occupied Algeria in 1830, Tunisia in 1881 and Morocco in 1912. Spain was given a small part of northern Morocco in 1912 and Italy took Libya from the Ottomans in 1911. The process of conquest took a long time. The last resistance in Algeria ended in 1871; there was a revolt in Spanish Morocco led by Abdel Krim from 1921 to 1926; and it was only in 1933 that the Italians brought Sanusiyya resistance to an end in Libya, and in 1934 that the French finally gained control of southern Morocco.

There was much animosity between conquerors and conquered. All Muslims tended to regard being ruled by non-Muslims as intolerable, and in Tunisia and Morocco especially there existed some sense of nationhood (if not in the modern sense) which made it doubly intolerable to have to endure French rule. A major source of conflict was the French law, known as the Senatus Consult (1865), which decreed that any Muslim North African who wished to become assimilated as a French citizen had to renounce Islamic law and adopt French law. Since Islamic law was so thoroughly entrenched, many thousands of people who might have become French citizens refused to do so. In Algeria, for example, only some 2500 Muslims ever became French citizens. They were ostracized by the Muslim community and they were never fully accepted into French society.

This was partly because of the presence of so many *colons*, white settlers, in the Maghreb. In the last years before independence, the *colons* of Algeria, numbering almost one million, the largest white population in Africa outside South Africa, formed some 10 per cent of the population; in Libya the figure was also 10 per cent; while in Morocco and Tunisia it was between 6 and 8 per cent. Like the settlers of Southern Africa, the *colons*, who were farmers, merchants, civil servants and also workers, fiercely resisted all plans for the economic, social or political advancement of the Arab and Berber majority. The *colons* competed with Arabs for jobs and their society was profoundly affected by racism. The major difference between Algeria and South Africa and the former Rhodesia was that, because of the French tradition of strongly centralized government, ultimate power always resided in Paris and not with the *colons*. Thus, while the *colons* were able to block and frustrate many reforms, when General de Gaulle's French government finally decided to quit Algeria, it was able to do so despite the fierce opposition of the *colons*, most of whom, like the whites of Angola and Mozambique, promptly fled back to the metropole.

Although Algeria, Tunisia and Morocco were all conquered by France the manner in which they were governed differed considerably. In 1871 Algeria was made part of metropolitan France and was divided into three 'departments' which elected deputies to sit in the French parliament in Paris. Because of the restrictions on Muslims becoming French citizens the vast majority of the country's population did not have the right to vote. As a result the Algerian deputies represented only the European *colons*, and in Paris they formed a powerful lobby against any reform or concession to the Muslim majority. European domination was based on their control of the best land in Algeria; in 1954 26 153 European families farmed 2 345 666 hectares of land whilst 630 732 Muslim families between them farmed 7 349 100 hectares. However, it was not the case that all of the *colons* were rich farmers for the majority of the million settlers lived in the cities, many of them in the poor suburbs of Algiers.

Neither Tunisia nor Morocco were ever incorporated into metropolitan France. Instead both were classified as 'Protectorates' and the French adopted a policy of 'indirect rule' using the existing authorities to do their work for them. In Morocco, Marshal Lyautey who led the conquest of the country, not only made use of the Moroccan sultan but also attempted to divide the Arab and Berber population against each other in a policy of 'divide and rule'. The different patterns of French colonial rule were to be of importance in shaping the nationalist movements in the Maghreb.

Labour migration and land alienation

The colonial Maghreb had two phenomena in common with Southern Africa: labour migration and land alienation. In Southern Africa people from the rural areas of countries such as Mozambique, Basutoland (now Lesotho), Nyasaland (now Malawi) and Northern Rhodesia (now Zambia) migrated south in search of work on the mines and farms of South Africa and Southern Rhodesia. In the Maghreb, and especially in Algeria, people migrated northwards, across the Mediterranean to France. During the First World War France conscripted hundreds of thousands of workers and soldiers from North Africa. In the inter-war years, rising population coupled with lack of land and economic opportunites at home compelled some 40 000 Maghrebians to seek temporary work in France each year. The numbers steadily grew, to a quarter of a million on the eve of the Algerian war in 1954, to one million by 1970. As in Southern Africa, North African workers over time became more and more reliant on getting work in the areas to which they migrated. By 1954 the cash remittances which these workers sent back to their families in Algeria equalled the amount earned in wages by Algerians on *colon* farms. As the French economy expanded during the 1960s, it became increasingly dependent on cheap, exploitable, foreign labour from the Maghreb and from southern Europe. As in Southern Africa, these migrants were not encourged to settle as permanent residents. Being mostly unskilled, they were given the worst paid and the dirtiest jobs; they were often harassed by the police and their legal rights were inferior to those of French citizens. Their situation, which became more precarious as the world recession hit France in the 1970s and 1980s, well illustrated the unequal relationship, born of colonialism, which was established between France and the Maghreb.

The alienation of land to settlers, always a major bone of contention in colonial Africa, was especially so in North Africa where much land was regarded by Muslims as sacred. The situation was worse in Algeria, where the *colons* seized some 2.7 million hectares. This amounted to one-third of all the land where adequate rainfall permitted cultivation, and a very high proportion of the most fertile land in the country. In the process, the local people were driven away from the coastal plains and valleys onto the highlands and steppes. Once they had been driven away as proprietors they were later encouraged to return, temporarily, as labourers on terms dictated by the new *colon* owners. The situation was comparable, though less severe, elsewhere. In Tunisia the *colons* took about half of the productive agricultural land, while in Morocco they took one-sixteenth of the cultivable area. All of this meant that, as elsewhere in Africa, land and labour grievances were to play a significant part in the protest and resistance movements against colonial rule in the Maghreb.

Religion and nationalism

Resistance also assumed a religious character. Muslims regarded it as a very retrograde step to be ruled by non-Muslims. The French compounded their unpopularity when they derided Islam as an inferior religion which, they claimed, was responsible for the technological backwardness and primitiveness of the Maghrebian peoples. In Morocco in 1930 they issued the famous Berber *Dahir*, which was an attempt to win the Berbers to their side. They believed that the Berbers were not true Muslims in their heart of hearts, but rather had professed their faith in Islam for centuries solely from fear of Arab retaliation. The Berber *Dahir* stated that the *sharia* (Islamic law) was no longer to apply to Berbers, who were to come under the jurisdiction of a combination of traditional Berber customary law and French criminal law. This was part of the French policy of 'divide and rule'.

Contrary to French expectations, the Berbers did not thank them. Rather, believing that the greatest harm had been done to them, they joined hands with their Arab brothers in protesting against the *Dahir*. The French added to their indiscretion by encouraging Roman Catholic missionaries to intensify their activities in Morocco. Crowds surged into the mosques to pray for deliverance from 'the time of peril'. In Fez, Moroccans performed pilgrimages to the shrine of Moulay Idris, founder and patron saint of the city, invoking his help and protection against the French. Outside Morocco, Muslim communities prayed for the Moroccan people who, it was rumoured, were in danger of being forced by Christians to renounce Islam.

In Algeria in 1928 Sheik Abdel Hamid Ben Badis began a reformist religious movement with a nationalist character, the aim of which was to restore Islam to its original purity. In 1931 he founded the Society of the Reformist Ulema, which was a religious, cultural and political organization. He forbade smoking, drinking and dancing. In 1938 he issued a proclamation labelling any Algerian who sought French citizenship as an apostate. The Society became particularly influential in the field of education. Since the French made only limited efforts to provide education for Algerian Muslims – only one in twelve went to school – and their schools neglected religious education, the Society founded Islamic modern schools, in which Arabic, mathematics, history and geography were taught. These were schools with a nationalist message for the rising generation, and pupils were taught the slogan 'my religion is Islam, my language is Arabic and my country is Algeria'. The Society published many journals which supported various political parties.

In Tunisia also religion played a part in early nationalist activity. As the French Resident-General and his officials in the provinces began to supplant the government of the Bey of Tunis, they started to seize *waqf* lands, religious endowments, the proceeds of which were traditionally used by

Muslims for schools, hospitals and mosques. Their preservation was thus essential in a Muslim community. In 1906 the *ulema* (learned men), whose religious centre was the Zaytuna Mosque, attacked the French concept of landownership. In the following year Muslims were embittered by the action of the French in persuading Tunisian Jews to accept French citizenship. Also, while the Berber *Dahir* was arousing discontent in Morocco, the French administration in Tunisia encouraged Christian missions to attempt to convert Muslims. In 1931 it made a grant of two million francs to the Eucharistic Conference which had been convened to meet in Tunis to celebrate the fiftieth anniversary of the French occupation of the country. The Catholic Bishop of Tunis described the proposed conference as a crusade against Islam. The people became so enraged at this that they demonstrated and protested against the conference being held at all. Dockworkers went on strike on the day the delegates were due to arrive, and they were joined by cotton merchants and their employees. The national press joined in the protest and the conference had finally to be abandoned.

Political nationalism in Tunisia

It was in the Protectorate of Tunisia that a westernized élite first began to express nationalist aspirations. Under the leadership of a French-trained lawyer, Ali Basah Hamba, the Young Tunisian Party was founded in 1908. A prominent member of this organization was Sheik al-Aziz al-Thaalbi, who became its leader in 1911. The party's ideals were similar to those of the Young Turks of Turkey, and they wanted to see Tunisia become part of a reformed Ottoman empire. In 1911 Hamba was deported by the Resident-General when the Young Tunisian Party presented him with a demand for constitutional reforms. In Constantinople, to which he had fled, Hamba disseminated anti-French feelings but he died in 1918 on the point of leading an expedition to attempt to liberate North Africa from European rule.

The First World War, in which the Tunisians had been compelled to fight on the side of the French, had an important impact on the thinking of the westernised élite, as it did in other parts of Africa. Particularly attractive was the principle of self-determination, proclaimed by President Woodrow Wilson of the United States.

Like Saad Zaghlul of Egypt, al-Thaalbi demanded the right to send a mission to Paris, where the Versailles Conference that ended the war was taking place. He too was refused. In 1920 the Young Tunisian Party was transformed into Hizb al-Dastur al-Hurr, the Destour or Liberal Constitutional Party. The nationalists put moderate demands before the Resident-General. They accused the French of violating the Protectorate Treaty of 1881 and asked for the establishment of parliamentary government. They declared that confiscation of land and immigration of *colons* should stop and requested the encouragement of Islamic education, the admission of Tunisians to high positions in the civil service and an end to the policy of assimilation.

The Resident-General, Lucien Saint, treated these demands with indifference. In 1921 the French President visited Tunisia and announced that the country would always remain linked to France. In the following year an attempt was made to deport the Destour leaders. When the Resident-General presented the Bey, Mohammed al-Nasir, with a list of proposed deportees, the Bey asked why his name had not been included and threatened to abdicate if the nationalists were exiled. However, he soon died and a pro-French Bey succeeded him. Al-Thaalbi was deported in 1923 and remained in exile until 1937. The party fell into disarray.

Habib Bourguiba and Néo-Destour

It was during this time that a French-trained barrister, Habib Bourguiba, entered the nationalist struggle. Born in 1903, he was educated at primary and secondary schools in Tunis. In 1924, like so many members of the North African westernised élite, he went to Paris for further studies. There he obtained a law degree and a diploma in political science and married a French woman. In 1927 he returned to Tunisia as a lawyer, and in 1930 joined the staff of *La Voix du Tunisien*, the organ of the Destour Party. When he observed that the party, as then constituted, lacked strong leadership and a programme that could attract the masses to the nationalist struggle, he started his own newspaper, *L'Action Tunisienne*, and began to campaign in the villages. In 1943 he formed the Néo-Destour (New Constitutional) Party, which was later to become the ruling party when Tunisia obtained independence in 1956.

After the founding of Néo-Destour the nationalist struggle in Tunisia centred largely around the personality of Bourguiba. He was essentially a realist and a pragmatist who possessed the rare gift of perceiving the best which the nationalists could hope to achieve in any given situation. He recognized that the French were unlikely to be forced out of Tunisia by violence alone, and he refused to issue anti-Allied propaganda during the Second World War when he was taken from a French prison by the Italians after their occupation of Vichy France at the end of 1942. He sought co-operation with the French in the granting of independence by

President Habib Bourguiba in 1958

stages. He was certainly no militant, believing that the investment of French capital and technology would be needed for the future development of his country. Similarly, he was not a fanatical Muslim; he believed that Islam would need to be modified as his country became more modernized.

But his moderation and willingness to co-operate with it notwithstanding, the French administration regarded Bourguiba and his followers as dangerous agitators and disturbers of the peace. The lot of these nationalists was frequent imprisonment or deportation. In 1945 the French at last agreed to establish a Legislative Assembly, but half the seats were to be reserved for *colons*. Supported by the masses, the Néo-Destourians, whose party had been banned, waged a successful boycott of the elections. The *colons* then opposed any further concessions to the nationalists, as did the administration in Algeria, which feared that any concessions granted in Tunisia would encourage nationalists in Algeria.

Tunisia achieves independence, 1956

The achievement of independence in both Tunisia and Morocco was to be greatly influenced by events in Indo-China and in Algeria. In Indo-China (now Laos, Vietnam and Kampuchea) the French fought the decisive and losing battle against the Viet-Minh from March to May of 1954 at Dien Bien Phu. Their defeat was a crucial turning point for the French empire, and it greatly encouraged anti-colonial movements everywhere. Dien Bien Phu, coupled with the outbreak of war in Algeria in November 1954, convinced the French of the need to come to terms with nationalists in Tunisia and Morocco, in order to avoid fighting three separate and very expensive wars in the Maghreb. (It also persuaded them to come to terms easily with nationalist leaders in French West and Equatorial Africa.)

Thus France granted internal autonomy to Tunisia in 1954, and brought Néo-Destour into government. In June 1955 Bourguiba negotiated internal self-government, though some radicals were opposed to its terms. Full independence followed in March 1956. In the end it was all relatively peaceful, but the threat of force locally and the reality of force elsewhere proved the decisive lever.

Morocco: the Moroccan League, Istiqlal and Mohammed V

In Morocco a nationalist movement led by a westernised élite emerged during the 1920s, at a time when Abdel Krim was organizing the Berbers of the Rif area against the Spanish rulers. The westernised élite in Morocco was certainly influenced by the post-war achievement of self-government by Middle Eastern countries such as Egypt, Syria and the Hijaz. Two members of this élite, independent of each other, founded nationalist movements almost simultaneously. One was Ahmed Balafrej, who had received university training in Morocco, Egypt and at the Sorbonne in Paris. In 1926 he summoned a group of men to Rabat and formed the Moroccan League. To escape the hostility of the administration, its title was changed to the apparently more harmless Supporters of Truth. The second was Mohammed Allal al-Fassi, who called another group of people to Fez. Son of a professor at the University of Qarawiyyin and a poet of some ability, he had been a student agitator and had written many nationalist songs. His organization soon merged with the Moroccan League, which was the ancestor of the Istiqlal Party, founded in December 1943. Istiqlal, recognizing the power and popularity of the Sultan of Morocco, determined to work with him to secure independence. This meant adopting a somewhat less modern political programme than nationalists elsewhere in the Maghreb.

The French jailed and exiled Istiqlal leaders, as was their policy in Tunisia and Algeria. Fortunately for the Moroccan people their Sultan,

Sidi Mohammed, or Mohammed V as he became on his accession in 1927 rose to the occasion by identifying himself with the aspirations of his people for independence from French rule.

Mohammed V was a shrewd ruler who contrasted with many of his contemporaries in Africa, who became tools in the hands of the colonial rulers. In fact he had been preferred to a better claimant to the Sherifian throne precisely because the French believed that he would be a reliable puppet who would carry out their wishes. For many years the French believed that they had judged him correctly. He co-operated with them, obeyed the orders of the Resident-General and showed no favourable disposition toward the westernised nationalists.

But both the French and the nationalists misjudged him. He was only being realistic, biding his time until he could join in the nationalist struggle most effectively. In fact he was already showing qualities which marked him out as the greatest Moroccan ruler of recent times. Knowing the deep chord which Islam struck in the hearts of his subjects, Mohammed V never outraged the principles of the Muslim faith. In public he performed the religious functions demanded of an Imam, regularly paid his official visit to the mosque on Friday, kept the fast of Ramadan as strictly as most of his subjects, and never appeared in public except in

Abdel Krim, symbol of Moroccan resistance to foreign rule

traditional robes. In private, however, he drove his own car, played tennis and wore western dress.

He wanted to see his people enjoy an education that would combine the best of the European and the Islamic systems. In order that traditional morality should not suffer, he advocated Islamic education for children. In later years they should learn the techniques of western education. His eldest son Moulay Hassan, who later became Sultan, obtained a degree in French law.

Mohammed V began to show the stuff of which he was made during the Second World War, when he sided with Charles de Gaulle's Free French Movement against the Vichy regime established by the Germans when they occupied France in 1940. Moroccan blood drenched the soils of North Africa, Corsica, Elba, Sicily and France. Some 300 000 Moroccans were mobilized in the struggle to liberate France, and de Gaulle honoured Mohammed V with the Cross of Liberation. The Sultan and Istiqlal, however, had helped the French in the expectation that France would recognize Morocco's right to independence. President Roosevelt of the United States encouraged the Sultan in this belief at their famous meeting in January 1943. He promised to do all he could to hasten Morocco's independence. Roosevelt's personal envoy, Robert Murphy, gave similar encouragement to the nationalist leaders Habib Bourguiba of Tunisia and Ferhat Abbas of Algeria. American support however tended to fade once the 'Cold War' against Russia got under way in 1947.

The French administrators of Morocco, however, showed no desire to leave, since they regarded the country as part of France. The inevitable clash with the Sultan occurred during the tenure of General Juin, who was Resident-General from 1947 to 1952. He encouraged the Kittaniyya *tariqa* and Thami al-Glaoui, the Pasha of Marrakesh, in their propaganda against the Sultan. Both the Kittaniyya sufi sect and the Glaoui family had been supporters of the French administration from the beginning. Glaoui was actually aiming at the Sherifian throne although he was not strictly eligible. Both were hostile to the nationalist aspirations of the Moroccan people. Juin encouraged Glaoui to organize propaganda against the Sultan in order to present to the outside world a picture that the Sultan was unpopular. Illiterate chiefs were compelled to sign petitions of whose content they were ignorant. These petitions were 'signed' in the presence of French administrators, who had summoned the leaders to Fez and Rabat on the pretext that they would be given anti-tuberculosis vaccinations and entertained to a great feast. When at last they realized that they had been duped into signing anti-Sultan documents, they were not amused. The people then began to protest in a way that bewildered Juin.

The French newspaper, *Le Monde*, described what happened:

> We are witnessing an intense and new phase of the Moroccan crisis. Since the middle of last week, groups of natives have been assembling quietly at the borders of the Berber country, south of Meknes. Without any noise or any kind of disturbance they are spending long hours outside the French administrative offices. When asked what their purpose is, they say that they want their pasha and caids dismissed, since these recently set themselves to oppose the Sultan. All this is done with such calm, such politeness, that the authorities are at a loss to know how to intervene.

Sultan Mohammed V was unmoved by the hostility of the French administrators. He refused demands that he should openly denounce Istiqlal, eliminate from his entourage all who sympathized with the nationalists, nominate a large number of candidates chosen by the French for posts of pashas and caids, and punish all who had shown opposition to Glaoui. He also refused to sign decrees which would have increased further the French hold over Morocco. In 1952 he communicated directly with Paris, demanding the abolition of the Protectorate Treaty and martial law, and the right to form a government of his own choosing. He declared that he wished to establish a parliamentary system of government without delay.

Morocco achieves independence, 1956

Confronted by such demands, the French decided to depose Mohammed V in 1953 and to replace him with a puppet ruler. At once armed opposition broke out in the working-class districts of the larger cities and then spread to the countryside. Even the Berber chiefs, whom the French had been encouraging so strongly to revolt against the Sultan, deemed it wise to call for his return. Like the Tunisians and the Algerians, the Moroccans had concluded that violence was the only language the French understood.

As in Tunisia, the situation was dramatically transformed by events in Indo-China and Algeria, which forced the French to make rapid concessions. In November 1955 Mohammed V returned to Morocco amid scenes of wild rejoicing. The French accepted the principle of independence, a new government involving Istiqlal was formed and the country moved rapidly to full independence in March 1956. The French hoped that the newly independent governments of Morocco and Tunisia would support them – or at least remain neutral – in the war they were fighting in Algeria.

148

Political nationalism in Algeria

The nationalists in Morocco and Tunisia had a relatively easy task in winning independence. This was partly because the French had always had to rely on the traditional rulers in these countries and so once the élite was won over to the nationalist cause there was little the French could do to stop them. The situation was very different in Algeria. The violence of the French conquest and the large settler (*colon*) presence had destroyed the traditional authorities. As a result Algerian nationalism could only succeed if it mobilized the masses. Furthermore, because Algeria was regarded by the French as part of France, the French government refused to contemplate Algerian independence. The ties that linked the European settler population in Algeria with people living on the French mainland were very strong. Algeria was very close to France and it was easy for Algerian settlers to visit their relations and friends in France. As late as 1954 when a 'liberal' prime minister, Pierre Mendès-France, was elected in France and began to negotiate independence with the nationalists in Indo-China, Morocco and Tunisia, the possibility of negotiating with nationalists in Algeria, or that Algeria would ever become independent was ruled out. In November 1954 Mendès-France told the French parliament: 'The departments of Algeria have been French for a long time and this situation cannot be altered ... Algeria is France'.

The failure of concessions, 1914–54

During the First World War conscription was imposed by the French, and 173 000 soldiers and 120 000 workers were sent from Algeria to support the French war effort. They were 'rewarded' with minor reforms in 1919, which gave greater representation to Muslims in local assemblies, abolished the special taxes on Arabs, and made it marginally easier for Muslims to become French citizens. In the same year Amir Khalid, a grandson of Abdel Kader, demanded the application of Woodrow Wilson's principle of self-determination to Algeria and formed the Algerian Federation of Elected Muslim Officials. He was deported in 1924. The best known Algerian nationalist of the period was Messali Hadj. He was born in Tlemcen in 1898 and served in the army in southern France from 1915 to 1918. He then went to Paris where he worked in the Renault car factory and joined others there in the formation of the Etoile Nord Africaine, a socio-political organization of North African migrant workers in France. Like Bourguiba, he married a French woman who was a communist. Until 1936 the Etoile Nord Africaine was associated with the

French Communist Party. In 1926 he attended an Anti-Imperialist Congress in Brussels, Belgium, where he campaigned actively against French occupation of the Maghreb. In 1937 he founded the Parti Populaire Algérien. Messali was totally opposed to the policy of assimilation; his ultimate goal was independence for an Islamic Algerian state.

Initially opposed to any conception of an Algerian nation were those who accepted assimilation. Among them were the so-called *beni oui oui* or 'yes-men'. They were councillors in the local assemblies and were mostly 'loyal' chiefs and large landowners. Among the pro-assimilationists was also Ferhat Abbas, whose career was in some ways a barometer of Algerian nationalism. Born in 1899 to a caid who was later decorated with the French Legion of Honour, Abbas received a French education and qualified as a pharmacist. Like so many of the Maghrebian westernised élite, he married a French woman. In his youth he knew more French than

Messali Hadj

150

Ferhat Abbas

Arabic; it was only later that he espoused Islamic culture. In 1936 he was bitterly disappointed when the *colons* blocked the Blum-Violette reforms, which would have allowed Muslims to become French citizens without renouncing Islamic law. The *colons* accused him of being an Algerian nationalist, a charge which he refuted in the often-quoted words:

> If I had discovered the Algerian Nation I would be a Nationalist and I would not be ashamed of it as if it were a crime. I will not die for the Algerian fatherland because it does not exist. I have not found it. I have searched history, I have questioned both the dead and the living, I have visited the graveyards; no one mentioned it, not even once.

In fact, the failure of the Blum-Violette reforms drove Ferhat Abbas and others into sympathy with the current Arab renaissance stemming from Egypt. When General de Gaulle and his Free French Movement took control of North Africa following the battle of El Alamein in 1942, he immediately offered Algerians the Blum-Violette reforms, only to find that Algerian opinion had moved ahead of him. In 1943 Abbas denounced assimilation and demanded a new constitution, equal political rights for all, land reform, recognition of Arabic as an official language, freedom of the press, the right to form political parties and trade unions, and free, compulsory education.

In March 1944 the French promulgated an ordinance in an effort to conciliate the nationalists. For the first time Muslims were to be given the right to vote nationally and were offered French citizenship, without having to renounce their Muslim status. In addition, the hated *indigénat*, which had made 'natives' liable to arbitrary arrest and summary trial, was abolished. A new assembly was to be established with half its members being elected by Muslims, and the other half by *colons* and assimilated Muslims. All these reforms were, as usual, bitterly contested by the *colons*, but before they could be implemented violence broke out in 1945 – as it did in so many African colonies. Algerian national flags were displayed during the celebrations to mark the end of the war in Europe. The police intervened, which provoked an unorganized uprising in which about one hundred *colons* were killed. The army retaliated massively, massacring some 20 000 Algerians. To make matters still worse, *colons* influence ensured that the first elections under the new system were 'rigged', thus giving democracy and notions of peaceful change a severe setback. As Abbas remarked, 'The Algerian personality, the Algerian fatherland, which I did not find in 1936 among the Muslims, I find there today. The change that has taken place is visible to the naked eye, and cannot be ignored.' As leaders were driven underground or into exile, a secret

Special Organization (OS) began to store arms to prepare for what seemed an inevitable armed struggle.

The Algerian War, 1954–62

The war which finally broke out in Algeria in November 1954 was the bloodiest war of liberation in Africa in the 1950s. By the time it ended nearly eight years later, some 250 000 Algerians had died, the same number had fled as refugees, and some 2 million people had been compulsorily 'regrouped' to ease the French war effort. The Algerians were able to call on some 20 000 regular guerrillas, while France despatched nearly a million men in a vain attempt to suppress them. The presence of nearly a million *colons* ensured that the war was bitter, bloody and racist. There were numerous atrocities, mostly perpetrated by the French. Ultimately the war discredited parliamentary government in France itself; the army and the *colons* overthrew the Fourth Republic in May 1958 and brought General de Gaulle to power, hoping that he would support the *colon* dream of *Algérie Francaise*. In this they miscalculated badly.

Initially the old nationalist leaders rejected the armed struggle. Messali always remained aloof, but Ferhat Abbas finally gave it his support in 1956 and became one of its most skilled propagandists. In 1958 he was responsible for persuading the Tunisian and Moroccan governments to give open support to the Algerian freedom fighters. The main organizers of the war were however very different from the earlier leaders. They were not well-educated; they were mainly soldiers, trained in the French army. They were of peasant origin and many had worked in factories in France in their youth. They were born after the First World War and did not see France as a great power, but rather as a country divided into bitter factions, which had been easily overrun by the Germans in 1940. They had no time for the battle of words; all they wanted was to fight for the independence of Algeria – not by slow stages, but immediately. Although they appealed throughout the war to the *ulema* (Islamic learned men) and to the Muslim feelings of the masses, they were not themselves Muslim fundamentalists. The best known among them is Mohammed Ben Bella, later first President of Algeria. Born in western Algeria of Moroccan parents, Ben Bella fought in the French army in the Italian and North African campaigns and was decorated for his bravery. In 1946 he returned to Algeria and was elected to the Municipal Council of Oran. Because of his nationalist stance he was framed on a murder charge, and so joined the underground (OS). When the OS was dismantled by the police in 1949, he fled to Cairo before he could be arrested. Under the inspiration of Nasser's

Mohammed Ben Bella, first President of independent Algeria

Egypt, Ben Bella and other revolutionary exiles planned the 'rebellion', constituting themselves into the Revolutionary Committee for Unity and Action. The name was later changed to the Front de Libération Nationale (National Liberation Front – FLN).

The FLN received the moral and financial support of Egypt, Morocco, Tunisia and the Arab League. Soldiers were trained in Tunisia, Morocco, Egypt, East Germany and Yugoslavia. Yugoslavia, which had itself experienced guerrilla war and was pursuing socialist policies whilst maintaining its independence from the Soviet Union, was an important model for the FLN. By 1956 the FLN had become superbly organized in Algeria and was receiving positive support from the great majority of the population. Without such support, the revolution could never have succeeded. The FLN was given a great boost by Nasser's seizure of the Suez Canal in 1956. Two years later it established a provisional government in exile in Cairo.

One important thing to note about the FLN is that by 1960 it was already advocating the kind of socialist policies that it wished to establish in Algeria after it came to power. As one of its leaders declared in that year: 'The Algerian revolution is not and cannot be a mere fight for the conquest of political power. It is an economic and social, as well as a political revolution. Independence cannot be an end in itself. The Algerian workers are fighting in order to guarantee land for the peasant, work for the worker and better living conditions.' By contrast, any mention of socialism was conspicuously absent from the manifestos of most African nationalist parties at this time.

Algeria achieves independence, 1962

Shortly after General de Gaulle came to power in May 1958, he announced at Constantine his plan to speed up political advancement in Algeria. In September 1959 he promised self-determination to Algeria. He offered Algerians three choices: integration with France, complete independence, or diluted independence in co-operation with France. As far as the FLN was concerned, there could be no question of compromising on the issue of complete independence. Faced with the prospect of Algeria becoming independent of France, the *colons* and some French generals attempted to overthrow de Gaulle in 1960–61. They formed a terrorist Secret Army Organization (OAS).

General de Gaulle, who commanded immense prestige in France, was undeterred by the armed opposition of the *colons*. His visit to Algeria from 9 to 13 December 1960 convinced him that the FLN represented the bulk of the Algerian people. Moreover, in spite of the fact that the FLN was outclassed in terms of the quality of weapons, its tactics were costing the French a great deal, in terms of lives lost and money spent. The FLN planted bombs in public places, raided isolated *colon* farms and destroyed newly-built French schools. It also organized a boycott of alcohol and tobacco, aimed at denying valuable tax revenues to the government.

In 1961 de Gaulle began talks with the Algerian provisional government in exile. This provoked a reign of terror by the OAS, but ultimately a cease-fire agreement was reached at Evian in March 1962. The agreement finally granting Algeria the right of independence was accepted in a referendum by 90 per cent of the French voters in April, and on 1 July it was approved in Algeria by a massive 5 975 581 votes to 16 534. Algeria became independent two days later. Ferhat Abbas became the first President of the Assembly and the following year, in a referendum, Ben Bella was elected first President of the Republic of Algeria.

Frantz Fanon and the Algerian revolution

It was largely through the writings of one man, Frantz Fanon, that opinion in Africa and the rest of the world was aroused against France's conduct of the Algerian War. Since Fanon has become an influential voice, especially amongst the young in Africa, it is worth saying something about his life and work.

Fanon was a black West Indian, born in Martinique in 1925. He attended schools there and in France before serving in the French army during the Second World War. Afterwards he studied medicine and psychiatry at Lyons, where he edited *Tom-Tom*, a black student's newspaper. In 1952 his first book, *Peau Noire, Masques Blancs* (translated as *Black Skin, White Masks*), which dealt with Martinique, was published. The following year he became Head of the Psychiatric Department at the Blida-Joinville Hospital in Algeria. In 1954 the war broke out, and Fanon's experiences in the hospital led him to support the 'rebels' unequivocally. He resigned in 1956, and took up an editorial position on the FLN's newspaper *El Moudjahid* in Tunis. In 1959 he was seriously injured by a mine on the Algerian–Moroccan frontier, and his second book was published. This was called *L'An V de la Révolution Algérienne*, which was later translated as *A Dying Colonialism*. In 1960 he was appointed as the Algerian government in exile's Ambassador to Nkrumah's Ghana but in 1961 he was found to be suffering from leukaemia. In the same year his most famous book, *Les Damnés de la Terre* (translated as *The Wretched of the Earth*), was published shortly before his death in hospital at the tragically early age of 36. A few months later Algeria was liberated. A fourth book, *Pour la Révolution Africaine*, was published posthumously in 1964.

In *Black Skin, White Masks* Fanon examined the ways in which blacks in Martinique were made to feel inferior and to imbibe notions of guilt just for being black. Later his experiences in hospital, especially of mental disorders, revealed to him how colonialism created a sense of alienation and denied humanity to its victims. In *A Dying Colonialism* he showed how the Algerian guerrillas, by resisting oppression, were able to break that mould and to start to create a new kind of society. In *The Wretched of the Earth*, written in great haste since he knew that he was dying, Fanon broadened his perspective to consider the liberation of the Third World. This book became a manifesto for all anti-colonial movements; it exposed the economic and psychological degradations of imperialism and pointed the way forward to a socialist future. Fanon was a 'radical pessimist' long before this became fashionable. He was highly critical of the new African ruling bourgeoisie, which had gained power without a struggle and was all set to exploit the masses. In short, Fanon was a champion of the oppressed peasants of the Third World and a damning critic of all authoritarian and élitist governments.

The path to independence in Libya

The huge, sparsely populated territory of Libya had a colonial experience very different from that of the three French-controlled countries of the Maghreb. Italy gained control of Libya from the Ottomans in 1911, but found herself fighting various wars of 'pacification' until 1933. A poor, backward country herself, Italy could offer Libyans little in the way of education or other social services. Unlike the rest of the Maghreb, no westernised élite emerged and genuine political consciousness was something which occurred only after independence. The Fascist dictator Benito Mussolini, seeking to relieve overcrowding at home, dumped 30 000 Italian peasants onto Libya in 1938–9. Shortly afterwards, the country became a battlefield during the Second World War, the Italians were driven out, and the Libyan 'problem' was handed over to the United Nations.

It was not an easy problem to resolve, since the country's three provinces had so little in common. Tripolitania contained some two-thirds of the population, was mainly Berber and was relatively advanced and prosperous. Cyrenaica, the home of the Sanusiyya sufi sect, was predominantly Arab and far more economically backward, while Fezzan in the Sahara comprised occasional oases frequented by nomadic Beduin.

After 1945 the British and French caretaker governments, which were given the responsibility of administering Libya, looked around for a suitable authority to whom power could be transferred. The obvious candidate was Idris al-Sanusi, the leader of the Sanusiyya, who had fought the Italians, had been exiled and had provided volunteers to fight alongside the British from 1940 to 1943. The country was then desperately poor and Idris felt the need to rely heavily on western financial support. There was some anti-western opposition from Bashwin al-Sadawi's National Congress Party centred in Tripolitania, but Idris was duly made King of the United Kingdom of Libya, which achieved a somewhat token independence in December 1951.

The Maghreb since independence

There has been much political, economic and social change in the Maghreb in the years since independence. No government has enjoyed

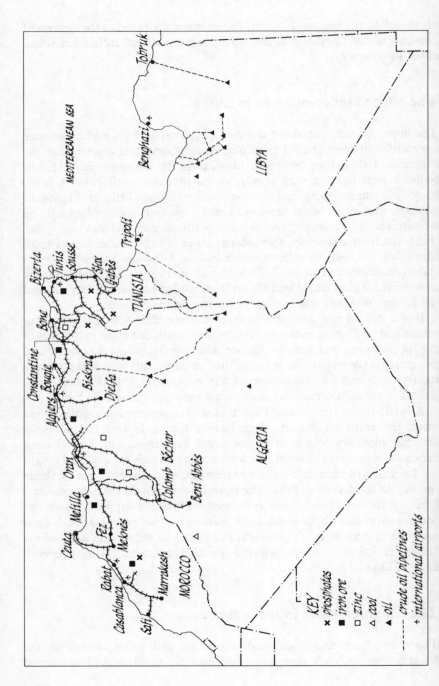

untroubled stability, and there have been successful military coups in Algeria and Libya. The monarchies in Tunisia and Libya have been overthrown, but King Hassan of Morocco has survived into the 1980s. The economies of Libya and Algeria have been transformed by the discovery of oil and gas. Oil revenues could be used to diversify the economy and to pursue socialist strategies at home and more non-aligned policies abroad. The much poorer states of Morocco and Tunisia remained closer to the west and adopted a much more moderate stance on the Arab-Israeli conflict than the richer, and more radical Libya and Algeria.

Although political relations between France and Algeria remained tense for several years after Algerian independence there were nonetheless strong economic links between the two countries. France, which has no oil supplies of its own, is particularly interested in Algerian oil and gas. With the arrival of a socialist, François Mitterrand, in power in France in 1981 political relations between the two countries have greatly improved. Presidents Mitterrand and Chadli met on several occasions in the first two years of Mitterrand's presidency and have signed a major agreement on the supply of Algerian gas to France. Indeed, in all respects the French presence in the Maghreb remains very strong.

The issue of the Western Sahara provoked conflict between Morocco and Algeria. There have been various attempts at land reform, but much of the Maghreb has in recent years witnessed rural depopulation with the young, as in so many parts of Africa, leaving the land for the 'bright lights' and greater economic opportunities of the towns. In the wake of rapidly rising populations, unemployment has become a major problem in Morocco, Tunisia and Algeria. The Moroccan government positively encourages people to seek work abroad, while nearly one million Algerians now work abroad. Everywhere there is growing inequality, which makes for political instability.

The oil revolution, and especially the higher prices since 1973, enabled Libya and Algeria to nationalize foreign-owned companies and to embark on ambitious plans for industrialization. Algeria, like Egypt, built a steel works with Russian help. But the reverse side of this was that agriculture tended to receive a very low priority. There were attempts at land reform. In Algeria all foreign-owned agricultural land was expropriated and large co-operatives were set up in the 1970s. But these proved ineffective and much of the land was subsequently returned to private ownership. A similar pattern had occurred earlier in Tunisia, in the 1960s. Here rural people resisted attempts at collectivization, and the minister responsible was imprisoned! More successful was King Hassan of Morocco's seizure of 200 000 hectares of foreign-owned land in 1973, and his subsequent distribution of it to local peasants. Throughout the Maghreb, agriculture tends to be divided into a dominant, large-scale, semi-capitalist 'modern' sector and a dominated, small-scale, backward 'traditional' peasant sector. Such a situation has encouraged serious rural depopulation and this, in conjunction with rising unemployment and growing inequalities, is likely to test to the limit the skills of all governments in the region, whatever their ideological and political persuasion.

Algeria since independence

The first military coup took place in Algeria. Here, the FLN never quite made the difficult transition from effective guerrilla force to effective government. As the end of the war and independencce approached, it became riddled by internal divisions, as former comrades fought each other for power. Ben Bella climbed to the top and became President in 1963, but he had spent much of the war in jail and was never quite trusted by those who had actually fought the war. Ben Bella pursued an active, flamboyant foreign policy, calling for Arab unity against Israel, the liberation of Southern Africa, and positive non-alignment. He played a leading role at OAU meetings, where he was an outspoken critic of neo-colonialism. He adopted various socialist policies and obtained support from Russia and Cuba. But many Algerians resented his dictatorial methods and felt he should concentrate more on home affairs. Consequently when the army, under Colonel Houari Boumedienne, rose against him in June 1965, the coup was successful and almost bloodless. The new government attempted to be broadly based and it gave higher priority to internal affairs. However, it continued to support the Palestinian cause and to offer assistance and military training to Southern African liberation movements. Boumedienne found himself facing considerable opposition from the left. In 1967 there was an unsuccessful armed rising and in 1975, when he tried to consolidate more power into his own hands, there was widespread opposition. He was forced to back down, and a new socialist constitution was offered to the people for public criticism and, duly amended, was passed by referendum. The first elections since the coup were held in 1977. Boumedienne died in 1978; the President since 1979 has been Colonel Bendjedid Chadli.

Libya since independence

The second coup in the Maghreb took place in Libya. Here the people of Tripolitania had never really been reconciled to a monarchy based in

Cyrenaica, while young Arab nationalists everywhere became increasingly critical of what they regarded as King Idris's subservience to western interests. Both the British and the Americans had military bases in Libya, and the country offered only lukewarm support for Arab states in conflict with Israel. Such criticisms intensified after oil was first discovered in 1959. Libya began its dramatic transformation from being one of the world's poorest countries to one of its major oil producers, but many Libyans felt that the western oil companies were being allowed too dominant a role. Thus in September 1969 King Idris, who was out of the country at the time, was overthrown in a military coup reminiscent of the Egyptian coup against King Faruk in 1952. A Revolutionary Command Council (RCC) was set up under Colonel Muamar al-Gadafy, which immediately adopted a more radical, anti-western stance, nationalized the oil companies and, in the 'cultural revolution' of 1973, attempted to run the country on strict Islamic principles. Gadafy proclaimed a jihad against Israel, attempted to force political unions with Egypt, Syria and Tunisia, offered strong support to the rebels in northern Chad, and acted generally as a volatile, disturbing force throughout the entire region. At first hostile to communism because of its atheism, after Sadat's break with the Soviet Union and his accord with Israel, Gadafy began to move closer to the Soviet Union. In 1975 he survived a coup attempt and two years later he abolished the RCC, renamed the country the Socialist People's Libyan Arab Jamahiriya (state of the masses), and became its Revolutionary Leader. This was an attempt to build a socialist Islamic state based on direct popular democracy.

Given the limelight that he has been enjoying for years as an unusual phenomenon in world politics, a pain in the neck of his neighbours and an irritant to a superpower like the United States, Gadafy deserves more than a brief mention. Son of a nomadic livestock trader, he was born in a tent in the desert near the Libyan town of Sierte in 1942. It was the bitter memory of Libya then occupied by the forces of Italian dictator, Benito Mussolini, and its people treated as fifth-class citizens, as much as his upbringing and education in Muslim schools, that shaped Gadafy. By 1956 he was organizing student groups in support of Egyptian President Gamal Abdel Nasser after the Suez Canal crisis and the Israeli invasion of Sinai. Expelled for starting a student strike, he finished secondary school with a tutor. He was devout, austere, puritanical and, from years of listening to Radio Cairo, a true believer in Arab nationalism. After graduating from Libya's military academy he spent several months at Britain's Army Signal School.

Shortly after Gadafy came to power in 1969, he proclaimed the principles of his governmental policy, which included the elimination of all

Colonel Muamar al-Gadafy, President of Libya

foreign bases, neutrality in foreign policy and national unity in a country that until then had been sharply divided along provincial and tribal lines. A year later, Gadafy announced that not only had these objectives been met but that the minimum wage had been doubled, huge development projects had been started and oil prices had been raised. Libya today ranks among the most prosperous of African states with an average per capita income of $7000.

Inside Libya Gadafy has been the sole spirit and voice of a revolution that has transformed the desert wasteland. He adopted from the beginning the policy of spreading the country's abundant oil wealth among the people. Apart from multiplying educational, health and other social facilities at a rate that has stupefied outside observers, the Gadafy administration has banned all private enterprise in favour of state-owned supermarkets which are the sole outlet for imported food, clothing and other goods, from gold watches to Italian shoes. In the area of accommodation the people were simply asked to move to the high-rise apartments and houses built by government. He has taken his people into partnership in the administration of the country, though final authority remains in his hands. Imitating Chairman Mao of China who attempted to educate the masses with his *Thoughts*, Gadafy penned the three-volume *Green Book*, the cornucopia of his thoughts and philosophy which Libyans should apply to their thoughts and action. With the aid of 'revolutionary committees', his ideological shock troops, Gadafy has been enforcing a strict Islamic code that outlaws adultery, homosexuality, alcohol consumption or 'scheming' against the state.

Morocco since independence

Morocco is the one country in the Maghreb where a monarchy has survived, though not without great difficulty. The title 'Sultan' gave way to 'King' in 1957, and in 1961 Mohammed V died and was succeeded by his son Hassan II. Like his father, Hassan became both supreme civil and religious leader. Following serious disturbances in Casablanca in 1965, Hassan attempted to form a government of national unity, failed, declared a state of emergency, suspended parliament and became Prime Minister for a while. There were unsuccessful army coups in 1971 and 1972. New constitutions were issued in 1970 and 1972 and approved in referenda, and while there was some resumption of political activity, no elections were held between 1964 and 1977. This was possible partly because Morocco remained largely a feudal society with virtually no experience of popular participation in government. In 1979 there were many strikes by workers, but the government held firm. Indeed, Hassan made skilful use of the Western Sahara issue in an attempt to increase popular support for the monarchy and to deflect attention from those calling for democratic reform.

In 1975 Hassan led a massive 'Green March' of his people across the southern border into the Spanish (now Western) Sahara. Spain agreed to quit and Morocco and Mauritania decided to partition the territory between themselves. But a local political movement, the Polisario Front, emerged to claim the territory and received armed support from Algeria. Guerrilla war began in 1976. The cost proved too great for Mauritania, which signed a peace treaty with Polisario in 1979, whereupon Morocco stepped in to grab the Mauritanian half of the country. Polisario retaliated by stepping up guerrilla raids inside Morocco, and Hassan was forced to buy more and more arms from Egypt and America, to the detriment of the Moroccan economy. As in Ethiopia, the war dragged on and on. It brought undoubted popularity to the King, but it poisoned inter-state relations in the region and proved a disruptive issue at meetings of the OAU.

Tunisia since independence

In Tunisia, where the old monarchy was quietly abolished in the year after independence, the government has thus far survived. Habib Bourguiba was made President for Life in 1974 and he remained President into his eighties. In 1964 Néo-Destour was renamed the Parti Socialiste Déstourien and there followed a brief flirtation with socialism, but economic disarray soon brought this to an end. Throughout the 1970s there were disturbances from workers and students who demanded, among other things, an end to the one-party state, to Tunisia's moderate stance on the Arab-Israeli question and to its close alliance with America. Those arrested were dealt with summarily. In 1978 following a major strike and riots, a state of emergency was proclaimed, fifty people were killed and hundreds injured and some two hundred trade union leaders were given long prison sentences following patently unfair trials. Undoubtedly Bourguiba has found Gadafy's Libya an extremely troublesome neighbour.

7   South Africa from the South African War to the apartheid election of 1948

Milner's grand design

At the end of the South African War in 1902, Viscount Milner was made Governor of the former Boer Republics, which were now known as the Transvaal and Orange River colonies, and High Commissioner for the whole of South Africa. To gain still greater control he wanted to suspend the self-government constitution of the Cape Colony but Joseph Chamberlain, the British Colonial Secretary, would not allow this. To help him with the immense tasks of reconstruction Milner brought out a number of young Oxford and Cambridge graduates as administrative officers. Because of their youth they became known as 'Milner's Kindergarten'.

Milner's aim was to ensure that South Africa should remain firmly British for all time. He also wanted to help the capitalist mining industry develop to the full. This would strengthen the prosperity of the empire as a whole as well as South Africa. It would provide the economic basis for his first aim. Apart from resettling Afrikaner prisoners of war and concentration camp inmates on the land and bringing the railways back into operation, Milner planned to encourage substantial British immigration. He wanted to plant enough British families on the land in the Transvaal to change the balance of power in the countryside. He also hoped to change the loyalties of young Afrikaners by anglicizing them through education. Many government schools were established in the ex-Republics where Afrikaner children would be taught through the medium of English. Dutch was allowed only as a language subject for a few lessons every week. As part of his grand design Milner planned to unite the whole of British-ruled Southern Africa, politically and economically. He formed a Customs Union for the four South African colonies and Southern Rhodesia (now Zimbabwe). He also achieved a railway agreement under which traffic was shared out between the different South African railway lines and that of

Mozambique. The Orange River and Transvaal railway lines were made into a single system as a first step towards a united South African railway. He looked forward to the introduction of a common native policy to provide for the control of the African population and to enable its labour to be exploited most economically. He set up a Native Affairs Commission to make recommendations on this.

The labour question

The success of Milner's policies depended on bringing the Johannesburg mines back into full operation as quickly as possible but this was hampered by a shortage of African labour. With the rebuilding of roads, railways and farmhouses there was a great deal of employment for Africans above ground. One of the main reasons, moreover, why mining magnates had wanted to see Kruger's government overthrown was their need for cheaper labour. On the outbreak of the war they had slashed African wages drastically. They raised them again to some extent after the war but they were not prepared to endanger the long-term profitability of the industry by raising them enough to attract Africans away from other opportunities.

To help with this problem Milner made an agreement with the Portuguese in 1901 which was called the *modus vivendi*. Under this the mines could recruit labour in Mozambique in return for a payment to the Mozambique authorities of a certain sum for each recruit. Furthermore, a fixed proportion of the railway traffic to Johannesburg would be allotted to the Mozambique rail line. Under this agreement and subsequent modifications of it the Johannesburg mines continued to draw the largest single contingent of their labour force from Mozambique until the victory of Frelimo in 1974–5. In the short run, however, not enough Mozambican labour was available to bring the mines back into full production.

While the development of mining was held up by labour shortage, poverty-stricken white families desperate for employment were gathering in large numbers around Johannesburg. In the last years of the Kruger regime, the market opportunities offered by the development of the gold mines made it increasingly uneconomic for the Transvaal 'notables' and land companies to continue to rent land to white client tenants (*bywoners*). They would do better to exploit the land themselves or rent it to Africans, who would engage in more intensive crop farming and could be forced to pay higher rents. After the upheaval of the South African War many landowners refused to take white tenants back again. Large numbers of landless whites were thus driven to the towns without resources or suitable skills for urban employment. Their most obvious hope was to obtain unskilled work on the mines. The mine owners, however, did not want to employ them. The whites did not have rural homes where their families could support themselves by agriculture as the African migrant workers did, and so they would have to be paid enough to support their wives and children. What is more, whites had political and legal rights. They could not be prevented from forming trade unions or subjected to the rigid discipline and exploitation imposed on Africans.

One mine manager, F.H.P. Cresswell, believed very strongly that the only way of keeping South Africa a white man's country was for whites to undertake all the work in the mines and industry themselves. He operated an experiment at the Village Deep mine using white labour only. Cresswell's views gained very wide political support from white South Africans but they did not convince the mine owners. The Chamber of Mines noted that the extra costs of white labour in Cresswell's experiment would make a large number of the Johannesburg mines uneconomic. Rather than endanger the long-term prosperity of the mine by employing the poor whites clamouring for jobs, they pressed for the importation of cheap Chinese labour as a stopgap. Milner gave them his support and during 1904 and 1905 many Chinese labourers were imported. This not only denied hope to the unemployed Afrikaner 'poor whites', it also frightened the mainly English-speaking whites who monopolized the skilled and semi-skilled jobs in the mines. They insisted that the Chinese should be restricted to unskilled work. This principle was later applied to Africans when the Chinese left.

Chinese labour rapidly restored the mines to full production and profitability but aroused widespread opposition among white South Africans. It led to increased agitation for a return to representative government, and undermined the credibility of the Milner regime. In Britain the conditions under which the Chinese were made to live became a national scandal, exploited by the Liberal Party to drive the Conservatives from office.

The rebirth of Afrikaner nationalism

At the end of the South African War British dominance throughout Southern Africa seemed unchallengeable. In the Cape many Afrikaners had lost the vote as a penalty for joining the Boer side in the war. Power was in the hands of the pro-British Progressive Party led by Dr Starr Jameson, the one-time leader of the notorious Raid (see Volume 1). Natal presented a similar picture with the Progressives firmly in charge while the two ex-Republics were under direct rule by Milner and his officials. Afrikaners on the other hand were deeply divided in the aftermath of

CAUTION!

Thanks to the Tories, thousands of cheap Chinese are being imported into the Transvaal. If any one had said two years ago that they would do this, the Tories would have said it was

A SHAMELESS FALSEHOOD,

invented to catch your votes by the Liberals.

The Tories tell you that when they were last in power the Liberals sanctioned, in the case of British Guiana, a law

ALMOST EXACTLY THE SAME

as the Tory Chinese Ordinance for the Transvaal. But this, so far from being true, is

A SHAMELESS FALSEHOOD,

which could only come from people who had never read both Ordinances, which differ in almost every vital point that is essential to the charge of

SLAVERY,

which Liberals bring against the present Tory Ordinance.

[OVER.

An election poster attacking the use of Chinese labour in South Africa issued by the Liberal Party in Britain

defeat. Those who fought to the bitter end, the *bitter-einders*, looked down on those who had surrendered earlier, the *hans-oppers*. They particularly hated and despised those who had joined the National Scouts and thus supported the British side.

Milner's anglicization policy, however, was seen as a threat to the whole Afrikaner community. The plight of the poor whites and the importation of Chinese labour won for the leaders of the Afrikaner 'notables' the loyalty of their impoverished fellow Afrikaners even though they were partly responsible for their lot in the first place. There was an upsurge of Afrikaner nationalist feeling which brought the factions together. This first took the form of a cultural and educational movement. A society for Christelike Nasionale Onderwys (Christian National Education – CNO) was formed and funds were collected to found schools in opposition to the government education system. The CNO schools could not afford to recruit enough good teachers and were not very successful. They did help to reinforce Afrikaner nationalist feelings, however. In the long run, also, the CNO movement continued to have an important impact on Afrikaner attitudes.

The reborn Afrikaner nationalism soon moved from the cultural to the political front. In 1905 two of the most outstanding generals of the war period in the Transvaal, Louis Botha and Jan Smuts, formed the Het Volk Party which campaigned for the restoration of self-government. In the Orange River colony, M.T. Steyn with the support of Abraham Fischer and J.B.M. Hertzog, formed the Orangia Unie Party which made similar demands. In the Cape the Afrikaner Bond was recovering confidence and could hope to win a majority once the ban on ex-rebels expired.

The failure of Milnerism: responsible government restored

Not only had Milner's policies led to a revival of Afrikaner nationalism but they had also alienated many English-speaking South Africans. His settlement schemes had failed to attract nearly enough English settlers to weaken the great preponderance of Afrikaner farmers in the Transvaal. His authoritarian attitudes and his preference for young expatriate staff angered British South African professionals. Divisions of interest between mining groups ensured that even in seeking to serve the interests of the majority of the magnates he would antagonize some of them. Finally by the fatal concession in the Vereeniging Treaty denying votes to Africans, Milner had excluded from political influence the one group who at that stage would have been sure to give full support to his pro-imperial policies against Afrikaner nationalism and its British South African allies. It thus became obvious even to the Conservative government in Britain that Milnerism had too little support in South Africa to be viable. Milner left and was replaced by Lord Selborne who was charged by the new Colonial Secretary, Alfred Lyttelton, with introducing constitutional reform to restore a limited measure of self-government to the whites in the two ex-republics. These arrangements never came into operation, however.

Before they could be implemented the Liberal Party, aided by the battle cry of 'Chinese slavery', defeated the Conservatives in a British general election. The Liberal Party had argued that the war had been wrong and the Boers unjustifiably deprived of their freedom. It had particularly opposed the concentration camps. It came to power with a bad conscience about South African affairs and a desire to make amends.

The Het Volk leaders, once Milner was replaced by the more amenable Selborne, also came to change their attitudes. They came to see that their interest as landowners had a lot in common with those of the British imperial authorities and the mine owners. A prosperous mining industry would not only create a growing market for farm produce but could provide the resources to enable government to provide loans and other subsidies necessary to turn their land holdings into profitable commercial farms. They were thus prepared to co-operate with English mine owners and to work within the context of the British empire provided they could gain full self-government. Smuts travelled to England and persuaded the new British Prime Minister that there was nothing to fear and much to gain from a generous policy towards the Boers.

The Liberal government acted promptly. The Transvaal was given responsible government in February 1907 and the Orange River in June of the same year. In the Transvaal one of the English-speaking groups allied with Het Volk and their coalition won the election. Botha became Premier with Smuts as his second-in-command. In the Orange River colony Orangia Unie won outright. Fischer was Premier with Hertzog as his deputy. Finally, in February 1908, in the first election after ex-rebels recovered the vote in the Cape, Jameson and the Progressives were defeated by the South African Party backed by the Afrikaner Bond but led by an Englishman, John X. Merriman. Thus five years after the end of a bitter war to establish British supremacy, all South Africa except Natal was controlled by predominantly Afrikaner governments.

The move to Union

The idea of a union of white Southern African states had long been promoted by Britain. It had also been advocated by the Afrikaner Bond from its first foundation by S.J. du Toit. The difference lay in who was to be in charge.

With the failure of Milnerism and the restoration of self-government to the ex-republics the possibility of unity being imposed by Britain was gone. Though British leaders of opinion, notably ex-members of Milner's kindergarten, took the initiative in arguing the case and forming closer-union societies, their chance of success depended on convincing the Boer leaders who now held the reigns of power.

From the point of view of the interests of all white people in South Africa the case for union was very strong. Once responsible government was restored the danger that clashes of interest between the colonies would lead to chaos was very obvious. For example, it was cheaper and more

The consolidation of white rule in South Africa

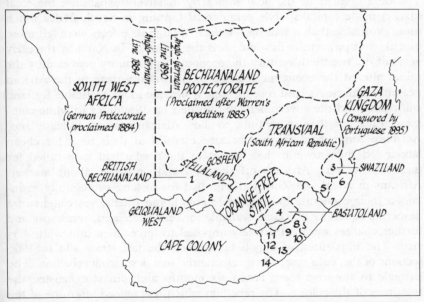

1 Proclaimed a Crown Colony after Warren's expedition 1885 subsequently attached to Cape

2 Annexed 1871. To Cape 1877

3 To Transvaal 1894. Subsequently restored to Imperial Govt

4 Annexed 1858. Joined to Cape 1871. Restored to Imperial Govt 1884

5 New Republic 1884

6 Thonga Land 1895

7 Zululand. Annexed and attached to Natal 1887

8 Griqualand East 1879

9 Xesibe 1884

10 Pondoland 1894

11 Thembu 1884

12 Fingoland 1879

13 Galeka Bomvana 1884

14 British Kaffraria (To Cape 1866)

profitable for the Transvaal to import all its needs by the shorter route from Delagoa Bay but this would spell ruin for the Cape, Natal and Orange River colonies. The Transvaal mines would benefit if the overseas imports they required could come in with only low customs duties, but the Cape and Natal derived most of their revenue from customs levies on such imports. Transvaal farmers wanted customs dues to be charged on agricultural goods imported into the colony from elsewhere in South Africa but farmers in the other colonies relied on supplying the Johannesburg market for their economic survival. Even more important from the whites' point of view was the need for a common approach to the control and exploitation of Africans and Asians.

The Bambata rebellion and Indian resistance in Natal

The development of the gold mines by massively expanding the local market made capitalist-style commercial farming in South Africa much more profitable than it had been before (though its effects were felt more quickly and powerfully in some areas than others). In Natal by the early years of the twentieth century the economic opportunity provided by the mines altered the economic balance to the disadvantage of the African peasant farmers. As land rose in value it became more profitable for land companies and the government to sell their land holdings to white commercial farmers than to continue to allow African peasants to lease land. As more commercial farmers became established their need for cheap labour led them to join their voices to those who had long called for measures to force Africans off the land and onto the labour market. Africans in Natal and Zululand who had for so long successfully maintained their economic independence now found themselves caught in a desperate squeeze. The land available for rent decreased, rents rose and further charges were deliberately imposed to force them into white service. The imposition of a poll tax proved the last straw and in 1906 sections of the Zulu rose, albeit reluctantly, in a despairing rebellion. The struggle to suppress them lasted six months and almost exhausted the resources of the colony. The rebellion which was named after one of the participating chiefs, Bambata, reawakened white fears of a wider African uprising and made them feel the need for a common 'native' policy.

Another threat to white interests and race superiority came from the Indians. Indians had been imported into Natal from the 1860s to provide cheap labour for the sugar plantations and other commercial farms. They were brought in because so many of the Natal Africans had succeeded in maintaining themselves and paying their taxes and rents through small-scale farming and refused to take service with whites. After the Indians

172

had worked for ten years they were entitled to stay on in Natal. A substantial Indian community thus grew up in Natal. While most remained very poor, working as labourers or small-scale market gardeners, others became skilled craftsmen. Many also took to trading. They displayed considerable business acumen and were satisfied with lower profit levels than whites. They also assisted one another more. Though most remained small traders some eventually acquired great fortunes.

After the discovery of gold they were naturally attracted by the commercial opportunities of the Transvaal. White traders there, however, feared this competition and the republic imposed complex regulations limiting their entry and right to trade and acquire property. The Orange Free State banned them altogether. Britain used the issue of the Transvaal discrimination against British subjects of Indian descent as a grievance against the Kruger government in the build-up to the South African War. After the war, however, the Milner regime not only maintained the discriminatory restrictions but even extended them. Resistance to these measures was led by a young Indian lawyer, Mahatma Gandhi. He first became involved in South African affairs on a visit in 1893 when he organized petitions against a bill in the Natal parliament designed to deny the vote to Indians. In 1894 he founded the Natal Indian Congress to defend Indian rights. That same year he successfully aroused public opinion in India against a discriminatory tax to be imposed on Natal Indians. On the intervention of the Viceroy of India the tax was drastically reduced. In 1906 the Milner regime introduced an Asiatic Law Amendment Ordinance further tightening the humiliating impositions on Indians in the Transvaal. It was in reaction to this that Gandhi first developed the concept and tactic of non-violent resistance aimed at winning over the oppressor by 'the force of truth and love' (*satyagraha*). In January 1908 Gandhi and over a hundred others went to jail for defying the law. Under pressure from the authorities in India Smuts on behalf of the Het Volk government in the Transvaal negotiated a compromise with Gandhi. When the Transvaal failed to carry out the bargain in full as Gandhi understood it, however, the struggle resumed and was still continuing at the time of South African union. Gandhi was later to use *satyagraha* on a much larger scale in the struggle for the independence of India. In South Africa it provided the inspiration for tactics of non-violent resistance employed by African as well as Indian political movements, most notably in the mass defiance campaign of the 1950s.

The Selborne Memorandum – Boer leaders accept Union

The high point of the British officials' campaign to convince white South

African opinion of the need for political union came with the circulation of a memorandum on the issue by the High Commissioner, Selborne. The memorandum stressed the problem of railways and customs and of policy towards Africans and Indians, pointing out that these could only be solved by white South Africans if they came together in a single state. Jameson at the Cape took the initiative by introducing a motion in the Cape parliament calling for closer union. The Boer leaders were not prepared to allow Jameson to lead the movement, however. They waited until the Cape election led to his replacement by Merriman. Then Smuts wrote almost at once to Merriman suggesting that the time for steps towards unification had come. In subsequent correspondence between the two leaders solutions to many of the key problems were agreed upon in advance.

The National Convention

In July 1908 the parliaments of all the white states agreed to the formation of a National Convention to draw up a scheme for closer union and the delegates met at Durban from 12 October to 5 November 1908, transferring to Cape Town from 23 November 1908 to 3 February 1909. When the Convention was summoned there was still no clear picture of the form unification should take. At this stage the Afrikaners were in a dominant position and favoured a unitary system while the British preferred federation. The majority at the Convention decided upon the unitary system; a national parliament of two chambers would have overriding powers and the colonies were to be reduced to provinces with separate councils presided over by administrators appointed by the national government. All

The delegates of the National Convention in Cape Town

hope of preserving the different institutions and ways of life in the separate states was gone.

The Convention also spent a great deal of time on the questions of a national language and the site of a capital. English and Dutch were made equal official languages and this could not changed without a two-thirds majority of both Houses sitting together. The problem of a capital almost caused a breakdown of the Convention but a compromise was finally reached whereby Cape Town became the legislative capital, Pretoria the administrative capital, and Bloemfontein the legal capital where the Appeal Courts would meet.

The struggle over the franchise

The most crucial issue at the Convention though not the one which took the most time was that of the franchise. The decision on who was to have the vote was to determine the future balance of power in the new state that was being formed. The situation in the colonies at the time was that in the Cape there was no race qualification but only economic and educational qualifications for the vote. A small proportion of the African and Coloured population could thus gain the vote and stand for election on the same basis as whites. The qualifications for voting rights had recently been raised, however, to ensure that whites would remain the overwhelming majority of the voters.

In Natal there was also theoretically no racial restriction on voting rights but complicated provisions made it so difficult for Africans to register that it was practically impossible. Indians were likewise excluded by provisions which did not openly mention race but achieved the purpose by other means. In the two ex-republics voting rights were confined to whites only. At the Convention some of the Cape delegates stood up strongly for the extension of the Cape system to the whole country. Most delegates from other areas were opposed to any voting rights for Africans or other non-Europeans at all. Even the delegates from the Eastern Cape tended to support this view. In the end a compromise was reached. Africans and Coloureds would retain their voting rights at the Cape but these would not be extended to other provinces. No non-white was to be permitted to stand for election to the Union parliament though they might do so for the Cape Provincial Council. Any reduction in the voting rights of non-whites would require to be accepted by a two-thirds majority of both Houses of Parliament sitting in joint session. This clause, like that prescribing equal treatment for Dutch and English came to be known as an entrenched clause.

In further decisions about voting rights and the distribution of political seats it was decided to favour the rural areas by giving them more seats per head of white population than the towns. This meant that the interests of white famers would be disproportionately represented. It also meant that Afrikaners would get proportionately more say than English-speakers who were much more predominantly townspeople. After a short session of the National Convention in 1909 in which minor amendments were made, the proposed constitution was ratified by all the South African states.

To come into operation, however, it still had to be ratified by the British parliament. An official delegation was sent from South Africa to London to argue for its acceptance. The franchise provisions of the proposed constitution, however, deeply alarmed the small literate and politically conscious élite of Africans and Coloureds in South Africa. They had hoped and anticipated that the non-racial voting system of the Cape would be extended to the rest of South Africa and that the way would be open to the gradual and progressive elimination of all racial discrimination at least as far as 'civilized' Africans were concerned. They now realized that they were threatened with the doors being shut on them for ever. Members of a number of small African political organizations in the four colonies came together to form an organization known as the South African Native Convention. They sent two delegates, John T. Jabavu and Walter Rubusana to London to rouse opinion against the racially discriminatory franchise provisions in the constitution and to press for the adoption of a 'colour-blind' system in their place. The African People's Organization, a political movement of the Coloured peoples, sent its founding president, Dr A. Abdurahman, on a similar mission. Finally the liberal Cape politician, W.P. Schreiner, organized a petition against the constitution and especially its franchise provisions.

These various groups received quite a sympathetic hearing in London and the Liberal government admitted that it would have preferred a franchise which did not involve racial discrimination. The government also, however, did not want to lose the chance of the peaceful unification of South Africa under the British flag. The international scene was growing more dangerous with the growth of German naval power and Britain did not want a divided South Africa with some areas anti-British. It was made clear by the South African delegates that a change in the franchise would destroy the union. The Liberals gave in, excusing themselves by predicting that the superiority of the colour-blind system of the Cape would become obvious and would be voluntarily accepted throughout South Africa. The South Africa Bill passed its third reading in parliament by a huge majority. On the 20 September 1909 it received royal assent and on 31 May 1910 the Union was formed.

Britain abandons her moral responsibility

Thus Britain finally abandoned almost all the responsibility she had for so long recognized towards the non-whites in Southern Africa. The way had been prepared by the Vereeniging Treaty and became final with the passing of the South Africa Act. Thereafter non-whites were left at the mercy of white settlers who made no secret of their prejudices. In only one respect did Britain draw back from abandoning all responsibility. This was in the areas of Basutoland (now Lesotho), Swaziland and Bechuanaland (now Botswana). It was anticipated that these areas would join the Union before long but Britain insisted on certain conditions to safeguard the rights of African peoples. It was also laid down that the inhabitants of the three states be consulted before any hand over took place. Thus these three High Commission territories as they came to be called remained separate from the Union. At the same time it was also expected that the new settlement in Southern Rhodesia would soon join the Union of South Africa and provision was made to make this possible.

South Africa after Union

The Union constitution gave whites a near monopoly of political power. Only in a few constituencies in the Cape Province could the votes of Africans and Coloureds have some significance and even then only in determining the balance between two white candidates. The policies that would be adopted and the way society would develop would thus depend on how different sections of the white population believed their interests could best be served.

The most powerful sections of the white population were the farmers, who had a particularly strong voice in the Union parliament, and the mine owners. Though the interests of these two sections differed in some respects, the health of the mining industry was of fundamental importance to the farmers and all sections of the white population. Mining profits were the only source from which the loans, subsidized services and cheap transport which farmers needed could be provided. Political leaders who represented farming interests thus had to be concerned for the well-being of the mines also.

Two other large sections of the white population were the white workers and the 'poor whites'. The white workers who held the skilled and many of the semi-skilled jobs in the mines, on the railways and in other industries, naturally wanted to improve their wages and conditions of service and their opportunities for employment. Above all they wanted to prevent employers replacing them with cheaper African or Coloured workers. The poor whites desperately wanted a system that would give them access to employment.

In addition to these economic divisions, the white population was also divided into Afrikaners and English-speakers. Language divisions cut across the economic ones to some extent but also coincided with them to a very significant degree. Afrikaners tended to be the less urbanized, less well-educated, poorer section of the white population. The great majority of the white farmers were Afrikaners but apart from a few wealthy landowners in the Transvaal and some of the wine-grape farmers in the Cape, they tended to be among the less wealthy of the farming community. The mine owners and industrialists were overwhelmingly English-speaking and for some time most of the skilled white workers were English. The poor whites, on the other hand, were predominantly Afrikaners.

The first Union government

On the formation of the Union, Het Volk with its British allies, the Orangia Unie Party and the South African Party in the Cape, came together to form the South African Party. This easily won the first general election in 1910 and Botha became Prime Minister with Smuts as his deputy. The government brought together leaders of the white farmers and of the mining interests. It was led by Afrikaners but had much British support. Opposition was provided by the remnants of the extreme pro-British, pro-capitalist Progressive Party, now called the Unionists, and by a small Labour Party formed and led by F.H. Cresswell to fight for the interests of white workers.

The main outlines of the policy the government pursued and the pattern which it and future governments were to impose on South African society was an expression of the common interest of the whites and particularly the farmers and mine owners. Both these groups depended for their prosperity on the exploitation of very cheap black labour. Both groups therefore wanted measures taken to force more Africans onto the labour market. Both groups also wanted Africans to be denied political and civil rights so that they could be subjected to rigid labour discipline that would otherwise be impossible. In the case of the mining groups, as well as other employers of migrant labour, it was vital that African reserves be retained. While most farm workers lived on their employer's property and many African urban workers were permanently settled in the towns, the bulk of the unskilled labour on the mines consisted of migrant workers who left their families in the reserves or in their home country while they served their contract period of employment. This meant that the mines did not have to pay wages sufficient to support the African miners' wives and families. They could be expected to maintain themselves by agriculture in the reserves. The system also meant that the white community did not have to pay retirement pensions, unemployment and sickness benefits, etc. Instead Africans who were too old, unfit or not needed for work could be simply pushed back into the reserves. The migrant labour system also reduced the possible physical and political danger to the white community of the development of very large permanent populations of Africans in the key economic centres of the country. The interests of the most powerful elements in the white community, therefore, dictated that instead of a policy of integration aimed at progressive development towards a common non-racial society, South Africa would pursue a policy of segregation and race discrimination.

This was already clear as early as 1906 when Milner's Native Affairs Commission published its report. It advocated limitation of African land owning rights to the reserves, reduction or elimination of African political rights, more pressure on African tenants on white-owned land to push them onto the job market, and control over urbanized Africans to ensure that they could live in the towns only when working for whites and when needed by them.

Foundations of segregation: the 1913 Land Act

The first major step along this road was taken in 1913 with the Natives' Land Act of that year. The tide had already been turning for some time against African farmers. Overcrowding and resulting overworking of the soils in the reserves was already resulting in serious deterioration. African farmers did not receive the loans, subsidies, and subsidized services available to whites. When the railways were built the fact that only whites had a political voice meant that African occupied areas were not served by branch lines and the cost of marketing their crops was thus much higher than for whites. Political measures had already resulted in a tough squeeze on African tenant farmers in Natal and the Cape. Even so a very significant part of the total agricultural production was still undertaken by African tenant farmers on private or company land in the Transvaal or Orange Free State as well as in Natal and to a lesser extent in the Cape. A large part of the total African population was still succeeding in keeping economic independence through farming. Many Africans were keenly aware of the advantages of owning their own land and some had succeeded in buying farms, either as individuals or community groups. The proportion of previously white-owned land that had been bought by Africans was very small but sufficient to cause a major white outcry.

The 1913 Natives' Land Act made it illegal for Africans to buy land outside the reserves. The final delimitation of these was to be undertaken by a subsequent commission. The law also banned the lease of land to Africans by whites outside the African reserve areas and the practice of share cropping known as 'farming on the halves' that was very widespread in the Orange Free State.

The introduction of the 1913 Natives' Land Act resulted in great hardship for many African families. In the Transvaal and Orange Free State many African tenants were turned off the land with nowhere to go. The law did not bring African tenant farming to a complete end, the practice was far too widespread and too profitable to many white landlords for that. Though the numbers were reduced many African tenants clung on. Those Africans who already owned land outside African areas were unaffected for the meantime and in the Cape the courts ruled that the Act was inapplicable as it affected African rights to acquire the vote. Nevertheless, the Act was a major step in the development of South African society, perhaps the largest single step in the whole history of the country since the Union. It marked the total rejection of the ideal of a common society as the ultimate goal of development. It meant that Africans were to be made aliens without rights of ownership in the greater part of their own country outside of the small, overcrowded reserves.

The Botha government and the Indians

In addition to tackling the land issue the Botha government faced the continuing Indian protest struggle led by Gandhi. In 1912 Indians in South Africa were further humiliated when the Cape Supreme Court decided that Indian marriages had no legal validity. Thousands of Indians now joined the *satyagraha* movement and courted arrest. Smuts once again negotiated with Gandhi and agreed to a compromise. Indian marriages were recognized and some other minor concessions were made. The campaign ended and Gandhi left for India. He had scored a minor victory but race discrimination against Indians remained almost as bad as before.

Conflict with white workers

The Botha government also ran into difficulties with white workers on the

Rand who took militant action in support of their right to form trade unions. The government, anxious to protect the profits of the mines, moved in to support the employers. After a series of upheavals the newly formed Union Defence Force was mobilized and in January 1914 rushed to Johannesburg where the white workers had seized control of the city. Army cannon were brought up to shell the trade union headquarters and the strike was crushed.

Origin of the National Party

By the time the Botha government enacted the 1913 Land Act the South African Party had split. From the outset some Afrikaners in the party were suspicious of Botha's and Smuts's attitude to English-speakers and the British empire. Their leader Hertzog feared that fusion of the two white groups would lead to the swamping of Afrikaner culture and language by English. In a speech in 1912 he declared that he favoured membership of the empire only so long as it was in the interests of South Africa. He said that the two white peoples should develop in separate streams and that South Africa must be ruled by true Afrikaners. This greatly embarrassed Botha who was campaigning for the support of English voters at the time. Botha then dropped Hertzog from the Cabinet and Hertzog and his supporters went on to form the National Party as the mouthpiece of Afrikaner nationalism. The formation of the party did not only express Afrikaner fears for their language and culture and continuing resentment against the English after the South African War but also rested on economic grievances. While some of the richer Afrikaner landowners were doing well and were happy with the results of their alliance with the mine owners, many smaller farmers were struggling with mounting debts. The growing number of poor whites, moreover, remained in a desperate and pitiful situation. There were thus many Afrikaners in the country and in the towns whose loyal support could be attracted to the new party.

Black political activity

The year 1912 which saw the split in the governing white party and the formation of an Afrikaner nationalist political movement also saw a development that in the long run will undoubtedly prove even more important. This was the formation of the first continuing national modern political organization of the overwhelming majority of the population, the African National Congress (known until 1923 as the South African Native

Botha (on the left) and Smuts (on the right)

National Congress). Indians, inspired by the national movement in their home country and led by Gandhi in agitation against the humiliating restrictions placed on them, had established the Natal Indian Congress as early as 1894. The Coloured peoples who overwhelmingly spoke Afrikaans as their mother tongue and practised a culture indistinguishable from white Afrikaners', were naturally drawn into modern political activity. In the Cape their more prosperous members had been able to acquire the vote. In 1903 they had formed a political organization of their own called the African People's Organization under the leadership of the widely respected Dr Abdurahman.

African resistance to white expropriation and exploitation initially and for many years took the form of frontier war or armed rebellion. This continued right down to the twentieth century. The Bambata rebellion of 1906 was the last major example of this. The educational work of missionary organizations had to some extent contradicted the efforts of the dominant whites to restrict Africans to labouring roles only. It had led to the emergence of a western-educated élite. Many of its members held junior positions in the mission churches. Some were teachers and a few succeeded in qualifying as lawyers or doctors. A few even studied abroad in Britain or America. The emergence of this élite was related to the success of many African farmers in adopting new methods and establishing small-scale commercial enterprises. A few of these became relatively wealthy, bought land of their own and lived a European life style.

The Ethiopian movement

The emergence of this élite provided leadership for two different forms of protest against white domination and race discrimination. One of these, which has its parallels throughout Black Africa, was a movement to form breakaway churches. In South Africa it was called the Ethiopian movement. It was provoked by the frustration of aspiring Africans within the mission churches. They became increasingly aware of the contradiction between the churches' teaching of equality of all men in the sight of God and the actual practice of the white missionaries. This was inevitably influenced by the race attitudes of the rest of white society. White missionaries were often reluctant to give significant authority to their African members and did not easily mix with them as social equals. The movement began in 1884 when Nehemiah Tile led a breakaway from the Wesleyan Mission and founded an independent Tembu Church. This was followed by a number of further breakaways from other churches.

As a result of subsequent splits among the breakaway churches several hundred independent African churches came into existence. In 1896 a link was established with the Black religious movement in the United States when the Reverend James Dwane established a branch of the American-based African Methodist Episcopal Church in South Africa. Among other things this made it easier for African students to study in America.

Though the Ethiopian movement was a religious movement it had a political element. It was an expression of African resentment at white domination. It long attracted much greater mass support than any political organization. It served to keep African self-esteem alive and to foster the belief in the possibility of African leadership. The independent churches also offered a training ground in administration, public speaking, committee work and so on.

On the other hand, the movement also may have had some effect in reducing African political protest by offering a safety valve for resentment and directing African eyes to the hereafter for redress rather than to action in the present world. Moreover, although the breakaway churches attracted large congregations, even more Africans remained members of the established mission churches.

Founding of the African National Congress

Some members of the western-educated élite were drawn into political rather than religious activity. This was encouraged in the Cape by the fact that there wealthier Africans could acquire the vote. In 1882 the first African political association, Imbumba Yama Africa was formed in the Cape. In the same year a Native Education Association was formed. In 1876 the *Isigidimi Sama Xhosa* (the Xhosa Messenger) edited by Elija Makiwane appeared. In 1881 the editorship was taken by John Tengo Jabavu and in 1884 he established his own paper *Imvo Zabantsundu* (African Opinion) which soon became a mouthpiece for African political views. In 1889 John L. Dube on return from the United States founded a Zulu Industrial School at Ohlange in Natal. The idea was based on Booker T. Washington's Tuskegee Institute in the United States.

In 1901, a Natal Native Congress was established. In the Cape two further organizations, a Native Vigilance Association and a South African Native Congress sprang up. After the end of the South African War, African organizations arose in the ex-republics also. A Native Vigilance Association was founded in the Orange River Colony and was later called the Orange River Colony Congress. In the Transvaal a Transvaal Congress was founded. In 1909 they came together in the South African Native National Conference to fight the franchise proposals in the draft constitution. After agreeing to send its delegation to England, however, the Conference dissolved. Then in 1912 Pixly ka Izaka Seme, a lawyer who had studied in both the United States and Britain summoned a conference to Bloemfontein which formed the South African Native National Congress which was renamed the African National Congress (ANC) in 1923.

The founders and leaders of the movement belonged to the mission-educated élite. They were firm believers in Christian liberal values and western ideas of progress and civilization. They did not want to overthrow white society in South Africa but simply to be accepted by it. Their ideal was a non-racial society based on individual merit. They did not press for political rights for the uneducated majority of Africans but simply wanted the selective franchise of the Cape extended to the rest of the country. The slogan used, however hypocritically, by Cecil Rhodes in the last year of his political career – 'equal rights for all civilised men' – was their ideal and they quoted it over and over again. On the other hand, they did also see themselves as the spokesmen for the grievances of all Africans where race discrimination was involved. They had a strong, even pathetic, faith that the values of reason and liberal humanism they held were shared by or could be instilled in the majority of whites.

They thus believed that their point of view would be bound to win acceptance if only they could explain it sufficiently clearly and convincingly. Reasoned petitions and deputations were thus their preferred methods of political action. It was their tragedy and that of South Africa that they did not meet the same reasonable attitude from the white authorities they approached. At the very first annual conference the new organization was faced with a shattering blow to its hopes and ideals, the 1913 Natives' Land Act. It lobbied MPs, petitioned the Governor-General and sent a deputation to Britain but all to no avail.

The First World War and the Boer rebellion

By 1914 the new Union of South Africa had seen the emergence of both an Afrikaner nationalist and an African nationalist political movement. The Botha government had laid the foundations of a policy of territorial race separation and was involved in bitter conflict with white workers when South Africa became involved in the First World War. Botha and Smuts decided at once to give Britain full support and prepared to launch an invasion of the German colony of South West Africa (now Namibia). This imposed intolerable strains on the loyalties of some Afrikaners who remembered earlier German friendship towards the republics and still thought of Britain as their enemy. A number of leading Afrikaner figures, including the commander-in-chief of the South African forces, General Beyers, protested against the planned attack on the German colony. The accidental shooting by the police of the revered Boer War leader, General de la Rey triggered off an ill-organized mutiny and rebellion. It was speedily crushed and the leaders were either arrested or killed. Over 5000 rebels were imprisoned. Most were soon released but one officer, Joseph Fourie, who had fought against government troops while still in uniform was tried and shot. The rebellion and its suppression evoked a great deal of Afrikaner nationalist feeling. Fourie was hailed as a martyr and in the 1915 election the National Party was able to establish a strong power base in rural districts.

South Africa's role in the First World War

South African forces captured South West Africa in a rapid and wholly successful campaign and then went on to play an important role in the campaign against the German forces in East Africa. Subsequently some South African forces also took part in the fighting in Europe. In all these campaigns Africans and Coloured South Africans took part alongside whites. White South African prejudices and fears of a threat to white supremacy, however, meant that they were refused the right to bear arms and were restricted to non-combatant though often just as dangerous roles.

Smuts as world statesman: the League of Nations Mandate for South West Africa

During the East African campaigns Smuts was made overall commander of the troops in the area. As his reputation grew he was invited to Britain for a meeting of the Imperial War Cabinet and then made a member of Britain's own War Cabinet. At the end of the war he played an important role in defining the organization of the League of Nations. To limit disputes between the powers over territories conquered he suggested that some of these might be placed under the authority of the League which would entrust the administration to a particular power under specified conditions. The power which received such a mandate would have to report regularly to the League. Smuts never intended that South West Africa should fall under this system. He wanted it to be fully incorporated into South Africa. As the promoter of the system, however, he was in a weak position to oppose its adoption in South West Africa. South Africa thus failed to incorporate South West Africa formally. Instead it received the right to administer it under a mandate from the League of Nations. This meant that South Africa was legally bound to promote the best interests and development of the inhabitants of the territory and had to make regular reports to the League of Nations Mandates Commission.

Post-war party realignments

In August 1919 Botha died and Smuts took on the leadership of the South African Party. In the general election of 1920 the National Party gained greatly increased Afrikaner support. It won more seats than the South African Party. Smuts, however, made an alliance with the Unionists. They agreed to dissolve their party and join the South African Party. This gave Smuts a continuing majority. In a further election in 1921 the enlarged South African Party won a majority but largely as a result of the votes of its English-speaking supporters.

The 1923 Natives (Urban Areas) Act

During the war increased economic activity and shortage of white labour had led to a substantial increase in the African population in the towns. They often lived in sordid and insanitary conditions. During 1918 South Africa was affected by the worldwide influenza epidemic. Many people of all races died but Africans as the poorest section suffered most. The epidemic drew attention to the unhygienic conditions in which many Africans lived in the towns and the danger of diseases which whites feared might spread to them. Two commissions, the 1921 Native Affairs Commission and the 1922 Transvaal Local Government Commission (known as the Stallard Commission) studied the problem. Both recommended that the African population in the towns should be segregated from whites and its numbers controlled. The Stallard Commission argued that the towns were the preserve of the white man. Africans had no right to be there except to serve the interests of the whites and must leave when they were no longer needed by them. This principle was embodied in law in the 1923 Natives (Urban Areas) Act. The Urban Areas Act, like the 1913 Natives' Land Act, was of fundamental importance to the development of South African society. It laid down the basic principle on which all subsequent legislation which has established ruthless control over African ubran populations has been based. The two acts taken together contain almost all the basic principles on which present-day apartheid is based.

Race relations in the gold mines: the Rand rebellion

During and immediately after the First World War a premium price was paid for gold. The war resulted in a shortage of white labour and white workers exploited the situation to gain improved pay and conditions. As many English-speaking white workers joined the army many semi-skilled positions came to be occupied by Afrikaner 'poor whites'. They had no particular mining skills but the mine owners gave them the jobs rather than face trouble with the rest of the white workers. They did employ some Africans in semi-skilled work that had previously been done by whites, however. Immediately after the war as white workers came back from the army they became alarmed at the prospect of losing their jobs to lower-paid Africans. They succeeded in forcing the mining companies to agree to a standstill agreement under which no job then performed by a white would be given to a non-white.

As the premium price for gold was reduced after the war, however, the costs of paying so many whites such high wages meant that many mines could no longer make a profit. As many Africans now had the skills to do the semi-skilled work and could be employed much more cheaply, the Chamber of Mines announced that it was abandoning the standstill agreement. This drove the white workers to desperation. After a series of bitter strikes they launched an attempt at violent revolution in March 1922 and seized control of Johannesburg. Smuts rushed in the army, however, and after two days of fighting which cost more lives than the South West Africa campaign the white miners were completely crushed. They had to accept the Chamber of Mines' proposals in full. Working costs were much reduced and the mines began to make a profit again.

The Labour Party–National Party alliance

Crushed by superior military force the white workers still had the weapon of the vote. They now turned to political action to protect their interests. The Labour Party which represented them sought an alliance with Hertzog's National Party. Although the leadership of the white workers was overwhelmingly English-speaking and Hertzog's party self-consciously Afrikaner, the alliance was a natural one. Both white workers and the less successful white farmers distrusted the big capitalists with whom Smuts was allied. Both had particularly strong motives to have Africans 'kept in their place' and not allowed to rise above the level of cheap, unskilled, manual workers.

The Pact government and its 'civilized labour' policy

The political strength of the new alliance was proved in 1924 when the Pact defeated the South African Party in a general election and was able to form a government. Faced with the problems of white poverty and unemployment it sought to increase the job opportunities available and give more of them to whites. A policy of active industrialization was undertaken. South Africa's second industrial revolution was launched with the establishment of a national steel industry at Vereeniging. This was operated by a national Iron and Steel Corporation (ISCOR) but private industry was also favoured through a deliberate policy of protecting home industries through customs charges on imports. The expansion of manufacturing industry developed slowly until it took off in a big way during the Second World War. The foundations for that take off were laid, however, in the earlier period. The policy which meant raising the prices of many goods was against the short-term interests of the mine owners. In the long run they benefited, however, through finding very profitable investment opportunities in the manufacturing sector.

Apart from trying to increase the number of jobs, the Pact government pursued a policy of giving preference to whites over non-whites in employment. This was called a 'civilized labour policy'. Africans, Coloureds and Indians were pushed out of jobs to make way for whites. This was done on a large scale in government corporations, notably the railways, where even the most menial jobs were given to whites. Private businesses were encouraged to follow the same line. The government would only help local manufacturers if they agreed to give a high proportion of the jobs in their factories to whites.

Hertzog's segregation policies

The 'civilized labour' policy was part of a wider plan by the new government to increase racial segregation. This did not mean any major change of direction in the policy of the South African Party but it did mean tightening segregation considerably even in ways that were not attractive to the mine owners and industrialists. Hertzog thus introduced legislation to support race discrimination in employment. The 1926 Mines and Works Amendment Act was popularly known as the Colour Bar Act. It gave legal support for the reservation of the skilled and semi-skilled jobs for whites. In addition to this the Native Administration Act of 1927 placed Africans outside the Cape under the unlimited authority of the government without the need to refer to parliament. Then the Immorality Act of 1927 made extra-marital sexual relations between whites and Africans a criminal offence.

These measures were related to four major pieces of legislation for increasing segregation introduced in 1926. A Native Land Bill proposed to tighten the 1913 Land Act and extend it to the Cape in return for some increase in the size of the native reserves. The Representation of Natives Bill aimed to remove the right of Africans at the Cape to vote on the same basis as whites. The Native Council Bill aimed to establish a Native Council which would have limited powers for the government of Africans in the reserves. While Hertzog wanted to increase the segregation of Africans and take their voting rights away, he believed that Coloureds as relations of the whites should eventually enjoy full citizen rights. He proposed a Coloured Persons' Rights Bill to improve their situation.

Hertzog's attempt to change the Cape franchise, however, involved the entrenched clause in the constitution. He tried to get a two-thirds majority in a joint session of the two Houses of Parliament but the South African Party was not prepared to allow him such a triumph. Hertzog was thus forced to withdraw his proposals.

The Black Peril election

In 1929 Hertzog fought a general election. He made the protection of white supremacy and privilege the main election issue. His party seized on a speech in which Smuts had talked about extending South Africa's influence northward to East Africa. Hertzog claimed that Smuts was planning to drown white South Africa in an expanded black state. The nationalists accused him of doing nothing to protect whites in South Africa from the threats posed by the blacks and even of believing in racial equality. In the Black Peril election, Hertzog won an overall majority. His Labour allies had split, however. One section of the party moved away from the support of a white labour policy towards the idea of fighting for the interests of workers of all races against their employers. This resulted in many white workers abandoning the Labour Party which ceased to be a key element in South African political life.

Hertzog's second government tightened segregation further. An amendment of the Urban Areas Act increased control over urban Africans. In the Transkei Native Reserves, local councils were brought together to form a United Transkeian Territories General Council with limited local government powers exercised under white supervision. This body, known as the *Bunga*, was the forerunner of present-day Bantustan governing bodies. Hertzog was still unable to get a two-thirds majority for his major segregation proposals, however. His government faced other serious problems, moreover. It came to office just before the Wall Street crash in America plunged the world into the worst phase of the inter-war depression. South Africa suffered even more than it might have because the National Party government clung to the idea of keeping its money on the gold standard which Britain had abandoned. As white bankruptcies and unemployment mounted the government rapidly lost popularity.

The birth of the United Party and the triumph of segregation

Then in 1933 South Africa went off the gold standard and Hertzog met Smuts to discuss a coalition of the National Party and the South African Party. There were no fundamental policy differences between them as both parties were firm supporters of white supremacy. The coalition was formed in March 1933. It won a massive victory in May, aided by the fact that with the abandonment of the gold standard the economy was rapidly improving. In 1934 the two parties in the coalition fused to form the United South African Party, known for short as the United Party, led by Hertzog with Smuts as his deputy. The way was now open for Hertzog to achieve his main segregation measures. In April 1936 the necessary two-thirds majority was obtained and the right of Africans to vote along with whites in the Cape was finally removed. In its place they were given the right to vote separately for special 'native' representatives who had to be white. A nationwide Native Representative Council was also set up. It was to advise government on matters concerning African interests but its powers were purely advisory. In the same year the Native Land and Trust Act consolidated the 1913 Land Act and extended it to the Cape. In return it provided for some slight extension of the reserves but these extensions had still not been fully brought into effect as late as the 1960s.

Afrikaner nationalism: the 'purified' National Party

The coalition between the National Party and the South African Party and their fusion in 1934 was unacceptable to a small group of National Party members of parliament led by D.F. Malan. They saw it as a sell out of the Afrikaner to British imperialism and capitalism. In July 1934 they broke away to form a group known as the 'purified' National Party which went into opposition. They were spokesmen for the increasingly bitter Afrikaner nationalist movement that had been developing in the inter-war years. Throughout the period many Afrikaners had continued to be forced from the land. Lacking adequate capital or education they were often bankrupted by natural disasters or economic downturns. As new farms could no longer be acquired by trekking, land had to be divided between heirs and this soon made units uneconomic. As they trekked in desperation to the towns, they entered a culturally alien and economically hostile environment. The availability of much cheaper African labour banned them from unskilled labour. Their lack of urban skills, sophisticated manners or grasp of the English language ruled them out of any higher employment and easily made them the object of ridicule. Large numbers were forced to live as paupers on government handouts with little hope of ever improving their condition. They were the object of general contempt. At the depth of the depression as much as a fifth of the total Afrikaner population had been reduced to this pathetic situation.

The fate of the poor whites and the fear among smaller Afrikaner farmers of being forced into this situation was reflected in the Afrikaans poetry and novels of the period. It led to a grim and bitter determination among Afrikaners to improve their situation by collective action on the political and economic fronts.

As early as 1918 a group of Afrikaner intellectuals had come together to form what soon became a secret society known as the Broederbond (Brotherhood). It sought to strengthen the bonds between Afrikaners by increasing their awareness of being a separate body with its own language and culture. It aimed to infiltrate supporters into key positions in all main branches of government and ultimately secure control of government by true Afrikaners. It wanted increased race segregation to give more jobs for poor whites and to prevent the possibility of their being absorbed by the African majority. It hoped to promote Afrikaner business enterprise and so conquer the capitalist world in South Africa for the Afrikaner.

Afrikaner nationalists used the symbol of the 'Great Trek', the celebration of the Day of the Covenant and the story of Blood River to hold Afrikaners together. They revived the costumes, songs and cultural activities of the rural past. They hoped to use this unity, however, to win a bigger share for Afrikaners in the urban industrial society of modern South Africa. In 1929 the Broederbond founded the Federasie van Afrikaanse Kultuurverenigings (FAK – Federation of Afrikaner Cultural Organizations). In the same year an Afrikaner nationalist alternative to the Boy Scouts was formed. It was called the Voortrekkers. In 1933 Afrikaner students broke away from the National Union of South African Students because it admitted African students. They formed the Afrikaanse Nasionale Studentebond (Afrikaner National Student Union).

The most dramatic advance of Afrikaner nationalism came in 1938 when it was decided to hold a national celebration of the centenary of the Day of the Covenant. A number of ox-wagons trekked through towns and villages from the Cape to Pretoria and Blood River where two simultaneous torch-lit memorial ceremonies were held. Two new organizations were formed. The first was a paramilitary semi-secret organization called the Ossewabrandwag (Ox-Wagon Sentinel). The second was a financial organization founded by means of voluntary contributions from Afrikaners to what was called a Reddingsdaad (Salvation Deed). The organization, known as the Reddingsdaadbond, used the resources to help establish an Afrikaner bank and Afrikaner businesses which would give preference in employment and in other ways to Afrikaners. These concerns also provided opportunities for the Afrikaner elite to break into the world of big business.

In the later 1930s the Afrikaner nationalist movement was much influenced by German Nazism. Hitler's racist philosophy appealed to many Afrikaners and belief in themselves as a master race was shared by most white South Africans.

African nationalism in the depression

The adverse economic circumstances between the two world wars affected Africans, Coloureds and Indians worse even than the poor whites. Not only were they overwhelmingly the poorest groups in society but far from helping them, government deliberately worsened their situation in order to help the whites. The extremely low wages they received and the high level of unemployment they suffered made it very difficult for them to sustain strike action for any length of time. Lack of resources made it difficult to maintain effective national organization. What is more, as they had no votes outside the Cape, such organizations could achieve little or nothing by constitutional means even if they had widespread mass support. Indeed, the more support African organizations acquired the more white opinion was likely to harden against offering them the slightest concessions. The alternative of open defiance or violence was unwelcome to most African leaders of the time and was bound to be ruthlessly crushed by the overwhelming power of the white state.

In 1918 the Transvaal branch of the African National Congress (ANC) gave support and encouragement to an African municipal workers' strike and in 1919 the ANC launched a mass movement on the Rand against the pass system. Thousands of Africans destroyed their passes in an attempt to break the system by defiance. Some limited wage increases for African municipal workers were achieved. The pass agitation was suppressed by police action, however. Over 200 Africans were put on trial. On several occasions white civilians violently attacked Africans who were holding meetings. In the anti-pass movement of 1919 the ANC reached the high point of mass support, on the Rand at least. It then went back to its usual policy of deputations and petitions and its supporters dwindled away.

The rise and fall of the ICU

In 1919 an African migrant worker from Nyasaland (now Malawi), Clements Kadalie, launched a new movement. This was the Industrial and Commercial Workers' Union, generally known as the ICU. It began by fostering strikes in the ports of the Eastern Cape but from 1923 developed into a nationwide mass movement. As it did so, however, it faced a problem of how to use its apparent strength in the face of an overwhelmingly powerful and ruthless white government which refused any concessions. While the majority clung to a line of a cautious moderation, a radical group, largely made up of members of the Communist Party, called for militant mass action. The radicals also attacked the wide powers of Kadalie in the organization and criticized his use of funds. Kadalie turned on them and had the communists expelled from his organization in December 1926. The ICU continued to grow and its membership reached a peak in 1928 but as it could still not find any means of effective action it then began to disintegrate. Personal quarrels between Kadalie and his most outstanding subordinate, A.W.C. Champion, resulted in Champion splitting away with the Natal branch of the organization. In spite of well-meant assistance of British trade unionists who sent W.G. Ballinger to act as an adviser to the ICU it rapidly collapsed.

Attempts at non-European unity

In the face of the threat to the rights of all non-whites posed by the Pact government and Hertzog's attacks on the Cape franchise, Dr Abdurahman summoned a joint conference of the African People's Organization, the ANC and the South African Indian Congress in 1927. Further conferences were held in 1930, 1931 and 1934. They demonstrated common opposition to the government's discriminatory policies. Some radicals called for militant mass action to back their protests but the majority insisted on moderation. Attempts to form a continuing common organization failed as the individual movements were unwilling to surrender their autonomy. Within the ANC a radical swing brought the Communist Party figure, James Gumede, to the presidency in 1927. In 1930 he was outvoted by more conservative members and replaced by the aged Pixley Seme. For some years the ANC became too weak even to hold annual conferences. The fusion of the National Party and the South African Party faced non-white political movements with a new threat. A new organization, the All-African Convention, was formed. It brought a number of African political organizations and the Communist Party together. It restricted itself to deputations and petitions which proved as useless as ever. The

All-African Convention was converted into a continuing organization in 1933 but it failed to maintain unity in the non-white political movement.

The ANC began to revive after 1936 and became once more the main mouthpiece of African political aspirations. The All-African Convention eventually gave birth in 1943 to a movement with both African and Coloured membership in the Cape, known as the Non-European Unity Movement.

South Africa in the Second World War

With the outbreak of the Second World War the United Party was deeply split. Hertzog supported a policy of neutrality but Smuts won a small parliamentary majority in favour of going in on the Allied side. South African forces played a major role in the liberation of Ethiopia and Somalia from the Italians. They also fought in the desert war in North Africa and in Sicily and in Italy. As in the First World War, many Africans and Coloureds took part but were refused the right to carry arms. The demands of South Africa's armed forces and the decline of imports caused by the war produced a boom for South African manufacturing industry which got South Africa's industrial revolution fully underway.

The shortage of white manpower led to the employment of Africans in some positions formerly held by whites. It also led to a massive growth of the African population in the towns. As the accommodation available was hopelessly inadequate they built unauthorized shanty towns for themselves. In some areas where expanding African settlements were next door to the white areas ugly race incidents took place. To facilitate the recruitment of black workers, pass laws and other controls on urban Africans were somewhat relaxed. A liberal wing of the United Party emerged, led by J.H. Hofmeyer, which looked forward to more far-reaching social reforms, and Smuts himself spoke in an increasingly liberal-sounding way.

This new liberalism did not extend to issues affecting the prosperity of mines and industries, however. Strikes by African workers were totally banned under an emergency war measure. As in the First World War Smuts gained a worldwide reputation. Just as he had helped establish the League of Nations, he now played an important role in the launching of the United Nations Organization. With the achievement of Allied victory in 1945 he appeared to be in an unshakeable political position.

Afrikaner nationalism in the Second World War

When Smuts took South Africa into the war and the United Party split, Hertzog and his followers after some delay joined the 'purified' National

Party which then came to be called the Herenigde Nasionale Party (HNP – the Reunited National Party, generally just the National Party). The reunion did not prove entirely successful. The ex-Minister of Defence, Oswald Pirow, broke away to found a short-lived movement called the New Order. It openly aimed at a system based on Nazi principles. A more long-lasting breakaway came to be headed by N.C. Havenga and became known as the Afrikaner Party.

The main rival to the National Party, however, was the Ossewabrandwag. This semi-secret organization was heavily influenced by Nazi ideals. It also advocated militant action and undertook many acts of sabotage against the South African and British forces and installations vital to the war effort. This in turn led to the arrest and internment of many extreme Afrikaner nationalist leaders. The National Party members, while holding racist views not much different from Nazism, did not accept Nazi leadership principles. They also disapproved of illegal violence and clung to constitutional action through the parliamentary system. A bitter struggle between the two organizations took place but as the tide of war turned in favour of the Allies, the Ossewabrandwag's militancy seemed futile and Malan's nationalists were able to win the full support of the Broederbond and consolidate their position as the political mouthpiece of Afrikaner nationalism. Athough the defeat of Germany made the National Party's opposition to the war appear misguided, the nationalists were able to appeal to white racial fears over the influx of Africans to the towns. They were also able to play on the issue of the dilution of white labour by the employment of non-whites. The fact that South Africa was an ally of the Soviet Union during the war enabled the nationalists to attack the Smuts government as betraying the white man in South Africa and opening the way to communism. The discovery that some Coloured women were employed in the textile industry doing the same work as whites was used to create a national scandal. The Dutch Reformed Church leaders called on all Afrikaners to unite in defence of their wives and mothers threatened with being placed on a level with Coloureds. This incident led in 1944 to the formation of a White Workers' Protection Society (Blanke Werkers se Beskermingsbond) under nationalist auspices.

Post-war problems of the Smuts government

Though an election held in July 1943 had given Smuts' United Party a massive majority, Malan's National Party had done quite well in the traditional Afrikaner areas. In the immediate post-war period the government's difficulties multiplied. Though much was done to help white servicemen settle back into civilian life, many felt it was not enough and developed a sense of grievance. The disturbed state of the world economy meant that many wartime restrictions and controls had to be continued. These included a ban on the use of white flour, a measure intended to save wheat imports.

South Africa, as one of the victors in the war, expected to hold a position of high international esteem. No sooner did the United Nations which Smuts had helped to establish meet, however, than South Africa found itself the subject of bitter criticism, led by India, for its racial policies. The treatment of Indians and the limitations on their rights to buy property and live where they pleased were the main points of contention. Compromise legislation which gave Indians, like Africans, the right to vote for special Indian representatives but confirmed the restrictions on residence rights was unpopular with many whites as being too liberal. It was rejected, on the other hand, by Indians who launched a passive defiance campaign. The Indian government withdrew its High Commissioner and started an economic boycott of South Africa.

India also led the attack in the United Nations against South Africa's proposal to incorporate South West Africa. South Africa suffered the humiliation of having its case rejected and being asked to submit reports on the territory to the United Nations Trusteeship Committee. In 1946 black miners on the Rand, who were still being paid almost exactly the same cash wages as in 1911 in spite of the inflation of prices in the meantime, launched a massive strike. They were ruthlessly suppressed and forced back to work with the use of troops. The African political élite proved more difficult for Smuts to deal with, however.

During the war years the ANC revived its organization quite successfully. Inspired by the principles of the Atlantic Charter it drew up a statement entitled *African Claims in South Africa*. It was a moderate document. It did, however, call for universal adult suffrage. When the ANC leaders asked Smuts to consider it in 1943, he dismissed their ideas as wildly impractical. In 1942 a Youth League was created within the ANC. It was to form a pressure group in favour of more militant action.

The ANC's dissatisfaction with the Smuts government came to a head in 1946 at a meeting of the Native Representative Council. When members wished to discuss issues raised by the African miners' strike they were ruled out of order. It was obvious that the Council had no effective voice in matters of real importance. One councillor said, 'We have been asked to co-operate with a toy telephone'. The members called on the government to abolish all discriminatory legislation forthwith and voted to adjourn their sessions until this call was acted on. The government was embarrassed particularly in the light of difficulties at the United Nations. These were made still worse by the fact that the ANC sent messages to the United Nations Committee opposing South Africa's claims to South West Africa on the grounds of injustice practised at home These problems made the Smuts government appear rather incompetent in handling non-white peoples at home and abroad. What is more the United Party's racial policies were far from clear and the fact that the liberal Hofmeyer was Smuts' deputy alarmed many whites.

The 1948 election: the coming of apartheid

In contrast to the United Party, the National Party put forward a race policy that on the surface at least, appeared clear and straightforward and which appealed to a very wide segment of the white population. The policy was called apartheid (separateness). The name was first used by some Afrikaner intellectuals in the 1930s and the concept was further worked out during the Second World War. The theory was that each race and nation had a unique destiny laid down by God. Each race must therefore be kept pure and allowed to develop separately along its own natural inborn lines. Racial mixing was against God's will and would lead to racial degeneration. Each race in South Africa should thus develop in its own territory. In the meantime social contact should be reduced to a minimum and sexual relations rigorously prevented. Supporters of the theory maintained that this would not only provide for the preservation of the white race but would also emancipate the African population from white cultural domination. In fact, however, the only territories considered for the African majority were the pathetically inadequate African reserves. In practice, therefore, the doctrine simply meant the continuation and tightening up of South Africa's traditional segregation policy under which overcrowded reserves served as reservoirs of cheap migrant labour and allowed white South Africans to avoid paying the full social costs of that labour. The fact that the policy was now supported by a theory of race separation meant that it would be followed much more dogmatically and rigidly than before. Helped by the appeal of apartheid as well as by promises to end restrictions and make white bread available again, the National Party together with its ally, the Afrikaner Party, succeeded in winning a small majority in the election. They had not won the majority of votes but the weighting of constituencies in favour of rural areas gave them just enough advantage to form the new government. The era of apartheid had begun.

8 South Africa from the introduction of apartheid to the introduction of the multiracial constitution

Baaskap apartheid

From 1948 to 1959/60 the National Party established the framework of its apartheid plans. At this stage National Party thinking was quite openly based on the idea that the African, Indian and Coloured peoples were racially inferior to whites. The policy said that African peoples should be allowed to develop to the full in the areas set aside for them. Such development however was to be along their own lines. It was assumed that this would involve no more than local government through a modified tribal system which would continue to need white supervision. The same

Apartheid: a segregated railway bridge

principle of racial inequality was made particularly obvious in the Separate Amenities Act which openly proclaimed that facilities provided for the different races need not be of an equal standard. This phase of apartheid is thus called *baaskap* (white supremacy) *apartheid*.

The major apartheid laws

The preservation of white racial purity was a major aspect of this stage of apartheid and in 1949 the Prohibition of Mixed Marriages Act made all marriages between whites and members of other races illegal. The following year the Immorality Act was amended to ban all sex relations outside marriage between whites and non-whites.

To achieve a separation of the races it was essential to classify South Africans in racial groups. The Population Registration Act of 1949 made provision for such classification after which all South Africans would have to carry documents stating their race.

A major concern of apartheid was to restrict Africans to their 'own areas' and limit numbers coming to the towns. This was to be achieved by tightening up the pass laws. The law which did this in 1952 was called the Abolition of Passes and Consolidation of Documents Act. The name

Apartheid: an African priest showing his pass. His photograph, name and reference number have been blacked out

was rather a sick joke. It substituted one passbook containing all the various authorizations required by an African living and working in town for the many separate pieces of paper previously required. The object however was to make control tighter and more efficient. This control was further strengthened by the Native Laws Amendment Act of 1952. This Act reduced the number of Africans who could claim their right to live permanently in the towns. In section 10 of the Act the only Africans who could claim that right were stated to be those who had been born in a particular town and lived there ever after or who had been employed in a town for fifteen years without a break, or who had worked in the town for ten years for the same employer. The right to live in one town did not give any right to residence in another. What is more under other laws even those with permanent residence rights could be deported to the rural reserves if they were political agitators, unemployed for long periods, or too old or ill to be of service to whites. Nevertheless those with these rights, often called the 'section 10 people' were better off than migrant workers and their advantages have continued to increase ever since.

Apart from greater control over urban Africans the National Party government launched a new attack on those Africans who were still maintaining their economic independence as tenant farmers on white-owned land in spite of the Land Acts of 1913 and 1936. In 1951 the Prevention of Illegal Squatting Act gave the government and local authorities powers to compulsorily remove such tenants. It also made provision for the establishment of resettlement camps to which they could be sent.

While reducing the number of Africans entitled to live in the towns and preparing the way to force them off the land in white-owned areas, the National Party government established the basis of limited 'tribal' self-government in the reserves. The nationwide elected Native Representative Council which had caused Smuts such trouble was abolished. The Bantu Authorities Act of 1953 provided for the exercise of local government powers in the reserves by Bantu Authorities which would be dominated by government-appointed chiefs.

One of the most damaging and far reaching apartheid laws was the 1953 Bantu Education Act. Previously African education though much less well supported had been operated on the same principles as that for whites or other racial groups and administered by the same Department of Education. Dr Hendrik Verwoerd then Minister of Education proclaimed, however, that the education given to Africans must not conflict with apartheid. Africans must not be educated to expect to hold positions they would not be allowed to occupy in white society. They should therefore be given a separate system of education aimed at fitting them for life in the reserves and menial service to whites. For this purpose African schools were to be placed under the administration of the Department of Native Affairs and new syllabuses were to be adopted in line with apartheid theory. In 1959 the principles of this law were applied to university education also, in the so-called Extension of University Education Act. Those universities, (predominantly the University of Cape Town and the University of the Witwatersrand) which had previously admitted students of other races along with whites were prohibited from doing so. Instead a series of separate 'universities' for Coloureds, Indians and for particular African 'tribes' were set up under rigid government control.

Within the towns Africans had long been segregated in separate locations and this segregation had been made a matter of law by the 1923 Urban Areas Act. Indians had also been subjected to residential restrictions in Natal and by custom most Coloureds lived in areas largely separate from whites. This separation was by no means universal and rigid however. Not only were there many areas of mixed residential settlement in some towns but Indians often owned businesses in city shopping centres. The Group Areas Act of 1950 aimed at strict racial segregation in the towns. It extended to Indians and Coloureds the segregationist principles already applied to Africans. The Act allowed the government to proclaim particular residential and business areas for the exclusive occupation of one race. Members of other races would then have to dispose of their property there and move to an area allotted to their own racial group. The Act allowed Coloureds to be pushed out of suburban areas that were attractive to

The main street of a shanty town near Johannesburg

whites. Indians were often forced to sell their city centre businesses and move to far less advantageous sites.

Though apartheid did not mark a new direction in the development of South African society it did mean the application of segregationist principles much more thoroughly than before. It caused a great deal of suffering and bitterness. It came moreover just as the rest of the world was moving in the opposite direction. Apartheid thus aroused almost universal international condemnation. It also caused the bitter resentment of the African, Indian and Coloured élite and of idealistic whites also. To give itself powers to crush this opposition within the country the government passed the Suppression of Communism Act in 1950. The Act outlawed the Communist Party but it also labelled as a communist anyone who pursued any of the aims of communism. This definition was so wide that it could include anyone supporting any change towards greater racial equality in South Africa. Persons named as 'communists' could be banned from political activities, ordered to move from their homes and restricted to particular areas of the country. It was the first step towards the subversion of the rule of law and the creation of a police state.

The attack on Coloured voting rights

One consequence of the racial philosophy of apartheid was the desire to segregate the Coloured peoples more rigorously. Hertzog had seen the Coloureds as cousins of the whites who should eventually share equal rights. Malan's National Party saw them as a possible source of race contamination and believed they should be strictly separated from whites. This principle was expressed in the 1950 Immorality Act and the 1950 Group Areas Act. It was also the basis of a major aim of the National Party – the abolition of Coloured voting rights at the Cape. This however required a two-thirds majority in a joint session of both houses of parliament. The Malan government's first approach was to argue that as South Africa was a sovereign state its parliament had unlimited power even to override its own constitution. He therefore simply ignored the provisions of the 'entrenched clause'. A Separate Registration of Voters Act was passed by a simple majority. Some Coloured voters appealed against the Act however and the Appeal Court declared it to be invalid.

Malan's government then tried another plan to get around the entrenched clause. A law was passed to make parliament itself into a court with overriding powers in constitutional matters. When this was passed the so-called High Court of Parliament sat on 25 August 1952 and solemnly declared the Separate Registration of Voters Act to be valid after all. The

Coloured voters appealed again, however, and the Appeal Court declared that since the law establishing the High Court of Parliament was clearly intended to subvert the constitution it was itself unconstitutional and invalid.

By this time white South Africans were deeply divided over the threat to the constitution and the issue was dropped for the meantime. After the 1953 election, attempts were made to remove Coloured voting rights by the means laid down in the constitution. Joint sessions of both houses of parilament were held but the two-thirds majority could not be obtained. Finally after Malan had retired and been replaced by J.G. Strijdom, a new and this time successful plan was adopted. The size of the Senate was artificially increased by the addition of large numbers of known National Party supporters. The Appeal Court was also enlarged by the appointment of sympathetic judges. The necessary two-thirds majority was then obtained. Coloureds lost their right to vote on the same rolls as whites in the Cape and instead became entitled to vote for special Coloured Representatives.

White opposition to apartheid

In Parliament opposition to apartheid was led by the United Party. The party was much weakened however by the death of both Smuts and Hofmeyr in 1948. Apart from its liberal wing moreover most United Party members sympathized with the ideals of apartheid. The party was thus unable to offer a convincing alternative to government policy and its electoral support steadily declined.

The attack on the constitution undertaken by the National Party government however carried a possible threat to the rights of English-speakers as well as Coloureds. The United Party was thus able to take a strong stand on this issue but the toughest opposition came from a new organization called the Torch Commando. It was formed in 1951 by a number of ex-servicemen led by 'Sailor' Malan who had been an air ace during the Battle of Britain. The Torch Commando organized demonstrations which attracted large crowds. Several violent clashes with National Party supporters occurred and there even seemed a possibility of civil war between sections of the white population. Support for the Commando however, was mainly based on English fears of what could happen if the Afrikaner nationalists could overturn the constitution. The Commando could not even agree to accept Coloured members. Once the government gave up the idea of overturning the constitution support for the Commando rapidly dwindled.

Black opposition to apartheid

A tragic consequence of increased white oppression was the increase of tensions between the oppressed peoples of South Africa. In January 1949

Women leaving jail after serving terms of imprisonment for taking part in the 1952–3 Defiance Campaign

violent riots between Africans and Indians broke out in Natal. The leaders of both communities hastened to try and heal the wounds of this upheaval and to plan joint action against the oppressive laws which affected both communities. In June 1952 the ANC and the South African Indian Congress launched a mass campaign of defiance of unjust laws. The idea was that well-disciplined volunteers should deliberately break apartheid laws and seek arrest on such a massive scale that the system would be unable to continue. Though Africans as well as Indians had been involved in passive resistance before, nothing approaching the scale and organization of the mass defiance campaign had ever been attempted. In the course of the campaign over 8000 people, mostly Africans and Indians but also including a few whites allowed themselves to be arrested. Enthusiasm among Africans was so high that ANC membership climbed to around 100 000. The government responded by refusing all concessions and arresting officials of both congresses who were charged under the Suppression of Communism Act.

Government's hand was also strengthened by the outbreak of violent riots in African townships near Port Elizabeth, Johannesburg, Kimberley and East London. The police suppressed the rioters with gunfire and at least forty were killed. The government blamed the riots on the defiance campaign though no connection was demonstrated and the leaders of the campaign had always stressed non-violence. African and Indian leaders blamed the riots on police provocation and called for a public enquiry which the government refused. The riots helped to harden white opinion against the defiance movement however. The government brough in new laws with harsher penalties including whipping for participation in passive resistance and the movement was finally suppressed.

After the collapse of the defiance campaign leaders of the ANC, the South African Indian Congress, the South African Coloured People's Organization and the White Congress of Democrats decided to hold a Congress of the People to work out a Charter for South Africa's future development. The Congress met at Kliptown near Johannesburg in June 1955. It adopted the Freedom Charter laying down principles for a non-racial South Africa. The government struck back brutally. Police swooped on leading participants of all races. On 5 December 1956 almost all the top leadership of the ANC and the South African Indian Congress along with a number of Coloured leaders and white radicals were arrested and charged with treason. Though substantial numbers were released at various stages in the course of the trial, proceedings dragged on until 29 November 1961 when the thirty still remaining were finally acquitted of all charges.

The trial thus kept many radical leaders of all races out of action for a prolonged period. By subjecting innocent people to prolonged suffering

Africans queue for taxis during their boycott of bus services on the Rand in 1957, one of a series of political protests which led up to the Sharpeville massacre of 1960

and deprivation it served to demonstrate the danger of expressing radical criticism of apartheid. The temporary removal of so many of its top leaders and the bitter frustration of ANC members at their impotence in the face of government repression created the atmosphere in which a split in the African nationalist movement occurred.

In November 1958 Robert Sobukwe and a number of his supporters walked out of an ANC conference in the Transvaal in protest at the association of the movement with the congresses of other races. They were particularly opposed to the left-wing radicalism of leading white members of the Congress of Democrats and formed a new nationalist organization, the Pan-Africanist Congress (PAC).

Organized political protest was not the only form in which black resistance to mounting oppression revealed itself. Enforcement of regulations requiring women to carry passes met with widespread resistance notably in the Western Transvaal. The most serious rebellion however was in Pondoland in 1958. It started in reaction to the introduction of the Bantu Authorities system. The rebellion was directed by a 'Mountain Committee'. It continued for many months and was only suppressed with the use of planes and tanks.

Consolidation and development of the Afrikaner nationalist government

After its first election victory in 1948 with a tiny majority the National Party government steadily consolidated its position. The small Afrikaner Party was persuaded to dissolve and join the National Party in 1951. The government's position was also strengthened by creating a number of seats for whites in South West Africa (now Namibia). Though declaring its defiance of the United Nations, the National Party government did not go to the length of annexing the territory outright. In the 1953 election in spite of the upheaval over the threat to the constitution involved in the Coloured voting rights issue the government won an increased majority. It was probably helped in this by white reaction to the defiance campaign and the African riots. In the next election in 1958, the government increased its majority again and for the first time won an absolute majority of votes cast.

It was not only in parliament that the National Party increased its control. The capture of political power created the opportunity for all the different Afrikaner organizations, cultural, educational, political and economic to be drawn together in a single network. Within this the Broederbond continued to play a vital coordinating role. As this happened it became much more difficult for an Afrikaner to break from the National Party. It could mean loss of employment, refusal of bank loans, exclusion from professional and cultural associations and social isolation.

Not only did the government's position become more entrenched throughout the period, its leadership also became more extreme in its devotion to apartheid. When Malan retired in 1954 he was succeeded by Strijdom. While head of the Transvaal branch of the National Party Strijdom was notorious as a hardliner and was often called the 'lion of the north'. When he died in 1958 he was succeeded by the most dedicated supporter of the system, Dr Verwoerd. Verwoerd had long been the major spokesman for the theory of apartheid. In his position as Minister of Native Affairs he was also the greatest architect of the system. In 1958 he came to the supreme position of power.

Pressures for change

Though the government's hold over the white electorate in South Africa had much increased and its own dedication to apartheid was stronger than ever, the wider world in which South Africa lived had changed very considerably. The emergence of India and other Asian nations on the world stage had been followed by the extension of decolonization to Black Africa. Ghana was already independent, Nigeria and other African countries were clearly following the same path. In Southern Africa itself, South Africa had no longer any hope of absorbing Basutoland, Bechuanaland and Swaziland and had to accept the fact that in the foreseeable future they would become independent states with seats in the United Nations. South Africa thus had to find a way of establishing relations with the new black states. South Africa had also to recognize that the idea that Africans were inherently suited to tribal government only and would find contentment and self-fulfilment through such a system was an illusion. Thus in 1959 Verwoerd introduced a Promotion of Bantu Self-Government Bill to parliament and declared that although white South Africans did not like it they must accept that the reserves would have to be allowed to develop into eventually independent states (Bantustans).

The Sharpeville massacre

In December 1959 the ANC decided to launch a mass campaign against the pass laws starting on 31 March 1960. The PAC, however, decided to get in first and announced the launching of its own anti-pass compaign on 21 March. On that day there were widespread demonstrations. One of these was at the small town of Sharpeville. A large crowd gathered outside the police station. Some had destroyed their pass books and were waiting to be arrested. Others came because they had heard that an important

Sharpeville, 21 March 1960: the crowd flees as police open fire

announcement about pass laws was to be made. Police reinforcements were brought to the station. Then suddenly they opened fire on the crowd. As the people fled the police continued firing, sixty-nine dead bodies lay on the ground, most shot in the back. A further 180 people were wounded.

Public opinion overseas was horrified. There were worldwide protests and a massive outflow of capital from the country. Albert Luthuli, the ANC leader, declared full support on behalf of the ANC for the PAC's campaign. He declared a day of mourning on 28 March and called for workers to stay at home. His call met with a wide response. Then on 30 March as police began making mass arrests, rioting broke out in a number of centres. The government declared a state of emergency and called out the white reserve army, the Active Citizens Force to seal off African townships near Cape Town. On 8 April it banned both the ANC and the PAC.

Beginning of the armed freedom struggle

Many African leaders now became convinced that there was no hope of bringing about change in South Africa by peaceful means. The ANC leader Nelson Mandela went underground and helped form a fighting wing of the ANC called Umkhonto We Sizwe (Spear of the Nation). It undertook a campaign of sabotage against public installations but tried to avoid loss of human life. The campaign began on 16 December 1961, the Afrikaner's Day of the Covenant. The PAC also formed a fighting wing. In 1962/3 it killed a number of policemen and informers. Both parties established bases in black Africa and London. From these they began to recruit and train freedom fighters for the struggle. The African leaders had resorted to violence very reluctantly. At first they were naturally ill-prepared, too idealistic and naive. It was some years before they could begin to become fully effective from a military point of view. Nevertheless the freedom war had begun.

South Africa becomes a republic

While African opposition in South Africa was forced into the path of violence and South Africa was being widely condemned abroad the government took a constitutional step which left it even more exposed. An aim of the National Party for many years had been to make the country a republic. In October 1960 this was put to a referendum of white voters and secured a clear majority. The change meant however that South Africa had to apply to the Commonwealth Prime Ministers' Conference to continue membership of the organization. Leaders of African countries raised such opposition that Verwoerd was forced to withdraw and South Africa ceased to be a Commonwealth country.

'Separate development': the new face of apartheid, 1960–74

Under the pressures which followed the Sharpeville massacre and South Africa leaving the Commonwealth the face of apartheid was considerably changed. Even the use of the name apartheid was largely abandoned in favour of 'separate development'. These changes began with Verwoerd's 1959 speech in which he explained that the Bantustans would have to be allowed to attain eventual independence. They became much greater after 1966. In that year Verwoerd was dramatically stabbed to death on the floor of parliament by a parliamentary messenger. His successor J.B. Vorster had been the Minister of Internal Affairs and responsible for the develop-

The Republic of South Africa today, showing some of the main areas of economic activity

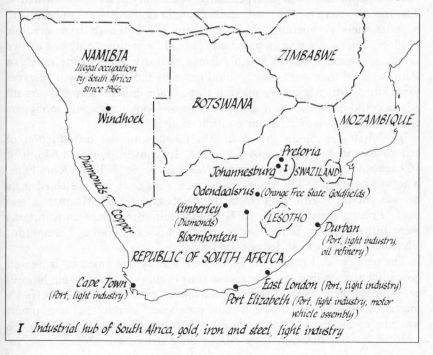

ment of the ruthless machinery of police repression. Verwoerd was undoubtedly a sincere believer in the philosophy of inherent cultural differences between different races and the overriding importance of race purity. Vorster and most of his colleagues did not seem to share these convictions. For them, apartheid was simply a practical means of keeping power in the hands of whites in general and Afrikaners in particular, so that they could continue to enjoy a grossly unfair share of the wealth of the country. They were thus prepared to change the face of apartheid so far as social contact between people of different races was concerned very considerably. On the other hand they enforced those aspects of the system which were essential to political and economic power more ruthlessly than before.

The 'homelands' policy

A central part of the new approach to apartheid was the idea put forward by Verwoerd that the African reserves or 'homelands' as they were now called should be encouraged to develop self-government and eventually full independence. Such 'independence' could only be a hollow formality. The reserves were far too small and lacking in resources ever to be able to support their populations. Most of them did not even have credible borders. They were simply fragments of land, sometimes only one or two farms, scattered about in South African territory. The 'homelands', or Bantustans as they were called, could never be more than labour reserves for white South Africa. By making them 'independent' however, South Africa could make the great majority of its own population into foreigners and thus justify denying them political or civil rights.

The first step along this road was taken with the introduction of self-government to the Transkei in 1963. Its constitution gave 64 out of 109 seats to government appointed chiefs however. When Victor Poto, who was opposed to the whole policy, won a majority of the elected seats he was outvoted with the help of the chiefs and Kaiser Matanzima was made Prime Minister. After 1971 similar self-government constitutions were introduced in Bophuthatswana, the Ciskei, Lebowa, Gazankulu, Vhavenda, KwaZulu and Basotho Qwaqwa.

The new policy towards the Bantustans was accompanied by increased government spending on these areas. Most of this was on housing, however, to make them more effective as dormitory reserves for South Africa's migrant labour force. Although some provision for industrial investment was made, the main emphasis was on border industries situated in the white areas but drawing their labour on a daily basis from across the frontier. In some cases Bantustan frontiers were extended to include existing African townships near major industrial centres. Umlazi, an African suburban township of Durban, was thus declared part of the KwaZulu Bantustan. The policy of separate development did mean that the political and administrative élite of the Bantustans would have to be treated formally as the social equals of their white counterparts.

The outward-looking policy

The requirements of foreign policy also pushed the South African government in the same direction. As increasing numbers of African states acquired independence they gained a significant voice in the United Nations. Within Africa they formed the Organization of African Unity and gave growing support to the freedom struggle in Southern Africa. What is more as South Africa's industrial revolution continued it needed to find expanding markets for its manufactured goods. The black African nations were the most obvious area where these goods might be sold. Within the borders of South Africa itself and on its frontiers Basutoland, Swaziland and Bechuanaland were headed for independence. In 1966 Vorster had a meeting with Chief Leabua Johathan of Lesotho and was photographed shaking his hand. This was a formal recognition of equality between a white and a black leader that shocked many white South Africans. In 1968 and 1971 similar meetings were held with Seretse Khama of Botswana and Prince Dhlamini of Swaziland.

Repeated attempts were made to persuade the black African states to establish diplomatic relations with South Africa and engage in dialogue over the subject of apartheid. South Africa's greatest success was in persuading Malawi to establish diplomatic relations. The high point of the outward-looking policy was reached in 1971 when Dr Kamuzu Banda, the President of Malawi, paid a formal state visit to South Africa.

A smile on the face of apartheid

The new policy of encouraging the Bantustans to progress towards formal independence and the outward-looking policy required some changes in the face of apartheid. Such changes were also required by a world situation in which non-white nations were becoming important trading partners of South Africa. They were urged on by the pressure of the international sporting world which subjected South Africa to wide-ranging boycotts. Provisions were thus made for leading Africans from independent states to be treated more or less as 'honorary whites'. Segregation was relaxed at Jan Smuts International Airport and at a number of top-class hotels. In the field of sport strict racial segregation was broken when South Africa accepted a Maori player as part of a New Zealand rugby team to tour South Africa and play against whites. These concessions, originally restricted to foreigners, came inevitably to be taken up by the African, Coloured and Indian élite within the country. The way was open for a progressive relaxation of social segregation which had been the main point of apartheid in its earliest days.

Mass removals

While the face of apartheid was relaxing however its fundamentals were being enforced more ruthlessly than ever. With the decision to push the Bantustans towards nominal independence went a massive drive to reduce the African population in the towns and white-owned areas and to force Africans into the Bantustans so that they could be denied political and civil rights in the white areas. This involved the forcible removal of huge numbers of Africans from their homes after which they were dumped in the so-called 'homelands'.

Large numbers of these were African peasants who had succeeded in holding on as independent farmers on land that had been bought before the 1913 and 1936 Land Acts came into operation. Apartheid laws overrode their property rights and they were forced off the land into the hopelessly overcrowded reserves. In addition to African peasants large numbers of urban Africans found their residence permits cancelled and they were driven into the 'homelands'. They often found themselves cut off from relatives, friends and the familiar surroundings of their hometowns to be stranded in a bleak and unfamiliar environment far from job opportunities or facilities necessary for a meaningful life. The lot of old people deported in this way simply because they were no longer able to work for whites was particularly pathetic. The conditions in the so-called resettlement camps to which many thousands were deported aroused worldwide concern but the government pressed on with its policy remorselessly. Between 1960 and 1972 well over a million people were forcibly uprooted and relocated in this way. By mid-1982 the number had increased to over three and a half million.

In addition to squeezing out 'black spots' in white rural areas and deporting Africans from the towns, controls over African movements were further tightened by the Bantu Laws Amendment Act of 1964. Africans were prevented from bringing their families to towns. A policy of providing hostels for single men rather than family homes was deliberately adopted. The social evils and suffering resulting from the migrant labour system were thus greatly increased.

Tougher police repression

Together with the more forceful application of the essentials of apartheid went a hardening of police repression. The shift to the policy of 'separate development' took place in the atmosphere created by the Sharpeville massacre which led to African nationalists adopting the tactics of sabotage and guerrilla war. In response the government introduced measures which greatly increased the power of the security police and reduced protection for the civil rights of citizens. In 1962 the police were given power to arrest and hold suspects in isolation for periods of twelve days. In 1963 this was extended to ninety days. In 1965 two periods of ninety days were allowed. Subsequently this has been further extended so that suspects can he held indefinitely. As suspects held under these measures had no access to legal advice they could be subjected to extreme pressures. Rumours of the use of torture and mysterious deaths of persons in police custody became commonplace.

The first major success of the police came with the arrest of Nelson Mandela. The leader of the fighting wing of the ANC evaded the police for so long that he was called 'the black pimpernel'. He was caught at last however and placed on trial at Rivonia in 1964. He used the occasion to deliver a famous condemnation of South Africa's racist system. He was sentenced to life imprisonment and detained on Robben Island until April 1982 when he was transferred to Cape Town. In 1968 the security police were reorganized in the Bureau of State Security (BOSS) and received still further powers. Against the inexperienced and untrained militants of the period the police measures proved successful. Radical opponents of the regime were imprisoned, psychologically broken or forced to flee the country. The African nationalist organizations were, however, able to keep alive abroad and to build up their forces for the liberation struggle from bases in black Africa.

White opposition to separate development

During the period from 1960 to 1970 the United Party continued to offer feeble opposition to the government's policies. The Liberal Party formed

Nelson Mandela, after his acquittal in 1961 on charges of treason. After a new trial in Rivonia, he was sentenced to life imprisonment in 1964

by a split in the United Party was driven out of existence by government harassment and a ban on multi-racial political organizations. For some years Helen Suzman, the sole member of parliament for the Progressive Party, was the only real opponent of apartheid in the House. From the government's point of view more serious opposition came from Afrikaners who thought that apartheid was being watered down. The relaxation of social segregation produced a split in National Party ranks between hard-liners, (*verkramptes*) and the more enlightened (*verligtes*). The leader of the *verkramptes* was Albert Hertzog who had played a key role in a number of Afrikaner organizations in the pre-1948 days. In September 1969 he broke away from the National Party to form the Herstigte Nasionale Party (HNP – the Restored National Party). Unlike Malan, however, Albert Hertzog was unable to win the support of the Broederbond. Vorster used the state security system to harass the new party and called an early election in 1970 to catch them out. Because of the divisions between Afrikaners, the United Party gained a brief increase in support but the National Party won a healthy majority and the HNP failed to win a single seat. The new party still remained alive, however, since its extremist race attitudes appealed to many whites. What is more there was an important group still within the National Party that shared its basic beliefs. This group of hardliners, the *houdende* Afrikaners, was led by Andries Treurnicht.

Black political activity in the era of separate development

The banning of both the ANC and the PAC soon after Sharpeville left the African majority with no legal nationwide political mouthpiece. Open political activity was largely confined to the Bantustans. The Bantustan political movements had to base themselves on the principle of separate development. To this extent they helped to support government policy and gave it some credibility. On the other hand to win support from their own electors the Bantustan leaders had to speak out against many aspects of apartheid. Even Kaiser Matanzima who had been chosen by the government as a supporter of its policy caused problems by rejecting the principles of Bantu education for the Transkei. Then he began demanding the inclusion of some neighbouring areas of white-owned land in the Transkei and more equal treatment for the Transkei people in the rest of South Africa. Among Bantustan leaders much the most outspoken to emerge was Gatsha Buthelezi of KwaZulu. He used the base of an apartheid Bantustan to denounce the whole system.

Black consciousness

In 1969 a new nationwide movement began with the breakaway of African students from the multi-racial National Union of South African Students. This was led by Steve Biko. He was influenced by the concept of 'black consciousness' developed in America. He used it to forge a new unity among Coloured, Indian and African students. They should all, he argued, think of themselves as black in contrast to whites. He first founded a black students union called the South African Students' Organization (SASO). Then this gave rise to a wider political and cultural black consciousness movement and the establishment of a political organization called the Black Peoples' Convention. It was open to Africans, Coloureds and Indians and rejected co-operation with white organizations whatever their racial attitude. It established its own network of social and cultural associations. Although it rejected the Bantustans and any co-operation with apartheid, the racial ideals of the movement seemed very close to apartheid theory. The government therefore adopted a tolerant attitude towards it for some time.

International complications for South Africa

During the 1960s South Africa became increasingly involved in two international situations. One was created by the unilateral declaration of independence made by the Ian Smith regime in Rhodesia (now Zimbabwe) in November 1965. The South African government gave vital help to the Smith regime by refusing to support the international trade boycott. With this help and that of the Portuguese authorities in Mozambique the illegal regime was able to avoid the effects of international sanctions to a very great extent. The South African government was anxious to avoid any greater involvement than this. Once the freedom struggle began to become a serious challenge to the régime from 1972, however, South Africa became drawn into offering growing military assistance. Units of the South African police were sent to assist the Rhodesian authorities. South Africa also gave some assistance to the colonial forces in Angola and Mozambique as the freedom struggle became more intense in those territories.

South Africa's role in South West Africa had been a subject of international criticism during the days of the League of Nations between the wars. The United Nations had scarcely been formed before it resumed the attack much more stridently. The end of the Smuts regime and the establishment of apartheid naturally resulted in heightened international pressure. Finally after many years of unavailing criticism the United Nations General Assembly voted in October 1966 to terminate the Trusteeship agreement giving South Africa administrative authority over the territory on the grounds that South Africa had failed to fulfil its obligations to the indigenous peoples. In 1969 the UN Security Council ratified the Assembly's decision and in 1971 the International Court of Justice confirmed the legality of the UN Assembly resolution and declared that the Security Council's decision was legally binding on all nations. South Africa refused to conform to the call to surrender control of the territory. Though South Africa was now in illegal occupation the western powers blocked any international action. In the meantime one of the African nationalist movements, the South West Africa People's Organization (SWAPO), had opened the guerrilla struggle in 1969.

Up to 1973 the white regimes in Southern Africa continued to grow closer to each other militarily, politically and economically. They appeared to be strong enough to defeat the freedom fighters and resist international pressure. South Africa indeed seemed likely to succeed in extending its influence far into black Africa and undermining the entire freedom struggle. It had established formal diplomatic relations with Malawi and the economic problems of Zambia made that country heavily economically dependent on the white south.

Economic pressures for change: the 1973 strikes

By the 1970s changes in technology were making some further changes in apartheid inevitable. With the new technology it was cheaper to employ more highly skilled workers even at higher wages rather than large numbers of unskilled workers however low their wages might be. This meant that the system of migrant labour would have to be changed as employers would want to have the continuous service of workers whom they had trained to operate their machines. In the new circumstances employers would be prepared to offer improved wages and conditions in order to have a more stable and contented work force.

In 1973 the South African economy was rocked by a series of massive strikes by African workers on the Rand and in Natal. Though the initial reaction was tough and troops were brought in in one case, the overall response was very different from the past. Significant wage rises were introduced. What is more, reforms of the labour laws to allow African workers some trade union rights including the right to strike in certain circumstances were promised. It was also openly recognized that provision for the education of Africans, Coloureds and Indians in industrial skills must be greatly expanded.

South Africa after 1974

In 1974 the strategic situation in Southern Africa was dramatically transformed by the revolution in Portugal and the resulting rapid movement towards decolonization of Mozambique and Angola. Though the revolution took place in Portugal itself, it was the long, brave, struggle of African freedom fighters in Angola, Mozambique and Guinea Bissau that undermined the dictatorship in Portugal. Mozambique became independent in June 1975 under the Frelimo government of Samora Machel. In Angola the departure of the Portuguese in November 1975 was followed by civil war between three freedom fighting movements, the FNLA, the MPLA and Unita. America gave support to the FNLA and South Africa supported Unita but the MPLA received Soviet aid and support from Cuban troops. As public opinion in America forced the government to stop intervention in the area, the MPLA was able to defeat the FNLA. It then defeated Unita also and South African troops that had gone into Angola in support of that movement had to withdraw with some losses.

The independence of Mozambique seriously undermined the position of Ian Smith's regime in Rhodesia. South Africa tried to disentangle herself from the situation. Vorster pressured Smith to achieve a negotiated settlement with the African nationalist leaders. The South African police units were withdrawn. An initial peace conference held in a railway carriage on the Victoria Falls bridge, on the border between Rhodesia and Zambia in 1975, came to nothing as Ian Smith was not prepared to consider a genuine transfer of power to Africans. A second peace conference held in Geneva in January 1977 also failed. The guerrilla struggle continued to expand, however, with ZANU's forces undertaking most of the action. Smith was forced to the expedient of reaching an agreement with Bishop Muzorewa which would establish nominal African majority rule but keep real power in white hands. This came into operation early in 1979. If failed however to stop the spread of the guerrilla war or to win international acceptance. Smith and Muzorewa were thus forced to accept a proposal made at the Commonwealth Heads of Government Conference in Lusaka in August 1979 for a new constitutional conference in London. This worked out the arrangements under which the Rhodesian regime handed over its authority to a British Governor thus ending the illegal independence of the country. Elections were held which resulted in a massive victory for the ZANU leader Robert Mugabe who was thus able to form a government and take Zimbabwe into independence in April 1980.

The Soweto explosion

In 1976 the pressures on South Africa arising from the drastic change in the strategic situation in Southern Africa were increased by even more serious internal problems. In June, the huge agglomeration of segregated African workers' townships near Johannesburg, known as Soweto (South Western Townships) exploded in an outburst of violence born of long pent up frustration, bitterness and hate. It began with a protest by schoolchildren against the imposition of Afrikaans as a medium of instruction. It soon spread to other African townships around the Rand and Pretoria and then to Natal and the Cape also. It came to involve Indian and Coloured youths as well as Africans. Though the police used firearms and a number of rioters were killed the violence did not die down quickly as it had in 1952. So great was the bitterness that the youths repeatedly braved gunfire to attack the police and the upheaval flared up again from time to time throughout the year. Though the riots may have owed something to the inspiration of ANC and PAC propaganda, and the rhetoric of the 'black consciousness' movement, they were essentially spontaneous and led by hitherto unknown young leaders. In the attempt to repress them the police made large numbers of arrests and this led even larger numbers of militant African youths to flee the townships and seek refuge in Botswana or Swaziland. Many of them would subsequently form willing recruits for the

Soweto: a row of single men's quarters

ANC and PAC guerrilla forces. South Africa was thus faced with the problem of massive black disaffection and simmering violence in the key industrial centres of the country combined with growing guerrilla infiltration across the borders.

The death of Steve Biko

The difficulties of the South African government were made worse by the crude reaction of its security forces. In October 1977 the Christian Institute and seventeen other organizations including almost the whole 'black consciousness' movement were banned. Fifty of their leaders were arrested and two newspapers with a large African readership were banned. World opinion was shocked at these developments and then horrified at the news of the death in prison of Steve Biko. The inquest revealed that he had died of brain damage suffered while in police custody and had been held for a prolonged period before his death, naked and in chains. Biko at once gained recognition as a martyr throughout the world as well as among black South Africans.

The funeral of Steve Biko

The reform programme

The growing security threat along South Africa's extensive borders soon placed such a heavy burden on military manpower that the long-maintained policy of refusing to allow African solidiers to carry arms had to be abandoned. Increasing use had to be made of black troops. The military authorities were thus forced to recognize that the white South African political system could only be maintained if it would win the loyalty of at least a substantial part of the population of other racial groups. Magnus Malan, then head of the army, repeatedly called for significant social reform to enable South Africa to fight a total war of survival.

The main features of the new approach to apartheid which resulted from these pressures involved the continuation and extension of some of the policies developed in the pre-1974 period but the radical change of others. The key idea was to buy the support of the Indian and Coloured communities and the urbanized blacks for the maintenance of white supremacy. This was to be done by the improvement of their social and economic conditions and by limited political concessions giving them some voice in national affairs while keeping ultimate power firmly in white hands. The policy was in line with the need for a more skilled, stable and well-motivated non-white work force.

Bantustan 'independence'

While the conditions of the urbanized African workforce were to be improved the majority of the African population was to be kept firmly out of the picture and denied the opportunity to share in improved economic conditions or to have any voice in South African politics. This was to be done by encouraging the Bantustans to accept 'formal' independence. Their 'citizens' would then become aliens in South Africa. The Transkei thus became 'independent' in 1976 and Bophuthatswana followed in 1977, Vhavenda in 1979 and the Ciskei in 1981. Though to call some of these fragmented scraps of territory independent nation states is blatantly absurd, the South African authorities persisted in doing so and imposing citizenship of the so-called African nations on thousands of people who have no direct connection with them, and no desire ever to reside in them. Having made the Bantustans foreign countries, the South African authorities have gone on to drop the populations resident in them from South African population statistics. The policy has not been altogether successful, however, as no other country in the whole world has recognized the independence of any of the Bantustans.

South Africa: 'black homelands' and the so-called 'independent states', 1982

Not all the Bantustan leaders have been prepared to accept so-called independence moreover. Chief Buthelezi of KwaZulu has been foremost in rejecting it. In 1982 South Africa adopted an alternative way of ridding herself of moral responsibility towards a significant part of her population. The idea was to give one of the larger fragments of the KwaZulu Bantustan, the territory called Ingwavuma, to the Kingdom of Swaziland. As Swaziland is a member of the United Nations the residents of Ingwavuma would then have to be recognized under international law as aliens in South Africa. The High Court however ruled that such a cession of territory and its inhabitants would be illegal and the plan was shelved.

Chief Gatsha Buthelezi of KwaZulu

Economic and social reforms for the urban blacks

A key aspect of the new policy towards urban Africans was the recognition that they would remain an important element in the life and economy of South Africa for the foreseeable future. This meant abandoning and reversing the previous policy of trying systematically to reduce the black urban population and convert permanent urban residents into migrant workers. From 1976 the previous policy of refusing to allow black urban residents to acquire long-term rights over their houses began to be abandoned. Leases first of 30 years then of 90 years were permitted. Finally in 1983 a scheme to allow and encourage urban Africans to buy their homes outright with the assistance of government-provided loans was launched. Provision was also made to allow Africans who possessed rights of urban residence under section 10 of the Urban Areas Act in one town to move to any other town. This greatly increased the freedom and economic opportunities of urban Africans and also served the interest of employers by increasing the mobility of skilled African labour. Not only were Africans allowed to move from one town to another but the barriers to their moving up the job ladder were also removed. Legal job reservation was virtually abolished. From 1979 further reforms opened the way to more open and effective trade union organization, even though provision was made for a wide measure of government control. As a consequence of these measures the economic situation of those Africans who have the right of urban residence as well as of Indians and Coloureds significantly improved from 1973 onwards. The wage gap between white and non-white workers while still huge significantly decreased. In 1970 the whites received 75 per cent of total personal incomes in South Africa. All other races combined, though they were the vast majority of the population, received only 25 per cent. In 1980 whites were receiving 60 per cent and other races 40 per cent. These measures were accompanied by further reductions in social apartheid. Hotels throughout the country were given the right to offer accommodation to all races. The Nico Malan theatre in Cape Town opened its doors to multiracial audiences. Multiracial night clubs offering multiracial dancing were discreetly winked at while still formally illegal. The repeal of the laws banning interracial sex and marriage was repeatedly suggested at the highest level though no action has been taken on this.

Political reform

The programme aimed at buying the support of key groups of other races for the white power structure had a political dimension also. Two different approaches were adopted towards the Coloured and Indian communities on the one hand and the urbanized Africans on the other. The difference was based on the assumption that Coloureds and Indians being minority groups threatened by the advance of the African majority might be persuaded to throw in their lot entirely with the whites in return for some subordinate say in the white-dominated political system. The urban blacks on the other hand because of their numbers and potential political danger to white domination were to be kept out of the national political system altogether though they were to be given increased local responsibilities in the black townships. Suggestions have also been made that some arrangement might be made for them through a confederal system which would bring the Bantustans and white-dominated South Africa together in a loose association of states.

For the 1977 election Vorster announced a plan for a major constitutional change. Instead of a single white parliament, three assemblies one for whites and one each for Indians and Coloureds would be created. Though ultimate sovereignty would remain with the white assembly, all three bodies would participate in the choice of a national cabinet and an executive president with wide authority. Though the National Party won the election with an overwhelming majority hardliner resistance within the Party led to the plan being quietly dropped.

The Muldergate affair

The next year Vorster announced his intention to resign as Prime Minister and seek election as State President. While members of his Cabinet were preparing to contest with each other for the position of Prime Minister a scandal concerning the Ministry of Information began to come into the open. Large sums of money had been spent in an undercover operation to gain control of South Africa's main English-language newspaper group. When this failed even larger sums were secretly spent to establish a pro-government English newspaper, *The Citizen*. Other projects involved attempts to gain influence over various publications and prominent persons in the United States, Britain and Europe. The money had been spent without authority from parliament. Indeed parliament had been assured that public funds were not being spent in this way. The scandal destroyed the chance of Connie Mulder, Minister of Information at the time, becoming the next Prime Minister. Instead P.W. Botha, previously Minister of Defence, was chosen. Mulder was eventually driven out of the National Party altogether and founded a right-wing Conservative Party. Vorster was also shown to have been implicated in the affair and had to resign his position as State President in disgrace. The scandal temporarily strengthened the position of the hardliner leader Andries Treurnicht who won the headship of the Transvaal Branch of the Party after Mulder was forced to resign.

The three-chamber parliament plan

After the original scheme for three separate parliaments was dropped, a government commission, the Schlebusch Commission, was set up to make proposals for constitutional reform. It recommended that the Senate be abolished and replaced with a President's Council with Indian and Coloured members as well as whites. It would have power to make further constitutional suggestions. Africans were not to be represented on this council but it was suggested that a separate council might be set up for them. The second council was never established however as Africans were not prepared to co-operate with the idea. The plan was adopted by the government. The Senate disappeared and the President's Council came into existence. It subsequently proposed a modified form of the earlier three-parliament idea. The parliament should be recognized with three different chambers, one for whites, one for Indians and one for Coloureds. The white chamber would have greater power than the others but the others would have some say. The white parliament would choose most of the national cabinet but some Coloureds and Indians would have ministries also. The head of government would be an executive president with very wide powers. He would be chosen by an electoral college on which whites would have the great majority of positions though Coloureds and Indians chosen by their chambers would also take part. The scheme was accepted by parliament in September 1983 and in November a referendum of white voters gave it overwhelming approval.

Namibia

In the aftermath of the Portuguese revolution the western powers began to take a more active part in trying to achieve a solution to the Namibia problem. The United Nations invited five western powers to form a contact group which would negotiate with South Africa for this purpose. Faced with this and the growing guerrilla movement in the territory, South Africa modified its earlier policy. Leaders of the ethnic 'homelands' and the white heartland of Namibia were assembled in a conference at the Windhoek Turnhalle (Sports Hall) to work out a constitution which would ead the country to independence as a federation of ethnic states. The onstitution would have given the whites the power to continue to control he economic heartland with the greater part of the resources of the ountry. As pressure from the United Nations mounted, South Africa greed to halt implementation of this scheme and to hold elections under Jnited Nations' supervision for a Constituent Assembly which would draw up its own constitution. Arrangements were held up by disagreements between South Africa and SWAPO over the conditions for a cease-ire. In 1978, Vorster suddenly broke off negotiations and went ahead to old elections in the territory without United Nations participation. The ;roups who had attended the Turnhalle Conference formed the Democratic Turnhalle Alliance (DTA) and obtained an overwhelming victory. SWAPO's call for a boycott failed and there was a large turnout of voters. Confident that the DTA would beat SWAPO in any open election, the outh African government then responded to United Nations pressure by greeing to hold another election under United Nations supervision.

Before this could be organized, however, South Africa opinion was hocked by the massive election victory of Mugabe in Zimbabwe and the otal defeat of Muzorewa who had previously looked secure. Implementation of the election agreement in Namibia was put off on a variety of pretexts and the negotiations dragged on until 1983. By this time the DTA had begun to break up internally and its popularity had greatly declined. The South African government thus seized on a pretext to dismiss the DTA administration and take over direct control while it looked for a more credible ally to place in charge of the country.

White opposition to the reform programme

In the period after the Portuguese collapse, the parliamentary opposition in South Africa became rather more effective. The feeble and divided United Party broke up. Some of its members formed a New Republic Party which had very similar views on race to the government and a power base in Natal. The larger part however joined the Progressive Party which changed its name to the Progressive Federal Party. It called for South Africa to be reorganized as an ethnic federation. The black majority would have overall power but there would be safeguards for white minority rights. The Progressives became the official opposition and maintained pressure on the government to widen its reform programme. Though they gained strength in successive elections after 1974, however, their numbers remained too small to threaten National Party control.

From the National Party point of view a more serious threat came from the Afrikaner hardliners. Though the HNP failed to win a parliamentary seat the level of its support among the electorate increased with successive elections. This pressure combined with that of the hardliners inside the party was sufficient to hold back the introduction of key aspects of the reform plan. Then in February 1982 Treurnicht openly challenged the Prime Minister's plan for limited power sharing. He was defeated and left the National Party with fifteen of his supporters. In March 1982 they launched the Conservative Party of South Africa. It was joined by Connie Mulder. The two right-wing opposition groups agreed to work together to fight two by-elections putting the government's electoral popularity to the test while its constitutional reform proposals were before Parliament in May 1983. White opposition to reform was not confined to parliamentary action. In 1980 an extreme right-wing terrorist organization the Wit Kommando (White Commando) bombed the offices of one of the Prime Minister's advisers and committed several other outrages. In 1983 another right-wing extremist group the Afrikaner Weerstandsbeweging (Afrikaner Resistance Movement) was found to have built up a number of illegal arms caches.

Continuing black opposition

The government's reform plan seemed likely to achieve some success in persuading at least a part of the Coloured and Indian communities to ally with the whites and support their continued political supremacy. In January 1983, the Coloured Labour Party voted overwhelmingly to enter into negotiations with the government over the three-chamber Parliament scheme, but many Coloureds were strongly against any such move.

The most crucial aim of the total plan, to win the support of a significant part of the African majority for the maintenance of the present system was unsuccessful. The contempt with which the palliatives offered by the government are held was evident in the pathetic turnout of only about 4 per cent of the voters for elections to the newly formed Community Council in Soweto in February 1978. Moderate constitutional opposition to the government's plan has been led by Chief Buthelezi of KwaZulu. Defying government opposition, he opened his Zulu cultural and political movement, Inkhata, to all Africans in South Africa and built up the largest registered membership of any political movement in the country. In January 1978 this movement was joined by the Coloured Labour Party and the Indian Reform Party in the South African Black Alliance to work for the summoning of a multiracial national convention to work out a new constitution for a non-racial South Africa. The alliance was severely damaged however by the Coloured Labour Party's decision to enter talks with the government in January 1983.

Apart from the organization of Inkhata, Buthelezi with the help of a number of experts prepared a well researched and reasoned alternative plan for the development of Natal to the government's apartheid schemes. Buthelezi's moderate approach was rejected by many Africans who see him as a tool of the system because he owes his position to the apartheid homeland' of KwaZulu. In May 1978 a new radical 'black consciousness' movement, the Azania People's Organization, was formed.

More significant still the guerrilla struggle directed by the externally based nationalist movement continued to expand and to enjoy a level of internal support which enabled freedom fighters to penetrate the heartland of white South Africa. In June 1980 ANC guerrillas pulled off a dramatic demonstration of their capacity for very high-level technical sophistication and strategic planning. They triggered simultaneous bomb blasts at the SASOL oil-from-coal installations in the Orange Free State and the Transvaal. This was followed by a steady build up of lower-level sabotage punctuated by periodic further dramatic incidents.

Internal repression and outward aggression

Faced with these threats and in the attempt to ward off right-wing criticism of the reform programme the South African government maintained a tough and repressive attitude towards even moderate criticism. Chief Buthelezi's proposals for Natal were brushed aside without serious consideration. The outspoken black churchman Bishop Tutu, who was awarded the Nobel Prize for Peace in 1984, was hounded and a commission of enquiry was established to examine the finances of the South African Council of Churches. In the more belligerent international atmosphere initiated by the Reagan administration in the United States, the South African government also adopted an increasingly aggressive stance towards its black neighbours. To the embarrassment of the government South African military personnel were shown to have been involved in an abortive attempt to overthrow the government of the Seychelles. More significant than this was the support given to the Mozambique National Resistance Movement which repeatedly sabotaged pipeline and rail links between Mozambique and Zimbabwe. In December 1982 it destroyed huge fuel storage installations at Beira in Mozambique.

The greatest South African military effort was devoted to Namibia and Angola. South African forces made increasingly far-reaching and long-lasting raids into Angola aimed not only at destroying SWAPO bases but also at rebuilding the forces of Unita in southern Angola. In August 1982 one of these raids was followed by prolonged military occupation of large areas of southern Angola.

In December 1982 South African forces made a direct attack on Maseru the capital of Lesotho aimed at ANC refugees there. South Africa is also believed to be supporting a guerrilla movement, the Lesotho Liberation Army, loyal to the opposition leader Ntsu Mokhehle. In February 1983 it destroyed a fuel depot and blew up a steel factory in Maseru.

Early in 1984 the diplomatic situation in Southern Africa was dramatically changed. The South African authorities negotiated an accord with Frelimo. Under this South Africa and the Mozambique government signed a non-aggression pact in March 1984. South Africa promised to give aid to Mozambique and stop support for the MNRM. Mozambique were to stop letting the ANC use the bases on its territory for military activity in South Africa. In a parallel agreement with the MPLA in Angola, South Africa said they would evacuate the southern provinces of the country and stop supplying Unita. The Angolan government agreed to stop SWAPO using military bases in Angola.

The introduction of the multiracial constitution

In the aftermath of these accords and after winning a two-thirds majority from white voters in a referendum, the Botha government introduced its new multiracial constitution in October 1984. Three separate assemblies were created for whites, Coloureds and Indians. An electoral college chosen by these, but with a large white majority, chose Botha as the first executive President. He appointed a mainly white Cabinet with just one Coloured and one Indian minister both without portfolio. Each House has the final say only over matters concerning its own community. Where they disagree over matters of national policy the decision is to be taken by the President's Council. This has representatives of all the Houses but a majority of whites. It also has fifteen members nominated by the President and ten by Opposition parties. Blacks were given no voice in the new arrangement.

Opposition to the constitution had hardened. In August elections were held for the Coloured and Indian chambers. The voters showed their contempt for the new constitution by a boycott: only 18.2 per cent of the Coloured electorate and 16.6 per cent of the Indian electorate voted. Active protest, in which Africans joined Coloureds and Indians, was brutally repressed by the security forces. It was clear that these limited reforms were not going to buy off the pressures for the elimination of apartheid altogether.

9 Central Africa, *c*.1900–53

Introduction

The establishment of colonial rule in Central Africa took place while the African peoples were experiencing great upheavals. The invasions of the Ngoni, Ndebele and Kololo and the expansions of the slave trade from the east coast had produced widespread disruption, misery and death. It is easy however to exaggerate the destruction of old societies and institutions. Even in what is now Zimbabwe after successive invasions and intrusions much of the old Shona political system survived. Outside of the area occupied by the Ndebele kingdom a number of Shona paramountcies maintained their independence and even the age-old Mwene Mutapa kingdom survived, though on a much reduced scale. Throughout the area the Ngoni and Ndebele invaders were actively building up new states embracing peoples of different ethnic origin and in the flood plains of the upper Zambezi a Lozi counter-revolution drove out the Kololo and restored the traditional dynasty. The slave trade also brought benefits to some. The Bemba kingdom for example made use of firearms to strengthen itself internally and engage in steady expansion. A new power balance was emerging in Central Africa but did not have time to establish itself before European intervention radically altered the situation.

The establishment of colonial rule in Southern Rhodesia

In Southern Rhodesia (now Zimbabwe) colonial rule was introduced by the British South Africa Company (BSAC) of Cecil Rhodes. He used his own vast financial resources and those of British capitalism to equip a column of predominantly South African whites with a few sons of wealthy and powerful English families who established themselves in Shona country in 1890. Rhodes used the mining concession he had gained from Lobengula to justify this although the Ndebele king had clearly not

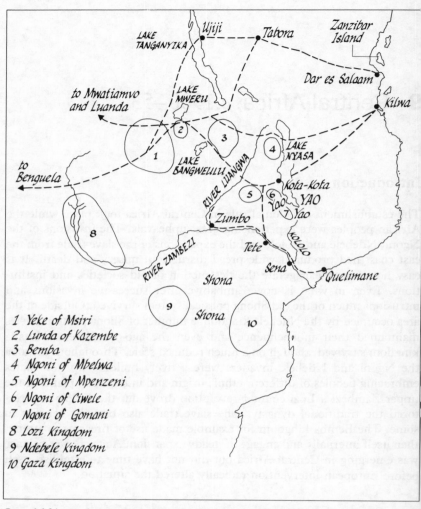

Central Africa on the eve of the colonial period, showing the approximate position of some of the more powerful African states and the main trade routes

1 Yeke of Msiri
2 Lunda of Kazembe
3 Bemba
4 Ngoni of Mbelwa
5 Ngoni of Mpenzeni
6 Ngoni of Ciwele
7 Ngoni of Gomani
8 Lozi Kingdom
9 Ndebele Kingdom
10 Gaza Kingdom

intended to give any right to settlement and was not in fact the overlord of the Shona rulers anyway. In 1893, a pretext was found for war with the Ndebele and Lobengula's regiments were mowed down with Maxim guns. The king fled to die in exile and since the pioneer column was mainly made up of whites from the south, the new colony, which was named Southern Rhodesia after Cecil Rhodes, was from the outset a northwards extension of the South African system of white domination.

The establishment of colonial rule in Nyasaland

In Nyasaland (now Malawi) colonial rule was preceded by extensive missionary activity. The African Lakes Company, a partly humanitarian, partly commercial venture was set up to keep the missionaries supplied, to tap the trade of the area and to replace the slave trade with legitimate trade. In the disturbed conditions of the time, the missions and the Company were bound to exercise considerable local political power. Mission stations tended to become little political states with quarrels, often leading to war, with Arab, Swahili and Yao traders. In these difficult circumstances the missions pressed for British intervention. Their political pull in Britain was sufficient to get the British government to give Portugal an ultimatum in 1890. It forced the Portuguese to abandon plans to occupy southern Nyasaland.

Colonial rule in Nyasaland was then established by Sir Harry Johnston acting as an official agent of the British government but partly financed by Rhodes in return for commercial concessions. Johnston's army was mainly made up of Indian troops lent him by the British government of India. He met with strong resistance but by 1894 most of the area was occupied. In spite of Rhodes's assistance the imperial government, under pressure from the missionaries and their supporters, refused to hand Nyasaland over to the British South Africa Company and it became the British Protectorate of Nyasaland, a name it retained until independence.

In Nyasaland Johnston confirmed large land grants to white settlers, especially in the south. Through exploiting cheap African labour some of these lands were later developed into plantations of tea and other crops. Though the white settlers were economically powerful and politically influential in colonial Nyasaland their numbers were very small and they were unable to gain a dominant position. The missions remained politically important and the imperial government was firmly in control of administration.

The establishment of colonial rule in Northern Rhodesia

In the area of Northern Rhodesia (now Zambia) as in Nyasaland, colonial rule was preceded by considerable missionary activity. In the eastern half of the country colonial rule was established on the basis of treaties obtained through Johnston and his agents operating from Nyasaland under his agreement with Rhodes. Troops from Nyasaland helped to crush resistance to the British South Africa Company's rule. In 1898 a pretext was found to justify an attack on Mpezeni's Ngoni. His regiments were easily smashed by Maxim guns. Huge herds of cattle were looted. In 1899 two Bemba chiefs were attacked and the Lunda King Kazembe driven from his kingdom. In western Northern Rhodesia colonial rule was established on the basis of treaties obtained by Rhodes's agents operating from the south. The most important of these was with the Lozi King Lewanika. It was used to justify the occupation of territory far beyond the borders of the actual Lozi kingdom. The area of Northern Rhodesia was first divided into separate territories known as North-Eastern and North-Western Rhodesia. In 1911 they were combined to become Northern Rhodesia, a name retained until independence.

From the beginning the British government insisted on its overriding authority in all areas occupied by the British South Africa Company but the day-to-day administration was left in the hands of the Company under the distant supervision of the British High Commissioner for South Africa.

The establishment of colonial rule in Mozambique (Portuguese East Africa)

In Mozambique competition with other European powers and the opportunity for expanding trade with the Transvaal made the Portuguese want to establish direct control over the territory. The Portuguese claim to Mozambique rested mainly on the influence of the *prazo* (estate) owners. But they were heavily involved in the slave trade and were in effect independent rulers. The Portuguese attempt to establish direct control concentrated largely on the Zambezi area. Their method was to ally with some of the *prazo* owners against others. They supported their allies with government troops as well as arms and ammunition. Even so they met fierce and determined resistance, especially from the Massangano *prazo*. Their strongest ally was the Gorongosa *prazo* owner, Manuel Antonio de Sousa, known as Gouveia. He sought to build up a large empire between the Zambezi and Manica in alliance with the Portuguese, but he came into conflict with Cecil Rhodes's British South Africa Company, which was attempting to gain control of areas in eastern Southern Rhodesia to which the Portuguese also laid claim. In 1890 Gouveia was seized and arrested by the British South Africa Company's police. The Shona kingdom of Barue took the opportunity to break away from Gouveia's control and he was killed the following year when trying to reassert his authority. In 1900 Barue supported a rebellion of people on the frontier between Southern Rhodesia and Mozambique, led by the outstanding Shona rebel leader Mapondera. In 1902 however a major Portuguese expedition finally subued Barue. This completed the conquest of the Zambezi area.

In southern Mozambique the ruler of the Gaza kingdom, Gungunyana, repeatedly sought to place his kingdom under the British to gain protection from the Portuguese. In 1895 however the Portuguese found a pretext for war. With the aid of machine guns, the mass regiments of the Gaza kingdom were mowed down. Gungunyana was captured and exiled to the Azores. Two years later his chief induna, Maguiguana, raised a desperate rebellion but was defeated by modern weapons and was killed. In northern Mozambique resistance was mainly led by the Muslim Arab and Swahili traders based on the offshore island of Angoche. The northern provinces were not fully conquered until 1912.

The First World War in Central Africa

Colonial rule had only recently been consolidated in Northern Rhodesia, Nyasaland and Mozambique when these areas became involved in the First World War. After a prolonged struggle for control of German East Africa (modern Tanzania) the remnant of the German forces there under the leadership of the brilliant General von Lettow-Vorbeck, evaded British forces and invaded northern Mozambique. He kept up the struggle through 1917 and 1918 and at the very end of the war broke into Northern Rhodesia and captured the administrative centre of Kasama before surrendering to British officers on the Chambeshi river. During the course of the prolonged campaign many Africans throughout Central Africa were recruited as soldiers and thousands more as carriers. The prolonged marches and arduous conditions led to a very heavy death toll. The strain imposed on African societies by the enforced absence of a high proportion of their young men was also very great. Many families were reduced to desperate circumstances.

Southern Rhodesia: the *Chimurenga* of 1896–7

The white settlers in Southern Rhodesia brought with them the racist attitudes of South Africa. Though no vast gold deposits were found, numerous small mines were opened. The settlers also staked out land for farms. As the BSAC could not afford an adequate system of native administration, individual settlers were appointed as officials and given a very free hand. In the Shona area they prevented the people from continuing to trade with the Portuguese. They took over their gold workings and demanded that chiefs supply them with labour. When their authority

was resisted they terrorized the people by punitive raids. In the Ndebe
country after the defeat of Lobengula, almost the whole of the core of t
kingdom was staked out as farms. The greater part of the total herds of t
community was seized on the pretext that it was the property of t
defeated king. Then most of those that were left died in an epidemic
rinderpest. Proud chiefs and indunas found themselves treated with arr
gant contempt.

In 1896 when the Ndebele heard the news that many of the BSAC
forces had been captured in the Jameson Raid fiasco they rose in
desperate struggle for freedom. Before the end of the year many Shor
chiefdoms joined in the uprising they called *Chimurenga*. Though the
were unable to capture the main centres of white power at Bulawayo an
Salisbury (now Harare) they forced the Company to face a long and costl
struggle. Rhodes thus felt forced to seek peace with the Ndebele short
completely defeating them. He held negotiations with them in the Mato
pos mountains and by promising them land for their people and amnest
for their leaders he persuaded them to give up the struggle by the end
1896. The Shona fought on until late in 1897 before all the resistance wa
crushed.

The establishment of settler political control in Southern Rhodesia, 1898–1923

The *Chimurenga* had greatly weakened the BSAC's position in Souther
Rhodesia and it became more than ever dependent on the settlers who ha
been called upon to do much of the fighting. It was also in a weak positio
with the British government after its scandalous behaviour in the Trans
vaal. The best way of preventing Britain from cancelling the Charte
seemed to be to win over the settlers who were mainly of British stock. I
1898, therefore, the Company agreed to set up a Legislative Council wit
four elected representatives of the white settlers. The vote was available t
adult male British subjects regardless of race, provided that they had a
income of at least £50 a year and buildings worth £75. In practice thi
meant that only a few Africans could hope to gain the right to vote.

Once the white settlers had gained some political representation the
pressed for more and in 1908 the BSAC allowed them to elect the majorit
in the Legislative Council. By 1923 when the BSAC finally laid down it
administrative authority in Southern Rhodesia the 36 000 settlers were i
virtual control over 900 000 Africans. When the BSAC's rule ended the
most important question was whether Southern Rhodesia should join the
Union of South Africa or become a separate country enjoying responsible

Two leaders of the Chimurenga – Mbuya Nehanda and Kaguvi – after their capture in 1896

government. At that time the whites were confident of maintaining their supremacy and saw little to fear from the African majority. They therefore saw no great need to ally with the South for protection and they feared that by joining South Africa they might be swamped by the Afrikaans-speaking majority among the whites there. They also feared that their economic interests would be neglected in favour of South Africa and that poor whites from the South would compete for the meagre opportunities of employment as skilled workers and craftsmen. A referendum was held in 1922 and the majority of the whites voted in favour of responsible government. Legally, Southern Rhodesia still remained under British authority and the British insisted that any legislation which discriminated against non-whites should be sent to London for approval but this did not prove a very effective safeguard. The white settlers were thus firmly in control.

Economic development of Southern Rhodesia

Though Rhodes's dreams of vast gold wealth in Southern Rhodesia never materialized, the mining of gold and other metals played an important part in the colonial economy. Much of the mining was undertaken by individuals or small companies with little capital, and as all mines faced greater transport costs than those in South Africa they were even more reliant on very cheap African labour. In the early period of white settlement white landowners were not in a position to exploit much of the larger areas of land they had acquired for themselves. They thus left African families on the land as tenants in return for part of the crop or a cash rent. Most of the agricultural production remained in African hands and as the mines and administrative centres provided a market for their produce, African small-scale farmers had something of a boom. They were often able to meet their tax demands without seeking employment from whites. Mines and other white-owned enterprises faced severe labour shortages. They had to rely on the Rhodesian Native Labour Bureau which recruited African workers on very unfavourable contracts from the poorer territories to the north. This contract service seemed to Africans the same as slavery. They called it *chibaro*.

In 1907 the BSAC finally officially recognized that there was no hope of finding a second Rand in Southern Rhodesia. It moved to a policy of encouraging white agriculture. This was continued by the settler-controlled government after 1923. Aided by cheap land loans and scientific assistance commercial farming by whites of maize and tobacco began to become profitable. As this happened pressure increased to push African tenants off white-owned land and restrict African land ownership to

The first train to arrive at Salisbury

limited reserves. This would help to make African labour available to whites and reduce their ability to compete as agricultural producers.

The two-pyramids policy

The racial policy developed in Southern Rhodesia thus followed the same segregationist principles as that of South Africa. It was called the two-pyramids policy. The country was to be divided into white-owned areas and African reserves. In the white areas the upper part of the social pyramid would be white, with Africans providing the unskilled workers at the base. In the African reserves, most of the pyramid would be black with only a few whites at the very top holding political and administrative power. The foundations of this policy were laid by the Land Apportionment Act of 1930 (similar in principle to the South African Natives Land Act of 1913). Provision for 'native reserves' had been made after the 1896-7 risings but their boundaries had not been clearly defined and many Africans lived outside them. Now the land was to be definitely divided into white and black areas. The limits of the reserves were defined and

Africans were denied the right to own land outside them. About half of the land including the most productive areas and all those with easy access to markets and railways went to the small white minority. All the towns were included in white areas and Africans could not acquire rights to permanent residence there. They could only live in segregated locations on the outskirts or in servant quarters, attached to their master's houses. Even to live in those places they needed official permission and had to be in white employment. As in South Africa they had to carry passes.

In Southern Rhodesia, as in South Africa, white workers were afraid that their employers might prefer to employ Africans at cheaper rates in semi-skilled and skilled positions. The Industrial Conciliation Act of 1934, the second main pillar of the two-pyramids policy, aimed to protect white workers from this. The Act was framed so as to avoid direct mention of race, but its intention was to deny Africans the right to join trade unions and to keep the higher paid work for whites only.

Though the policy of segregation reduced the opportunities for African farmers and forced increasing numbers on to the labour market, the land available to Africans was still sufficient to allow many to avoid working for whites. Those who did, moreover, could travel to South Africa where wages were often better. African farmers also still succeeded in offering some competition to whites. Measures were thus taken through, for example, the Maize Control Act of 1935 to ensure that whites would get better prices for their produce. To counter the problem of labour shortage without raising wages, large numbers of African workers were brought in as migrant labour from Nyasaland, Northern Rhodesia and Mozambique. As a result the real wages of black workers hardly increased at all for thirty years after 1923.

Impact of the Second World War in Southern Rhodesia

During the war years, 1939–45, Southern Rhodesians of all races saw military service in many parts of the world. Africans in particular returned with many new ideas and could not easily reconcile themselves to racial discrimination in their own country. Southern Rhodesia enjoyed an economic boom during the war which continued afterwards and this was accompanied by a great increase in white immigration. White farmers began to make use of the remaining land in white areas that they had previously not directly exploited. African tenants who had lived there were driven into the reserves where poverty and overcrowding were producing a serious situation. Manufacturing industries, though still on a small scale, began to expand and together with the growth of white commercial farming created an increased demand for African labour. After the war, moreover, the ferment of political activity heralded the collapse of the European colonial empires. The white settlers in Southern Rhodesia recognized the threat. While South Africa took the road of apartheid, in Southern Rhodesia the settlers' need for assured supplies of cheap African labour, more capital and wider markets for industry and enhanced security, led the governing party to think in terms of federation with Northern Rhodesia and Nyasaland to create an economically powerful white-controlled state.

The Land Husbandry Act, 1951

In Southern Rhodesia by 1951 the continuing boom had produced a situation in which the supply of African labour through immigration was not sufficient. By this time too the economy of the country as a whole had greatly expanded. To help meet the need for cheap labour the Southern Rhodesian government introduced the Land Husbandry Act. The Land Husbandry Act was perhaps the most revolutionary measure since the setting up of Southern Rhodesia. It provided for the abolition of the traditional system of land tenure in African areas. Instead of a share of tribal land, individuals could acquire outright ownership of small areas of land. These farms had to be a minimum size and could not be subdivided. The main object was to provide that those unable to acquire land would have to work in the towns and provide the whites with the cheap labour they needed. It was also hoped that those who did get land would feel that they had a stake in the existing political system. The result of the act was that large numbers of Africans found themselves in a desperate position without security in either town or in the country. Inevitably they turned to political activity and formed the basis for the development of African nationalism as a mass movement.

Origins of African nationalism in Southern Rhodesia

The defeat of the *Chimurenga* left Africans disillusioned and it seemed clear that whites could not be driven out by force of arms. There were thus no more serious uprisings and Africans accepted the need to adapt themselves to the new society and to direct their political activity into modern forms. The missions began to make converts on a large scale; the ever-increasing drive for western education had begun. In the mines, on the farms, in the industries and homes of the whites Africans acquired new skills and experience of the modern world but also a sense of humiliation and frustration. They suffered indignities like the pass system and social segregation in buildings, offices and transport similar to that in South Africa. At the same time they made contact with Africans from other parts of Southern Africa who were involved in political activity and, since many workers were migrants from outside Southern Rhodesia, the new experiences and ideas were carried into rural areas and spread a growing consciousness of the nature of the new white settler-dominated world into even the most remote villages.

Since the Ndebele had been less severely crushed in the course of the *Chimurenga* than the Shona and their own political system had survived to a considerable extent, it was natural that they should be the first to recover their political awareness and confidence. They also found that they had been cheated by Rhodes's promises at the end of the *Chimurenga* and were deprived of most of their traditional and best land. Their first political activity was aimed at the restoration of the Ndebele kingship and the return of sufficient of their lost land to give them a definite national home in which they could develop a degree of Ndebele self-government. Their method of action was to present petitions to the British High Commissioner and King George V. Though they failed in their objectives, the movement continued to be popular among the Ndebele, and in the 1920s the Ndebele Home Society was formed to press for the same concessions. Their political methods were modern and they enjoyed wide support but their ideas were very conservative. Apart from requesting more land than the whites would give, their ideas were not very far from the whites' policy of the 'two-pyramids'.

The beginning of a different type of political organization came in 1923 when the small number of African voters came together to form the Rhodesian Bantu Voters' Association. This association and a number of other societies known as Welfare Associations were thoroughly modern in outlook and concentrated on getting increased voting rights for Africans together with educational and social reforms. They were much influenced by the tactics of Jabavu and the Cape Voters' Association from which they gained much inspiration. Their weakness lay in the fact that they were confined to a tiny educated élite and were not very successful in communicating with the masses and gaining their support. At first their leaders were Africans from South Africa and Nyasaland but by the 1930s educated Africans from Southern Rhodesia were beginning to take over the leadership of these associations.

In 1934 an attempt was made to form a nationwide nationalist movement. In that year Aaron Jacha founded the Southern Rhodesian African National Congress, the first attempt in British Central Africa at forming a

uly national political movement. For a long time however it continued to
ct very cautiously and to have little appeal except to the educated élite.

The religious expression of discontent

Before the Second World War, African discontent tended to express itself
a religious rather than political form. The religious movement was really
art of the Ethiopian Movement described in Chapter 7. In the 1920s the
African Watchtower Movement which began in Nyasaland spread into the
Shona areas of Southern Rhodesia. A host of other breakaway sects also
spread into the country from South Africa. By the 1930s the movement of
religious independency had become a mass phenomenon among the Shona
and since then the country has remained an important centre of the
movement. These religious movements provided an outlet for the discontent and frustration of Africans. They helped to keep their dignity alive
and fostered the realization that they were not inferior to their white
overlords. This resistance and defiance would eventually be channelled in
a political direction. In the short run the breakaway churches also served
as a safety valve preventing African resentment from expressing itself in
openly political and violent ways. Many Africans who rejected white
superiority, however, remained within the mission churches and gained
their education and preparation for future nationalist activity there.

African industrial organization

The idea of industrial organization for Africans was born in South Africa
where Clements Kadalie founded the Industrial and Commercial Workers'
Union (ICU). It rapidly grew into a mass political organization in Southern Africa. In the late 1920s Kadalie, who came from Nyasaland, sent a fellow
Nyasa, Robert Sambo, to Southern Rhodesia to found a local branch
of his union. He was deported but the idea caught on and branches were
established in Bulawayo and Salisbury. Mass meetings of urban workers
were held where their wrongs were denounced and unity called for. They
attracted much wider support than the Welfare Associations but also the
attention of the police. The leaders of the movement were arrested and
imprisoned in the 1930s and with the break up of the South African
Industrial and Commercial Workers' Union, the Southern Rhodesian
branch was also gravely weakened. The idea lingered on however and in
1945 a Reformed ICU was a significant African organization in Salisbury.

African nationalism in Southern Rhodesia becomes a mass movement

The Second World War was as much a turning point for Africans as for the settlers. Ex-servicemen returned with experience of a world where a man's social standing did not necessarily depend on the colour of his skin. New white immigrants displaced African workers and as more and more Africans drifted to the towns social problems and discontent there grew more and more intense. The numbers of Africans receiving western education rapidly increased and with this the number of potential political leaders was greatly increased. Nationalist progress in other colonial territories became known in Southern Rhodesia through the radio and newspapers. The awakening of political consciousness showed itself in the emergence of the Reformed ICU and the revival of the Southern Rhodesia African National Congress (SRANC) after 1945. That year the African railway workers staged a successful strike which led to official recognition of their union. In 1948 Africans joined a nationwide strike which was joined by domestic servants. As the effects of the Land Husbandry Act of 1951 made themselves felt, the SRANC became a real mass political party. Reinvigorated in 1957 under the leadership of Joshua Nkomo, it united almost all the streams of discontent behind the effort to win political advancement from the white minority.

Northern Rhodesia under colonial rule

Like Southern Rhodesia, Northern Rhodesia was first administered by the BSAC. At first the number of white settlers was very small indeed. A certain amount of mining especially around Broken Hill was begun from the early years. Many copper deposits were discovered and numerous small copper mines were opened up. The oxidized ores which were discovered near the surface proved relatively poor however. They were not nearly as rich as those found in neighbouring Katanga. Mining them was only barely profitable and many of the early mines soon closed. In addition to copper mining a number of small gold mines were opened. The deposits found were all relatively small however and no major gold-mining complex developed. Though all mining remained on a relatively small scale, minerals had become the chief export by 1906. The most important economic development of the time was the extension of the railway. By 1906 the line had reached Broken Hill from Bulawayo and by 1909 it had linked up with the railway system of the Belgian Congo. Apart from improving the economy of mining operations this also helped the development of comnercial agriculture in the country. An increasing number of white farmers started farming on land alongside the rail line, others settled on lands taken from the Ngoni of Mpezeni to the east. Another smaller group of settlers established farms in the north of the country. Altogether far the greatest number of whites settled near the railway. For the most part the line ran through areas of sparse African population so European settlement was not as disruptive as in Southern Rhodesia.

Though the white population in the country was small the whites' self-confidence was very high and they had no doubt that it would eventually become a white settler-dominated country like Southern Rhodesia. They so seriously underestimated the African majority that they saw little reason to ally with their neighbours across the Zambezi. In 1924, when the BSAC gave up the administration, the settlers opposed amalgamation with Southern Rhodesia. Northern Rhodesia thus came under direct British administration.

The development of the Northern Rhodesian Copperbelt

The extensive deposits of oxidized ores in Northern Rhodesia at first proved an economic disappointment. In the 1920s however it was discovered that vast deposits of sulphide ores lay under the oxidized layers. The so-called 'flotation' process had just been discovered which made it profitable to mine these sulphide ores. Large capitalist companies were thus attracted to Northern Rhodesia and the result was an economic boom which revolutionized the country. After a brief initial setback caused by the worldwide depression, the Copperbelt mines have remained by far the main source of wealth of the country. The growth of the Copperbelt affected the life of the country in many ways. It attracted greatly increased white migration including large numbers of skilled and semi-skilled mine workers. Many of these came from South Africa and almost all of them shared a determination to protect their privileged financial position by preserving a white monopoly of the more highly paid jobs. The new wealth stimulated trade and brought considerable development not only to the Copperbelt towns but to the whole area along the line of rail. This area became one of high economic development and white domination while much the greater part of the country remained a poverty stricken rural slum but much less directly affected by white racism.

The development of the copper mines added to the existing demand for labour from Southern Rhodesia, South Africa and the white farmers in Northern Rhodesia. The economic boom resulting from mining development also suggested the possibility that substantial numbers of white settlers would be attracted to come to the country. The government thus set about dividing the land into areas for white settlement and African reserves. Very large areas were set aside for white settlement and though most of this land was never taken up, Africans were kept out of them for a long time. The creation of these reserves put increasing pressure on African agriculture. In some areas, notably in the Eastern Province, serious soil deterioration resulted. Under pressure of land shortage and the demands of taxation increasing numbers of Africans were forced on to the labour market. In some areas it was not unusual for as much as 70 per cent of the total available male workforce to be absent from the rural areas as migrant workers. This situation exacerbated the economic decline of the rural areas compared with the progress of the area around the mines and along the railway line.

Many workers from the rural areas of Northern Rhodesia went to work at the copper mines. At first they were employed for short periods only as migrant workers. In time however the mines began to encourage them to settle more or less permanently in the towns. The process of urbanization which still continues had begun. Social attitudes in the towns were racist, but since there were insufficient whites to do all the jobs, Africans had rather better opportunities in skilled and clerical work than they had in the

Early urbanization in Northern Rhodesia: one of the towns that grew up in the Copperbelt

countries to the south. There were also better opportunities for Africans in government service and with the mining companies. Thus a small but important African élite grew up with the education to understand modern political methods and ready to take a lead in the development of modern African nationalism.

White politics in Northern Rhodesia

As in Southern Rhodesia, the white settlers fought for and won political representation under the administration of the BSAC and in 1924, when the Company's rule ended, they looked forward to a rapid advance to self-government. They were bitterly disappointed when the British government made it clear that it could not possibly entrust power over an African population of one million to a mere 4000 whites. Though they were given a voice the British government kept them in the minority on the Legislative Council. The settlers thus soon began to feel that they had made a mistake in not joining with Southern Rhodesia. They began to press for amalgamation. In 1929 the white settlers in Northern Rhodesia received a shattering blow to their self-confidence when the British Colonial Secretary, Lord Passfield, announced that in Northern Rhodesia as in East Africa the interest of the Africans were to be regarded as paramount. The settlers were deeply alarmed and began actively to seek union with their southern neighbours.

In 1938 they met informally with representatives of Southern Rhodesian whites to discuss the amalgamation of the three British Central African territories. As a result of settler agitation the Bledisloe Commission was sent out to the area to investigate the possibility of uniting the territories. White settlers in the whole region were enthusiastic, but the Africans in the two northern territories expressed a dislike for the idea of being handed over from the care of the imperial government to a settler-dominated regime. As a result the Commission was unable to recommend an immediate amalgamation.

The Second World War was a major turning point for Northern Rhodesia. It meant a great increase in the demand for copper from Britain. The weakening of imperial governments throughout the world and the upsurge of non-European rule caused the settlers to feel that their supremacy was by no means certain and that they must act swiftly to protect it. During and immediately after the war, the white settlers in Northern Rhodesia pressed more vigorously for increased political power and a link with Southern Rhodesia. During the war a so-called 'national government' was formed in the country. Then in 1945 the settlers were given a majority position in the Legislative Council. Led by Roy Welensky, originally a trade union leader of the white railway workers, the settlers were ready to make an all-out effort to gain complete control of the country.

African political activity in Northern Rhodesia

As in Southern Rhodesia, mass expression of political consciousness by Africans first took the form of religious movements. The African Watchtower movement which began in Nyasaland spread widely but was only one of a number of sects. Among these was a movement started by Tomo Nyirenda who taught that the country must be cleansed of witches and that he had an infallible method of detecting them. He was responsible for the death of a large number of people before he was finally arrested and hanged in 1925.

Modern-style political activity first took the form of voluntary Welfare Societies formed by the more highly educated African élite. Because of the higher level of education provided by the missions in Nyasaland it was Africans from there who first provided leadership for these organizations in Northern Rhodesia, but as educational opportunities in Northern Rhodesia increased they fell into the background. By 1933 there were Welfare Associations in Abercorn, Kasama and Fort Jameson. Their policies were moderate at first; they pressed for minor reforms but did not question the general principle of white rule. However the settlers' attempts at amalgamation with Southern Rhodesia forced Africans to unite their political opposition to the settlers' ambitions. In 1946 the members of fourteen Welfare Associations joined to form the Federation of African Societies of Northern Rhodesia. It was a loose-knit but national organization which could grow into a truly mass party.

Industrial unrest in Northern Rhodesia

The development of the Copperbelt gave Northern Rhodesia a larger scale of industry than anywhere else in Central Africa with a huge concentration of African labour. Low wages, poor housing, racial discrimination and humiliation inevitably bred discontent. In 1935 there was a series of strikes accompanied in some cases by violent riots. Government troops had to be brought in to control the situation. Six miners were killed and twenty-two injured. In 1940 after the white mine workers had held a successful strike for improved pay and conditions, African workers also went on strike. These protests were spontaneous since Africans did not ossess a permanent trade union. This time seventeen were killed and xty-four injured. After the Second World War, however, provision was ade for Africans to have a union and William Comrie, a Scottish trade nionist, was sent out to establish a permanent organization. Thereafter e African Mine Workers Union and the African Railwaymen's Union ecame powerful organizations and were the main elements in the Fed- ration of African Trade Unions. For a long time however African trade nions held back from committing themselves to any active political role.

ndirect rule and the African Representative Council

s more highly educated Africans in Northern Rhodesia began forming Velfare Associations and criticizing many aspects of white race domina- ion in the country, the Northern Rhodesian authorities recognized the eed to involve Africans in the government of their country. They looked owever to the traditional chiefs to counterbalance the critical attitude of he African educated élite, and treated them as the true representatives of he mass of the people. After 1930 the system of indirect rule was intro- luced through which chiefs were given a definite role in local administra- ion. Thus just as traditional systems were being overtaken by the impact f European rule and economic activity the government tried to revive the old order. After the Copperbelt disturbances of 1935, the authorities saw he need to maintain contact with African workers and set up Urban Advisory Councils. By 1943 the government realized the need for a further ncrease in African consultation and some direct involvement of the edu- cated élite. That year a series of African Provincial Councils was set up. Their members were largely drawn from traditional chiefs but a small number of elected representatives was permitted. In 1946 these measures were extended even further and an African Representative Council was formed consisting of twenty-five members selected by the Provincial Councils and four appointees of the paramount chief of Barotseland. Thus the government had set up a system for African consultation but consist- ing mainly of the more conservative elements, traditional chiefs who had strong reasons for favouring the continuation of white rule. The Federa- tion of African Societies of Northern Rhodesia formed in the same year and soon to be renamed the African National Congress was not regarded by the government as truly representative.

Nyasaland under colonial rule

Unlike Northern Rhodesia, Nyasaland had no rich mineral deposits. It remained an agricultural country in which much of the land was poor.

Compared with the Rhodesias moreover it had a relatively dense population and this was increased by the migration of large numbers fleeing from the oppressive Portuguese regime in Mozambique. Land hunger was a serious problem in some parts of southern Nyasaland, and this was increased by the grant of substantial areas to white settlers who established plantations for cotton, tobacco and tea.

Apart from the small number of white settlers, the coming of colonial rule also saw a substantial immigration of Indians. Johnston had a high regard for Indian initiative and business acumen. He once said, 'Nyasaland should be ruled by whites, exploited by Indians and worked by blacks.' Indians soon came to dominate the internal trade and opened stores even in the remotest areas of the country. Some went to Northern Rhodesia also and most of the country stores there were Indian-owned. Indians tended to form very tight communities and did not easily take Africans into partnership in their businesses. Because of their wide network of business contacts, thrifty habits and commercial skills, Africans found it very difficult to compete with them. Like the whites Indians tended to treat Africans as inferiors. On the other hand their business skills and their willingness to operate on low profit margins enabled them to offer their African customers a better deal than they would probably have been able to get any other way. Their enterprise in opening businesses all over the country played, moreover, an important role in the economy of the country.

Though Nyasaland was pitifully poor it had the strongest mission

An Indian-owned store in Nyasaland

enterprises in all of British Central Africa. The educational work of the missions, especially the Livingstonia Mission in northern Nyasaland, was outstanding. This resulted in Nyasaland, though more backward than Northern or Southern Rhodesia in other respects, developing a larger body of western-educated Africans with modern skills. The result of this and of the overpopulation of much of the country was that throughout Central, Southern and East Africa Nyasas came to perform many of the clerical, teaching and other skilled roles available to Africans in the colonial period. They also supplied much of the early leadership for African political activity throughout Central Africa. This was true of the religious breakaway movements and of the African Welfare Associations in both Southern and Northern Rhodesia. In South Africa also, Clements Kadalie, the founder of the ICU, was a Nyasa. Even when Africans from other territories took over the greater part of the leadership in their own areas, Africans from Nyasaland continued to exercise considerable influence.

The colonial government encouraged the development of white-owned plantations. It also made some effort to encourage Africans to grow export crops. The poverty of the country and the debts incurred in building a railway to link with the Rhodesian rail route to Beira, however, meant that the government had to pressure the African population to seek work on the plantations and on the mines in Northern and Southern Rhodesia and South Africa. This provided the tax revenue to maintain the white administration and pay the debts. Throughout the colonial period much of Nyasaland thus remained a labour reserve for the white-dominated south. Its economy was overwhelmingly dependent on the export of its people as migrant workers.

White politics in Nyasaland

The white population of Nyasaland was always tiny compared to that of either of the Rhodesias. In 1907, two representatives of the white settlers were chosen by the governor to sit on his Legislative Council and thereafter the settlers sought to improve their political position. They joined together to form the Convention of Associations but there were never enough of them to win political control of the country which remained in the hands of the British government. The majority of the settlers therefore sought ways of linking with a larger body of whites in Northern and Southern Rhodesia, but these attempts failed until after the Second World War when the situation in Central Africa as a whole changed radically.

The development of African political activity in Nyasaland

Africans in Nyasaland did not suffer such severe shocks from the establishment of white rule as in Southern Rhodesia. Nevertheless, in the Southern Region much of the land was taken over by white men and land hunger became acute. Thousands of refugees from harsh Portuguese rule in Mozambique added to the problem of overcrowding. White settlers brought racial prejudices with them and in the towns Africans lived in separate locations. There were also often separate counters for Africans in European and Indian stores. Even the missionaries who did so much for African education and who sometimes supported Africans against the settlers were infected with the same spirit. Though they preached equality of men in God's eye, they rarely gave full responsibility to their African preachers or mixed with them socially.

Mass protest in Nyasaland as elsewhere in British Central Africa first took a religious form. Nyasaland indeed took the lead in this respect and the idea of breakaway churches spread from there to other territories. The idea of religious protest was, in fact, first introduced by an Englishman, Joseph Booth. His idea was to build African religious communities which would be economically self-sufficient and in which Africans could prosper without Europeans. He was horrified by the racist attitudes of most whites and in a long and troubled period during which he maintained his connections with Nyasaland he founded a whole series of different missions and gave help and encouragement to breakaway African church leaders, especially the Watchtower.

The Chilembwe rising, 1915

One of Booth's assistants at this first mission in Nyasaland was John Chilembwe. Booth took him to America where he was able to study at a black university. Chilembwe came back to Africa in 1906 and founded his own mission, called the Providence Industrial Mission. He soon despaired of the treatment of his people and failed to see how the whites could reconcile this with sending Africans to fight European wars. As his letters and petitions were ignored he decided to lead a rising to show that Africans could not be treated with such contempt. In 1915 his followers killed two whites but the rising was soon suppressed and he was killed while trying to escape. However, his memory remained as an inspiration to African leaders in later years.

Elliot Kenan Kamwana and African Watchtower

The largest movement expressing rejection of white domination in religious form was the African Watchtower Church founded in Nyasaland between 1908 and 1909 by Elliot Kenan Kamwana. The African Watchtower Church gained its inspiration from the American-based worldwide Watchtower organization of Jehovah's Witnesses, but the Nyasaland Church was entirely African-controlled, and interpreted the Jehovah's witnesses doctrine in its own way. It preached that the end of the world was at hand, that white rule would then be destroyed and that Africans would enjoy all the material goods and luxuries denied to them. The movement did not itself give rise to rebellion but rather served as a safety valve for African feelings of frustration and humiliation. The Nyasaland government was so alarmed by Kamwana's preaching that he was exiled in 1909 and not allowed to return until 1937. The movement he founded, however, remained strong, gained mass support in Nyasaland and spread into both the Rhodesias. There were other independent African sects also whose attitudes varied; some represented a direct protest against white domination, others were an attempt to adapt the values of white society but without white control, others sought the preservation of traditional beliefs and customs, others the complete rejection of African tradition.

John Chilembwe baptising at Mbombwe

The voluntary associations

African political activity of the modern type developed more rapidly and extensively in Nyasaland than in other parts of British Central Africa. As early as 1912 educated Africans in northern Nyasaland formed the North Nyasa Native Association, which from 1919 began to press for direct African representation in the Legislative Council. In 1920 a similar association was formed in the south of the country and after that a whole series of associations sprang up. By 1933 there were fifteen. These voluntary associations tended to have a rather narrow membership drawn from the educated African élite and their policies tended to be moderate and cautious. However, they did give Africans the experience of modern political action, and social and political awareness could spread from them through the general African population. The government paid little attention to their petitions but the associations did express African feelings about the possible federation of Nyasaland with Southern and Northern Rhodesia, and their representations, especially to the Bledisloe Commission, helped to frustrate the achievement of this idea before the Second World War.

In Nyasaland, as elsewhere, the war changed the whole of political life and Africans began to prepare for the struggle to decide a future pattern of society. In 1943 an attempt was made to unite the voluntary associations into a common organization and in 1944 the Nyasaland African Congress was formed. It inherited the narrow membership of the bodies which made it up and expressed moderate policies. But it did mean that Nyasaland had a national African voice to focus African feelings in the struggles which lay ahead.

Early resistance to the Portuguese in Mozambique

Even before the conquest of Mozambique had been completed, rebellions took place in areas which had already been subjugated. As early as 1884 a serious uprising broke out on the Massingire *prazo* on the Lower Shire river. In 1892 there were widespread risings in the neighbourhood of Gouveia's former *prazo* of Gorongosa. In 1898 another broke out on the *prazo* of Bororo under a chief named Namisella. Between 1900 and 1901 a serious rising broke out in the frontier area between Mozambique and Southern Rhodesia. It gained inspiration from the leadership of Mapondera, a Shona chief who earned a reputation as a warrior in resistance to the Ndebele. When Rhodes's BSAC occupied Zimbabwe he led opposition to it in the eastern districts. Later he crossed the border and raised rebellion against the Portuguese. As mentioned above he joined forces with the still independent kingdom of Barue and was finally captured and imprisoned when that kingdom was defeated in 1902. Only two years later the kingdom of Barue broke into rebellion and tried to involve neighbouring peoples in a general uprising against the Portuguese. This initial Barue rebellion was rapidly repressed however.

The 1917 Barue rising: the first Mozambican liberation war

The involvement of Portugal in the struggle with Germany during the First World War resulted in the burdens of forced labour in Mozambique being greatly increased. In 1914 the construction of a strategic road through the Barue kingdom was begun and thousands of young people were forced to work on the project under appalling conditions. In addition able-bodied young men of military age were conscripted into the army. Nongwe-Nongwe, one of two rival claimants to the Barue throne, was inspired by the prophetic messages of a young girl spirit medium to raise a rebellion. He built a widespread coalition including the Tavara led by Chiramanzi, a claimant to the Mwene Mutapa throne. Thonga and Sena chiefs were also involved. The Chikunda and Nsenga were drawn into the struggle. The inhabitants of Gouveia's previous *prazo* of Gorongosa led by sons of Gouveia and one of his lieutenants also took part.

The rising took the Portuguese by surprise and early in 1917 quickly liberated most of the Tete and Sena districts of Mozambique. The two main centres were placed under siege and Zumbo was captured. Initial counter-attacks by the Portuguese were defeated. The Portuguese however succeeded in winning the support of the Ngoni by offers of money and the right to loot rebel areas. With this support the tide was turned and the Portuguese succeeded in suppressing the rebellion by October 1918. Even then small numbers of guerrillas fought on until 1920. With the collapse of the rebellion about 100 000 refugees fled to neighbouring Nyasaland and Southern Rhodesia.

Economic and political development of Mozambique

As Portugal was a very poor country it could not afford to invest much in the development of its African territories. Until 1930 much of Mozambique was administered by two chartered companies, the Niassa Company, largely British-owned, in the northern provinces and the Mozambique Company in Manica and Sofala. The Zambesia Company although it did not have administrative powers was given the right to exploit and develop the lands around the Zambezi.

These companies and the Portuguese administration rented *prazos* to smaller companies and individual settlers. Africans were subjected to heavy hut taxes and rents. In some areas (especially the northern provinces) they were forced to grow export crops like cotton and sell them to the companies at very low prices. The Portuguese regulation of 1899 openly provided for forced labour by the African population of the colonies. In 1928 it was modified to allow forced labour for public purposes only, but this made little difference in practice. Africans were forced to work on estates and plantations as well as on roads and public works. Thousands more were exported to South Africa and Southern Rhodesia as migrant workers. Under agreements with South Africa the Mozambique authorities received payment for every African recruited by the Witwatersrand Native Labour Association (WNLA). This was a major element in the finances of the colony. Portuguese rule was exercised by poorly paid and often under-educated white officials supported by poorly trained, ill-disciplined and underpaid African levies (*sepais*). Not surprisingly, local populations were frequently treated with great brutality. Throughout the colonial period refugees migrated out of the territory to the shelter of the milder colonial regimes in Nyasaland and the Rhodesias.

The Salazar dictatorship and its policies

In 1926 the army seized power in Portugal and two years later Antonio de Oliveira Salazar, an economics professor at Coimbra University, was made Minister of Finance. It proved the beginning of a personal dictatorship which lasted until he suffered a crippling stroke in 1968. Under Salazar's so-called New State, central government authority was greatly increased. The colonial administration was directly controlled from Lisbon. The chartered companies lost their administrative powers in Mozambique to government officials.

It was not however until after the Second World War that Portugal was able to undertake any major new development in Mozambique. Then major efforts began to be made in the hope of building a new prosperity in Portugal on the wealth of the colonies and settling Portuguese immigrants in them to relieve unemployment at home. It was also hoped to prevent the growth of colonial nationalism. In the 1950s the Portuguese undertook major developments in the Limpopo valley. Dams were built for irrigation as well as hydroelectric power. Portuguese settlers were established to farm the irrigated land and grouped around a number of new villages modelled on those in Portugal. A small number of Africans were also given farmland on the schemes. In the 1970s work began on the huge

Cabora Bassa complex on the Zambezi river. Apart from supplying cheap hydroelectric power to South Africa the dam was intended to allow irrigation of a huge area and to sustain massive further white settlement. While these schemes brought significant economic development to Mozambique, Africans saw them as means of reinforcing and increasing white domination. Between 1930 and 1973 the white population of the colony increased from 19 800 to about 200 000.

African nationalism in Mozambique

Even before the imposition of colonial rule was complete some educated Africans and persons of mixed descent began writing critical accounts of the Portuguese regime. One of these was Alfredo de Aguiar, a soldier of part-Angolan, part-white descent. He started a newspaper on Mozambique Island in 1885. From 1886 to 1894 it was published in Lourenço Marques (now Maputo). It was called *Clamor Africano*. It bitterly attacked forced labour and lack of education and job opportunities for Africans. In 1911 Jose Albasini published a paper *O Africano* in Shangana and Portuguese. It was suppressed in 1920. After 1911 associations of educated Africans arose in the main centres in Mozambique. Their members criticized discrimination and hoped to advance within the colonial system. One of these associations the Gremio Africano (African Guild) published a paper called *O Brado Africano* from 1918. Edited by the Albasini brothers it attacked discrimination and forced labour.

With the establishment of Salazar's New State, repression became more severe. After a critical editorial *O Brado Africano* was briefly suppressed. Jose Albasini then revived the name of Aguiar's paper and briefly published *O Clamor Africano*. Soon however the government moved in and took control of all African papers. It did the same to African societies and associations. The Associao Africano (African Association) which had grown out of the Gremio Africano was purged. The radicals on the Associao then formed the Instituto Negrofilo in the late 1930s. The government however purged this also and then allowed it to continue under government supervision as the Centro Associativo dos Negros de Moçambique. Even then the organization continued to be regarded with suspicion.

After the Second World War a number of black Mozambican writers expressed nationalist ideas but they were soon repressed. Workers expressed their resentment at the harsh working conditions in dockyards strikes in 1947 and 1956. They were forcibly suppressed with considerable loss of life.

The whites' drive for federation in Central Africa

Immediately after the establishment of colonial rule in British Central Africa, the whites in the three territories were confident of maintaining their supremacy over their African populations and of obtaining self-government. They saw no need to link up with South Africa or with each other. After the ending of the BSAC's administration this attitude changed however. Northern Rhodesian settlers began to fear that they would not be able to entrench their position and settlers in Southern Rhodesia became anxious to extend their control northwards after the discovery of Northern Rhodesia's mineral resources. They felt it would be safer to unite the territories to protect the whites from increasing African political activity. The small body of white settlers in Nyasaland was ever more keen for unification and so the long campaign for amalgamation began. As early as 1929 the Hilton Young Commission was appointed to look into the possibility of uniting the three territories together or joining them to the British East African territories. The commission was unable however to recommend immediate steps towards unification.

The Passfield Memorandum of 1929 was a great blow to settler confidence in the British government. They became convinced that their only hope of maintaining their supremacy was in uniting together and shaking off British rule. Plans were laid at an informal Victoria Falls Conference in 1936 and in response to settler agitation the Bledisloe Commission visited Central Africa in 1938. The Commission noted the economic interdependence of the territories and recommended unification in principle. It could not make any firm recommendation however because of its obligation to the African peoples in the northern territories and their strong opposition to any link with settler rule to the south.

During the war the idea of unification was not allowed to die. An inter-territorial council, the Central African Council, came into existence which in the years after the war launched a number of inter-territorial services like the Central African Airways.

The end of the Second World War brought the whole situation to a head. The war had exhausted Britain and the break up of her empire was only a matter of time. Northern Rhodesian copper was more important to Britain than ever and the settlers were therefore in a position to exert strong pressure on the British government. At the same time non-European nationalist movements were growing all over the world and the settlers would have to move quickly. Moreover racism had been condemned by world opinion. The settlers would have to make some concessions to Africans so that their policy would not be seen as openly racist.

By 1948 the settlers were ready for a second, attempt at achieving amalgamation. In Northern Rhodesia they had gained virtual control of the government. In Southern Rhodesia the governing party under Godfrey Huggins had won a resounding political victory. At the same time the victory of the Afrikaner nationalists in South Africa in 1948 with their openly racist philosophy of apartheid and their strong anti-British attitudes placed further pressure on Britain. The British government was very anxious to stop the settlers in the two Rhodesias joining with South Africa. White leaders in the three British Central African territories held a second conference at the Victoria Falls in 1949. They realized that an outright demand for the amalgamation of the three territories would be too much for the British government to accept and so they put forward the idea of a federation. To make their plans appear non-racist, they proclaimed a policy of multiracial partnership and co-operation. Africans in Northern Rhodesia and Nyasaland were not convinced however and the Secretary of State for the Colonies in the British government assured them that no move to join the three territories would be made until all the peoples had been consulted.

The settlers continued and increased their agitation and the Labour government in Britain saw itself in a perplexing position. There were strong arguments to show that federation would increase the prosperity of all the people of the area and would be most important in preventing the settlers from joining up with South Africa. The great copper companies saw federation as the greatest hope for economic stability and progress in the area and they put the weight of their influence behind the idea. The British government finally allowed British and Central African civil servants to meet in London to look at the technical aspects of the idea. By so doing they were partially committing themselves to federation.

The London conference met in 1951. It gave its approval to the federal scheme and drew up detailed proposals. A third conference was then held at Victoria Falls to which, at British insistence, some Africans from Nyasaland and Northern Rhodesia were invited. They showed themselves totally opposed to federation. During the conference the British Secretary of State for the Colonies heard that the British parliament was about to be dissolved and he therefore brought the conference to an abrupt end. Before leaving, however, he encouraged the conference to vote in favour of the principle of federation despite the strenuous opposition from the African delegates.

261

The establishment of the Central African Federation, 1953

The Conservative Party won the election in Britain and the new government announced its strong approval of the federal scheme for Central Africa. In spite of continuing African protests, the Central African Federation was brought into existence in 1953. Under the scheme each territory was to have its own government responsible for local administration. These separate territorial governments would be responsible for 'native affairs' within their territories. In addition, the British government would remain directly involved in the administration of the two northern Protectorates. As a further safeguard for African interests, an African Affairs Board was to be a Standing Committee of the Federal Parliament with power to intervene if any legislation was found to be racist. The legislation

The Central African Federation

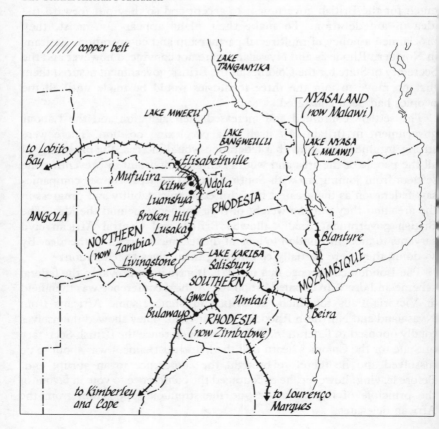

in question would then have to be referred to London for approval. The Federal Parliament had powers covering all matters involving more than one territory and was also responsible for foreign affairs.

The Federal Parliament was made up of thirty-five members. Seventeen came from Southern Rhodesia, eleven from Northern Rhodesia and seven from Nyasaland. Of the thirty-five members six were Africans, two from each territory. The African delegates from Northern Rhodesia and Nyasaland were chosen by the African Representative Councils in each territory. The two African delegates from Southern Rhodesia, however, were elected by the voters on the ordinary voting role, that is, whites.

The scheme was received with enthusiasm by the settlers in the two northern territories but met with considerable criticism from some whites in Southern Rhodesia. In a referendum of voters in Southern Rhodesia held to approve the introduction of federation the scheme was approved by a large majority. Nevertheless, about a third of the white voters in Southern Rhodesia voted against it as being too liberal.

The effect on African nationalism

The European drive for the creation of the Central African Federation stimulated the development of mass nationalist movements in Northern Rhodesia and Nyasaland, where Africans had long been strongly opposed to amalgamation with Southern Rhodesia. As the negotiations for federation proceeded, African nationalist movements turned from moderate to more outspoken and radical attitudes. They now found the mass of the African population eager to follow them. In Northern Rhodesia the Federation of African Societies which had become the Northern Rhodesian African National Congress was led by Harry Nkumbula. With the aid of a number of militant leaders, including Kenneth Kaunda, the party began creating a mass organization and launched an outspoken campaign against the Central African Federation. Nkumbula called for African self-government and warned that if a federation was imposed by force life would be made intolerable for whites in the territory. The Nyasaland African Congress developed along similar lines. In Britain a Malawian, Dr H. Kamuzu Banda, who had left his country early in youth for a long and successful career of study in Britain and America before settling in Britain as a doctor, gave the Congress movement full support and tried to persuade British public opinion against the federal scheme. With the establishment of the Federation however African opposition appeared hopeless and the settlers seemed sure of victory.

10 Central Africa since 1953

White politics in the Central African Federation

With the achievement of Federation the settlers in Northern Rhodesia (now Zambia), Southern Rhodesia (now Zimbabwe) and Nyasaland (now Malawi) had gained the first major step on the way to consolidating their dominance. Final victory still lay ahead however. It would only be secure when they had established their control over the whole Federation and could win independence from Britain. It had been agreed that the status and constitution of the Federation would be reviewed in 1960 and the settlers were determined that they would achieve their independence then. For this purpose it was necessary both to strengthen white control and to make such concessions to Africans as would convince Britain and the world at large of their good intentions. Apart from very limited African representation in the Federal Parliament, probably the most important concession was the establishment of the multiracial University College of Rhodesia and Nyasaland in Salisbury. But due to the limited educational opportunities for Africans, the student population was predominantly white and an increase in secondary education for Africans was not considered a high priority by the white-dominated government.

Under the principle of racial partnership, open racial discrimination in public places became illegal. A campaign was launched to break down the traditional colour bar. Even the Salisbury (now Harare) swimming baths were finally declared open to all races though this created extreme white antagonism. In spite of these concessions the main direction of policy under the Federation was towards strengthening the settler position. Federation led to an economic boom for Southern Rhodesia. The price of copper stayed high and profits increased in Southern Rhodesian industries which could now rely on an assured market in the two northern territories. Salisbury blossomed into a modern town of skyscrapers and the Kariba Dam was built on the Zambezi to provide power for industry. It created what was then the largest man-made lake in the world.

The Kariba Dam.

While Southern Rhodesia profited from Federation and Nyasaland may have made some gains Northern Rhodesia was the greatest loser. It saw the money earned from its mines drawn away to Salisbury and enjoyed relatively little development in return. Southern Rhodesia continued to encourage the immigration of white settlers on an unprecedented scale.

In 1957 and 1958 the Federal Parliament passed two measures designed to consolidate and increase white control of the Federation. These were the Constitution Amendment Act and a Franchise Act. These Acts increased the number of African representatives in the Federal Parliament but changed the way that they were to be chosen so that all of them would be elected by a mainly white electorate instead of by Africans as had been the case with those from Nyasaland and Northern Rhodesia. The African Affairs Board queried both measures but its protests were overruled in Britain. The settlers now looked forward to complete victory in 1960.

African nationalists destroy the Federation

Just as the settlers saw victory ahead the tide began to turn against them.

This was largely the result of events outside Central Africa. British experience of the Mau Mau in Kenya and French experiences in Indo-China and Algeria showed that attempts to suppress political ambitions of the majority in colonial countries could lead to expensive and futile struggles. In West Africa, Ghana was granted independence in 1957 and Nigeria and other colonies were clearly moving along the same road. Britain needed only to be convinced that the African majority in Nyasaland and Northern Rhodesia were likely to offer serious resistance to continued federal rule and were capable of forming viable governments which would not be too harmful to British interests. This the African leaders succeeded in proving.

Nationalism in Nyasaland

The situation in Nyasaland offered the most favourable opportunity for African nationalism. There were relatively few white settlers (3800 in 1950 rising to a peak of 9500 in 1960) and its people had experience of working in South Africa and Southern Rhodesia. They had no doubt of the danger of allowing their country to fall permanently under settler rule. As there was little white investment in the country moreover the supporters of the Federation would not be too upset to see Nyasaland leave so long as the two Rhodesias remained joined together. The introduction of the Federation sparked off violent riots in southern Nyasaland. Though suppressed, they showed the depth of African antipathy. After an initial setback following the establishment of Federation, the Nyasaland African Congress revived under the leadership of a set of new young leaders and spread widely through the country.

The young men who led the Congress felt they needed a leader who could command world respect and bring the struggle to a climax. Their thoughts turned to Dr H. Kamuzu Banda who had taken an active interest in the struggle against Federation when he was in England. At first he was reluctant to come but in July 1958 he accepted their invitation and arrived in Nyasaland. He soon gained overwhelming popularity with the people. Huge crowds turned out to listen to him denounce the 'stupid so-called federation'. By early 1959 it was clear that the vast majority of the people were behind him and the authorities felt that unless drastic action was taken they would lose control of the situation altogether.

Nationalism in Northern Rhodesia

In Northern Rhodesia also a more radical movement of African national-

Dr H. Kamuzu Banda

ism was developing. This was led by Kenneth Kaunda. He was the son of
a Livingstonia mission teacher, David Kaunda, who had come into the
country from Nyasaland to establish a mission at Lubwa. Later he had
taken part in forming the very first modern-style political organization in
the country, the Mwenzo Native Welfare Association in 1912. Like his
father, Kenneth worked as a primary school teacher. He became one of
Harry Nkumbula's chief supporters in the period of the struggle against
Federation. After the formation of the Federation, however, Kaunda and a
number of other young leaders in the Northern Rhodesian African

Dr Kenneth Kaunda, first President of Zambia, at the independence celebrations

National Congress (ANC) became frustrated with Nkumbula's increasingly moderate leadership. IN 1958 the governor, A.E.T. Benson, introduced a new constitution for the Protectorate. Kaunda and the young radicals felt it was unsatisfactory and called for a boycott. Nkumbula insisted on participation in the elections called under the new scheme. Kaunda and his supporters then broke away and founded a new party the Zambia African National Congress (ZANC) to struggle for full independence. Though Nkumbula's ANC kept support in the Tonga area of southern Zambia, ZANC spread rapidly in the rest of the country especially the Bemba-speaking areas. The administration was seriously alarmed.

Nationalism in Southern Rhodesia

By this time African nationalism had become a powerful movement in Southern Rhodesia as well. Stimulated by the upsurge of the movement to the north and by the effect of the 1951 Land Husbandry Act, the African National Congress (ANC) revived after 1957. Led by Joshua Nkomo it was rapidly growing into a formidable mass organization with support both in the towns and the countryside.

The authorities felt that the situation in Nyasaland had become so rious that it could only be brought under control by the use of troops om Southern Rhodesia. They feared, however, that this might trigger off a uprising in the south. A State of Emergency was thus declared in outhern Rhodesia though no violence had occurred. The ANC was anned and its leaders arrested. Then an emergency was declared in Nyasaland too, troops were flow in from Southern Rhodesia and Banda nd many other leaders were arrested. In Northern Rhodesia no state of mergency was declared but Kaunda and his followers were arrested and ne new ZANC was banned.

The Devlin and Monckton commissions

These measures were intended to preserve the Federation by destroying he leadership of African nationalism in the three territories. They had the pposite effect however. The British Parliament and public opinion were lerted to the dangers of the developing situation in Central Africa. A ommission under Lord Devlin concluded that the supposed plot which ad been the prextext for the arrest of Banda was a fabrication. Another ommission under Lord Monckton was sent out to consult public opinion hroughout the Federation and advise on the best way to maintain it. The Commission found that African opinion was bitterly opposed to the Federation. It concluded that the only hope of winning popular support for the Federation was to allow Africans in the two northern territories to enjoy elf-government and have the opportunity to leave the Federation if they wanted to.

The British government decided to come to terms with Banda, a relatively moderate leader, rather than allow more extreme elements to come o the fore. While he was in jail a new movement, the Malawi Congress Party, was formed and soon demonstrated that it had mass support. Banda vas released in 1960 as the British government had already decided to negotiate with him as the effective political leader of the majority of the people of Nyasaland. In June 1960 in London a constitution was agreed which put the country well on the way to majority rule. It was clear that the Federation could not possibly gain independence under settler rule in 1960.

In Northern Rhodesia the settlers were in a much stronger position than in Nyasaland. There too however the arrest of the ZANC leaders proved the beginning of the end of settler power. The arrested leaders became political martyrs and two new parties were formed to carry on the tradition of the banned ZANC. On 1 August 1959 they joined together to become the United National Independence Party. The new party spread like

wildfire and on his release Kaunda was able to take the leadership of
party clearly establishing itself as the main political movement for th
masses. This and the evidence of African opinion in Northern Rhodes
collected by the Monckton Commission convinced the British governmer
that there could be no peaceful solution to the problems of the countr
without giving Africans a far greater say in the territorial government an
winning Kaunda's support. Though the settler leaders under Roy Weler
sky, Prime Minister of the Federation, still hoped to gain independent a
the Federal Review Conference in London, they were wholly dis
appointed. The British government insisted that the constitution of th
territories had to be modified in a more democratic direction before an
major changes in the status of the Federation could be considered.

The achievement of independence in Nyasaland and Northern Rhodesia, 1964

In Nyasaland progress to majority rule was now straightforward. A cor
stitution based on majority rule was introduced and Banda won an over
whelming victory in the elections. He was uncompromising in his deter
mination to leave the Federation and make Nyasaland an independen
country. In Northern Rhodesia, however, the settlers were still deter
mined to fight for their supremacy and the salvation of the Federation
Early in 1961, the British Secretary of State for the Colonies, Iain Mac
leod, proposed a complex constitution for the country which would en
sure African majority rule in the Legislative Council but Welensky an
others brought pressure to bear so that it was modified to give the settler
continued dominance. This change brought widespread alarm and frustra
tion. Kaunda announced that unless the new proposals were withdrawn h
would 'paralyse' the government. Though Kaunda insisted that protest
should be peaceful, violent upheavals and a rash of acts of sabotage too
place over wide areas of the country. The upheaval was called the Cha
Cha-Cha. It was suppressed with the use of troops but the British govern
ment was now convinced that African nationalism was too strong to b
repressed without severe bloodshed. The constitutional proposals wer
again altered to give Africans a small majority.

Faced with the final constitutional change, the settlers fell back on on
last hope; to accept the inevitability of an African-led government fo
Northern Rhodesia and to work for an alliance with the ANC in the hop
that this would still be controlled by whites and would agree to remain in
the Federation. This seemed a hopeful idea because of the role which
Moise Tshombe was playing in Katanga at that time. As a result of the

elections held in 1962, the two African parties between them held a slight majority of seats but the settler party remained the largest single group. If Nkumbula had agreed to go along with the settlers' plan, they might have succeeded. His loyalty to African nationalism and pressure from within his own party however led him to form a coalition with Kaunda's UNIP. The triumph of African nationalism in Northern Rhodesia was assured and the Federation was doomed. On 31 December 1963 the Central African Federation, which had been established ten years earlier to consolidate settler rule in Central Africa, was dissolved. On 6 July 1964 Nyasaland became the independent state (later Republic) of Malawi and on 24 October 1964 Northern Rhodesia became the Republic of Zambia.

Southern Rhodesia: the 1961 constitution

When the Southern Rhodesia ANC was banned and its leaders were arrested under the State of Emergency declared in 1959 a new party, the National Democratic Party, was formed in January 1960. It soon demonstrated that it had mass support. Thus the development of African nationalism seemed to follow a path similar to the two territories to the north. The situation in Southern Rhodesia was very different however. The country was in many ways a small South Africa. Above all the settlers were self-governing and had their own military forces. African nationalism therefore did not face a British government which was primarily concerned with trade and disinclined to enter upon an expensive war of colonial repression. Instead they faced a government of settlers determined to preserve their supremacy and racial privileges. Thus in the constitutional conference of 1961 the territory did not gain majority rule like Zambia and Malawi but only a new constitution which provided for African representation but aimed at maintaining settler control for a prolonged period.

Joshua Nkomo first agreed to accept this new constitution but then changed his mind. This proved an important turning point in Southern Rhodesia's history, for Whitehead's United Federal Party, deprived of the support of African voters, was defeated by the even more racist Rhodesian Front (RF). The National Democratic Party was banned but once again emerged in a new form as the Zimbabwe African People's Union (ZAPU). It found however that while the two northern territories were moving towards independence under African rule, Southern Rhodesia was controlled by the more extreme supporters of white dominance. Frustrations and a distrust of Nkomo's leadership led to a split in the African nationalist opposition in 1963. Ndabaningi Sithole and a number of other young leaders broke away from ZAPU and founded the Zimbabwe African National Union (ZANU). In the short run the split gravely weakened African nationalism in Southern Rhodesia. As the two parties struggled with each other for the allegiance of the people they lost any chance they might have had of influencing the course of political development at a crucial stage.

Triumph of the Rhodesian Front, 1962

The settlers in Southern Rhodesia had been attracted to the idea of Federation to gain access to the mineral wealth of Northern Rhodesia and because they believed it to be the best means of continuing white supremacy. For these objectives they had been prepared to make some concessions to the African majority. Even at the time of Federation however a substantial body of whites in Southern Rhodesia opposed these concessions. They doubted the wisdom of linking with the north and tended to look to closer relations with South Africa. With the loss of the northern territories by the settlers it was inevitable that Southern Rhodesian whites would turn their political direction to the south. It was thus not surprising that the ruling United Federal Party was defeated in the 1962 election by the RF with its strong racist attitude and pro-South Africa bias.

The unilateral declaration of independence, 1965

The direction of British policy north of the Zambezi led white Rhodesians to believe that any connection with Britain, however slight, was a dangerous lever which might be used in favour of African political advancement. They decided that full independence was the only way of obtaining white supremacy forever. The British government however insisted on five principles which would have to be adhered to before independence was granted. One of these was unimpeded progress to majority rule. The whole point of independence for the settlers however was to prevent such a political development. An agreement was clearly impossible and the party began to think of declaring independence unilaterally. The first RF Prime Minister, Winston Field, drew back from such action and was replaced by Ian Smith. Smith waited for the outcome of the British general election in 1965. The result was a victory for the Labour Party which would certainly not give the Rhodesian settlers what the Conservatives had refused. But its majority was very small and it was therefore in too weak a position to take very strong measures against any action by the settlers. As the crisis came

Released temporarily from detention, Joshua Nkomo (*right*) and other African political leaders were able to talk to British Prime Minister Harold Wilson (*left*) in October 1965. The whites, however, were resolute, and UDI followed in November

to a head the Britain Prime Minister, Harold Wilson, warned white Rhodesians of the tragic consequences of a unilateral declaration of independence. At the same time, however, he assured them that Britain would not use force against them. This was all that Smith needed and on 11 November 1965 he declared independence unilaterally.

Consequences of Rhodesia's unilateral declaration of independence

Smith's unilateral declaration of independence (UDI) was an act of rebellion against the authority of Britain. His regime was not recognized by any other country. From the point of view of international law Britain remained responsible for Rhodesia as the country was now called – Northern Rhodesia having become Zambia. Smith and his associates were just a gang of outlaws. Nevertheless Smith had many supporters in Britain as most of the white settlers had kith and kin there. Wilson, with his tiny parliamentary majority, was in an awkward position. He had already promised not to use force so he had to rely on economic pressures. He was

A Rhodesian newspaper on the day after UDI

even reluctant to apply any meaningful economic sanctions. It became clear, however, that Smith was not going to give up UDI easily and Britain felt bound to apply economic sanctions and ask the United Nations to make them binding on the whole world community. For the campaign of economic sanctions to have any appearance of seriousness it was essential that Zambia be persuaded to take part. Wilson urged Kaunda to do so, promising that the Smith regime would be brought down in 'weeks rather than months'. However, so long as the Portuguese authorities in Mozambique together with the government of South Africa gave their support to Smith and helped him evade sanctions the whole system was very ineffective.

In spite of a British naval patrol off Mozambique the Smith regime continued to be supplied with ample petrol and other essentials. By raising the price of imports the sanctions actually gave a boost to manufacturing industry in Rhodesia. Instead of Rhodesia it was Zambia that felt the main impact of the economic sanctions. Just as the newly independent government was beginning to try to tackle the problems of its colonial heritage, the Rhodesian regime cut off essential supplies of petrol. Zambia's entire development was very badly damaged by the need to concentrate on the problems of finding alternative routes for essential imports and exports. Zambia was also faced with serious problems by the influx of many refugees from Rhodesia as well as from Mozambique and Angola.

Beginnings of the freedom struggle (*Chimurenga*)

With the declaration of UDI and the British refusal to use force to end the rebellion, both ZAPU and ZANU prepared to launch an armed freedom struggle. Early in 1966 the first armed clash between ZANU freedom fighters and troops of the illegal regime took place at Sinoia. The first attempts of the freedom fighters were poorly organized and ill-prepared however. Inadequate political work had been undertaken in the African villages before the freedom fighters went in. They sometimes found a very poor reception and were even betrayed to the security forces. It would be several years before adequate training of guerrilla fighters and satisfactory political preparation in the villages could be completed. In the meantime the freedom fighters did not pose a serious threat and the whites openly mocked their efforts.

Talks, talks about talks, and more talks

Though the Smith regime was in open rebellion, the British government under Wilson was very anxious to reach an agreement with it that would allow Britain to grant legal independence and so be rid of responsibility. To do this, however, Britain had to insist on conditions which at least looked like conforming to the five principles it had always demanded.

Very soon after UDI British officials began 'talks about talks' with the Smith regime. These were followed by a summit meeting between Smith and Wilson on the British warship *Tiger*. Wilson agreed to settlement proposals that were very favourable to the white minority but the Smith regime felt so strong that members of his cabinet refused to accept the deal. After more 'talks about talks' a second summit meeting was held on the warship *Fearless* but no agreement was reached. The high point of the Smith regime's drive to gain internationally recognized independence and consolidate white minority rule for the indefinite future came in 1971. In Britain the Labour Party had been defeated by the Conservatives. While the new government still formally insisted on the five principles, it was more sympathetic than Labour to the Rhodesian whites and was determined to reach an agreement with them. After more lengthy talks the Foreign Secretary, Sir Alec Douglas-Home, succeeded in reaching an agreement with Smith. The settlement proposals appeared to offer progress to majority rule over a fairly lengthy period but contained several loopholes which would allow the whites to stop this and keep their domination indefinitely. Smith seemed to have achieved his object.

The Pearce Commission and the ANC: Africans say no

One of the principles that Britain had insisted upon had been that an settlement must be broadly acceptable to 'the people of Rhodesia as whole'. The Smith regime was confident that most Africans apart from few agitators were happy under white rule. They agreed that a British Royal Commission should visit Rhodesia and hold discussions with a sections of the population. Even when Bishop Abel Muzorewa of th African Episcopal Church began organizing a movement (later called th African National Congress – ANC) to encourage Africans to say no, th regime was still confident.

When the Pearce Commission met African communities however an explained the meaning of the settlement they were answered by a stron loud and clear 'No!' The Smith regime tried to maintain that this was th result of intimidation and misinterpretation by members of Muzorewa' organization. The Pearce Commission was accompanied by televisio reporters, however, and the behaviour and attitude of the crowds could b seen by the whole world. The Pearce Commission had to report that th settlement terms were not acceptable to the majority of the population an the British government had no option but to drop them. Smith had failed to achieve his aim just when he appeared certain of success.

The whole Pearce Commission exercise proved a disaster for the Smith regime in other ways as well. It showed Britain, South Africa and th world at large the depth and extent of African rejection of white minority rule in Rhodesia. It showed that the regime would be unlikely to survive for very long even if it gained legal independence. Finally it showed Africans who disliked the regime that this hatred was shared by almost every other African throughout the land. It thus played a very important part in preparing the ground for the spread of the liberation struggle.

The freedom struggle (*Chimurenga*) takes hold

The Pearce Commission exercise exposed the weakness of the Smith regime but freedom would not have been achieved without the heroic efforts of the freedom fighters. By 1972 ZANU infiltrators organized in the Zimbabwe National Liberation Army (ZANLA) had done enough ground work in the north-eastern districts of Rhodesia for a new phase of the freedom struggle to be launched. From then on the guerrilla war took hold and never stopped until liberation was achieved. The new phase in the freedom struggle depended on careful political preparation among the African villages. It also depended on the progress of the freedom struggle against the Portuguese in neighbouring Mozambique.

Nationalism in Mozambique

In spite of Portuguese repression in Mozambique, a number of small nationalist groups came into existence in the 1950s and 1960s. They were inspired by the achievements of Kwame Nkrumah in Ghana, Julius Nyerere in Tanzania and the struggle against Federation in Zambia and Malawi. By 1960 African migrants and refugees from Mozambique had established several political movements in exile. One of these was called the União Nacional Democrática de Moçambique (the National Democratic Union of Mozambique – Udenamo). Its founders came mainly from southern and central Mozambique. The movement was formed in Salisbury in 1960. Another though smaller movement called União Africano de Moçambique Independence (African Union of Independent Mozambique — Unami) was formed by Mozambican exiles in Malawi.

The Makonde peoples who lived in the northernmost districts of Mozambique had particularly bitter experiences of colonial exploitation. They were forced to grow cotton which the Niassa Company bought at very low prices. In the 1950s they formed a co-operative organization to try and get a better return but the government repressed this in the interests of the Company. In 1957 the Makonde migrants from Mozambique living in Tanganyika created the Tanganyika Mozambique Makonde Union. In 1961 inspired by the success of the Tanganyika African National Union (TANU) under the leadership of Nyerere, the Makonde Union turned itself into a national movement called the Mozambique National Union (MANU). Agitation in the Makonde area was followed in 1961 by the arrest of a number of leaders by the Portuguese. The authorities then invited the people to come to the administrative centre at Mueda where the district governor would listen to their grievances. When the people gathered, however, any leaders who spoke out were immediately arrested. The crowd became angry and troops opened fire, killing 600.

In December that year, following the achievement of independence by Tanzania, Udenamo and Unami as well as MANU set up headquarters in Dar es Salaam. They were encouraged to get together by Nyerere and Nkrumah. In June 1962 they held a conference and agreed to form a common Frente de Libertação de Moçambique (Front for the Liberation of Mozambique – Frelimo). Eduardo Mondlane was chosen as the movement's first president. From the outset the movement planned to launch a guerrilla struggle for the liberation of its country. In 1963 the first small group of recruits was sent for training as freedom fighters to Algeria and Egypt. That year the Organization of African Unity (OAU) recognized the movement and it was the only one in Mozambique to be aided by the

Dr Eduardo Mondlane on his arrival in Dar es Salaam in March 1963

organization. By August 1964 it had infiltrated about 250 freedom fighters into the Makonde district. Frelimo adopted a policy of undertaking political work in the villages to win the loyalty of the people and explain the need for the struggle before starting military action. Then the freedom fighters would operate in small groups from bases inside the country using arms smuggled in advance. In the aftermath of the Mueda massacre Frelimo freedom fighters met a warm welcome in the Makonde country. They were able to start active operations in September 1964 and soon gained a further hold over most of the area outside of the main centres and started setting up their own administration, schools and health services. They were aided by the fact that the area was remote from the main centres of Portuguese authority and had very few roads. On the other hand it lay close to the Tanzanian border. During 1965 Frelimo also began to make progress in winning over the Nyanja-speaking people who occupied a narrow strip down the eastern shore of Lake Malawi. With their support the war spread south towards the Tete district around the Zambezi where the main Portuguese development effort was concentrated.

Divisions and setbacks: the assassination of Mondlane

In spite of its early successes Frelimo suffered considerable internal political problems. Soon after it was formed Mondlane had to return to the United States to complete his teaching commitments at an American university and during his absence conflict led to a number of breakaways. On his return in 1964 the organization recovered but some of the rebels would not come back and formed a rival movement. It was called the Comite Revolucionario de Moçambique (the Revolutionary Committee of Mozambique – Coremo). Coremo established headquarters in Zambia and engaged in limited guerrilla fighting in Tete district. It failed to gain recognition or support from the OAU however and without this support could not mount a major war effort. It remained very small and never became a significant rival to Frelimo.

Conflicts and rivalries still persisted within Frelimo and culminated in 1969 when Frelimo dissidents conspired with the Portuguese to assassinate Mondlane in Dar es Salaam with a parcel bomb. His death on 3 February seriously weakened the organization. He was replaced by Samora Machel who came from the area of the Gaza kingdom in southern Mozambique and had originally left the country as a medical student. He had been one of the early recruits sent for military training in Algeria.

The Portuguese counter-offensive: Operation Gordian Knot

In 1969 to 1970 the Portuguese commander, General de Arriaga, launched a massive military exercise called Operation Gordian Knot to smash Frelimo's hold in northern Mozambique. A force of 35 000 troops was used and military action was backed by a major programme of road building. Thousands of Africans were resettled in protected villages. To meet the demand for military manpower the Portuguese had to rely increasingly on African soldiers. They came to constitute 60 per cent of the total Portuguese army in Mozambique. By the end of 1970 de Arriaga claimed to have broken the guerrilla movement. Though it had certainly suffered severely and could not operate as openly as before, Frelimo's political hold on the northern districts remained strong. It was also able to keep open its corridor down Lake Malawi and in 1971 began to extend operations in the Tete districts. During 1972 it established a sufficient hold in areas adjoining north-eastern Rhodesia to provide liberated bases for ZANU to start guerrilla warfare in that area. During 1973 and early

Samora Machel (*right foreground*) with fellow Frelimo freedom fighters

1974 Frelimo continued to expand its activities southwards into the areas occupied by Shona-speaking peoples. A major effort was made to halt the completion of the Cabora Bassa dam project. This was not successful but forced the Portuguese to expend massive resources on its defence.

The 1974 revolution in Portugal and the independence of Mozambique

By 1974 the strain on Portuguese resources created by the guerrilla struggle in Mozambique, Angola and Guinea Bissau reached breaking point. While the majority of the Portuguese population was desperately poor, far the greater part of Portugal's budget was going on its colonial wars. To keep up military manpower the dictatorship was forced to conscript all young men of military age for a period of service. Most resented this and saw no point in endangering their lives in far away African countries they had no interest in. Many officers came to realize that the struggle could never be won and was bleeding their country to death for no purpose. In April 1974 young officers who formed an organization called Movimento das Forcas Armadas (Movement of the Armed Forces) led a military coup, overthrew the dictatorship in Portugal and opened the way to democracy. The new government hesitated at first to give full independence to the African colonies. In Mozambique the Portuguese negotiated with Frelimo with a view to a compromise solution of semi-independence. Frelimo would not accept this however and took advantage of the cease-fire to extend its political activities rapidly throughout the southern districts of the country. Finally the Portuguese agreed to grant full independence in June 1975. Settlers in Mozambique then attempted a coup to prevent this. They did not have army support, however, and their attempt quickly collapsed. It resulted in a large number of the white settlers fleeing the country or being expelled. On 25 June 1975 Mozambique became independent under a Frelimo government headed by Machel.

The tide begins to turn in Rhodesia

In north-eastern Rhodesia, meanwhile, the guerrilla struggle launched in 1972 by ZANLA, the military wing of ZANU, took a firm hold. Benefiting from the experience of Frelimo, the ZANLA freedom fighters took care to prepare the political ground before undertaking military action. Once they had the political loyalty of the villagers it proved impossible for

ZIPRA forces undergoing instruction near the Rhodesian border

the security forces to root them out. ZAPU, which had its base in Zambia, also built up its military wing, the Zimbabwe People's Revolutionar Army (ZIPRA). Its forces were aided in equipment and training by the Soviet Union. Unlike ZANLA, however, they did not take much active part in guerrilla warfare within the country until a very late stage in the struggle. As the strain on the Smith regime became more serious it needed to lean on the help of South Africa, and units of the South African police became involved in the struggle against the freedom fighters. Co-operation with the Portuguese was also stepped up. Rhodesian forces took part in attacks on Frelimo in the border areas. Top military officers of South Africa, Rhodesia and Portugual held regular planning meetings.

The collapse of the Portuguese regime and the independence of Mozambique however altered the whole strategic picture. The Smith regime's main import/export route to Beira was now cut and Rhodesia was open to infiltration along its entire lengthy frontier with Mozambique. The South African Prime Minister, B.J. Vorster, realized that white Rhodesia was unlikely to survive. There was therefore no point in South Africa continuing to support it. South Africa's best policy was to get a moderate black government established by negotiation. Vorster thus negotiated with Kaunda who also wanted to see the war ended by negotiation as quickly as possible. Vorster pressured Smith while Kaunda, together with the presidents of the other 'frontline' states – Tanzania, Botswana and Mozambique – urged the African political movements to negotiate. Under this pressure Smith released ZAPU's leader Joshua Nkomo and ZANU's Ndabaningi Sithole. Meeting in Lusaka they agreed to join together under the chairmanship of Bishop Muzorewa in a single movement called the African National Congress. A meeting was arranged between the Zimbabwe African leaders and Smith. Arrangements were also made for Kaunda and Vorster to meet in a railway train halted in the middle of the bridge over the Zambezi at the Victoria Falls. Though Vorster and Kaunda met, Smith was not prepared to consider handing over to African rule. He used disagreement between the African leaders as an excuse for aborting a meeting. Nkomo then went on to negotiate with Smith on his own. Smith however was not prepared to make significant concessions and the talks collapsed.

Leadership changes in the liberation movement and the Kissinger initiative

The union of the liberation movements in the ANC did not prove very long-lasting. Nkomo broke away to pursue negotiations with Smith. With-n ZANU there were differences of opinion on whether negotiations offered any hope or whether the war should be stepped up. In 1975 ZANU's national chairman, a supporter of a tough line, was assassinated in Zambia. A number of ZANU leaders were then arrested in connection with this and in an attempt to force the party to keep to the cease-fire that had been agreed with Smith. In this period the political leadership headed by Sithole became increasingly out ot touch with fighting men in the ZANLA camps in Mozambique. Sithole was finally rejected and leadership passed to Robert Mugabe. Sithole continued to led a splinter group claiming to be the true ZANU.

In September 1976 the US Secretary of State, Henry Kissinger, launched a new attempt to bring an end to the war in Zimbabwe. After the disastrous failure of American intervention in Angola he felt that the interests of the United States could best be served by backing the movement towards majority rule. He hoped that this would prevent the liberation movements from drawing closer to the Communist world. Kissinger held talks with Vorster and the leaders of the 'frontline' states. He then talked to Smith. Under pressure from South Africa, Smith agreed to proposals for a change to majority rule in two years. A conference under British chairmanship was held in Geneva from October to December. In this situation the two liberation movements came together in a loose alliance called the Patriotic Front. At the conference Smith insisted that whites should hold the key ministries giving control of the security forces in the transitional government. He also insisted that this transitional government should hold power for almost all the two-year period. The African leaders, however, had copies of a secret Rhodesian cabinet paper which seemed to suggest that the transitional arrangements might be used as a blind to build up and re-equip the Smith regime's forces and lead the African leaders into a trap. They insisted on changes which Smith rejected and the talks collapsed.

Thereafter the pace of the freedom struggle rapidly expanded. Young Zimbabweans abandoned school classrooms in growing numbers and crossed the frontiers to joint the fight. Guerrilla activity spread to all parts of the country and ZIPRA forces coming in from Zambia and Botswana began taking an active part alongside ZANLA. The Smith regime responded with stepped-up military action and a massive programme of population resettlement in protected villages. It also launched terror raids into Mozambique and Zambia. Despite the impact of these measure which gravely disrupted the freedom movements and their host countries, guerrilla activity continued growing. Mounting insecurity forced many white farmers to abandon their land and increasing numbers of whites began leaving Rhodesia altogether. The Smith regime was forced to rely increasingly on African soldiers for its army. The cost of the military effort and equipment became too great for the Rhodesian economy, hampered by international sanctions, to bear.

The internal settlement

The Rhodesian military leaders saw that a political solution was essential. Smith was forced to realize that a changeover to a black government was inevitable. He was still determined not to let real power slip from white hands however. So he rejected a new Anglo-American peace plan and instead held negotiations with those African leaders who had no military backing. He believed they would be likely to accept a compromise arrangement. They were Bishop Muzorewa, Sithole and Jeremiah Chirau. Chirau was a government-appointed chief who had been a minister in the Smith government and then resigned to form a pro-government party, the Zimbabwe United People's Organization (ZUPO). In March 1978 Smith and the three African leaders agreed on proposals for a new constitution. They provided for a changeover to black majority rule but with such checks and restrictions that white privileges would be fully protected. Whites would also continue to hold the key positions of power in the civil service, army and police for a long time.

In the meantime the 'frontline' states had agreed to give exclusive support to the Patriotic Front, and this was supported by the OAU. Britain and the United States also refused to recognize the internal settlement regime. After the agreement a transitional government was set up consisting of the three African leaders and Smith. In April 1979 elections were held for the first government to be formed under the internal settlement constitution. For the first time all adult Africans were able to vote. The Patriotic Front called for a boycott of the elections but the regime succeeded in persuading and forcing a very high proportion of the voters to turn out. They gave Bishop Muzorewa's United African National Council a big majority and he became Prime Minister. The name of the country was changed at this time to Zimbabwe–Rhodesia. The successful election exercise gave a great boost to the internal settlement regime. It gave the impression that it had the support of the majority of the population of all races. Africans who had voted for Muzorewa, however, had not had the opportunity of voting for either of the Patriotic Front leaders. It was obvious also that Muzorewa had little real power to change things in favour of Africans. When Byron Hove, a member of his cabinet, called for rapid Africanization of the army, police and civil service he was forced to resign. When Muzorewa wanted to appoint an African to a top official position he found that constitutional provisions protecting the rights of seniority in government service made this impossible. The world at large still refused to recognize the internal settlement regime. Most important of all the freedom struggle continued and the level of violence continued to grow. To counter this, Muzorewa and Sithole were encouraged to organize their supporters as armed auxiliaries. These private armies further increased the violence and disruption affecting the lives of the mass of the population.

Zimbabwe achieves independence, 1980

In Britain many Conservatives favoured recognizing the Muzorewa regime and ending British responsibility for Rhodesia. The Prime Minister, Margaret Thatcher virtually promised to do so. During the August 1979 meeting of the Commonwealth Heads of Government in Lusaka, however, she changed her mind. In response to the wishes of the 'front-line' states she agreed to call a constitutional conference of all parties. The internal regime authorities badly needed a political settlement to end the war. After the recent election triumph they were confident that Muzorewa would win in an open vote. They agreed to take part and the conference was held at Lancaster House in London. At the conference a new constitution was agreed which removed many of the restrictions in the internal settlement system. New elections were to be held for a government to lead the country to independence. In the meantime the regime formally surrendered its independence and a transitional government headed by a British Governor, Lord Soames, was set up. A cease-fire came into effect and all freedom fighters had to go to a series of camps where they gave up their arms.

White Rhodesians were confident at first that Muzorewa would win and that the Patriotic Front leaders would lose all basis for continuing the struggle. White confidence was increased by the fact that the two sections of the Patriotic Front decided to fight the elections independently. This confidence was badly shaken however when they saw the massive crowds who turned out to welcome the return of Nkomo. Their anxiety turned to panic when the still larger and obviously overjoyed crowds who greeted Mugabe were seen. There was talk of a white coup and frantic efforts were made to get ZANU banned. It was too late however. In the elections ZANU's wing of the Patriotic Front won an overall majority. It received 63 per cent of all the votes cast. Nkomo's ZAPU branch of the Patriotic Front came next but very far behind. Between them the two wings of the Patriotic Front took no less than 87 per cent of all the votes in an

Robert Mugabe, Zimbabwe's first
Prime Minister

exceptionally high poll. Muzorewa's UANC and the supporters of other
internal settlement leaders were humiliatingly defeated. White voters
however still clung to Smith and his Rhodesian Front. He won all the
twenty seats reserved for whites. After the election, Mugabe became
Prime Minister and led the country to independence on 18 April 1980. He
promised a policy of reconciliation and set out to unite all sections of the
population in the task of national reconstruction.

Zambia since independence

The long struggle beginning with Rhodesia's UDI posed serious problems
for the newly independent nations of Zambia and Malawi. They responded in very different ways.

Zambia had the advantage of relative wealth provided by its copper-
mining industry. On the other hand the colonial period had left the
country with very serious problems. Probably the most basic was the grave
difference between the prosperity of the Copperbelt and line of rail areas
and the great poverty of the rural areas. Most of these had been allowed to
degenerate into little more than breeding reserves for migrant workers.
Zambia's economy had been developed as an integral part of the white-
ruled Southern African complex. Its transport and communication systems were overwhelmingly oriented towards the south. It was almost
entirely dependent on a single product, copper, for its foreign exchange
and it imported almost all manufactured products, many of them from
Rhodesia. The copper mines were owned by foreign companies, one of
which was very closely linked to South Africa. Then there was the acute

problem of the great difference in income and life style between the previously dominant white minority and the African majority. Bitterness over this was made worse by open race discrimination. Because of this discrimination Zambia at independence had pathetically few of its citizens with advanced education or technical skills. It had only about a hundred Africans with university degrees and hardly any with advanced mining or other related skills. A massive educational effort was essential and in the meantime the economy of the country would be heavily dependent on the continued services of white expatriates, many of whom were deeply racially prejudiced.

In addition to these problems, the peoples of Zambia had had little opportunity to develop a sense of nationhood. There were natural rivalries and suspicions between the peoples belonging to different language groupings. As independence approached, the Litunga, traditional head of the Lozi kingdom, fearing for the loss of his kingdom's special position, had sought separation from Zambia. After the formation of UNIP, Harry Nkumbula's ANC had remained strong among the Tonga and related peoples. Within UNIP itself, there were barely concealed rivalries between the members of different ethnic communities.

During the colonial period many Zambians had reacted to white colonial oppression by turning to religious cults which rejected any participation in the state. The African Watchtower (Jehovah's Witnesses) was the largest of these. On the eve of independence however it was another such cult, the Lumpa Church headed by Alice Lenshina, which posed the most serious threat. The Lumpas not only rejected participation in politics but tried to set up a government of their own in the areas where they were strong. The army had to be used to suppress them and 700 were killed.

Hardly had the Lumpas been crushed when Smith's UDI posed a further series of desperate problems. Once Zambia agreed to comply with sanctions against Rhodesia the country had to seek alternative sources for the many products previously imported from there. The Smith regime moreover retaliated by refusing to allow essential petrol supplies to be transported through Rhodesia to Zambia. Zambia was thus placed under siege and had to develop new routes with great urgency.

Problems following UDI

The situation following UDI moreover greatly increased racial tension in Zambia. Many whites openly favoured the Smith regime. The situation was particularly serious in the security forces where many white officers continued to feel loyalty to their fellows south of the Zambezi. It thus became necessary to replace many senior police officers at short notice. Their African replacements had not had adequate training. Police efficiency and morale slumped severely just as problems of crime, law and order were escalating. In these circumstances only the outstanding leadership of Kaunda prevented the country from disintegrating. Strict petrol rationing was introduced. Supplies were flown in and carried on lorries and trucks over the difficult routes of the untarred Great East Road from Malawi and the Great North Road (known as the hell run) from Tanzania. Massive road works to convert these to all-weather highways were launched. An oil pipeline was built through Tanzania. Plans were also made to break the stranglehold of the Southern African routes by building a new railway from the Tanzanian coast. With Chinese aid the Tan-Zam (Tazara) Railway was completed in 1974. Through these measures Smith's attempt to bring Zambia to its knees was defeated. The total dependence of the country on southern routes was alleviated.

At the same time the shortage of African trained manpower was vigorously tackled. Secondary education was massively expanded. In 1966 the University of Zambia opened and in a few years was training top-level manpower for almost every aspect of national life. Technical education also received a tremendous boost. Dependence on Rhodesian-controlled power supplies was much reduced by building a hydroelectric dam on the Kafue River and a further set of generators on the northern side of the Kariba dam. Zambia also found and developed its own coal mines to replace supplies from Rhodesia's Wankie coalfield. A major effort was undertaken to diversify the country by establishing a manufacturing industry which produced textiles and a wide range of consumer goods.

The economic reforms

To give the nation greater control over the economy most major businesses were brought wholly or mainly under government control, starting with the Mulungushi Reforms in 1968. This programme was extended in 1973 to give the nation a controlling share of the mining industry. By the 1980s virtually all mining, manufacturing, insurance and large-scale commercial activity as well as public transport and communication services were controlled and coordinated through a series of massive national corporations.

On the other hand the urgent need to build new transport routes and educational institutions left few resources available for the development of the rural areas. The situation in these areas was made even worse by reforms aimed at limiting trading licences to Zambian citizens. This was intended to open opportunities for Africans and break the near monopoly of Indian traders. The result however was that in many rural areas Indian traders were forced out of business but no Africans had the capital or business skill to replace them. Shopping centres just closed down and the people were made poorer than ever.

The pressures of UDI made racial tensions worse and in that atmosphere it was out of the question to force Africans who took over senior posts to accept lower incomes than their white predecessors and colleagues. The emerging black élite thus inherited the life style and consumption patterns of the departing whites. Elite members soon came to share many of their attitudes as well. It was also impossible in the circumstances to hold back the demand from black mine workers for large pay rises to narrow the gap between them and the white skilled workers. Massive pay rises were thus given in 1966. This reduced the profits of the mines and discouraged employment. In the explosive political situation it was also impossible to impose a sufficient degree of discipline on African workers at all levels of the economy or among UNIP party workers themselves. Slackness, inefficiency, drunkenness and abuse of position became notoriously widespread. In this situation the gap between urban and rural living standards became even greater than in colonial times. People abandoned the rural areas and flocked into the towns in uncontrollable numbers. As urban housing and employment could not be expanded fast enough, slum shanty towns multiplied. Growing numbers remained unemployed or underemployed and crime boomed. These problems were made worse by the immigration of large numbers of refugees from Rhodesia, Angola and Mozambique. At this time the efficiency of the police had declined. Crime became very largely out of control.

Divisions within UNIP

At the political level Kaunda faced an early problem when he dismissed a Lozi member of his cabinet, Nalumino Mundia. Mundia formed a breakaway party. This did not pose a very serious threat until after the UNIP annual party conference at Mulungushi in 1966. At that conference there was open voting for senior party officials. Bemba-speaking members led by Simon Kapwepwe and Tonga-speakers lined up against Lozi- and Nyanja-speakers from the Eastern Province. As a result of the changes in the balance of power in the party the senior Eastern Province leader Reuben Kamanga lost his position as Vice-President to Kapwepwe and the senior Lozi in the cabinet, Arthur Wina, lost the ministry of finance. The Lozi were also suffering the consequences of the ending of migrant labour to South Africa and had so far seen little development in their area. They turned increasingly to Mundia's party. As the ANC remained in control of much of the Tonga area the breakaway party was a serious threat to UNIP. Because of the Rhodesian situation, Kaunda felt that security was at stake. Mundia was detained and his party banned.

Another more serious crisis occurred in 1971. By this time the peoples of the Eastern Province, loosely organized as the 'unity of the east' (Mmodzi wa mawa), had linked up with Lozi and Tonga against the Bemba-speakers. They repeatedly protested against Bemba predominance. Kapwepwe responded by protesting against the persecution of the Bemba and eventually walked out of UNIP with a number of followers. He founded the United People's Party (UPP). Tension in the country was very high. Kapwepwe and a number of other members of the new party were arrested and detained. Then in December 1972 legislation was passed making Zambia a one-party state. The following year Kapwepwe and most of his colleagues were released. The creation of a one-party state was intended to reduce the danger of ethnic rivalries. It was also hoped that it would enable the party to mobilize the whole population for the work of development. The measure may have had some success in keeping the country from breaking apart on ethnic lines in the difficult times that followed. Unfortunately the second objective was not achieved. Attempts to impose discipline on party members were not very successful. They became increasingly cut off from the mass of the people.

After 1973 Zambia's problems became more severe. The Rhodesian border was completely closed. The rail line to Angola was also constantly threatened by Unita guerrillas. This put an excessive burden on the northern routes. The Tan-Zam (Tazara) railway when finally opened was not able to cope with the burden of traffic. Its problems were worsened by inefficiency and hold-ups in the Tanzanian ports. In 1973-4, moreover, a massive rise in oil prices began and the recession in western economies which followed led to a drastic fall in copper prices. The combined effect of these two developments was a massive reduction in Zambia's prosperity and an increase in its debts. As discontent rose a national State of Emergency was proclaimed in 1976. To help strengthen unity Nalumino Mundia was taken back in to the party and government in February 1976. In 1978 Kapwepwe also rejoined the party. He died however in January 1980. In the last years of the Zimbabwe freedom struggle Zambia was repeatedly hit by raids mounted by the white Rhodesian regime. They produced considerable loss of life, disruption and expense. When the struggle in Zimbabwe was finally over. Zambia had survived as a nation and made great progress in developing the skills and abilities of its people. It had been prevented however from overcoming the most serious prob-

ems of its colonial heritage. Its main source of income was drastically
reduced and its debts to the outside world constituted a mounting burden.

Malawi since independence

When Malawi became independent in July 1964 its economy was closely
tied to white-ruled Southern Africa. South Africa and Rhodesia were the
country's main trading partners and the main source of foreign exchange
was provided by the thousands of Malawians working there. There was no
way that Malawi could make a radical break with the south without a
disastrous drop in its already very low living standards. Kamuzu Banda
moreover soon proved to have strongly conservative tendencies. His long
years in Africa and Britain had left him with a concern for standards little
different from that of many colonials. He was in no hurry to Africanize
senior positions in the civil service. He also openly pursued a policy of
friendship with the white supremacist regimes to the south. He argued
that this was more likely to break down apartheid than confrontation.

The young Malawi leaders who had originally invited Banda to be the
figurehead of their movement became increasingly frustrated. In September 1964, six senior members resigned from the cabinet. One of these,
H.B.M. Chipembere, started a rebellion in the Mangochi Hills to the east of
Lake Malawi. In February 1965 he made a successful raid on Fort Johnston (now Mangochi) but soon after was defeated at the Liwonde ferry. He
left Malawi and went into exile in the United States, where he died in
1975. In 1967 another attempted uprising was launched by Yatuta Chisiza,
ex-Minister of Home Affairs. He and fourteen other members of his band
were killed. The rebellions and the fact that they were successfully
crushed gave Banda both the opportunity and the justification for increasing his personal power to an extraordinary degree. The organization of the
Malawi Congress Party has been closely controlled by the President, while
the National Assembly became little more than a rubber stamp for his
decisions. In each election since 1971 members were personally chosen by
Banda himself from a list of candidates drawn up by local committees of
party members and civil servants.

Banda's policy of friendship with the south led him openly to reject the
adoption of sanctions against Rhodesia. In 1967 he opened formal diplomatic ties with South Africa. The following year he received a large
loan from South Africa to help establish the new capital at Lilongwe. In
May 1970 Vorster paid a visit to Malawi and in August 1971 Banda in
return made a state visit to South Africa. He was feted grandly all over the
country and the visit ended with a state banquet in his honour. Banda's

attitude to the white states in the south made him unpopular with many other African leaders. Banda was also suspicious that ex-ministers in exile might launch a new rebellion from Tanzania or Zambia. Relations were further strained in 1967 and 1968 when Banda claimed large areas of Tanzania, Zambia and Mozambique for Malawi. After 1971 however relations improved somewhat. Nyerere exchanged messages with Banda in 1972. In 1974 Kaunda paid a brief visit to Malawi. In 1975 Banda visited Zambia and diplomatic relations were established between the two countries.

Economic development

In economic development Malawi turned out to gain some advantages from having so few resources other than agriculture. Development efforts had therefore to be largely concentrated on improving crop production and expanding agricultural exports. This met with significant success. The wide range of Malawi's agricultural export crops also protected the country to some extent from the effects of price fluctuations in particular commodities. The small but growing manufacturing sector was helped by the fact that much of its energy could be provided by hydroelectric power coming from dams that were built on the Shire river.

In 1974 following an air crash in which seventy-five Malawian migrant workers were killed, Banda banned further recruitment of labour for the south. After long negotiations with South Africa this was relaxed, but the number of Malawians working on the Southern African mines was reduced to a fraction of the previous total.

The pattern of development favoured by Banda's government was to allow freedom of opportunity to the individual. In farming the more successful farmers were given every encouragement to get ahead. Members of Parliament and officials including the President were able to invest in agriculture with full government support. The result was the emergence of an élite of rich farmers. Wages paid to farm workers on the tea and tobacco plantations remained very low however.

As time went on Banda's personal grip continued to tighten. Any of his ministers who showed any promise as possible successors were promptly demoted if not detained. All potential opposition, even if non-political, was also suppressed. The Watchtower (Jehovah's Witnesses) in Malawi was severely persecuted and their church eventually banned. In 1977 a plot against the President was alleged and in a secret trial the Secretary-General of the Malawi Congress Party and the Head of the Police Special Branch were condemned. In spite of his pervious attitude to Portugal and the

Smith regime, Banda succeeded in establishing good relations with Mozambique and Zimbabwe when they became independent. A major problem facing the country remained the concentration of all powers in the hands of a man advancing into old age with no obvious successor in sight.

11 Middle Africa 1900–30

The extent of European control

By 1900 the European colonial governments were in commanding positions throughout most of Middle Africa with the exception of northern and southern Angola. The Kwanyama warriors in the south remained self-confidently independent of the Portuguese until 1915, while in the north the Ndembu and other peoples held out until the painful advance of the Portuguese between 1907 and 1909. However the European colonial powers had not imposed their system of government upon all the peoples in the territories they claimed. Nor had they established peace and order. For many the colonial governments' victories brought freedom from former masters but few were able to use that freedom in so positive a way as the Ganda chiefs after the destruction of the Kabaka's power in what is now Uganda. In most cases freedom quickly turned to confusion and uncertainty, followed by the exactions of the colonial government as it set up its taxation system.

The colonial governments extended their rule gradually and unevenly during the first two decades of the twentieth century. Even by 1920 the process was by no means complete. The fact that colonial rule was not imposed at once on all the peoples of Middle Africa is worth noting for it accounts for much of the uneven development and its later serious repercussions. The colonial governments tended to adopt and extend the use of existing languages and political systems. In German East Africa and Kenya, Swahili was much used in both administration and education far beyond the coastal area where it was habitually spoken. The Congo Free (Independent) State government made the Kongo, Lingala and Luba languages play a similar role. The Germans took up the system of ruling through *akidas* or appointed chiefs which they had met in their first years of activity when confined to the coast and trade routes. The British also had a trade routes mentality in their first years in Kenya and they forced the Kikuyu and other peoples to accept men they described as chiefs but who were in fact merely former caravan leaders or trading administrators. In Uganda this tendency to extend existing political systems and personnel was even more marked. Not only did the British extend the boundaries of the Ganda kingdom, but Ganda officials, clerks and teachers were given posts in all the surrounding areas and Ganda dominance in the colonial administration continued well into the twentieth century.

The first railways: the Congo

The colonial powers had established their rule in Middle Africa to develop and exploit its resources and consequently found it necessary to improve

Railway construction in the Congo

the existing transport system, for only the most valuable products could be economically transported by headloading. Only by building railways could transport costs be reduced sufficiently to bring European manufactures into the heart of the continent and to bring out African products on a large scale for export. In the Congo Free State a comparatively short stretch of railway between Matadi and Kinshasa, where the river was unsuitable for steamers promised to link a vast natural communications system with the sea. The building of this line, which began in 1889, placed a heavy burden on the Kongo people. Although the Congo Free State was not slow to force all those who could to work, there were still not sufficient men available since they were already heavily involved in the porterage business and in the construction of the State's administrative centre at Boma. Shiploads of labourers were brought in from Sierra Leone and Nigeria on contract. The work was hard and widespread disease brought death to a substantial proportion of the workmen. Many fled before their contracts expired, and few renewed their contracts. Men were imported from China but the Kongo people had to bear the greater part of the work. When the line was complete thousands of men were suddenly released from employment. New burdens were soon to be imposed but the railway construction had abruptly changed the life of the peoples of the Lower Zaire river and drawn them forcefully into the colonial economy.

The first railways: East Africa

The British government, anxious to have a better line of communication with the Upper Nile, started construction of the much longer Mombasa to Uganda railway in 1895. Whereas the Congo line passed through fairly populous districts, the Uganda line, after the first forty kilometres inland, went through country which was almost uninhabited. Large numbers of Indian labourers were brought in and few Africans were employed. The railway construction teams crawled slowly cross the Kenyan plains and mountains almost in isolation until the last year when they descended toward Lake Victoria and entered the populous Luo districts before reaching the line's terminus on the lake in 1901. Apart from creating some demand for domestic servants and providing a new market for the foodstuffs produced by the Kamba and Kikuyu peoples, the railway building had little direct impact on the lives of the Kenyan peoples. Once complete the line made possible the development of a cotton exporting industry and the British colonial administration began to look around for additional goods to transport in order to make the railway pay its way.

The Germans took twelve years (1893–1905) to build their first line rom Tanga to Usumbara which was only about 130 kilometres long. Consequently it had less effect on African life and on trade than did the British or Belgian lines. Their next venture, however, was more ambitious and made a serious impact on African life both during and after construction. In 1905 the Central Railway set off from Dar es Salaam and by 1907 t had reached Morogoro. In 1912 it entered Tabora and by 1914 it had reached its terminus on Lake Tanganyika. Between 1906 and 1912 the Northern Railway was extended from Usumbara to Mount Kilimanjaro, more than doubling its former length. These large and quickly constructed railways placed a substantial burden on the resources of the colony. Several years before the idea of building a central line was approved by the German government, the colonial administration in German East Africa had tried to show that such a railway would be feasible by forcing an increase in the colony's revenue and exports. They raised taxation and compelled people to grow cash crops. The people of Tanzania therefore began to pay the price of the Central Railway long before the first line was laid.

The rubber boom

Finance was a continual problem to all the colonial governments in Middle Africa for, unlike the governments in many parts of West Africa, most were unable to benefit from and build up existing trade but had to start from scratch. By 1890 the colonial administrations were in severe financial difficulties. The German Colonization Society and the Imperial British East Africa Company sank under their debts and had to be rescued by their respective governments. The Congo Free State saved itself by persuading the European powers at the Brussels Conference in 1890 to allow it to collect import duties. Thereafter it improved its financial position by establishing what amounted to a commercial monopoly within its territory. Had it not been for the sudden and dramatic rise in rubber exports all the governments, but most particularly the Angolan and the Congo Free State governments, would have been in an even more difficult position. Angola had exported rubber from the mid-1870s onward. But the trade increased extremely rapidly from 1886. By 1893 the port of Benguela was exporting almost nothing but rubber and the new product compensated for the decline of the ivory trade. But after 1900 the price of rubber began to fall. Exports had to be increased to maintain the previous level of income. The rubber itself became more difficult to obtain as the more accessible sources were worked out. A decline set in and although prices recovered somewhat before the First World War, Angolan exports

Beating rubber in the Congo

had almost dried up by 1912. The Congo went through a similar cycle. King Leopold, whose organization was almost bankrupt in 1894, was a rich man by 1900 and was using money made from the Congo to build palaces and finance public works in Belgium. Rubber exports grew from two tons in 1891 to six thousand tons in 1901. When prices began to fall the Free State tried to save itself by making it difficult for producers to sell to anyone but government agents. People were forced to collect rubber and deliver it as taxes to government stations. Prices to the producer were artificially lowered in 1901 so that the State and its subsidiary companies could maintain their profits. These abuses had existed before but they became harsher and more obvious after 1900. Finally, after a storm of protest in Europe in 1908, the Belgian state assumed control of the Congo Free State from King Leopold. East Africa was less affected by the rubber boom. Rubber production contributed to the revenue of the colonies of German East Africa, Uganda and Kenya in the first decade of the twentieth century but it never played such as dominant role as in Angola and the Congo.

The rubber boom was another event, like the construction of the railways, which disrupted the life of the people without producing any clear-cut new historical movement. Hundreds of thousands of men were mobilized all over Middle Africa for rubber collection. The 1880s and 1890s had been a golden age for the Ovimbundu people in Angola but with the decline in 1900 they, who had formerly employed others, had to sell their labour. In German East Africa, Morogoro became an important rubber collecting centre but by 1907 there was no more rubber there. This cycle was repeated all over the Congo Basin, in western Uganda and along the coastal strip of East Africa. Between 1906 and 1912 many European companies hired men to clear land and plant trees to establish regular rubber plantations but most of these proved unprofitable and many went bankrupt. The growth of the colonial economy, like the early industrialization of Europe, proceeded by fits and starts with frequent failures for which Africans often had to pay. The rubber boom and collapse was an outstanding example of this.

The revolts

As the colonial governments extended their rule they constantly encountered resistance: robbery of caravans, refusal to pay taxes, refusal to provide compulsory labour. Sizable forces were maintained to deal with such situations. The Congo Free State's *Force Publique* numbered 16 000 men in 1905. The German security force in East Africa was some 2300 strong and the British military force about 2000 excluding police. These men were quick to shoot and burn villages at the first sign of opposition. Away from the main centres their annual tax-gathering expeditions closely resembled the old marauding raids and their columns came back to base with herds of cattle or crowds of conscripted labourers. These military activities led to many small incidents but there were few major military engagements. There were two battles between the British and the Nandi in 1900 and 1905. Some 200 men were killed in a serious struggle between the Chagga and the tax-gathering Germans in 1900. There was more serious fighting between the Portuguese and the peoples of southern Angola between 1904 and 1915. These were isolated incidents.

But the Bailundu rising on the Bihe Plateau in Angola in 1902 presented a rather different form of opposition. It rose from widespread economic grievances among people severely affected by falling rubber prices and governmental exactions and was not the struggle of a community trying to maintain its sovereignty. For several months battle flared across the plateau until the weight of Portuguese arms brought it to an end. In 1904 in the Sankuru district of Kasai several formerly distinct and often mutually hostile communities among the Lele, Kuba and Pende united in a politico-religious movement and rose against the Free State regime. The rising was suppressed with heavy bloodshed as was another rising in the Lulonga district in 1905, but not before 145 agents of the hated 'Abir' rubber trading company had been killed between January and July.

Maji Maji

In 1905, in southern German East Africa, the most widespread revolt of all broke out in an area where German administration had been particularly harsh in its tax collection and most active in carrying through its compulsory cotton growing schemes to provide a substantial cash-crop export and prove the viability of railway projects. Artificially low prices were paid for the crop when harvested. A portion of the proceeds was taken by the government to finance the administration of the scheme and another portion was assigned to local authorities. Consequently many of the men who had actually produced the crop received nothing for their labour. This fraud drove men to despair and a movement arose to rid the country of colonial rule. Priests and messengers spread the word from village to village that deliverance was at hand. They claimed to have found a medicine which would turn the bullets of the colonial forces to water – hence the name of the movement, *maji*, meaning 'water'. Claims of this sort were not uncommon in Africa at this time and even later. What was remarkable was that the movement crossed ethnic and other boundaries. So strong was the solidarity against colonial rule that the German administration in the south collapsed between July and September 1905. The revolt reached as far as Morogoro and spread to the outskirts of the colonial capital at Dar es Salaam. Then the Germans rushed in reinforcements and took the offensive. Resistance was bitter but ineffective. By the end of 1905 the colonial administration was again in control of most of the areas where the revolt had broken out. Fighting continued up to 1907 in the Songea area until the Germans finally defeated the once powerful Ngoni warriors. The failure of the rising and the famine left the whole of the area in a depressed state. Much wealth and trade were destroyed, a quarter of a million people had died and game and tsetse moved in to make the devastated areas unfit for future settlement.

Years of reappraisal

During the years between 1905 and 1909 most of the colonial governments, their bitter rivalry and mutual suspicion having by then largely died away, were anxiously reconsidering their achievements, aims and methods. The crude frontiers of colonial states had been replaced during the last years of the nineteenth and the first years of the twentieth centuries by more realistic boundaries which took account of African political systems, removing possible causes of misunderstanding and friction between the colonizers and producing more co-operative attitudes among their officials. The era of competitive grasping at territory was not over but adjustment of boundaries was now once more a matter for high diplomacy in Europe and no longer preoccupied officials in the colonies. At the same time the high hopes of the early colonialists had suffered some severe shocks. All the colonial governments were more or less insolvent and dependent on inflows of money from metropolitan governments or loans from financiers. The railways often had insufficient traffic even to pay running costs; the rubber boom was fading away; the revolts had shaken the colonial rulers and produced serious debate on colonial policy in Europe. Among colonial officials there was serious discussion as to whether better results could be obtained by waiting for African producers to develop cash crops or by encouraging the development of European plantations, for of the few European plantations which had been set up many had failed. The British decided to stimulate African cotton-growing in Kenya in 1906. The Belgians, determined upon reform, reduced the number and size of the large concessions that had been made to private interests, notably the private domain of King Leopold in the central Congo, and in 1910 restored the right of producers to sell their crops freely and suppressed the system of paying taxes in products of the soil. In German East Africa Governor Rechenburg (1906–12) favoured African agriculture and having removed planters from the Legislative Council, went ahead with the Central Railway to open up the large centres of African population in the north-west to trade, rather than building a line in the north-east where the European planters had their plantations.

The growth of the plantation economy

At this time it was still uncertain whether Middle Africa would become a society of free cash-crop producing farmers, as was much of West Africa, or become a society dominated by great European-controlled estates where Africans worked as labourers. Nevertheless, although colonial policy seemed to be moving in the direction of the former solution, the period between 1908 and the First World War was one during which the plantation economy grew in a strong and sustained fashion. Plantations, mines and railway projects got under way in the Congo and put increasing pressure on the labour supply. In 1910 the first of many labour recruiting agencies – the Bourse du Travail – was set up in Katanga to bring men from distant places to work in the mines. The work of these agencies was backed up by the action of the administrations. By 1916, 46 000 labourers were working in mines and plantations in the Congo. In German East Africa the number of wage earners rose from 70 000 in 1909 to 172 000 in 1912–13. A large proportion of these labourers, who were engaged on comparatively short one or two year contracts, had to trek long distances on foot to reach their places of employment. Many spent several months going to and from work. Although the colonial governments considered it their duty to ensure that every man was fully employed, there was a constant shortage of labour in many European enterprises. Consequently the growth of plantation agriculture stifled the development of African cash-crop production. It is possible that the labour shortage produced by the forcible diversion of men from the Luo districts of Kenya to settlers' farms on the Highlands caused the disastrous failure of the African cotton growing experiment there in 1907. The rise in the prices of agricultural products in the 1920s enabled the planters and plantation companies to push forward towards a dominating position in the field of export production and despite their policy declarations the colonial governments were unable to stand up to the forces of expanding European capitalism. Big companies could offer impoverished colonial governments and their servants immediate financial and other benefits. King Leopold had been lavish in granting concessions for immediate financial gain in such companies as the Abir rubber company and the Société Anversoise. In 1907 the Société Minière was formed to exploit the resources of Katanga and a vast concession was handed over to the Lever company to establish oil-palm estates in the northern Congo Basin. The demands of these organizations for labour and other favours soon resulted in a weakening of the Belgian reform measures both in theory and in practice. Governor Rechenberg fought his private war against the planters in German East Africa but they were able to exert pressure on the German government at home and the colonial government was soon spending money on railways to serve their interests. In Kenya the settlers were already well-organized by 1908 and successfully put pressure on the government to force low-cost labour to work on their estates.

The impact of the First World War

Middle Africa was more heavily affected by the First World War than any other part of the continent. Elsewhere the campaigns were fairly brief. In Middle Africa German forces continued to resist until armistice day in November 1918. The main battlefield was German East Africa, although there was war also between Portuguese and Germans in southern Angola. Once more East Africa saw bands of fighting men scouring the land, burning, destroying and eating up the small food supplies of impoverished villages. Throughout the whole of Middle Africa recruiting agents were out in strength seeking men to act as carriers for the warring forces. The colonial powers were at war and no moral scruples about forced labour deterred them from raising every man they could. The main battles were fought close to the railways but whenever the armies moved away from them enormous numbers of carriers were required. At the beginning of the war the comparatively small German force operating in the north-east, where there were many railways, had 8000 carriers constantly engaged in bringing up supplies. The British and Belgians counted their carriers in hundreds of thousands. Thousands died of disease, exhaustion and malnutrition and had to be replaced. The war was followed by a wave of famine and disease. Spanish influenza swept across Middle Africa in 1918–19 carrying off an estimated 25 000 people in Uganda alone and severely affecting Tanganyika (where the British had replaced the Germans as rulers), the Belgian Congo and Kenya. Finally, there was a further outbreak of rinderpest which reached catastrophic proportions in some parts of Uganda, while in many countries the tsetse fly advanced across the ravaged lands.

A wave of unrest

In the early 1920s there were a number of political protests in different parts of Middle Africa. The general background conditions for these outbreaks were similar to those behind the revolts of the early years of the century. At the end of the war the prices of African exports rose sharply but then suffered an equally sharp fall in 1920–21. In British East Africa rapid changes in the value of currency added to the dislocation. Again people were baffled by the confusing world economic system and again Africans were called upon to pay the cost of economic upset through lower prices for their products and, in Kenya, through sharp reductions in the wages of plantation employees. But this time there were no concerted armed risings. A significant change had taken place in people's thinking and reactions and the strength and weaknesses of the colonial regime were better understood. In the Lower Congo popular discontent found its leader in Simon Kimbangu who first demonstrated his power by healing the sick and dying, and then set out to lead the people into a new society. Polygamy, idols, even dancing were rejected, schools were set up, a new day of rest was proclaimed, the end of the colonial regime was prophesied and an organization was set up to provide food for those who came to be cured. The colonial government was not attacked but ignored by the tens

Wood-carving at N'Kamba, showing three people on the way to Calvary. Simon Kimbangu carries the cross

of thousands who came to hear Kimbangu. He was arrested but later escaped and remained in hiding for several months before giving himself up. He was tried and deported to Elisabethville but his movement went on and was to reappear strongly later in the century in a modified form as the 'Church of Jesus Christ as revealed to Simon Kimbangu'. In 1921 the moral power of Kimbangu's teaching was such that it not only won over those who had been working with the colonial regime but also shook the self-confidence of the colonial rulers themselves, for they were uncomfortably aware that his arrest and trial were without legal or moral justification. Kimbangu's boycott of colonialism was not the only protest against Belgian rule in this period. Another movement spread from Sankuru to Equateur and the Kwango.

In Kenya, Harry Thuku, organizer of the Young Kikuyu Association, led a movement which demanded the abolition of the newly introduced pass system, the reduction of the poll tax and the return of Kikuyu lands. His programme appealed both to workers whose wages were threatened and to squatter farmers on European-owned lands who were being forced to give their labour instead of paying rents for the land they occupied. His method of 'Associations' with the object of influencing government policy was similar to that used by the settlers themselves. Between 1920 and 1922

Middle Africa: railways and the dates of their completion

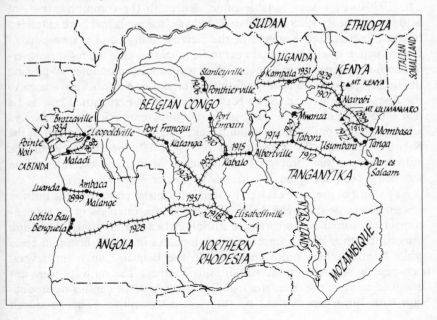

Thuku placed his demands before the authorities and held great meetings in Nairobi and elsewhere. In March 1922 he was arrested and a demonstration in Nairobi was broken up by police firing on the crowd. After these events unrest died down but Thuku's movement was also to reappear later in modified form. There was trouble too in Uganda but there the pattern was rather different. In the Buganda kingdom the control of export production was largely in the hands of the *saza* ('county') chiefs who had secured freehold property rights by the 1900 Uganda Agreement and the 1907 land settlement. In 1918 the traditional *bataka* clan heads, the guardians of old clan rituals, came forward as spokesmen of the people, agitating for a revision of the land settlement in their favour. The Bataka Association they formed in 1920 also drew attention to the increasing exactions (the *envuju* payments in produce and the *busulu* periods of compulsory labour) which the chiefs were imposing on those in *saza* lands. The *bataka* chiefs had much popular support, including that of the young Kabaka. Their agitation failed to alter the land settlement but in 1927 a limit was imposed on the exactions which chiefs could demand of the people.

More railway building

The 1920s saw a very notable improvement in the communications of Middle Africa. By 1928 the Benguela railway in Angola had been extended to the minefields of Katanga in the Belgian Congo and a new port of Lobito which was constructed next to Benguela became the most prosperous commercial centre in Angola. Work was continued on lines by-passing the unnavigable sections of the Congo river and on lines from Katanga to the Angolan border and to the Kasai river at Port Francqui. Eight and a half million pounds were spent on improving communications in Kenya and Uganda by building lines round Lake Victoria to Kampala and in the Kenya Highlands. In Tanganyika too, by 1929, the extension of the railway system was complete from Moshi to Arusha and the central line was being extended from Tabora to Mwanza on Lake Victoria.

As a result of pressure exerted by the white settler politicians the railway systems were deliberately designed to serve the interests of European-controlled economic enterprises in Middle Africa. Rather than integrating the country they greatly improved the amenities in certain favoured areas while leaving others quite unserved. In the Belgian Congo the several networks were not even linked with one another. The railways were not designed to draw the countries together but to link the centres of production with European markets by the most direct routes. This produced uneven development with a few prosperous modern centres being served with foodstuffs and with migrant labour drawn from neglected and backward hinterlands.

Road construction

This situation was somewhat improved by extensive road building programmes during the decade following the First World War. Up to 1920 there was little road construction. In the Belgian Congo the total network of what were classed as roads amounted to only 2240 kilometres. By 1947 there were over 100 000 kilometres of roads most of which had been constructed before 1937. The period of rapid road construction began in 1921. The 1400 kilometres of roads which existed in Orientale Province in 1922 grew to 16 000 kilometres by 1929. This sudden increase in road construction was due to the great wave of motor vehicle imports during the period 1925–30, making possible a more flexible transportation system than that provided by the railways. In Angola the Portuguese were quick to see the advantages of motor transport and started an intensive road building programme in the 1920s. In Uganda the old pre-war road tracks and ox-wagon trails were replaced during the 1920s by a reasonably satisfactory system of dirt roads and by the end of the decade most of the more populous districts were accessible by road. Kenya and Tanganyika with overall vast distances and low population density were less well served but even so there was a great deal of road building during this period.

The importance of the road building and the increasing use of motor vehicles during this period for the history of the people of Middle Africa can hardly be overestimated. It brought a revolution in the life of countless communities as social, economic and cultural transformation became possible in concert with other communities. At first road building was simply another colonial imposition. The roads were constructed with local labour, usually unpaid and forcibly recruited. But once open to motor transport they greatly diminished the necessity for head porterage of goods. Men were now able to return to more rewarding activities. In Tanganyika by 1938 hardly anyone could be found who was willing to trek by foot over anything but short distances. The long journeys on foot from south to north were a thing of the past. People now went by lorry. The lorries could also penetrate to villages away from the main centres and collect their cash crops for export. The reduced cost of transporting foodstuffs put an end to the age-old fear of local famine in this part of Africa where the rainfall was inadequate and undependable over the greater part of the land. The roads opened up new horizons for men in formerly isolated communities. Some villages moved or, as in the Belgian Congo, were moved by administrators up to the road to form new communities which could take advantage of the new facility. The neglected countryside and rural areas slowly began to make progress.

Plantations and settlers in the ascendancy

It was one of the misfortunes of Middle Africa, in the short term at least that large-scale European-controlled enterprises secured a dominating position in society just before the road and motor transport revolution began to open up new prospects. Mines and plantations in Angola and the Belgian Congo and white settler agriculture in Kenya moved into a period of comparative prosperity in the early 1920s when, after the sharp boom and slump of 1920–21, the world demand and prices for primary products rose once more. In the Belgian Congo the great Katanga copper mines got into their stride. Tin and diamond mining got under way. The great plantation companies such as Lever could now depend entirely on the production of their large European-managed plantations for supplies of palm oil, rubber and other goods. In Angola diamond mining began and soon became one of the colony's major exports, together with sisal, sugar and coffee from European-run estates. In Kenya the white settlers in the Highlands finally mastered the problems of farming, and plantation-produced coffee and sisal became the main exports backed by the settler-produced maize. The settlers, planters and companies were consequently able to wield an even greater influence than before over the colonial governments during these years.

In Kenya the white settlers were bent on nothing less than complete control over the colony. They demanded the right to elect their own government to rule the two and a half million or more people in the country and when this was refused in 1922 they planned to seize the railway and kidnap the Governor. The British government, anxious to avoid a repetition of the Boer War situation, was conciliatory. However, the government of India, affronted by the settlers' attacks on the rights of Indians in Kenya, exerted pressure on the Colonial Office in London and the path to settler rule was blocked and the policy of 'paramountcy of native interests' promulgated in London. However, the Legislative Council, which had existed since 1906, was now given European and Indian elected representatives and in effect became dominated by settlers. This was reflected in the strongly pro-settler bias in most of its policies. For a while it seemed as if Uganda might go the same way. In 1920 the British

Colonial Office inclined towards a policy of permitting more land purchase by Europeans and labour legislation favourable to their interests. In 1920 the establishment of a Legislative Council with members chosen exclusively from among planters and representatives of large companies formed part of a movement towards a settler- and company-controlled regime. But this movement was arrested by London in 1923 when it became clear that African productive enterprise was more successfully strengthening the country's economy than the weak and unsuccessful efforts at plantation agriculture. In Tanganyika where, before the war, the settlers and companies had become almost as strong as their Kenyan counterparts, the situation was radically changed by the destruction of the estates during the war and the removal of their German owners. The settlers, many of whom were not British, had difficulty in recovering their position after the war. But the press supported their interests, settlers in neighbouring Kenya sought to bring pressure to bear and the weak governors who ruled the country up to 1926 were often swayed by their arguments. In many ways the early 1920s represented the heyday of settler power, and what defence of African interests there was within the colonial system was conducted by the missionaries and humanitarian opinion in Europe.

The proletarianization of African labour

As European enterprise expanded in the early 1920s it put an increasing demand on African manpower. In the Belgian Congo the number of men employed by European firms, construction schemes and plantations rose from 147 000 in 1922 to over 400 000 in 1925. An additional 40 000 men were engaged on government public works and in the ranks of the *Force Publique*. Nevertheless the labour supply still fell short of demand and government officials were ordered to ensure that every able-bodied man was working for either the government or some European employer. Forced labour became the order of the day. By the middle of the decade the government were talking in terms of the 'total mobilization of labour' to meet the incessant demand. But upon investigation it was found that the point of 'total mobilization' (estimated at 15–16 per cent of the total population in wartime Europe) had practically been reached. Much has been written about the exploitation of the Belgian Congo during King Leopold's reign. The exploitation was more comprehensive and systematic during the 1920s, but being better organized and less violent it gave rise to less criticism in Europe. The burden placed on the African community in Kenya was, if anything, greater than in the Belgian Congo. There too the government forced men to work on European farms. In 1919 Governor

Northey issued his famous circulars to administrative officers telling them to 'encourage' men to work on European estates. After missionary criticism the circulars were eventually withdrawn but much courage on the part of the administrators was needed to resist the demands of the settlers who were in such a strong position in the 1920s. In Uganda also, where African chiefs were the main landowners, there was a heavy demand for labour as production rose and migrant workers came in from Rwanda and elsewhere.

At the same time, in the Belgian Congo and in Kenya especially, measures were taken to prevent Africans from earning money by gathering and producing cash crops on their own farms. In Kenya they were forbidden to produce the most valuable crop, coffee; it was said that African production of coffee would encourage the spread of diseases affecting the crop. The discouragement of African cash-crop production was a method of keeping wages down, for wages were so low that a man could earn in a few days gathering crops what he would be paid for a month's work on a European plantation. Africans were being made into a proletariat without property and without control over the means of production. This was already true of trade and commerce. In Angola Africans were forced out of trade by a system of licensing of traders. In the Belgian Congo the large firms controlled the purchase of cash crops and much of the distribution of imported goods. In East Africa, Indian traders were able to beat the small African traders out of business because of the financial support and trading connections they maintained with the big Indian trading companies which themselves were linked with the commercial power of western India and the wider world of business and finance. During the 1920s the situation began to change. Whereas the majority of workers had been casual labourers whose energies were used for short periods in the main centres after which they returned to their villages, now urban communities began to grow up in the new centres. Luba workers began to reside permanently in towns such as Luluabourg and Elisabethville, while Kongo peoples settled permanently in Leopoldville. Such urbanization was eventually to be of great political significance.

The exceptional Ganda

As has already been noted, African society suffered from the colonial regime up to the middle 1920s but it was not transformed by it. Inter-state warfare was stopped, but inter-village warfare still went on in many areas. The expansion of states was stopped but the few colonial administrators made only occasional, though disruptive, political interventions. Colonial-

ppointed chiefs wielded petty dictatorships over many villages which had
been autonomous but states like Rwanda continued much as before. One
tate which *was* transformed and which played an active role throughout
his period was Buganda. The chiefly oligarchy which came to power there
n the late nineteenth century regarded itself as the partner of the British
administration – not as its subordinate agent. The chiefs, who were either
Christian or Muslim, were mainly educated men, prosperous from their
cotton estates and anxious to modernize. The corporate strength of the
oligarchy was most clearly expressed in the new *Lukiko* (Parliament) and
he self-confidence of the Ganda ruling class, exemplified by Sir Apolo
Kagwa, *Katikiro* (chief minister) until 1926. Kagwa, who left behind him a
mass of correspondence equal to any contemporary European statesman,
was at once a reformer and a stout defender of his state against colonial
encroachment. While gladly accepting advice and technical assistance he
was not prepared to tolerate uninformed or unwanted interference. He
took his stand on the Uganda Agreement which defined the relationship
between the Buganda state and the British government. When in 1910 the

Sir Apolo Kagwa
(*right*) in 1902

British interfered in the delicate question of chiefs' property rights he engaged a solicitor to fight the Ganda case. From the 1890s to the 1920s the British were careful not to offend him. Buganda was the heart of the British Protectorate in Uganda and although the British administration was secure there, elsewhere it was not firmly established. But after the First World War, as other districts were organized under British administration and officials grew accustomed to more high-handed dealings with weaker states, so the British wanted closer control of Buganda. Kagwa insisted that the Provincial Commissioner should deal only with him and the other ministers of Buganda and not give directions on his own account to local authorities. But by then Kagwa was old and unwell; his relations with the young Kabaka were uneasy and his political position weakened. In 1926 he resigned and an era in Ganda affairs came to an end. Buganda began to look more like other colonial-administered states.

The economic slump

The middle 1920s marked the high-water mark of the post-war economic expansion. In 1927 and 1928 prices began once more to fall and by the end of the decade the worldwide economic slump occurred. The whole colonial economy stopped expanding and governments reduced their activity to a bare minimum. It was the final discontinuity in a period filled with false starts of various kinds. It principally affected European government activities and by slowing them down it gave Africans a much needed breathing space and allowed them to take stock of their position and set about recovering control of the destinies of their countries.

12 Building a new society in Middle Africa, c. 1930–65

The years around 1930 can in many senses be regarded as a turning point in the history of Middle Africa. It was then that the balance began to swing from the thrusting forces of colonialist imperialism toward resurgent African enterprise. After the confusions and turmoil of the previous period, new dynamic forces began to emerge which were progressively to transform Middle Africa and create a new society. This is not to say that from 1930 onward the colonial regime began to falter or fade away. In many respects it was to become more active than before. But its activity was increasingly outweighed by the constructive forces of a modernizing, progressive African society which finally engulfed and threw off colonial control during the early 1960s.

Demographic dynamism

In 1926 many of those concerned with the administration of the Belgian Congo felt that a crisis was at hand. There was a general belief that under the impact of the colonial regime the population of the country was declining and would continue to decline unless serious measures were taken. It is debatable whether the population had indeed declined but certainly some areas of the country had been depopulated since the 1880s and the population generally speaking was not rising. In East Africa, although there was not the same alarm, the picture was not very different. Large areas such as southern Tanganyika had been depopulated and most of the evidence pointed to a stagnant or declining population. But from the middle 1920s the picture began to change. Although we have no very reliable figures, there is every indication that the population began to rise and in some areas rose fast. For example, it is estimated that in Kenya the Kikuyu population was expanding at the rate of 1.5 per cent every year between 1925 and 1935 and the population of Tanganyika nearly doubled between 1921 and 1950. All the evidence points to the period just before and just after 1930 as being that when the 'population explosion' which is now such a marked feature of African life in Middle Africa began.

There were many reasons for this development. As the colonial regime, having secured a monopoly of the use of force, established more peaceful conditions there was a substantial extension of farms in many areas. The Sukuma people moved out into Zinza Province to take up new land. In eastern Tanganyika men came down from the mountains and out of palisaded villages to cultivate fields which were formerly abandoned. In Kenya, Kamba had been coming down from the hills into the plain since the first decade of the century. Kikuyu cut into the defensive forest fringes of their territory. People in Nyanza Province spread out from their villages. In the Belgian Congo also, Luba and other peoples began to move into lands along the line of the Port Franqui–Katanga railway. Road building and the increasing trade in foodstuffs also permitted a more rapid and efficient development of agriculture. Farming extended rapidly, more food was produced and a growing population could be sustained. At the same time a more determined effort was made to stamp out the recurrent famines and epidemics which had in former years decimated the population. In 1918–19 the Uganda government, alarmed at the onset of famine, distributed 800 tons of food in Busoga. Its efforts were not entirely successful but thereafter it was able to act with greater effect to prevent sudden droughts from ruining communities which lived on the border of subsistence.

In 1925 the government of the Belgian Congo became alarmed in a more general way about the living conditions of the people. It took up the question of public health more vigorously and began to build up a network of dispensaries and health centres throughout the country. These, together with the efforts of the missions and the companies in the same field, soon provided the Belgian Congo with one of the best medical services in Africa. In East Africa also the governments turned more actively to the fight against disease. The Uganda government's expenditure on its medical department expanded fourfold in the years between 1919 and 1928. In 1928 there were fifty-nine dispensaries in Uganda; by 1938 there were 108. In Tanganyika there were 310 dispensaries by 1934, most of which had been set up during the previous ten years. These services gradually improved general health and above all guarded against the spread of the major epidemic diseases. Inevitably the rapid growth in population radically changed its composition. The proportion of children and youths in relation to the rest of the community began to grow. The young men who were to fight for independence in the 1940s and 1950s were born around this time and they, together with the larger families, brought optimism and self-confidence to replace the frustration and depression of the previous period.

Educational progress

It was in this optimistic atmosphere that an extensive movement towards new schools took place in many parts of Middle Africa. The movement was uneven since mass demand for the new education occurred among different peoples at different times. Whereas in Buganda many thousands of schools set up before the First World War continued to expand, the education system established before the war in Tanganyika was severely disrupted during the war and by 1930 was only reaching the position it had attained in 1914. On the other hand by 1945 education had still not started to spread on any substantial scale among the Maasai. In many parts of the Belgian Congo, Tanganyika and Kenya in the late 1920s and early 1930s schools began to spring up in large numbers in villages at a distance from the main mission stations.

Up to 1910 in the Belgian Congo the Catholic missionaries especially and followed the *ferme chapelle* system of gathering together small communities of ex-slaves and social outcasts around a few missionary centres apart from and usually in opposition to the rest of society. Since the missions were the main organizers of education and the chief suppliers of teachers, education tended to be narrowly focused rather than widely spread. By 1930 this situation had profoundly changed. The central mission stations still provided the bulk of the teachers, but among whole peoples the acquisition of literacy and the new ideas that went with it had become a popular movement. It was no longer necessary to bribe children to go to school. Villages built their own schools and engaged their own teachers, sometimes with the aid of whatever missionary organization they preferred, or with the aid of the African churches and educational organizations that began to appear. In Kenya, where there had been forty schools in 1912, there were 2000 in 1930. Many of these schools were condemned as 'bush schools' by the educational departments of the colonial governments who measured them against the yardstick of formal European education and found them wanting. But these schools cannot be judged by the range of their very limited and often heavily religious curricula, for this overlooks the important movement of the human spirit that they represented. The teachers were men of vision who opened up new perspectives, created new aspirations and indulged in serious social criticism at a local level. The rapid growth of these schools was part of the hungry search after a better order of society which was so characteristic of

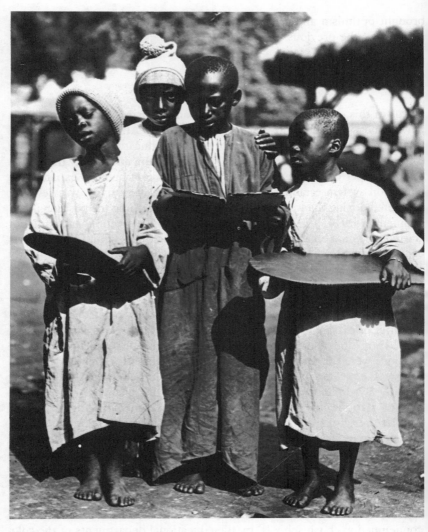

Children at a mission school in the Congo

this period. The years between 1920 and 1940 were rich in movements of this kind. In the Lower Congo, Simon Kimbangu and his disciples provoked a widespread popular movement which extended beyond the boundaries of the Belgian Congo to the French-held territories to the north. In Buganda the Abamaliki movement working outside the missionary organizations satisfied the widespread demand for baptism which appeared among the Ganda poor in the early 1920s. In 1929 a revivalist movement within the Christian church affected Rwanda, Uganda and Kenya. In 1933 the primate of the African Orthodox Church of South Africa, Archbishop Alexander, was invited to Kenya and baptized large numbers of Kikuyu. Throughout this period the Wata wa Mungu – the people of God – were also at work among the Kikuyu. These movements went hand-in-hand with the rapid development of education and when the first surges of energy had passed they left behind them a larger number of more vigorous schools.

While the proliferation of schools, religious revivals and baptisms changed the outlook of village communities there was another aspect of the movements which was concerned with social criticism on a broader plane. Kimbangu was concerned not only with changing local customs but with removing the colonial burden from the shoulders of the whole Kongo people. Archbishop Alexander was brought to Kenya to found an independent African Orthodox Church which would organize and gather together many local communities under solely African control. The initiative to do this had been taken by a number of teachers who, impatient with the missions' unsympathetic attitude and failure to undertand Kikuyu customs, had set up their own school organizations – the Kikuyu Independent Schools Association and the Kikuyu Karinga Educational Association. These movements and the ideas behind them produced a growing solidarity among the Kikuyu people as a whole just as the Kimbanguist movement produced a sense of unity among the people of the Lower Congo. The slow development of secondary education played a similar role within the framework of the established educational system. Whereas village and elementary schools mainly produced local change, secondary schools produced an élite which could seriously challenge the colonial order. Consequently the colonial governments mostly discouraged the growth of secondary schools and preferred to provide agricultural training or trade schools and attempted to restrict higher instruction to their own requirements for medical assistants or public works engineers. But the colonial governments were not always able to exercise firm control over the educational system. The bulk of education was in the hands of the missions which themselves had to be responsive to African demands since so many of their schools were the result of African enterprise. In Uganda the attempt between 1925 and 1934 to stifle the growth of secondary education and create purely vocational schools was blocked by missionary and African resistance. Makerere College emerged in 1933 as a fully fledged secondary school and by 1939 there were 1335 secondary schools in Uganda. Since the missions in the Belgian Congo were more dependent on government finance they conformed more closely to what the government required. But there, as elsewhere, the missions were anxious to produce priests and pastors and the seminaries provided another avenue to higher education. But generally speaking between 1920 and 1940 the number who received higher education was small. Primary education was dominant and secondary education still something for the future. The educated élites had not yet emerged as a significant force and such bodies as the Tanganyika African Association formed in 1929 had a very restricted membership. In Angola education had scarcely reached the village level. There were schools in the coastal cities and some Ovimbundu districts but discouragement by the colonial government and the constant activity of labour recruiting agents severely limited the possibility of educational development.

The consequences of the economic slump

From 1928 to 1938 the demand for products exported from Middle Africa and the prices paid for them fell to an unprecedented low level. For example, from 1929 to 1933 the price of cloves – Zanzibar's principal export – fell from twenty-four rupees a frasilah to six rupees, and prices remained low until the Second World War. This dramatic fall, while striking a severe blow at the major industry in Zanzibar, also hastened a social revolution. The Arab planters who had dominated the island were ruined and many Indian capitalists suffered a severe setback. Many estates had to be sold and were bought by Swahilis who could work on smaller profit margins. This shift in economic power was reflected in the increasing involvement of Africans in the administration and in 1934, when local government was reorganized, more power was placed in the hands of local, mainly African, communities. Elsewhere in Middle Africa the economic depression had a similar effect. It hit hardest at foreign planters who spent heavily on imported goods to maintain a high standard of living and affected least the African farmers who were engaged in subsistence farming. Although these farmers earned less from their export products they also paid less for cotton textiles, their main import, as large quantities of cheap Japanese cloth were appearing on the markets. However, whereas in Zanzibar the administration did little to save the Arab planter aristocracy, elsewhere the colonial governments took measures to ease the foreign settlers' and companies' difficulties and continued policies which reduced the benefits Africans might have derived from the new situation.

The plantation economy in danger

In Kenya the effects of the economic depression were worsened by attacks of locusts and droughts between 1931 and 1934. But the government assisted the settlers with loans and a Land Bank was set up in 1931 with a capital of £500 000. The settlers turned increasingly to the production of wheat and dairy produce which could be sold profitably behind the tariff barrier. Africans still had to pay the same taxes as before even though their wages were reduced from fourteen shillings to eight shillings a month and the price of their export articles such as hides and ghee had fallen further than the prices of other exports. However, after some initial losses the African farmers began to profit from the situation by taking over the production of crops such as maize which the settlers were no longer able to produce profitably. The old distinction between African 'subsistence' farming and settler cash-crop production began to disappear. In Tanganyika in the early 1930s as the area of plantation land was reduced, coffee growing by the Chagga people and in Bukoba continued to develop. Cotton production extended, especially on the southern shore of Lake Victoria, and tea planting began in the Southern Highlands. As the Chagga farmers became comparatively wealthy, better systems of organization such as the Chagga co-operative society were set up and education extended rapidly. In central Tanganyika, however, where the soil was poorer, there was not the same progress. Many communities found their cash incomes severely reduced and being unable to find the money to buy cotton textiles began to clothe themselves in bark cloth once more. In 1939 they were still struggling against the age-old enemy of periodic famine. Uganda, mainly because the cash economy was almost entirely African-based, suffered less from the depression. Despite falling prices, coffee production increased without a break. Cotton production fell between 1929 and 1932 but then rose faster than before as farmers in more remote areas began to see the advantages of securing a cash income in this way. Better houses were built, co-operative societies were formed and schools were set up. In the Belgian Congo and Angola the slump checked the vigorous growth of the plantation economy. The completion of the major railway projects just before the slump reduced the demand for construction labour and carriers. More men were able to return to their villages to develop their own farms although taxes remained high and forced labour was still exacted for road construction and government service. Like governments in East Africa, the Congo administration began to encourage African cash-crop production. In 1933 the *paysannat indigène* policy was adopted by the Belgians. African farmers were to form the backbone of society and the Congo was not to be a place for large-scale European settlement. In the ensuing years the colonial governments paid consider able attention to the development of African production and their effort resulted in a substantial extension of cotton cultivation by African far mers. In areas where the soil was suitable for cotton the farmers became quite wealthy even though the prices was kept artificially low. In other areas, such as the central Congo where yields were less, the crop was hardly worth growing and forced cotton cultivation became a major grie vance against the colonial regime.

Indirect rule

Between 1925 and 1940 there was much anxious discussion by colonial rulers about systems of 'native administration'. There was a major con troversy concerning the relative advantages of 'indirect' and 'direct' rule (see Chapter 1). Indirect rule, 'invented' by Lugard in Northern Nigeria, owed something to British experiences in India and was also a response to growing nationalism in Ireland, India and Egypt. By giving some powers to 'traditional' rulers it was hoped to undermine the future role of the educated, westernized élite. Sir Donald Cameron, a disciple of Lugard, was sent out as Governor of Tanganyika (1925–31) to introduce indirect rule there. He was convinced that the Germans had smashed up the 'tribal' systems, which needed to be restored. Much effort went into 'finding the chief', even among chiefless societies, while ambitious Africans, anxious to obtain positions in the new institutions, sometimes invented entirely bogus 'tribal' histories which completely deceived colonial administrators. Thus new 'tribes' were invented and a new political geography was cre ated.

In reality, although the British and the Belgians tried hard, it proved impossible to impose a completely uniform system of 'native administra tion' over such wide areas containing such diverse forms of social organiza tion. In Tanganyika the Chagga people fitted fairly well into the system of indirect rule. But in the coastal areas it was difficult to find a better authority than that of the nominated chiefs, whom the Germans and, before them, the Arabs had appointed. Indirect rule worked best in places like Buganda and Rwanda, where strongly centralized state systems had existed in precolonial times. It could not be imposed so easily over, for example, the small Kikuyu communities where no authority could claim to rule more than a few villages.

Indirect rule – for all that the British proclaimed its superiority over French direct rule – became a means of social control rather than social progress and often resulted in a much deeper penetration by the colonial state. District officials now learned far more of what was really going on, while 'Native Authorities', instructed by European 'advisers', began ordering people to leave their homes in the name of soil conservation, to reduce their cattle holdings and so forth. In short, chiefs became more rather than less autocratic and indirect rule in many ways served to disguise the underlying violence of colonial states.

Local government becomes more African

Whether colonial rule was direct or indirect, however, there was one feature common to most of Middle Africa during this period – except Angola. A more meaningful dialogue was begun between the colonial government and African society. During the 1920s and 1930s administrators began to make serious studies of the organization of African societies and began to take African political and legal institutions into account more seriously, asking Africans how they thought local government should be organized. Europeans now became more conscious than ever before of the richness of African culture. Here and there administrators and missionaries turned from breaking down African customs to the preservation and development of the traditional institutions. The 1920s and 1930s saw an increase in work such as that of the Reverend Van Wing who in 1921 produced his 'Bakongo Studies' and contributed much to the development of Kongo self-consciousness through his studies of the history and institutions of the Kongo people. Much of this kind of work was done for practical reasons to produce information for colonial governments. But, whatever the motivation, Africans found that they were being more frequently consulted. In time, communities began to identify themselves with the administrative areas to which they were assigned, and for those who had formerly lived within the narrow bounds of closed village societies this often meant the opening up of wider perspectives. In other cases, precolonial systems which had been broken down in the early colonial period were now resuscitated and precolonial tendencies toward the creation of wider unities were given new scope. The Hehe people were able to unite again under their paramount chief. The Sukuma and Nyamwezi peoples were drawn together into federations in 1927 and 1928 and although internal disputes led to the breakdown of the central councils in 1930 the two federations remained as judicial and administrative units. In Kenya the system of rule through appointed chiefs was gradually brought to an end from 1924 onward and Local Native Councils were established whose members were to some extent determined by popular choice. Although colonial administrators supervised the working of these new bodies there was now some opportunity for the people to discuss how administration should be run and to decide how the growing funds at the disposal of local government treasuries should be used. After the political paralysis and petty tyrannies of earlier years, this represented some considerable advance.

Looking backward and looking forward

The development of local government and the restoration of old political structures had certain inherent dangers. There was the possibility of old precolonial divisions being restored. The re-establishment of the traditional ruling families often meant that power was placed in the hands of old men with old ideas leaving few opportunities for progressive, younger men. The constant search for the oldest institutions gave the new system a conservative if not a reactionary character. For example, Buganda could be regarded as having been successful in retaining some autonomy while remaining under colonial control. Or it could be seen as a society where an established ruling class of chiefs were anxiously preserving their own power and social and political inequality. But as well as basing local administration on traditional institutions, the colonial governments were also trying to create administrative areas of fairly equal and manageable size. While some former states like that of the Hehe were reunited, others were broken up as was the old Lunda empire. The Buganda kingdom remained intact but the areas adjacent to it, such as Busoga and Toro, which Buganda had been about to take over before the British invasion, now became more markedly autonomous as the colonial government of Uganda in the late 1920s made the administrative boundaries of the various native authorities more rigid. On the other hand new unities emerged as the colonial government gathered small communities with similar institutions into new administrative districts, as was the case with the Tetela people in the central Congo, the small separate Kongo communities, the Sukuma communities and the Chagga chiefdoms. A number of societies along the northern stretch of the Zaire river traced their descent back to a common ancestor, Mongo, and as administrators collected their several histories they began to acquire a solidarity which was based on tradition but was nevertheless not traditional. Loyalty towards these broader communities made co-operation easier in building roads and schools, in marketing cash crops and also provided a framework in which African culture could flourish and develop more vigorously. In the early stages they represented an opening up of men's minds. If the ethnic lines began to harden later that was the response of another generation to the trials of other times.

Many of the disputes and discussions that went on in the centres of colonial government before and during the Second World War were however still nearly as remote from the life of the people as had been the discussions at the Berlin Conference of 1885. Africans seldom participated in the debates and they had no say in determining the shape of government as a whole. There were Legislative Councils in each of the East African territories after 1926 but they had no African members before 1945. Selected missionaries and Secretaries of Native Affairs were expected to protect African interests. In the Belgian Congo unofficial members were added to the Councils in 1933, but they were all Europeans until 1947.

Closer union in East Africa

One of the major issues discussed by the governments of East Africa during this period was the question of closer union. From 1924 onward the British Colonial Office pressed for the establishment of some form of co-ordinating authority which would lead ultimately to the amalgamation of the East African territories into a single federation, hoping in this way to make possible economies in defence, customs administration, railway development, postal services and other such matters. There was much opposition to the scheme in Zanzibar, Uganda and Tanganyika. In Kenya the settlers at first resisted the idea but in 1926 began to support closer union provided that it would be accompanied by the concession of an elected European majority on the Legislative Council. Their enthusiasm, however, made Indians and Africans more suspicious of the scheme than before and when Sir Hilton Young's commission investigated the question in 1928 it reached the conclusion that the climate of opinion was not in favour of any major change. In 1931 a Select Committee of Parliament, after hearing Indian and African objections, again decided that the time was not opportune. The three states, four including Zanzibar, continued to co-operate in running various common services but no political step was taken to bring them together until after the war. By then the states were too firmly fixed and the East African High Commission, set up in 1948, was too weak and too settler-dominated to attract the loyalty of rising nationalist opinion.

German colonial ambitions

The colonial governments in Middle Africa were also troubled in the last years before the war by Germany's demands for compensation for the colonies she had lost in 1919. Germany was particularly interested in Middle Africa where there were German settlers in Tanganyika, formerly

German East Africa. In 1938 the fates of Tanganyika and the Belgian Congo were the subject of diplomatic discussions between Germany and Britain and there was much uneasiness in colonial circles but the onset of war put an end to all uncertainty.

The impact of the Second World War

The Second World War did not have the same disastrous effect on Middle Africa as the First World War, and no military campaigns were fought there, apart from the British and Italian troops' battles on the northern Kenyan frontier, preliminary to the Italian defeat in Ethiopia. Nevertheless, the war had a great impact on the life of the people and the war years

Service in the Second World War widened the horizons of many Africans: British East African troops examine a statue in a bomb-damaged Buddhist temple in Kalewa, Burma, 1944

were a period of crucial change throughout most of the area. Kenya became the base for military operations and later a rest centre for troops engaged in the Middle East. This created a large demand for foodstuffs and the settler farms were more profitably active than ever before. The Belgian Congo and Middle Africa provided supplies on an equally large scale to the Allied nations as a whole. With the Japanese invasion of South East Asia in 1942 came a serious reduction in the supply of certain tropical products and Zanzibar cloves were now in great demand. Formerly unprofitable rubber plantations could now sell all they produced and wild rubber was even gathered in the forests again. There was an enormous demand for copra, sisal, cotton, palm oil and minerals of direct military value. The period between 1940 and 1945 was reminiscent of the early 1920s. There was a scramble for labour and the government intervened to force people to work more. In the Belgian Congo compulsory cultivation, mainly of cotton, was increased to 120 days of a man's working year. Rubber collection and food growing was speeded up by forced labour and emergency powers were taken to deal with the problem of labour shortage. Labour legislation was used to prevent absenteeism and to keep wages low. In East Africa, government action was less harsh but there was a return to compulsory labour after May 1940 to increase the production of maize and other food crops. In Uganda some 77 000 men were recruited for military service. In Kenya the figure reached 75 000, about 20 per cent of the adult male population. Nevertheless, despite this outflow of men, export production was stepped up and the production of food crops maintained. The Second World War put a strain on Middle Africa's resources which was probably equal to if not greater than anything previously experienced.

Middle Africa's vigorous response

The effect of the Second World War was rather different from previous plunderings by the colonial governments of Middle Africa's manpower resources. This was a more mechanized war than the First World War. The army did not want carriers and other totally unskilled labourers. Many soldiers received some form of technical training – if only as drivers. They saw other societies in other parts of the world where the supremacy of the white man was not an accepted fact as at home. In Middle Africa itself there was a great increase in the demand for skilled and semi-skilled labour. Many secured jobs as clerks or mechanics with government or private enterprise. Even for those who went to do unskilled tasks in the mining centres there was the challenge of entering a new society – the society of the big city. The Belgian Congo copper mines were already an established industry when war broke out. But the war effort extended their production from 122 000 tons in 1939 to 165 000 tons in 1944. Tin production, already well established before the war, was doubled. The mining towns no longer resembled the depressing chaos, the semi-slave camps of early days. Since 1928, in an effort to stabilize their labour force, the Belgian Congo mining companies had been providing more attractive social conditions, proper accommodation and medical services, and a new urban society was emerging. People began to regard a working visit to these new cities less as an imposition and more as an interesting and exciting experience and, within a few years of the outbreak of war, the colonial administrators began to be worried by the beginnings of a rural exodus. Men were now going to work in the cities by choice and not by force. No doubt the enforced collection of rubber and cultivation of cotton in rural areas was partly responsible for the exodus but the attraction of the cities played an important role. The jump from 536 000 wage earners in the Belgian Congo in 1940 to over 700 000 in 1945 did not involve the same amount of human misery as the increase from 125 000 to 421 000 between 1920 and 1926.

This growing African preference for town life started the rapid growth of cities in Middle Africa which was to continue throughout the next two decades. Between 1940 and 1945 the population of Leopoldville rose from 47 000 to 96 000 and that of Elisabethville from 27 000 to 65 000. The pattern of protest against colonial rule also changed significantly. Revolts now began to occur in the cities rather than in the rural areas. There was a dock strike in Mombasa in 1939, a strike by Union Minière workers in Elisabethville in 1941, a mutiny of the Congolese *Force Publique* at Luluabourg in 1944 and a dock strike at Matadi in 1945. These were not peaceful strikes and the colonial governments regarded them as a serious challenge to their authority. They were accompanied by bloodshed and stirred the whole populations of the affected towns. Trade unions were still very weak and were not even allowed in the Belgian Congo. The strikes represented real economic grievances for, although the prices of Middle Africa's products were rising on the world market, the real income of the people did not rise appreciably. Economic controls had been set up to limit the consumption of the people. Africa was producing more but the industrialized nations now involved in war production had not the manufactured goods to send in return. Also, the supply of cheap textiles was cut off from Japan when that country entered the war in 1941. Consequently, higher wages and higher prices for export crops would merely have led to inflation and the colonial governments kept down wages as much as possible and limited the producer price of crops through the operation of

Building houses for workers at the Owen Falls scheme in Uganda

marketing boards and other controls. Nevertheless, the cost of living rose rapidly, foodstuffs were often in short supply and Tanganyika had to import substantial quantities of maize to avert famine. Although Portugal was not involved in the war, Angola was also affected by the increased demand for her export products. African coffee farmers were able to sell their crops at a better price and the diamond mines and the port of Lobito were more active than ever before. But Angola was now lagging behind its neighbours in many respects and there was a flow of labour away from Angola towards the neighbouring Belgian Congo and even towards distant South Africa.

The post-war boom

After the period of post-war reconstruction, the Korean War gave a further boost to world consumption of minerals which Middle Africa produced. The colonial governments now had substantial sums of money, accumulated marketing board surpluses and loans from the controlling states in Europe, which could be invested in economic development. In the 1940s and 1950s many major projects were undertaken, some of which, like the groundnut scheme in Tanganyika failed miserably, but many of which were successful. Railway networks were improved, many roads were tarred, hydroelectric schemes were carried through, notably the Owen Falls dam in Uganda and those in the Katanga area of the Belgian Congo. Secondary industries such as brewing, textile manufacture and shoe making, were established – especially in the Belgian Congo where by 1950, less than half the population was engaged in agriculture. Leopoldville became a sizable city with a population exceeding 100 000. Although the other countries of Middle Africa still remained primarily agricultural, the city of Nairobi rivalled Leopoldville in size and industrial activity, and the populations of the major cities continued to grow rapidly throughout the whole area, including Angola. The excitement and adventure of the city had taken hold of the popular imagination and a new urban culture was emerging.

The gap between city and village in terms of amenities and opportunities steadily widened during these years. The best job opportunities were in the towns. In 1946 the minimum workers' wage was raised in the Belgian Congo and in the ensuing years the Union Minière gave a series of wage increases to its employees. In the 1950s the proportion of the population in clerical employment increased rapidly as clerks could earn substantial wages compared with other workers. The shops and warehouses were now filled with a wider range of consumer goods. Imported radios, bicycles, motor vehicles, sewing machines and other items found their way through retail channels to the villages. Social links between town and village remained strong as town associations often had branches or connections in the villages. The rapid extension of national education systems tended to produce a common set of values across the land. The most remote areas were drawn into the cash economy. Money became the principal measure of a man's worth and money seemed easier to make in the town than in the village. The change in social values was made easier by the fact that the population was predominantly youthful. The birth rate continued to rise and the death rate fell due mainly to the improvements in public health. The development of medical services was by no means even throughout the area, for whereas the Belgian Congo had a medical assistant for every 3000 inhabitants, the Angolan health service was very weak. It was out of this thrusting, changing and vigorously expanding society that the nationalist movement grew during the eventful decades of the 1940s and 1950s.

The colonial system begins to crack

While this rapid social and economic development was in progress the system of colonial rule was beginning to crumble. The Second World War altered the shape of world politics. The Soviet Union and the United States emerged as the major world powers and both were opposed to the continuance of European colonial rule. Britain had more or less lost control of politics in India before and during the war and had little alternative but to grant independence to India and Pakistan in 1947. Thereafter, the dissolution of the British imperial system was merely a matter of time. In 1946 Governor Ryckmans of the Belgian Congo had declared 'The days of colonialism are past', indicating a very remarkable change of mind among the colonial rulers.

Imperialism was now on the defensive. It felt it had to justify its existence and begin reforms leading ultimately to the emancipation of the peoples subjected to its rule. However, the first concessions made were quite paltry. In 1945 the first Africans were admitted to the Ugandan Legislative Council and in 1950 they secured parity of representation with Europeans and Indians on that body: eight Africans balanced four Europeans and four Asians. But none of these were elected and on the other side of the table were sixteen official members. The government had not begun to transfer power; it had merely provided an official channel through which people could make petitions and question what was done. Tanganyika, being a United Nations trust territory, was more affected by the changing climate of world opinion for it was open to inspection by the United Nations. The United Nations had a broad membership and was more critical of colonial administration than the League of Nations had been. It was anxious to see that trust territories advanced towards independence. United Nations missions visited Tanganyika periodically and provided emerging nationalist opinion with a platform for expressing its views. But, until 1955, African unofficials on the Legislative Council still numbered only three and these were chosen by the Governor from chiefs who were regarded as 'loyal' by the administration. In the Belgian Congo reform took much longer to materialize. Under the cumbrous system of government, reform legislation passed from Provincial Councils to the Government Council in the Congo and from there to the Ministerial Council and Consultative Council in Belgium and from there back to the Congo and so on for nearly ten years. And then, the central piece of reform legislation entailed the introduction of representative government at the local level only. Nationalist opinion had to put strong pressure on colonial governments before any real political concessions were made. In Kenya there were two Africans on the Legislative

329

Council by 1946. This was in any case less significant than the changes in the Ugandan or Tanganyikan Councils for in Kenya independence would have to mean independence not only from the colonial power but also from the ambitious white settlers in Kenya itself. Since before the First World War the political associations of the settler group had maintained constant pressure on the administation. Their elected representatives on the Legislative Council spoke frequently and forcefully. During the war settler members had acted as semi-official ministers. In 1945 one was made Minister of Agriculture. Although the settlers had no formal control of the instruments of government, they were so strong that the colonial government felt obliged to negotiate with them before deciding any significant change in the country's constitution. They represented a serious obstacle to African advance.

Nationalist politics in Kenya

African nationalist movements were stronger and more active in Kenya than anywhere else in Middle Africa. The Kikuyu Central Association which was so active in the 1920s extended its activity to bring in an Ukamba Members' Association in 1938. It was backed up by other movements with similar aims. In the religious field there were the African Independent Pentecostal Church and the African Orthodox Church and a number of sects such as the Dini ya Yesu Kristo. In the field of education were the Kikuyu Independent Schools and the Kikuyu Karinga Educational Associations. The very existence of these movements, committed to African control in religion and education, represented a protest against the colonial regime. There were also some less militant political groups centred on the Kikuyu Association and, after 1934, the Kikuyu Provincial Association founded by Harry Thuku. The growth of membership of the Kikuyu Central Association from 300 in May 1938 to 2000 in March 1939 was symptomatic of the spread of popular discontent. The expanding population was suffering increasingly from land shortage. Overcropping was resulting in soil erosion in the more heavily populated areas. Increasing cattle herds were destroying the pastures they fed on. From 1930 onwards European settlers began to turn Africans out of rented farms on their estates which they had tilled for many years and had come to regard as their own. The Europeans were now using the land themselves and wanted labour rather than rents. The fate of these farmers created anxiety even among those living outside the settler areas. The Carter Land Commission of 1932 attracted attention to the problem and its limited consultation of the people raised some hope that there would be an improvement.

But in ended with a firmer demarcation of the boundaries of the settler areas, parts of which were claimed by African families as their ancestral lands. The atmosphere of suspicion of government intentions thickened. In the late 1930s the government began to reduce cattle herds with a view to making the cattle industry more productive. The final objective was worthwhile but the immediate result was the slaughter of a proportion of the people's animals. As a result there were violent demonstrations, petitions to government and riots during the late 1930s and 1940s. Government schemes for soil conservation also placed a burden on the people, and added to the general unrest. The demobilization of soldiers at the end of the war added a new group of determined men to the number of dissatisfied, for many former soldiers were unable to get jobs and others were frustrated by the limitations the colonial regime placed on African enterprise.

Jomo Kenyatta and the Kenya African Union

In 1946 a man appeared who could unite almost all the anti-colonial elements and direct them in a purposeful fashion toward nationalist objectives. Jomo Kenyatta was born at the end of the nineteenth century and had been involved in the nationalist movement from its beginnings in the 1920s. He was a well-educated and forward-looking man who maintained contact with and respect for the traditional customs of the Kikuyu people to which he belonged. He remained a radical nationalist and never lost contact with the rising new generations. He had followed Thuku in 1921, was general secretary of the Kikuyu Central Association in 1929 and editor of its newspaper. He then went to Britain to put the people's grievances before the British government and public. He visited Moscow and also wrote a study of Kikuyu life, *Facing Mount Kenya*. In 1946 he was hailed as the leader of Kenyan nationalism and became the unchallenged President of the newly formed Kenya African Union (KAU) in 1947. From his headquarters at the Githunguri Training College he directed the dissemination of nationalist ideas through the independent schools organization, through trade unions and through public meetings. The strength of the nationalist movement steadily grew but few political gains were made.

The Mau Mau rising

While Kenyatta was organizing public opinion in conventional fashion, another movement, Mau Mau, was also at work. Its connections with the

KAU remain obscure because Mau Mau worked in secret and was proscribed by the government. But both movements worked for the same ends and there was personal contact between the two organisations. From 1950 Mau Mau began administering oaths to persons requiring them to support the organization and to fight the government until independence was achieved. In 1951 Mau Mau's activity became sufficiently marked for the government to declare it an unlawful society but by 20 October 1952 the situation was so serious that a State of Emergency was declared. British troops were called in and strenuous measures were taken to arrest the Mau Mau leaders and destroy the movement. By this time Mau Mau was a powerful organization with its main area of activity in Kikuyu districts. It was committed to violence as a means to independence and the oaths symbolized this violence. Several thousand people were killed as a result of assisting the government. But the bulk of the population sympathized with the Mau Mau aims. War camps in the mountains were supplied with

Detained Kikuyu suspected of having taken part in Mau Mau activities undergo 're-education'

food from villages by willing helpers and with arms and ammunition purchased or stolen from the security forces themselves. In Nairobi hidden arms factories manufactured weapons. In spite of the State of Emergency the oathing ceremonies were increased. The government's action in closing the independent African schools drove more men into Mau Mau's ranks. Many unemployed and even criminal elements from the towns went out to join them in search of adventure. The colonial government used armoured vehicles and artillery; war camps in the hills were bombed; whole villages were uprooted and moved to cut off food supplies from the fighting bands. The government forces killed some 7800 people and lost some 500 of their own men. The Mau Mau fought a mainly defensive battle, only attacking to secure supplies of arms. Few settler farms were attacked and only thirty European civilians were killed. Mau Mau's offensive was carried out mainly on the political front through the oathing ceremonies which struck at the people's psychological acceptance of the dominance of colonial power. The government forces took three years to isolate the fighting men in the hills and after that sporadic guerrilla warfare continued until 1960 when the State of Emergency ended. Nevertheless, the Mau Mau rising had important political consequences. The settlers realized how great was their dependence on British arms, and the presence of British troops put real power back into the hands of the colonial government. The campaign cost the British some £50 million and tied down a large number of British troops that were needed elsewhere. It was a heavy burden which the colonial government was anxious to lose and unwilling to repeat elsewhere in Africa. The days of one-sided, small concessions were now ended. The days of negotiations with nationalist leaders with force behind their words were about to begin.

Divisions within Kenyan society

When the Emergency was declared in Kenya in 1952 Kenyatta was arrested, together with nearly 200 other political leaders. He was tried, convicted of managing Mau Mau and imprisoned. All political activity was paralyzed and between 1953 and 1955 African political parties were banned. But the colonial government knew it had to tread carefully and seek to conciliate the African people. It attempted to produce a multiracial constitution which no one group would be able to dominate. Pressure was exerted first of all on the settlers to make them give up the idea of seeking ultimate control of the country. Their ranks were split into two factions by the decision to appoint an African minister in 1954; one faction led by Michael Blundell favoured the move; the other led by Group Captain L.R. Briggs opposed it.

Jomo Kenyatta – handcuffed to Fred Kubai – after his arrest in 1952. Convicted of 'managing' Mau Mau in 1953, he was detained until 1961

The Asian community was also divided because of the 1947 partition of the Indian sub-continent into the independent states of India and Pakistan. In 1951 this split was recognized by the creation of separate constituencies for Muslims and Hindus. Africans were also divided as a result of a number of government measures. First, all those connected in any way with Mau Mau were removed from power. A campaign emphasizing the negative aspects of Mau Mau was mounted while all those who had fought against Mau Mau were accorded favours and rewards. A myth was created that the Kikuyu alone were principally, if not wholly, responsible for the movement and the government encouraged anti-Kikuyu feeling among the other ethnic groups. In 1954 when appointing the first African minister, the government passed over the moderate and longest-standing African member of the Legislative Council, Eliud Mathu, a Kikuyu, and gave the post to a Luo. When, in 1955, the ban on African political parties was ifted, their activity was restricted to the district level, thus encouraging a number of competing organizations each more or less identified with an ethnic group. In the mainly Kikuyu Central Province, politics were not permitted. When, in 1957, the first elections for African members of the Legislative Council were arranged they were run on the basis of the so-called 'fancy franchises'. Apart from educational and property qualifications, those who were thought to be disloyal to the government were not given the vote while others were able to secure up to three votes. The result was an election run almost entirely on ethnic lines. In the Central Province the administration helped a man from the Meru minority into the seat against a strong Kikuyu candidate. Meanwhile, the promotion of some Africans to higher places in the administration, the police and the army, caused a certain amount of dissension amongst those who felt they were being left behind. It is surprising that any political unity survived this period of careful government diplomacy.

The revival of nationalist politics

However, despite divisions over personalities and group interests, the African political parties were united on the crucial issues connected with progress towards independence. All those elected in 1957 campaigned against the constitution which provided for only two African ministerial posts compared with the four held by European unofficial members. They joined the Legislative Council but refused to accept office as ministers. Meanwhile in the cities a powerful movement had emerged which largely avoided the dangers of factionalism. With the ban on political parties in 1953 the Kenya Federation of Labour became the spokesman for popular grievances. Its connection with international labour organizations enabled it to survive attacks from the administration. Its ability to organize and secure better conditions for its members secured it widespread support among the workers. Two major strikes, one in Mombasa, the other in Nairobi in 1955, showed its bargaining power. The careful policies of Tom Mboya, its General Secretary, ensured that it did not become identified with any one ethnic group. The trade unions represented a unifying force at a time when the political parties were in disarray. The other major unifying force was Kenyatta, whose stature had been enhanced by imprisonment. A Luo politician, Oginga Odinga, was the first to call for his release and soon Kenyatta's return became the main slogan for all parties in the 1961 election. Even Blundell began to speak in favour of Kenyatta's release. It soon became clear that Kenyatta alone could head a government which could claim anything like general African support. His release in

August 1961 caused general rejoicing. He immediately became the centre of political discussion and by the end of the year he was a member of the Legislative Council.

The last step to freedom in Kenya

A very complex situation faced Kenyatta on his return. The Lancaster House Conference of 1960 had brought substantial changes in the constitution and Kenya was already halfway along the road to independence. There was now a wholly elected Legislative Council in which a united African front could have obtained control but unfortunately there was no unity. In early 1960 the Kenya African National Union (KANU) was founded as a successor to KAU, with Kenyatta as President although he was still a detainee. Mboya was General Secretary and Oginga Odinga Vice-President. The minority ethnic groups, fearing that KANU would be Kikuyu–Luo biased and neglect their interests, set up a rival body, the Kenya African Democratic Union (KADU). In the 1961 elections KADU, benefiting from a delimitation of constituency boundaries favourable to minorities, won eleven seats with 150 000 votes. KANU won nineteen seats with just under 600 000 votes. At first both parties refused to take office until Kenyatta was released. But finally KADU agreed to form a government with Blundell's party and a few other specially elected members. Even then KADU could not secure a majority in the Legislative Council and the Governor used his power to add eleven more members. Thus when Kenyatta returned a minority party was in power and the African members of the Legislative Council were split. The question of minority rights had been raised and with it the more dangerous question of regionalism, for KADU was encouraged by Blundell and others to seek ultimate security from Kikuyu–Luo domination through a regionalist constitution. Within KANU itself there were bitter personal rivalries, notably between Mboya and Oginga Odinga. The problem still remained of the continued exclusion from politics of former Mau Mau sympathizers. In the cities there was serious unemployment and in rural areas continuing land hunger. Meanwhile, the settlers, although no longer representing a serious political danger, from 1960 onwards had begun to realize their assets and send them out of the country, presenting a serious threat to the economy. Kenya needed more, not less capital investment to create more profitable employment for its people.

Kenyatta's first attempts to unite the rival groups failed. However, by making concessions to KADU's regionalism at a further constitutional conference in London in 1962 he was able to draw KADU into an uneasy

Jomo Kenyatta and Tom Mboya leaving for London to take part in talks on Kenya's independence

coalition. A general election in May 1963 gave KANU a majority in the Legislative Council and in June Kenyatta became Kenya's first Prime Minister. He distributed ministerial offices to most of the different factions; feelers were sent out to the Mau Mau men in the hills; even the settlers were conciliated through social contacts and were soon acclaiming the man they had formerly condemned so bitterly. Discussions were begun with a view to establishing a wider East African Federation. By the end of the year 1963 Kenya had become entirely independent. Kenyatta had produced an impressive measure of national unity out of an extremely confused situation. His dominating personality enabled the people of Kenya to call for freedom with a single voice and to replace colonial rule with an African government to which all but a very few on the Somali border were prepared to give their loyalty.

Politics in Uganda

The situation in Uganda was very different from that in Kenya for the major problem was not settle domination but rather what form independence should take. Some parts of Uganda had already secured virtual self-government by 1945. The policies pursued by Sir Charles Dundas Governor during the wartime period, had enabled the kingdom of Buganda to secure a position of virtual autonomy. Dundas had pursued a policy of non-interference with the result that Buganda was practically ruled by its Kabaka and Lukiko. The kingdoms of Toro, Ankole (Nkore) and Bunyoro although less free from colonial interference, were moving in a similar direction. The way forward politically seemed to many to consist in protecting Ganda institutions from outside interference and securing control of the foreign-dominated economy. After the war, more African-owned shops and commercial enterprises began to appear and co-operative societies were rapidly organized. However, while Buganda insisted on confining its ambitions to securing and maintaining its own autonomy, the problem remained as to the fate of the other inter-lacustrine kingdoms and the smaller groups in northern Uganda. The neighbouring presence of settler-dominated Kenya and fears of an imposed East African Federation made leaders of opinion in Buganda concentrate on conserving and extending what independence they had rather than seeking to build a broader national unity in Uganda.

Conflict between Buganda and the colonial government

From 1945 onward the policy of the colonial government altered. Concessions were stopped and there was renewed colonial interference in the internal affairs of Buganda. The Protectorate administration introduced policies of economic and social development designed to benefit the Ganda lower classes and the neglected northern areas. Consequently a new educated élite began to emerge which was more interested in broader nationalist ideas. But Buganda resented the colonial government's interference. Relations steadily deteriorated until in 1953 there was a complete rupture, occasioned by a statement by the British Colonial Secretary which suggested that the principle which had led to the establishment of the settler-dominated Federation in Central Africa might be extended to East Africa. The reaction was immediate. The Lukiko demanded that Buganda be transferred from the Colonial Office to the Foreign Office – a method of securing a status similar to that of Middle Eastern countries which had treaty relations with the British government. The request was refused and e colonial government deposed the Kabaka. All factions in Uganda allied to the Kabaka's defence. In 1955 the colonial government had to admit defeat and the Kabaka was restored. Loyalty to the Kabaka became the most powerful political force in Buganda and the possibility of Ganda co-operation with nationalists elsewhere in Uganda was greatly hampered. After this, paradoxically, constitutional advance became the colonial government's main weapon, for its easiest means of recovering control was to offer a more Africanized central government which would be more attractive than Ganda autonomy. At the same time the Ganda leaders, while blocking the path of constitutional progress at the centre, made increasing attacks on alien, especially Asian, businesses.

Uganda moves towards independence

Political parties had begun to emerge in other parts of Uganda. The nationalist Uganda National Congress (UNC), founded in 1952 and mainly Ganda-based, identified with the 'out' groups in Buganda politics and was supported by the lower classes of Ganda society, young intellectuals and others who were dissatisfied with the existing system. The UNC was gravely weakened by the Kabaka crisis, losing many supporters as the ranks closed behind the Kabaka. The Democratic Party, urged into existence in 1956 by the Catholic bishops as a counter to the allegedly communist ideas of some UNC members, benefited from the existence of Catholic action organizations within and beyond the Buganda kingdom and sought to identify itself with the underprivileged. The UNC began to increase its support by recruiting members outside Buganda and by 1958 was largely a non-Ganda party. A general political awakening was beginning throughout Uganda. In 1957 a demand was made that the system of direct election to the Legislative Council, already conceded to Buganda, should be extended to all. The government agreed and in 1958 the first elections were held.

Out of these elections emerged a new organization – the Uganda People's Union – which was anti-Ganda in outlook, channelling the old grievances against the formerly powerful Buganda state and the new resentment against Ganda obstruction of constitutional progress. The colonial government then determined upon a new measure of political advance and a new constitution was promulgated in 1960. At last something like a truly representative legislature was provided for in place of the previous multiracial bodies with their large representation of European and Asian interests. The way to independence now lay open but it was not the sort of independence that was wanted by Buganda. The Lukiko replied to the announcement of the constitutional changes with a unilateral declaration of Bugandan independence and an order to all Ganda citizens to boycott the subsequent elections. The Democratic Party, with its leader, Benedict Kiwanuka, won the 1961 election. Only 30 000 of the million Buganda voters participated in the election and all but one of the Buganda seats went to the Democratic Party.

Meanwhile, Milton Obote became leader of the opposition. Obote had been the leader of the non-Ganda wing of the UNC, but prior to the elections of 1961 he had amalgamated with the Uganda People's Union to form the Uganda People's Congress (UPC), whose membership and outlook was generally anti-Ganda. Observing from the 1961 elections that a party with no support in Buganda was doomed to perpetual opposition, Obote reached an agreement with the Buganda political organization, the *Kabaka Yekka* (Kabaka only) to work together against the Democratic Party. This collaboration secured for Buganda substantial concessions at the 1961 constitutional conference in return for which Buganda agreed to co-operate with the Uganda state. Buganda was allowed greater autonomy than any other administrative region and the members of the central legislature were to be selected by the Lukiko and not elected. The result of these arrangements was that the UPC emerged the victor from the 1962 elections. In alliance with *Kabaka Yekka* it beat the Democratic Party at the polls in the elections to the Lukiko and the Lukiko selected members who supported the UPC government for the central Legislature. On this basis Uganda secured its independence in October 1962 and Milton Obote became Prime Minister. The alliance of non-Ganda, nationalist UPC and Buganda loyalists was an extremely uneasy one and did not stand the test of time.

Tanganyika secures independence

Tanganyika's path to freedom was comparatively smoother and less disturbed by internal dissension, for the colonial government, anxious to avoid crises like the Mau Mau rising or the Kabaka affair, co-operated in the end with nationalists. And the United Nations exerted pressure to speed up political progress. That independence came early was largely due to the efforts of Julius Nyerere and the Tanganyika African National Union (TANU). Established in 1954, TANU aimed at creating a spirit of national unity by breaking down local and sectional feelings and mobilizing opinion in favour of independence. It took up local grievances against colonial rule and people were encouraged to look on TANU as their protector against injustice. It was regarded by the government as subver-

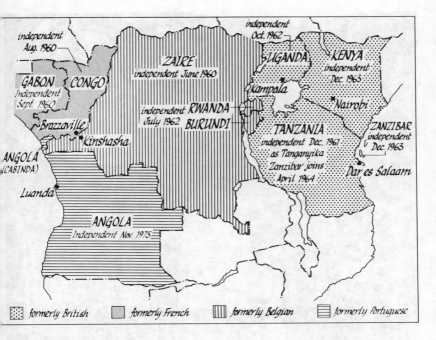

Middle Africa today

sive and banned in many areas. In 1956 the unofficial members of the
Legislative Council united to form a rival organization – the United
Tanganyika Party (UTP). Nyerere persistently pursued moderate policies
and sought above all international support for his nationalist cause.
TANU forged close links with the rapidly growing trade unions and by
1958 had secured 250 000 members. The government recognized its political force in that year by nominating Nyerere and Rashidi Kawawa, the
General Secretary of the Tanganyikan Federation of Labour, to the Legislative Council. The colonial government then decided to allow elections
of the official members of the council but stipulated that each constituency
should elect one member for each racial group. Nyerere, although at first
opposed to this multiracial system in a country with a 98 per cent African
population, persuaded TANU to make use of this arrangement and to
select its own European and Asian member for each constituency.

The result was a sweeping victory for TANU. No UTP candidates were
returned and the UTP quickly disintegrated. The number of TANU
branches increased rapidly as the public realized that the party now had
real power. Prolonged strikes during the next two years on the railways
and the sisal plantations made the government aware of the necessity of

President Julius Nyerere announcing the union of Tanganyika and Zanzibar in 1964

negotiating with TANU and brought about discussions concerning future advance between Governor Sir Richard Turnbull and Nyerere. In 1960 a new round of elections for a legislature which was to be mainly African once more proved TANU's strength. All but thirteen TANU candidates were returned unopposed. A one-party state virtually existed *de facto* in Tanganyika. Independence came almost as a matter of course in December 1961.

The union between Zanzibar and Tanganyika

Politics were brought to life amongst the 300 000 or so inhabitants of Zanzibar and Pemba with a new constitution in 1956 which provided for the election of six members to the Legislative Council. The radical Zanzibar Nationalist Party (ZNP) which grew out of the old Arab Association had links with Egyptian nationalism and Communist China. The Afro-Shirazi Party (ASP), an amalgamation of the former African Association and the Shirazi Association, was almost prompted into existence by the administration and by TANU on the mainland. However, racial politics and personalities played a major role in the election campaign of 1957 and in the end ASP numbers won the day. As a result, interracial bitterness and strife were greatly increased. Further elections were held in 1961. They were accompanied by much interracial violence and bloodshed, and resulted in a draw between the ZNP and ASP, producing constitutional deadlock. For two years Zanzibar had a caretaker government until further elections in 1963 paved the way for independence. This time the ZNP won twelve seats, the ASP thirteen and the Zanzibar and Pemba People's Party (ZPPP) – a party which broke away from the ASP before the 1961 elections – six. A coalition was formed between the ZNP and the ZPPP and Zanzibar became independent in December 1963 with the leader of the ZPPP, Muhammad Shamte, as Prime Minister. In January 1964 a police mutiny led by John Okello deposed the Sultan and a republic was proclaimed. Much rioting followed the revolution. Large clove estates were confiscated and large businesses were taken under government control. These policies alienated the western powers and the new regime sought support from Eastern Europe, Russia and China. This successful revolt triggered off other mutinies in the armies of Tanganyika, Uganda and Kenya, and British forces had to be called in. Nyerere, realizing the dangers which the Zanzibar revolution could create for East African governments, entered into an agreement with the government of Zanzibar effecting a union between the two states. Thus in April 1964 Tanzania came into being. However, for most purposes Zanzibar maintained its autonomy and the revolutionary government remained master in its own house.

Political dissension in the Belgian Congo

The transfer of authority from the colonial power to an independent African government took place more suddenly in the Belgian Congo than in any of the East African countries. Up to the middle 1950s the colonial administration was still vigorously in control. Enlightened paternalism was the order of the day. Government, missions and companies concentrated on improving social conditions while resisting African attempts to rise beyond subordinate positions. In 1954, however, the explosive schools issue, which so seriously divided opinion in Belgium itself, was transferred to the Congo. The Belgian Colonial Minister, a Liberal, ordered the establishment of state schools in the Congo to break the missions' virtual monopoly of education. Much bitterness was aroused between the mainly clerical Flemings and the largely anticlerical Walloons and each side turned to the Congolese for assistance. The previously stifled voice of Congolese opinion was now encouraged to speak. The development of higher education which had lagged behind that of African countries of comparable size, was hastened forward by the dispute as each group created new institutions. The Catholic Church, long a supporter of the colonial regime, began to speak of political reform. From 1957 onwards an economic recession producing unemployment and popular discontent further weakened the colonial regime.

The Belgian Congo moves towards independence

In 1956 the Leopoldville journal, *Conscience Africaine* which represented the views of one of the rapidly expanding groups of educated men (*cercles des évolués*) produced a manifesto demanding progressive advance towards independent African government. A few weeks later the Abako organization produced a counter-manifesto calling, in a more radical fashion, for advance towards Congolese independence. There were many cultural and ethnic organizations like the Abako in the towns which claimed to represent and defend the interests of a particular ethnic or linguistic group. The Abako represented the Kongo people of the Lower Congo as well as those living in neighbouring Angola and French Moyen Congo. It aimed at developing the Kongo language and cultural institutions. In 1957, after the long deliberations over local government reform in Belgium and the Congo, pilot elections for a new form of municipal government were held in Leopoldville and Jadotville. In Leopoldville the Abako won the election and its leader, Joseph Kasavubu, became the Burgomaster (Mayor) of one ward in the city. His inauguration speech in April 1958 in which he declared that democracy would not be complete until the Belgian Congo secured at least autonomy made a considerable impression. More people were drawn into political discussion as further elections were held in other large cities during 1958. The first elections were also held for the reform and democratization of local government in rural areas. Public political debate was further activated by a government working party sent to the Belgian Congo to consult public opinion about the pace and direction of political advance. Also many Congolese represented their country at the Brussels Exhibition in 1958 where they were able to exchange ideas and hear all kinds of nationalist opinions. After the virtual political silence of the previous period, 1958 was a year of most vigorous political discussion at all levels of society in the Belgian Congo, stimulated in August when de Gaulle, just across the river in Brazzaville, granted autonomy within the French Community to the Moyen Congo.

The turning point in Congolese political development was 4–6 January 1959. On 4 January a riot broke out in Leopoldville after an Abako meeting had been banned. Disorder reigned for two days. European shops were broken into and burned and over forty people were killed. The administration was faced with the alternatives of repression or political concession. They chose the latter. On 13 January a statement was issued that the Belgian Congo would now move towards independence. The nationalist leaders, observing that the formerly dictatorial colonial government was completely losing its nerve, clamoured for an early date for independence. In April 1959 at Luluabourg a congress of political parties

A poster in Leopoldville (now Kinshasa) market announcing the date of independence of the Belgian Congo

dominated by the recently reorganized Mouvement National Congolai (MNC) under the dynamic leadership of Patrice Lumumba, demanded independence by 1961. The Abako demanded independence by March 1960. From then on events moved with increasing rapidity. Politica parties sprang up all over the country making wildly irresponsible prom ises. The government began to lose control of rural areas, especially the crucial Leopoldville–Matadi area where the main transport systems con verged. Farmers began to pay dues to the parties instead of paying taxes to the government. The government, terrified that an Algerian-type situation might develop, decided to decolonize as rapidly as possible. It called a 'Round Table Conference' in Ostend in January 1960. The Congolese leaders were expecting a five-year transition to independence; instead the Belgians imposed an independence date of 30 June 1960 on the reluctant, and still bitterly divided, Congolese. The first national elections would be held in May. It was to prove a recipe for disaster.

What form of state?

There was considerable difference of opinion among the nationalist leaders as to the form of the constitution. The MNC stood for a unitary state, for its supporters came from the smaller societies in the centre of the country which would benefit from a national union. They had no important economic resources and had suffered much from compulsory cotton cul tivation and consequently tended to be politically and socially radical in outlook. In contrast the Katanga Province held the greater part of the economic wealth of the country. But although the mine workers enjoyed a comparatively high standard of living, the inhabitants of the Katanga region felt they had not adequately benefited from the wealth around them. A large proportion of the cities' inhabitants were stranger Lubas from Kasai and it was they who had dominated the 1958 municipal elections. In reply the people of Katanga Province organized themselves into the Conakat party to push Kasaians out of city government. At the same time, the white European residents, who were already hostile to the Leopoldville government, formed an alliance with Conakat in the hope that by detaching Katanga from the rest of the Congo they would be able to maintain their privileged position and preserve some measure of white supremacy. Under their influence Conakat began to demand a federalist constitution giving Katanga virtual autonomy. The Abako party stood roughly midway between the MNC and Conakat. Abako had always been a movement of the Kongo people, and it wanted some degree of local autonomy to enable it to develop Kongo culture – especially with the Kongo people across the frontiers. The unitarism versus federalism de-

Members of the UN peacekeeping forces in the Congo

bate, begun in 1959, was the main subject of controversy at the 1960 conference. No clear-cut decisions were made and the matter was left for final determination after independence. At the May elections no party emerged with a clear majority. Lumumba's party had the largest number of seats, thirty-three out of a total of 137. A coalition was formed by the MNC and the Abako together with the Parti Solidaire Africaine and other small groups. Lumumba became Prime Minister and Kasavubu the Abako leader, President.

Political crisis

Within a week of independence the *Force Publique* mutinied. A large proportion of the panicking European population left the country. At the same time the Conakat government in Katanga Province seceded. Belgian troops were sent to stop the mutiny and Belgian technical assistance strengthened the Katanga regime. Katanga held on to the receipts from its exports which continued to flow out through Angola and the Conakat leader, Moise Tshombe, commanded a powerful, rich and effective government while Lumumba's central government was virtually paralyzed. In response to Lumumba's call the United Nations sent advisers and later military forces to his assistance but the situation continued to deteriorate. On 5 September Kasavubu dismissed Lumumba from office and called on Joseph Ileo to form a government. On 12 September the army commander, Joseph Mobutu, announced that he was neutralizing both President and Prime Minister and the government was placed in the hands of a body of commissioners chosen from among university students. In November Antoine Gizenga, a supporter of Lumumba and the ex-Vice Premier, set up a provisional government in Stanleyville where he received the support of the provincial government and declared that his government would stand for Lumumbist principles. In January 1961 Lumumba was assassinated in Katanga where he had been flown as a government prisoner. The Gizenga government continued to stand by its dead leader's principles of a unitary state and a more radical outlook in internal and external affairs. Thus by the beginning of 1961 there were three governments in the Congo – the secessionist regime in Katanga, Mobutu's commissioners in Leopoldville and Gizenga's government in Stanleyville. Gradually the Leopoldville government got the upper hand as it remained the only internationally recognized government. By 1963 Katanga had been brought back within the Congolese Republic (later called Zaire) by force. In 1965, with the politicians thoroughly discredited, the army, under Mobutu, seized power.

Rwanda and Burundi

The precolonial kingdoms of Rwanda and Burundi became part of German East Africa and in 1919 were transferred to Belgium under a League of Nations Mandate. Both colonial powers found it expedient to rule indirectly through the Tutsi aristocracy, which continued to extract taxes and labour from the Hutu majority. Thus, little social change took place. There was also little economic development, and as the dense population soared from 2.3 million in 1918 to 4.4 million in 1956, to 8.5 million in 1975, the people had to look for work in neighbouring Uganda, Tanganyika and the Belgian Congo.

As in the Congo, the Belgians made no effort to prepare the people for independence. In 1959 they suddenly announced a plan for independence and dramatically switched their support to the Hutu. This led to the formation of rival Hutu and Tutsi political parties, and in Rwanda hundreds of Tutsi were killed and thousands fled as refugees. The United Nations, which supervised the transition to independence, hoped the two kingdoms would unite, but, as elsewhere in Africa at this time, those hoping to gain high office opposed the idea, and so they became independent as separate states in July 1962. In Rwanda, elections had produced a Hutu majority and the overthrow of the monarchy. In Burundi the Tutsi retained control with the monarchy made more democratic. But in neither country did independence produce stability. After massacres in Rwanda in 1962, over 100 000 Tutsi fled into exile. Later in the 1960s Hutu were butchered in Burundi and the exodus of refugees was even greater. As in Zaire, both countries eventually fell under military rule.

The French Congo and Gabon

The French possessed two small colonies in Middle Africa, to the northwest of the Zaire (formerly Congo) river. These were Gabon and Moyen (Middle) Congo. From 1910 they formed part of the vast Federation of French Equatorial Africa. In the early years of the century, large concession companies had brutally compelled people to grow cotton and collect rubber. Forced labour was indeed only abolished after the Second World War in response to the Federation's support for de Gaulle's Free French movement. Promises of reform were made at Brazzaville in 1944, and, in general, because of the highly centralized nature of French rule, political developments followed a very similar pattern to that already described in the chapters on West Africa. French Equatorial Africa was however far less economically advanced than French West Africa, which itself lagged far behind British West Africa. Political parties tended to be local and traditionalist, and there was much factional violence, especially in Moyen Congo. As late as 1957 virtually all politicians preferred the maintenance of strong economic links with France to any form of independence. It was events elsewhere, notably Guinea's 'no' to de Gaulle's 1958 referendum, which ultimately swept Moyen Congo and Gabon to an independence in 1960 which neither of them wanted. Gabon, by far the richest of the four states of Equatorial Africa, resisted attempts by the other states to keep the Federation intact; it feared this would mean subsidizing its poorer neighbours. The end result was that both countries achieved a very nominal form of independence. The major economic assets were in French hands, they were almost entirely dependent on French aid, and their early governments were consequently almost embarrassingly pro-French. Indeed when Léon M'Ba, President of Gabon, was toppled in a coup in 1964, he was promptly restored to power by French troops.

The Angolan liberation struggle

Unlike the British, the French and the Belgians, the Portuguese in Angola (and in their other African colonies, Mozambique and Guinea-Bissau) did not agree to decolonize when confronted with pressures from African nationalists. Instead they chose to fight, which in turn meant that the people of Angola had to fight for their own liberation. Portugal was a Fascist state which tolerated no democracy at home and ran a brutal regime in her colonies. She was economically too weak to decolonize; she knew that, unlike France, she would be unable to retain economic control over her colonies if once she let them go.

It took a thirteen-year guerrilla war followed by a civil war to liberate and bring independence to Angola. The war started (like Maji Maji) in the cotton fields, where compulsory cultivation (to the detriment of food crops), low prices and delayed payments provoked despair and finally violence, in January 1961. The Portuguese air force responded by bombing villages indiscriminately. This war soon ended but the following month violence erupted in the capital, Luanda. Here the Movimento Popular de Libertação de Angola (Popular Movement for the Liberation of Angola – MPLA), which had been formed in 1955 as little more than a debating society for the educated few, tried to free its leaders from the local gaol. Armed groups of whites, no doubt influenced by recent atrocities in the neighbouring (former Belgian) Congo, ran amok through the black slums, killing hundreds of people. In March, violence spread to the coffee fields of the north. Here too there was forced labour and local Kongo people found their land increasingly given to poor, unskilled Portuguese immigrants, who came flooding into the country, attracted by the coffee boom of the 1950s. (The white population of Angola rose from 80 000 in 1950 to 170 000 in 1960, to 300 00 in 1970.) When the workers-at one plantation asked for wages which were six months overdue, bloody violence broke out and spread to much of northern Angola. Kongo people killed hundreds of white settlers and Ovimbundu migrant workers, and were themselves killed in thousands. Over 100 000 fled as refugees to neighbouring Zaire, and the Portuguese began their war to reconquer the territory.

In the initial phase of the war, the Portuguese found themselves confronted by two enemies. The northern Kongo-speaking refugees who fled to Leopoldville (later Kinshasha) in Zaire formed the Frente Nacional de Libertação de Angola (National Front for the Liberation of Angola – FNLA) under Holden Roberto. Leopoldville was a Kongo city, where for decades Kongo people from Angola had crossed the colonial border in search of education at local Baptist schools. MPLA, though it tried hard to broaden its base, was predominantly a Luanda-based Mbundu party. Education in Luanda derived largely from Methodists. In 1961 MPLA established a small guerrilla base some 80 kilometres out of Luanda, which it was never to lose throughout the entire war, but many of its leaders were forced into exile, to Conakry in Guinea and later to Brazzaville in the former Moyen Congo. From 1962 its leader was Agostinho Neto. After the independence of Zambia, in October 1964, MPLA was able to mount a campaign in eastern Angola. It was a source of weakness and division that the liberation movements were forced to operate largely outside Angola under different patrons who were often in conflict with each other.

By 1963 Portugal, given decisive military help by the United States and the NATO countries, had reached a virtual stalemate with both FNLA and MPLA. The liberation movements found that although they could tie down the Portuguee army of 50 000, they could not achieve decisive victories, since their bases were so far away from the main cities and plantations of Angola. They could attack the Benguela Railway – but their patrons, Zaire and Zambia, both used it to export their vital copper. About 20 000 people died in the first two years of the war.

After 1963 Portugal, in response to the mounting cost of the war, abandoned its earlier policy of economic nationalism and sought investment in Angola from countries such as the United States, West Germany, France, Britain and Brazil. In return for economic concessions, these countries were required not to support the liberation movements openly. It was hoped that foreign investment would create an improved infrastructure and transport system and so ease the task of counter-insurgency. The plan worked reasonably well, and at the same time the Portuguese secret police (PIDE) paid informers in the liberation movements to maintain and indeed to widen the splits between them. Thus in 1965 União Nacional para a Independência Total de Angola (National Union for the Total

Liberation of Angola – Unita) under Jonas Savimbi broke away from FNLA and began organizing among the Presbyterian Ovimbundu of the Central Highlands.

In the final phase of the war, from 1970 to 1974, the Portuguese belatedly attempted to win over the hearts and minds of some black Angolans. They offered new economic and educational opportunities to those who renounced the liberation struggle. New schools were established and an élite of master farmers was created in the north and north-east which would later oppose the socialism of MPLA. The Portuguese army was extensively Africanized in order to reduce the white casualty rate. It herded a million people into so-called 'protected villages', dropped napalm bombs and poisoned crops in MPLA-held areas in eastern Angola. By 1974 the cost of fighting simultaneous wars in Angola, Guinea-Bissau and Mozambique brought about the collapse of the Portuguese dictatorship. Africans had helped to liberate Europeans.

Independence and the Angolan civil war

The new government in Lisbon found it relatively easy to agree independence with the PAIGC in Guinea-Bissau and with Frelimo in Mozambique.

In January 1975 – with help from President Kenyatta – the Portuguese attempted to set up a power-sharing arrangement to take over in Angola. Leaders of the Angolan political movements are pictured here with Kenyatta: *left*, Holden Roberto (FNLA), *second from right*, Agostinho Neto (MPLA), *right*, Jonas Savimbi (Unita)

Angola, with its great potential wealth in oil, diamonds, iron and coffee and with its three rival movements divided by ethnicity, religion and geography, proved far more difficult. With the aid of the Kenyan President, Jomo Kenyatta, the Portuguese set up a power-sharing body and announced a date for independence, in November 1975. But President Mobutu of Zaire, fearing that a socialist MPLA government in Angola might inspire his own brutally repressed opposition and possibly seeking to resurrect the old Kongo kingdom, encouraged Holden Roberto's FNLA to make a unilateral grab for power. This failed but the attempt destroyed the fragile coalition. All three groups engaged in bitter street fighting in Luanda, from which MPLA emerged victorious by July. Then South Africa intervened. It was also afraid of an MPLA victory, since this would greatly encourage SWAPO guerrillas fighting South Africa in Namibia. South Africa reached an agreement with Unita and the United States, and began to invade southern Angola in October. Faced by such blatant Afrikaner imperialism, MPLA sought Soviet assistance and, in a dramatic airlift, some 10 000 Cuban troops were sent out to help.

Thus independence day arrived, on 11 November 1975, amidst a civil war. Confronted by the Cubans, the South Africans withdrew (to the delight of their own black population), complaining that America had not supported them. After a disastrous attack on Luanda, FNLA and the Zaire army were driven back across the border, amidst much recrimination between Roberto and Savimbi. An American-financed rabble of mercenaries was brought to trial and convicted of murder after which some of its members were shot – amid howls of protest in the western media. Thus Neto eventually became President of an Angolan government in control of much of the country and recognized by most of the world – though not by the United States.

The cost was enormous. The vital north–south economic links had been torn apart, greatly hindering agricultural exports. All the important roads had been mined repeatedly. And thousands of people, particularly those with skills and education, had been killed when caught on the 'wrong' side. Unita remained strong in the Central Highlands, where Ovimbundu farmers traditionally distrusted the city planners of Luanda. Almost a decade after independence South African troops continued to operate sporadically and destructively inside Angola, supporting Unita guerrillas, seeking to destabilize the country and thus hinder SWAPO. With great hypocrisy, South Africa and the United States demanded the withdrawal of Cuban troops as a precondition for a cease-fire and elections in Namibia. But since the stunning electoral victory of ZANU in Zimbabwe in 1980 (which surprised South Africa, which had given vast financial support to the 'internal settlement' regime of Bishop Muzorewa), the South

Africans have backed away from any kind of open election in Namibia.
Thus, the MPLA government has found itself embroiled in both the
Southern African and the East–West conflicts.

Agostinho Neto, President of Angola, seen here speaking in May 1st Square in Luanda,
1975

13 Middle Africa since independence

Introduction

As in the case of West Africa (see Chapter 3), Middle Africa since independence has been desperately searching for political stability and economic development. Military coups have toppled governments in Uganda, Rwanda, Burundi, Zaire (formerly the Belgian Congo) and the

Angola has continued to be plagued by civil war since independence: anti-government Unita troops backed by South Africa on the march near the Benguela railway.

Congo (formerly French Moyen-Congo), while civil war and the war against South African troops have devastated Angola. Even the politically stable regimes in Kenya, Tanzania and Gabon were facing severe economic problems in the early 1980s which seriously threatened that hard-won stability. Throughout the region countries were suffering the effects of the 'oil revolution' and the major world economic recession of the 1970s. As populations continued to grow rapidly, notably in Kenya, governments found it hard to maintain basic services and impossible to promote economic growth, especially in rural areas. By the 1980s it was difficult to recall the spirit of optimism and enthusiasm which had greeted the attainment of independence in the 1960s. Particularly was this so in countries like Uganda, Zaire, Rwanda and Burundi, which had witnessed the wholesale slaughter of innocent people and the almost complete absence of any rule of law for many years.

The four countries in the western part of Middle Africa, Angola, Congo, Gabon and Zaire, had all become oil producers by the 1970s and thus were in a position to take advantage of the huge rise in oil prices. But for the countries to the east, Burundi, Kenya, Rwanda, Tanzania and Uganda, which had no oil and very few mineral resources, the oil revolution was a major catastrophe. Thus, for example, the cost of Tanzania's oil imports in 1972 was 269 million shillings. By 1981, despite a 30 per cent reduction in the amount of oil imported, the cost had risen almost tenfold to an astronomic 2053 million shillings. During the same period both the value and the volume of Tanzania's agricultural exports declined. As a result the country plunged heavily into debt. By 1982 it owed an estimated £1500 million. Such a crippling burden obviously placed severe constraints on the government's ability to improve the lot of its people.

Despite significant regional differences, there are a number of themes common to Middle Africa as a whole. Typically Middle African countries export agricultural commodities and raw materials at low prices which are fixed in the west. They import, at high cost, western manufactured goods whose prices are also determined in the west. Even when Middle African countries export minerals, these tend to be dominated by huge multinational corporations over which it is difficult for small countries to exercise control. The sudden post-independence discovery of minerals, as in Gabon, has tended to increase dependence on foreign capital, technology and personnel. Moreover, countries are often critically dependent upon world markets over which they have no control. For example, the collapse of the world price for copper in 1974–5 was a severe blow to Mobutu Sese Seko's government in Zaire. Up to that time it had brought a creditable recovery from the chaos and anarchy of the early 1960s. But after the copper crash Zaire has slid steadily downhill year by year. By 1984 it was acing the most severe political, economic and social crisis in the region. Further south, Zambia too suffered acutely from the slump in copper.

All of Middle Africa has witnessed urban growth and rural decay. The high hopes at independence and the rapid expansion of jobs in the civil service and parastatal organizations produced a massive migration to the towns, especially to major cities such as Nairobi and Kinshasa (formerly Leopoldville). Rapidly government ministers, civil servants, doctors, lawyers etc. became urban men who had no wish to serve in the less developed rural areas. The vast majority of new development projects were located in the towns, which widened further the rural-urban gap. Lavish prestige buildings of dubious value were often constructed. A large urban working class emerged, including very many who were unemployed or partially employed in the so-called 'informal sector'. Since governments tended to rise and fall in the cities, they feared opposition from this urban population far more than from the more dispersed and relatively powerless peasantries. Thus typically governments have paid low prices to rural producers in order to provide cheap food to urban workers. Often they have heavily subsidized maize. The result has frequently been that farmers have given up producing for the regular market and have either taken to smuggling or else have left the land and joined the ceaseless drift to the towns. By the 1980s rural societies almost everywhere had become demoralized and, with population rising rapidly, governments were having to import food at enormous cost. In the urban areas workers continually demanded higher wages and better services. It was economically difficult to afford these, but politically difficult to deny them. Everywhere rural people had come to feel deprived and had become aware that their interests and those of the state were in conflict.

People also tended to become more impatient with governments, especially those which were feeble, corrupt or vindictive, because of the 'crisis of expectations' aroused by politicians at independence and whenever new governments seized power. People believed the often extravagant promises of politicians and felt cheated when they failed to deliver. Such alienation encouraged people to challenge the legitimacy of the new governments, especially those whose actions heightened ethnic tensions. Corruption became endemic in such countries as Zaire. Inequalities and the formation of new classes were as apparent in 'socialist' Tanzania and the Congo as in 'capitalist' Kenya and Zaire. In all these countries huge inefficient and loss-making parastatal organizations contributed to the economic crisis. Throughout Middle Africa, but especially in Uganda and Zaire, the infrastructure of government and communications began to break down and sometimes to disappear altogether. In extreme cases the state was seen as a crude oppressor from which all rational people fled.

Zaire: the unending crisis

Zaire is one of the largest countries in Africa and, with its vast mineral and hydroelectric resources, potentially one of the richest. But its history since independence in 1960 has been a deeply troubled one. The years 1960-6 were dominated by insurrections and civil wars during which the province of Katanga (now Shaba) which produced 70 per cent of the country's minerals, tried unsuccessfully to break away. When the army under General Mobutu took over in 1965 it found a country deeply scarred by foreign interference, with its economy in tatters and with administration over large parts of the country non-existent. Gradually, helped by high copper prices, Mobutu's government restored a measure of stability and strength to the country during the period 1965-73. In particular, it succeeded in bringing runaway inflation under control and agricultural production, severely hit by the troubles of the early 1960s, showed signs of recovery. The country had come to depend heavily on American aid but the benefits gained seemed to justify this. Then Zaire was hit by a series of disasters, some of them self-induced, which plunged the country into a downward spiral of misery and impoverishment.

In 1973 oil prices increased dramatically. In 1974-5 the price of copper collapsed. In 1975, as a result of the civil war in Angola, the Benguela railway, Zaire's main export route, was closed and has remained closed ever since. During the Angolan civil war, as noted in Chapter 12, Mobutu tried unsuccessfully to install his client Holden Roberto and the FNLA in power. The Zairian army was also involved but performed disastrously, leading to great loss of morale. Mobutu became unpopular throughout Africa, since he had unilaterally destroyed a power-sharing formula which had been constructed with great difficulty and which had the support of the Organization of African Unity. Between 1973 and 1975 in an ill-timed move, the government tried to 'Zairianize' the economy by seizing a large number of foreign-owned stores, businesses and farms. The results were disastrous, for not only was there much corruption in the distribution of these assets but the new owners proved quite incapable of managing them. There was massive dislocation of commercial life, intensified by the fall in copper prices and the rise in oil prices. In 1977 and again in 1978 refugee dissidents from Shaba invaded the province from Angola, and Mobutu's regime survived only because French and Belgian paratroops and soldiers from Morocco, Senegal, Ivory Coast, Togo and Gabon came to his rescue. America and Saudi Arabia paid the bills.

By this time the regime had become brutal and corrupt, there was severe economic and social disintegration, runaway inflation had returned, and the country was importing huge amounts of food and had incurred a

Mobutu Sese Seko, President of Zaire

stupendous foreign debt, amounting in 1980 to some £3000 million. Yet Mobutu was widely believed to be one of the richest men in the world. He plundered public resources for his own profit and to reward his followers. Corruption had become endemic throughout Zaire. The army and police were not paid and so were forced to steal food from farmers and whatever they could from civilians. In a manner reminiscent of early responses to colonial rule, farmers responded by growing fewer crops, by fleeing to more inaccessible parts of the forest or by seeking escape in the towns. Rural revolts broke out almost annually, but were easily repressed by the use of helicopters and modern weaponry supplied by the west, for whom the staunchly anti-communist Mobutu had become an invaluable ally. By 1976 real urban wages had slumped to 26 per cent of their 1960 value and have dwindled still further since then. As authority became more random, more irrational and more corrupt, everyone felt exploited and powerless and crisis behaviour had become the norm.

Chaos in Uganda

A comparable breakdown in society took place in Uganda during the 1970s. Following independence in 1962, the country's first prime minister (later president), Milton Obote, seemed to be making some success of ruling a country containing many regional divisions and rivalries. Obote imposed a unitary constitution in 1966, deposed the Kabaka of Buganda, who fled into exile, abolished all the kingdoms and declared the country a republic. His 'Common Man's Charter' of 1969 alarmed members of the

Idi Amin   Milton Obote

ruling élite and foreign investors alike. By 1971 all opposition had been banned and Obote had become increasingly reliant on the army and secret police. In February 1971, while attending the Commonwealth heads of state meeting in Singapore, Obote was overthrown in a bloodless military coup led by the army commander, General Idi Amin. There was rejoicing in Buganda. But not for long. After an initial period of relative stability, it soon became clear that Amin was a crazed psychopath who vented his bloodlust on the entire population. As the army was encouraged to run amok, perhaps half a million people were slaughtered, often with obscene brutality. No-one will ever know the exact number killed. There was terror throughout the land. Amin also expelled virtually the entire Asian population of 70 000, including Ugandan citizens. As in similar circumstances in Zaire, this resulted in commercial chaos. Agricultural production, especially of export crops, declined markedly in the Amin years, as people concentrated on their own survival. Following a long history of border friction, Amin's army invaded Tanzania in October 1978. The Tanzanians, helped by Ugandan exiles, fought back, entered Uganda and overthrew the Amin regime in April 1979. Amin's well-paid and well-equipped army performed dismally when put to the test. Following a series of complex political manoeuvres, elections were held in December 1980 and Obote's Uganda People's Party returned to power after a truly disastrous decade. In 1985, after several troubled years, Milton Obote was once again overthrown.

Gabon and Kenya: the capitalist road

Both Gabon and Kenya pursued pro-western, capitalist paths of development and explicitly sought western investment. The path proved much smoother in Gabon, thanks to the discovery of substantial deposits of crude oil, uranium, manganese ore and natural gas. These resources tended to be exploited by large multinational corporations which employed few Gabonese and exported raw materials unprocessed. But the state extracted high royalties and export taxes and its revenues increased tenfold between 1960 and 1973. By 1979 Gabon had become Africa's fifth largest producer of crude oil with the second highest per capita income on the continent. Naturally this concealed great inequalities and as mining boomed so agriculture, especially the cocoa industry, declined. But prosperity did allow political stability, notably in the volatile 1970s – when Zaire and Uganda were enduring major political upheavals. The Gabonese government of Omar Bongo could afford to pay its civil servants well and to provide facilities for its rural population. As a further guarantee of political stability there was a defence agreement with France, whose nuclear energy programme relied heavily on uranium from Gabon.

Kenya too was often hailed as a model of capitalist development.

Daniel arap Moi, President of Kenya

Despite the assassinations of Tom Mboya, Pio Pinto and J.M. Kariuki, the country enjoyed relative political calm. After a long tenure of office, Jomo Kenyatta died in 1978 and there was much relief when power passed peacefully into the hands of the former vice-president, Daniel arap Moi. But by the early 1980s the country was facing severe economic and political problems, as an ill-organized attempted coup in 1982 illustrated.

Perhaps because it possessed no substantial mineral resources, Kenya sought western investment and participation in her economy. There was thus no nationalization of assets while land redistribution in the former 'White Highlands' was limited in scale. Departing whites were paid generous compensation, and their farms tended to fall into the hands of the ruling political élite. Within the Kenya African National Union (KANU) the struggle between the moderates led by Kenyatta and Mboya and Odinga's radicals was decisively won by the moderates. Odinga tried to form a rival party but it was banned in 1969. Increasingly political and economic power came to reside in the office of the president. Economic inequalities widened, and the landless flocked to Nairobi where unemployment spiralled and the new shanty towns were bulldozed. By the end of the 1970s to the problems of landlessness, unemployment and the population explosion were added rampant inflation and a growing shortage of food. Massive purchases of imported maize were made in 1980–81. The government conceded a military base to the Americans at Mombasa. This enraged some Kenyan intellectuals, a number of whom were imprisoned while others fled into exile. By 1979 the country's public debt amounted to £578 million. A note of optimism was struck in 1983, however, when the border with Tanzania, closed during the 1970s, was reopened and politicians spoke of the need to revive the East African Community, which had existed between 1967 and 1976, but had foundered in the wake of much bickering.

The Congo and Tanzania: the path to socialism

Very different approaches to development were attempted in the Congo and Tanzania. In August 1963 the young workers of Brazzaville succeeded during three days of street fighting in toppling the corrupt neo-colonial regime of the Abbé Youlou, whose servility to France was an embarrassment to all. The new Congo government, headed by Alphonse Massemba-Débat, allied itself to Ghana, Guinea and Mali, adopted anti-imperialist rhetoric, offered a base to the MPLA and sought friends and aid from the Eastern bloc. The Chinese built a textile factory and the Russians offered some assistance, but insufficient to break the chains of dependency. The

362

tate took over a number of enterprises, generally those of marginal profitability. But the government was in constant need of French assistance, the youth and labour movements in Brazzaville remained highly volatile and in 1968 there was a military coup led by a northern army officer, Marian Ngouabi. The following year Ngouabi declared the Congo to be a 'People's Republic' guided by Marxism-Leninism. The coup brought about a significant shift from southern to northern dominance of Congo politics. Political stability remained elusive however, and there were constant purges within the ruling Congolese Workers' Party. In 1977 Ngouabi was assassinated. Two years later his successor was removed by the Party's Central Committee, to be replaced by Sasso Nguesso.

Throughout all these changes Congolese politics were characterized by the visible contrast between public radicalism and private moderation. After a decade and a half of 'Marxism-Leninism', it was clear to all that the French business community in Brazzaville remained as powerful as ever. The civil service and parastatal organizations were characterized by over-manning, inefficiency and gross corruption. A desperate search for revenue to pay the wage bill was partially met by the discovery of offshore oil. Production and prices fluctuated violently however. When both were low there were political crises, while tensions eased when prices rose.

Tanzania's experiment in village socialism was first proclaimed in the Arusha Declaration of February 1967. This followed conflicts with both trade union leaders and university students. In the Declaration Nyerere committed himself and the TANU leadership to a policy of socialism and self-reliance, with severe constraints being placed upon political leaders. They were not to earn more than one salary, not to own shares or houses rented to others and not to employ workers in any business. This was followed by the nationalization of banks, insurance companies, import-export houses and a number of manufacturing enterprises and the creation of new parastatal organizations.

Clearly this was a different approach to that of Kenya and Zaire. Nyerere, the leader of one of the world's poorest countries, was patently a man of great integrity and intelligence. His vision of a socialist Tanzania, expressed in many elegantly written policy documents, aroused the sympathy of scholars and economic planners throughout the world. In the 1970s more was written on Tanzania than any other country in Africa. Yet by the end of the 1970s the Tanzanian economy was in desperate straits and it was clear that the attempt to impose socialism from the top had failed. In part Tanzania was the victim of events outside its control, in part the wounds were self-inflicted.

On the land a bewildering array of agricultural policies was pursued at various times – spontaneous settlement schemes, planned settlement schemes, *ujamaa* villages, planned villages, state farms and then, in 1983 in response to pressure from western creditors, a return to capitalist farming with farms being offered to the Asian community. It is hardly surprising that there was much confusion and that agricultural productivity declined. Agriculture provides 75 per cent of the country's foreign exchange earnings, but during the 1970s production of each of the seven major export crops declined by an average 17 per cent. In the vigorous 'villagization' programme of 1973–6, virtually the entire rural population of 13 million was moved into some 8000 villages. The intention was to give everyone access to schools, dispensaries and the like. In reality the state lacked the resources to mount such an ambitious programme, numerous mistakes were made and much hardship ensued. The programme coincided with a severe drought in 1974–6, and was followed in 1977 by the collapse of the East African Community from which Tanzania had derived many important services, the war against Uganda in 1978–9 which cost 684 lives and over 4000 million shillings, and by yet more poor rains in 1980 and 1981. All this, coupled with the increasing cost of oil and of all imports from the west, placed very severe strains on the Tanzanian economy. Between 1977 and 1982 the government was forced to spend 640 million shillings importing food, the external debt mounted annually, and by 1982 the purchasing power of Tanzania's exports was half what it had been five years earlier. Even the volume of exports was less than it had been in the early 1970s. Prices to farmers for both food and cash crops fell. The government continued to subsidize the price of maize, the main food crop, but in 1983 announced that it would have to phase out this subsidy within four years. This would have obvious implications in the towns. In Dar es Salaam tension was already high following the repeated forced removal of the unemployed to the rural areas. Throughout the country there was an acute shortage of imported spare parts for agriculture and industry while the transport infrastructure had begun to decay.

Tanzania's inefficient government and parastatal sector, motivated neither by more than superficial socialist commitment nor by financial incentive, had become an immobile parasite quite incapable of responding urgently to the country's many desperate problems. When Nyerere announced, on being re-elected in October 1980, that this was to be his final five-year term in office, it seemed that he too had despaired of ever creating socialism in Tanzania. Like its 'capitalist' neighbour Kenya, the country was massively in debt and at the mercy of western creditors. Though two decades of political independence had passed, economic independence seemed as far away as ever.

Index